The **Rough Guide** to

Dubai

written and researched by

Gavin Thomas

www.roughguides.com

Contents

◀◀ Dubai Fountain with the Burj Khalifa in the background ◀ Sheikh Zayed Road

Introduction to Dubai

Dubai is like nowhere else on the planet. Often claimed to be the world's fastest-growing city, in the past four decades it has metamorphosed from a small Gulf trading centre to become one of the world's most glamorous, spectacular and futuristic urban destinations, fuelled by a heady cocktail of petrodollars, visionary commercial acumen and naked ambition. Dubai's ability to dream – and then achieve – the impossible has ripped up expectations and rewritten the record books. Stunning developments such as the soaring Burj Khalifa, the unforgettably beautiful Burj al Arab and the vast Palm Jumeirah island are embodiments of the ruling sheikhs' determination to make the city one of the world's essential destinations for the twenty-first-century.

Modern Dubai is often seen as a panegyric to consumerist luxury: a self-indulgent haven of magical hotels, superlative bars and restaurants and extravagantly themed shopping malls, although this one-eyed cliché does absolutely no justice to the city's beguiling contrasts and rich cultural make-up. Look beyond the popular perception and you'll find that Dubai has much more to offer than is generally supposed, ranging from the fascinating old city centre, with its higgledy-piggledy labyrinth of bustling souks, interspersed with fine old traditional Arabian houses lined up along the Creek, to the memorably quirky postmodern architectural skylines of southern Dubai.

The city's human geography is no less memorable, featuring a cosmopolitan assortment of Emiratis, Arabs, Iranians, Indians, Filipinas and Europeans – a fascinating patchwork of cultures and languages which gives the city its uniquely varied cultural appeal. Headline-grabbing developments like the record-breaking Burj Khalifa and Palm Jumeirah have also deflected attention from Dubai's massive but largely unappreciated role in providing the Islamic world with a model of political stability, religious tolerance and business excellence in action, serving as the ultimate symbol of what can be achieved by a peaceful and progressive pan-Arabian global city in one of the world's most troubled regions.

The recent credit crunch may have signalled the end of some of the city's more extravagant mega-projects, but announcements of Dubai's demise are likely to prove premature, and the city remains one of the twenty-first century's most fascinating and vibrant urban experiments in progress. Visit now to see history, literally, in the making.

What to see

At the heart of the metropolis on the south side of the Creek, **Bur Dubai** is the oldest part of the city and offers a fascinating insight into Dubai's traditional roots. The area is home to many of the city's most interesting traditional Arabian heritage houses, clustered in the beautiful old Iranian quarter of **Bastakiya** and the waterfront **Shindagha** district, as well as the excellent **Dubai Museum** and the atmospheric **Textile Souk**. On the opposite side of the Creek, the bustling district of **Deira** is where you'll find most of Dubai's traditional commercial activity, much of it still conducted in the area's vibrant array of old-fashioned souks, including the famous **Gold and Spice Souks**.

Fringing Deira and Bur Dubai lie the city's **inner suburbs**. Attractions here range from the entertainingly workaday suburbs of Karama and Satwa, home to dozens of no-frills Indian curry houses, low-rent souks (including the infamous **Karama Souk**, epicentre of the city's thriving trade in designer fakes) and some of the city's most entertaining street life, through to more upmarket modern developments like the kitsch Egyptian-themed **Wafi complex** and the atmospheric **Khan Murjan Souk** next door, one of the city's most accomplished exercises in faux-Arabian nostalgia.

◀ Traditional carpet shop

A few kilometres south of the old city centre, modern Dubai begins in spectacular style with **Sheikh Zayed Road**, home to a neck-cricking array of skyscrapers, including the glittering Emirates Towers. This strip is an essential stop for lovers of postmodern architectural whimsy, and also is home to many of the city's **best restaurants**, **bars** and **pubs**. Further south lies the massive new **Downtown Dubai** development, centred on the stupendous new **Burj Khalifa**, the world's tallest building, flanked by further record-breaking attractions including the gargantuan **Dubai Mall** and the spectacular **Dubai Fountain**.

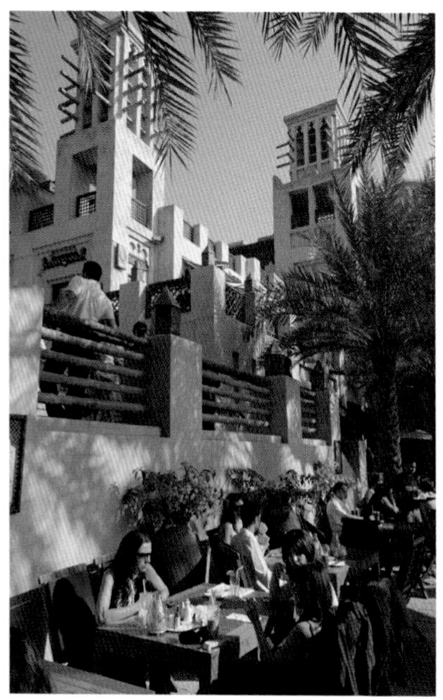

◀ Madinat Jumeirah

West of the Sheikh Zayed Road, the sprawling beachside suburb of **Jumeirah** is the traditional address-of-choice for Dubai's European expats, with an endless swath of walled villas and a smattering of low-key sights including the beautiful **Jumeirah Mosque** (open to non-Muslims for entertaining and informative tours) and the kitsch, Italian-themed Mercato mall.

At the southern end of Jumeirah, the sleepy suburb of Umm Suqueim is home to a trio of iconic Dubai sights: the wave-shaped *Jumeirah Beach Hotel*; the extraordinary mock-Arabian **Madinat Jumeirah** complex, where you'll find some of the city's most memorable hotels, restaurants and bars; and the unforgettable **Burj al Arab** hotel. South of the *Burj al Arab* stretches the spectacular new **Dubai Marina** development, with its densely packed forest of glassy skyscrapers, while offshore lies the **Palm Jumeirah**, the world's largest man-made island, which ends in a flourish at the gargantuan new *Atlantis* resort.

There are a number of rewarding **day-trips** beyond the city, all of which offer an interesting alternative take on life in the 21st-century Gulf. Just 10km down the coast, the famously conservative city of **Sharjah** hosts a good selection of rewarding museums devoted to cultural and religious matters, including the excellent new **Museum of Islamic Civilization**. To the southeast and on the border with Oman is **Al Ain**, the UAE's only major inland city, which offers a complete change of pace from life on the coast, with traditional mud-brick forts, old-fashioned souks and the country's finest **oasis**. A short drive beyond lies the even more laidback **East Coast**, with a

Dubai: second among equals

Given the city's soaring international profile, many people unfamiliar with the region think Dubai is a country, which of course it isn't. It's actually just one of the seven statelettes which collectively form the United Arab Emirates (UAE), a loose confederation founded in 1971 following the departure of the British from the Gulf. Technically the seven emirates are considered equal, and perserve a considerable measure of legislative autonomy, rather like the various states of the US – which explains, for instance, why local laws in Dubai are so different from those in neighbouring Sharjah. In practice, however, a clear pecking order applies. Abu Dhabi, the largest and wealthiest of the emirates, serves as the capital (despite Abu Dhabi city being barely half the size of Dubai) and wields the greatest influence over national policy, as well as providing the UAE with its president. Dubai ranks second, followed by Sharjah and then the other emirates of Umm al Quwain, Ras al Khaimah, Ajman and Fujairah, which remain relatively undeveloped and even surprisingly impoverished in places.

string of beautifully (and still largely deserted) beaches, backdropped by the dramatic **Hajar mountains**. Last but not least, the UAE's capital **Abu Dhabi**, offers an intriguing contrast to freewheeling Dubai, and is home to two of the UAE's most impressive landmarks in the shape of the extravagant *Emirates Palace* hotel, and the even more spectacular **Sheikh Zayed Mosque**.

◀ Beach, Dubai Marina

When to go

Camel safari outside Dubai

The best time to visit Dubai is in the cooler winter months from December through to February, when the city enjoys a pleasantly Mediterranean climate, with average daily temperature in the mid-20s°C. Not surprisingly, room rates (and demand) are at their peak during these months, though the weather in January and February can sometimes be rather overcast, and even surprisingly wet at times. Temperatures rise significantly from March through to April, and in October and November, when the thermometer begins to nudge up into the 30s on a regular basis, though the heat is still relatively bearable, and shouldn't stop you getting out and about.

During the summer months from May to September the city boils – especially in the suffocating months of July and August – with average temperatures in the high-30s to low 40s (and frequently higher). Although the heat is intense (even after dark), room rates at most of the top hotels plummet by as much as seventy-five percent, making this an excellent time to enjoy some authentic Dubaian luxury at relatively affordable prices – so long as you don't mind spending most of your time hopping between air-conditioned hotels, shopping malls, restaurants and clubs.

Average temperatures and rainfall

	Jan	Feb	Mar	Apr	May	Jun	Jul	Aug	Sep	Oct	Nov	Dec
Dubai												
Max/min (°C)	24/14	25/15	28/17	32/20	37/24	39/26	41/29	40/29	39/26	35/23	31/18	26/15
Max/min (°F)	75/58	76/58	82/63	90/68	98/74	102/79	105/84	105/85	102/79	95/73	87/65	79/60
Average rainfall												
mm	11	36	22	8	1	0	0	0	0	0	2	8

things not to miss

It's not possible to see everything that Dubai and the neighbouring emirates have to offer in a short trip – and we don't suggest you try. What follows, in no particular order, is a selective and subjective taste of the city and surrounding area's highlights, from traditional Arabian heritage houses and museums through to modernist landmarks, as well as the most spectacular malls, restaurants and bars. All are arranged in colour-coded categories to help you find the best things to see, do and experience, and all entries have a page reference to take you straight into the Guide, where you can find out more.

01 Bastakiya Page **45** • One of the city's best preserved heritage areas, with a fascinating little warren of old-fashioned houses topped by innumerable wind towers.

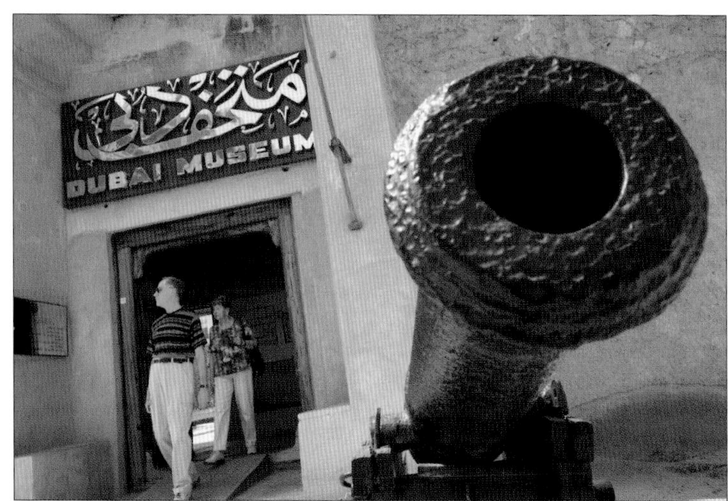

02 Dubai Museum Page **43** • An unbeatable introduction to the city's history and traditional culture, housed in the old Al Fahidi Fort.

03 Burj Khalifa Page **72** • The world's tallest building at 828m, rising like an enormous space rocket above the streets of Downtown Dubai.

04 Malls Pages **93** & **143** • Dubai has taken retail therapy and raised it to an art-form. Many of the city's malls rank as tourist attractions in their own right, ranging from the kitsch, Italian-themed Mercato through to the outlandish Ibn Battuta Mall, themed after the journeys of the legendary Moroccan traveller.

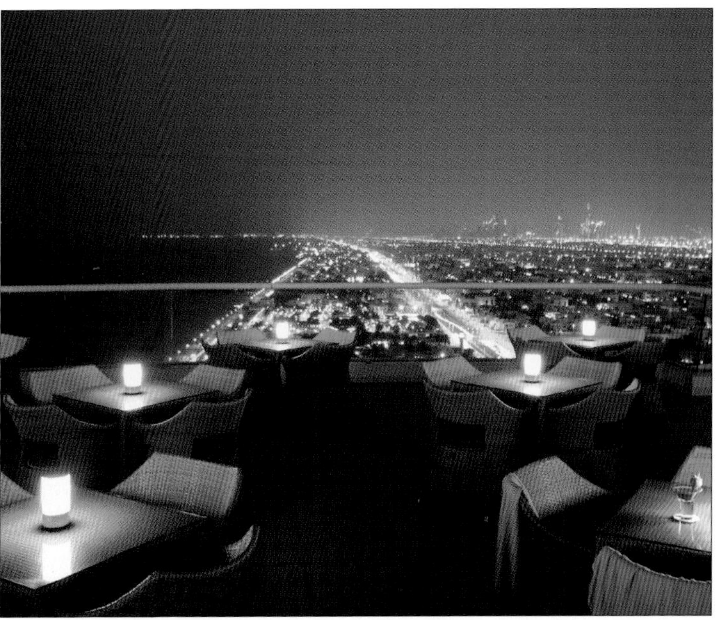

05 **High-rise bars** Page 123 • Sip on a cocktail in one of Dubai's chic high-rise bars, with sweeping views of the modern city outside.

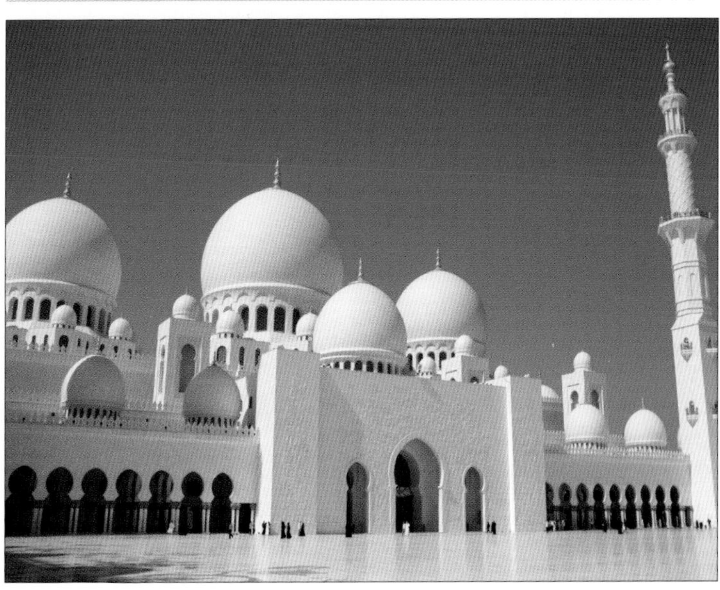

06 **Sheikh Zayed Mosque, Abu Dhabi** Page 174 • Abu Dhabi's most spectacular landmark, this monumental mosque is one of the world's largest, with huge courtyards, domes and minarets enclosing a marvellously opulent prayer hall within.

07 **Jumeirah Mosque** Page **77** • Dubai's most beautiful mosque welcomes visitors for insightful guided tours.

08 **Sheikh Zayed Road** Page **69** • Dubai's most futuristic road, lined with a sequence of neck-cricking skyscrapers ranging from the unquestionably wonderful to the irrefutably weird.

09 **Desert safaris** Page **26** • Go dune-bashing, try your hand at sand-skiing or quad-biking, then settle down over a shisha for a spot of traditional belly dancing.

10 **Arabian food and shisha** Pages **110** & **129** • Explore the Middle East's wonderful cuisine, from tempting mezze to succulent grills and kebabs, rounded off with an aromatic puff on a traditional shisha.

11 Al Ain oasis Page **159** • An idyllic retreat from the heat and dust of contemporary Al Ain, with peaceful little pedestrianized roads running through shady plantations of luxuriant date palms.

12 Dhow wharfage Page **58** • Home to hundreds of superb Arabian dhows moored up along the Deira creekside – one of central Dubai's most incongruous but magical sights.

13 Ski Dubai

Page **85** • Go skiing, snowboarding or snowball-fighting at Ski Dubai, a surreal slope of Alpine mountainside attached to a mall in southern Dubai.

14 Abra ride on the Creek Pages **23** & **48** • Hop aboard a traditional abra for a breezy ride across the Creek, with marvellous views of the city centre waterfront en route.

15 Deira Souks Pages **53, 57** & **59** • At the heart of old Dubai, the central district of Deira comprises a labyrinth of absorbing bazaars, ranging from the Gold Souk's glittering shop windows to the aromatic alleyways of the Spice Souk.

16 Wafi and Khan Murjan Souk Pages **64** & **65** • Check out the quirky Egyptian-themed Wafi mall and leisure complex – complete with obelisks, hieroglyphics and huge pharaonic statues – and the atmospheric Khan Murjan Souk next door, a sumptuous recreation of a traditional Arabian bazaar.

17 Sharjah Islamic Museum Page **151** • State-of-the-art museum, showcasing the rich history of Islamic science, arts and culture.

18 Sheikh Saeed al Maktoum House Page **51** • Former home of the ruling Maktoum sheikhs, now housing an absorbing collection of atmospheric old city photographs.

19 Madinat Jumeirah Page **84** • Astounding mock-Arabian city, home to a string of lavish hotels and leisure facilities – the quintessential Dubaian example of opulent kitsch on an epic scale.

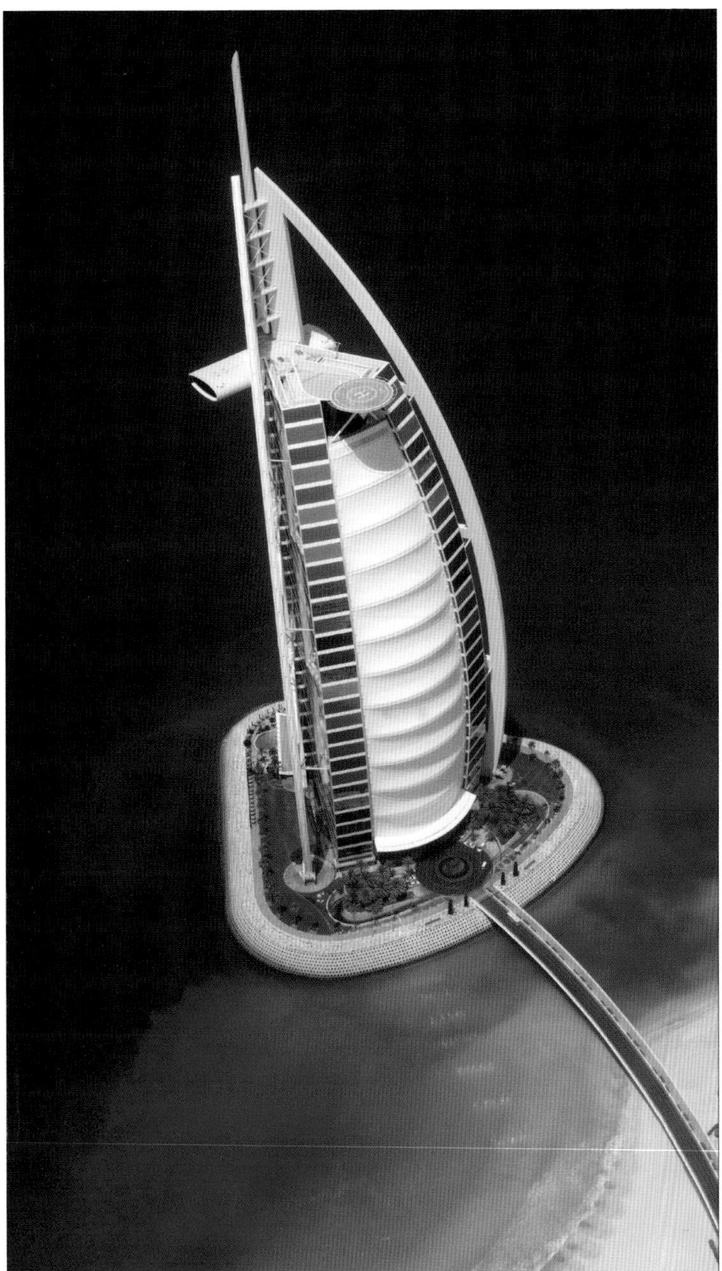

20 Burj al Arab Page **81** • One of the world's most instantly recognizable contemporary buildings, this superb, sail-shaped hotel towers gracefully above the coast of southern Dubai.

Basics

Basics

Getting there

Dubai is the Middle East's largest airline hub, boasting excellent connections worldwide with the city's own Emirates airline and other international carriers. These include numerous direct flights to various destinations in the UK, plus a couple of places in the US and Australia.

Other options for getting to Dubai are contrastingly limited (for Western visitors, at least). It's possible to travel **overland** into the UAE from several points in neighbouring Oman, but not Saudi Arabia. There are no regular **ferry** services to Dubai, although the city is a popular stop on many cruise itineraries.

Flights from the UK and Ireland

Several airlines offer **non-stop flights** between the UK and Dubai; outbound flying time is around 7hr (slightly longer on the way back), with return fares starting at about £300–350. There are currently non-stop flights from Heathrow with Emirates, Virgin Atlantic, British Airways and Royal Brunei Airlines, plus indirect flights with many other European and Gulf airlines. Emirates also operates direct flights to Dubai from a number of regional UK airports including Birmingham, Manchester, Newcastle and Glasgow.

Flights from the US and Canada

There are currently non-stop flights to Dubai with Emirates from New York, Houston, Los Angeles, San Francisco and Toronto, plus innumerable other one- and two-stop options with a host of other carriers. Flights from the east coast take around 13–14hr; from the west coast around 16hr; and 15–17hr from Houston. Fares start at around $1500 return from New York and Toronto, and $1700 from Houston, LA and San Francisco.

Flights from Australia and New Zealand and South Africa

There are non-stop flights to Dubai with Emirates from Perth (11hr), Sydney and Melbourne (15hr), Brisbane (16hr), plus one- and two-stop flights from Auckland (via Brisbane, Sydney or Melbourne; 22hr) and Christchurch (via Sydney and Bangkok; 20hr). Return **fares** start at around Aus$2000. There are also numerous alternative routings via Asia, usually at slightly lower fares.

Travelling from South Africa, there are direct flights from Johannesburg, Cape Town and Durban (taking around 8–9hr), plus a few one-stop options including, most conveniently, Kenya Airways via Nairobi and Ethiopian Airlines via Addis Ababa. Return fares start at around 7000 ZAR.

By land

The UAE shares land borders with Oman and Saudi Arabia, though only the Oman border is open to visitors from outside the Gulf. There are currently four border crossings between the **UAE and Oman** open to non-Emirati and Omani citizens: at Tibat between Ras al Khaimah emirate and Oman's Musandam Peninsula; at Al Ain/Buraimi in Abu Dhabi emirate; just east of Hatta in Dubai emirate; and at Khatmat Malahah between Oman and Fujairah emirate on the east coast of the UAE. For details of visa and entry requirements, see p.35.

It's about a five-hour drive from Muscat to Dubai, and there are also several daily buses operated by the Oman National Transport Company (there's a timetable at Ⓦwww.omanet.om/english/useful/transport.asp, but don't assume it will be up to date) leaving from the bus station in Ruwi.

Airlines

Air Canada Ⓦwww.aircanada.com.
Air New Zealand Ⓦwww.airnz.co.nz.
British Airways Ⓦwww.ba.com.
Emirates Ⓦwww.emirates.com.

Six steps to a better kind of travel

At Rough Guides we are passionately committed to travel. We feel strongly that only through travelling do we truly come to understand the world we live in and the people we share it with – plus tourism has brought a great deal of **benefit** to developing economies around the world over the last few decades. But the extraordinary growth in tourism has also damaged some places irreparably, and of course **climate change** is exacerbated by most forms of transport, especially flying. This means that now more than ever it's important to **travel thoughtfully** and **responsibly**, with respect for the cultures you're visiting – not only to derive the most benefit from your trip but also to preserve the best bits of the planet for everyone to enjoy. At Rough Guides we feel there are six main areas in which you can make a difference:

- Consider what you're contributing to the **local economy**, and how much the services you use do the same, whether it's through employing local workers and guides or sourcing locally grown produce and local services.
- Consider the **environment** on holiday as well as at home. Water is scarce in many developing destinations, and the biodiversity of local flora and fauna can be adversely affected by tourism. Try to patronize businesses that take account of this.
- Travel with a purpose, not just to tick off experiences. Consider **spending longer** in a place, and getting to know it and its people.
- Give thought to how often you **fly**. Try to avoid short hops by air and more harmful night flights.
- Consider **alternatives to flying**, travelling instead by bus, train, boat and even by bike or on foot where possible.
- Make your trips "**climate neutral**" via a reputable carbon offset scheme. All Rough Guide flights are offset, and every year we donate money to a variety of charities devoted to combating the effects of climate change.

Ethiopian Airlines Ⓦwww.ethiopianairlines.com.
Gulf Air Ⓦwww.gulfair.com.
Kenya Airways Ⓦwww.kenya-airways.com.
Qantas Ⓦwww.qantas.com.
Royal Brunei Ⓦwww.bruneiair.com.
South African Airways Ⓦwww.flysaa.com.
Virgin Atlantic Ⓦwww.virgin-atlantic.com.

Agents and operators

North South Travel UK Ⓣ01245/608 291, Ⓦwww.northsouthtravel.co.uk. Friendly, competitive travel agency, offering discounted fares worldwide. Profits are used to support projects in the developing world, especially the promotion of sustainable tourism.

STA Travel UK Ⓣ0871/2300 040, US Ⓣ1-800/781-4040, Australia Ⓣ134 782, New Zealand Ⓣ0800/474 400, South Africa Ⓣ0861/781 781; Ⓦwww.statravel.co.uk. Worldwide specialists in independent travel; also student IDs, travel insurance, car rental, rail passes, and more. Good discounts for students and under-26s.

Trailfinders UK Ⓣ0845/058 5858, Ireland Ⓣ01/677 7888, Australia Ⓣ1300/780 212; Ⓦwww.trailfinders.com. One of the best-informed and most efficient agents for independent travellers.

Travel CUTS Canada Ⓣ1-866/246-9762, US Ⓣ1-800/592-2887; Ⓦwww.travelcuts.com. Canadian youth and student travel firm.

USIT Ireland Ⓣ01/602 1906, Northern Ireland Ⓣ028/9032 7111; Ⓦwww.usit.ie. Ireland's main student and youth travel specialists.

Arrival

Unless you're travelling overland from neighbouring Oman or sailing in on a cruiseship, you'll arrive at Dubai's sparkling modern international airport. Once you've cleared customs and the crowds, getting into town is fairly straightforward.

The airport (ⓦwww.dubaiairport.com) is very centrally located in the district of Garhoud, around 4km from the city centre. There are three passenger terminals: Terminal 1 is where most international flights arrive; Terminal 3 is where all Emirates airlines flights land; and Terminal 2 is used by smaller regional carriers, including FlyDubai. All three terminals have numerous car rental agencies and currency exchange; there are also plenty of ATMs.

There are several ways of getting into town from the airport and some hotels offer free airport transfers as part of the room rate; check when you book. Both Terminal 1 and Terminal 3 have dedicated **metro stations**, offering quick and inexpensive transport into the city centre and beyond to southern Dubai. Alternatively, there are plentiful **taxis**, although the 20dh flag fare (see p.22) taxis levy for airport pick-ups is a major turn-off. There are also various **buses** running from the airport into the city centre, although these are only really useful if you're staying in Deira or Bur Dubai and know where you're going; you'll also have to buy a Nol card or ticket (see p.22) before boarding the bus. The two most useful services (every 15–30min, 24hr; 3dh). are airport bus #401, which travels via Baniyas Road to Al Sabkha Bus Station in central Deira, and airport bus #402, which runs to Al Ghubaiba Bus Station in the middle of Bur Dubai.

City transport

Dubai is very spread out – it's over 20km from the city centre down to Dubai Marina – but getting around is relatively straightforward and inexpensive, thanks mainly to the city's brand-new metro system. Taxis offer another convenient and relatively inexpensive form of transport, while there are also buses and boats, as well as cheap car rental.

Full information about the city's public transport is available on the Roads & Transport Authority (RTA) website at ⓦwww.rta.ae. The RTA also provide an excellent **online travel planner** at ⓦhttp://wojhati.rta.ae.

By metro

Opened in September 2009, the **Dubai Metro** (ⓦwww.rta.ae) has already revolutionized transport within the city and offers a cheap, fast and convenient way of getting around, with state-of-the-art driverless trains running on a mixture of underground and overground lines, and eye-catching modern stations. The popularity of the system means that it's surprisingly difficult to get a seat.

The metro will eventually consist of two lines (see Greater Dubai colour map), although only

Nol cards

Almost all Dubai's public transport services – **metro**, **buses** and **waterbuses** (but not abras) – are covered by the **Nol** system (®www.nol.ae), which provides integrated ticketing across the entire transport network. To use any of these forms of transport you'll need to buy a pre-paid Nol card or ticket ahead of travel; no tickets are sold on board metro trains, buses or waterbuses. You swipe the card or ticket as you pass through the metro ticket barriers or as you board a bus or waterbus, and the correct amount is automatically deducted from your pre-paid account. Cards can be **bought** and **topped-up** at any metro station; at one of the machines located at 64 bus stops around the city; or at branches of Carrefour, Spinneys, Waitrose and the Emirates NBD bank.

Types of cards and ticket

There are three types of Nol card; all three are valid for five years and can store up to 500dh worth of credit. The **Silver Card** costs 20dh (including 14dh credit). The **Gold Card** (same price) is almost identical, but also allows users to travel on Gold Class compartments on the metro (see below). The **Blue Card** costs 70dh (including 20dh credit) and offers additional benefits, including the ability to top-up online and to earn loyalty points. The caveat is that Blue Cards aren't available over the counter – you'll have to submit a written or online application, so casual visitors probably won't find them of much use. An alternative to the three cards is the **Red Ticket** (a paper ticket, rather than a card). This has been specifically designed for tourists, costs just 2dh and is valid for 90 days, although it has to be pre-paid with the correct fare for each journey and can only be recharged up to a maximum of ten times. If you're going to be using public transport regularly while you're in the city it's worth investing in a Silver or Gold card.

one has so far been opened. This is the 52km-long **Red Line**, which runs from Rashidiya, just south of the airport, via the airport and city centre and then south down Sheikh Zayed Road to Jebel Ali. There are 29 stations along the line, although only 18 had opened at the time of writing; the others were due to come into service in October 2010. The 22km-long **Green Line** (scheduled to come into service in August 2011 according to latest estimates) will arc around the city centre, running from Al Qusais, north of the airport, via Deira and Bur Dubai and then down to Oud Metha and Jaddaf.

Trains run every 10min from 6am to 11pm Saturday to Thursday, and 2pm to midnight on Friday. **Fares** are calculated according to the distance travelled ranging from 1.8dh up to a maximum of 6.5dh (or from 3.6dh to 13dh in Gold Class). **Children** under 5 or shorter than 0.9m travel free. All trains have a dedicated carriage for **women and children** (look for the signs above the platform barriers) plus a **Gold Class** compartment at the front of/back of the train – these have slightly plusher seating and decor, although the main benefit is that they're usually fairly empty, meaning that you're pretty much guaranteed a seat.

By taxi

Away from areas served by the metro, the only way of getting around Dubai quickly and conveniently is by **taxi**. There are usually plenty of taxis around pretty much everywhere in the city and at all times of day and night with the important exception of Bur Dubai and Deira, where you might sometimes struggle to find a cab, particularly during the morning and evening rush hours and after dark. Large malls and big hotels are always good places to pick up a cab; if not, just stand on the street and wave at anything that passes. Taxis are operated by various companies (see box opposite) and come in assorted colours, though all have yellow taxi signs on the roof, illuminated when the vehicle is available for hire.

Fares are pretty good value. There's a minimum charge of 10dh per ride, with a basic flag fare of 3dh (or 3.5dh from 10pm–6am), plus around 1.6dh per kilometre; the exception is in taxis picked up from the airport, where a 20dh flag fare is imposed. Booking by phone (see box opposite) adds an extra 3dh to the fare (or 4dh from 10pm–6am). If you want a taxi to wait for you, it costs 0.5dh per minute. You'll also be charged an extra 20dh if you take a taxi into Sharjah. For a full list of fares and charges, visit ⓦhttp://dtc.dubai.ae and click on the "Fare" tab.

Taxi drivers are reasonably well trained and will be familiar with all the main city landmarks, although if you're going anywhere more obscure you might have to help them find the way; if in doubt, try to have directions or a full address to hand. Rumours of taxi drivers inflating fares by driving newly arrived tourists five times around the block occasionally surface, but appear to have no basis in reality; the whole industry is stringently regulated, and drivers are unlikely to risk their jobs for the sake of a few extra dirhams. Be aware, though, that Dubai's labyrinthine traffic systems often add considerably to the distances between A and B. If you get into a cab and the driver heads off in completely the wrong direction it's likely because he has to turn around or find the correct exit/entrance to a particular road. If you think you have a genuine grievance and you wish to lodge a **complaint**, phone the RTA call centre (ⓣ800 90 90). Make sure you take the driver's ID number before you leave. **Tips** aren't strictly necessary, though many taxi drivers have got into the slightly annoying habit of automatically keeping the small change from fares. That said, a few extra dirhams probably means a lot more to them than they will to you.

Taxi drivers might occasionally **refuse to take you** if you're travelling only a short distance. The only other occasion when a driver may refuse your fare is if it's likely to get them stuck in a massive traffic jam (such as when crossing the Creek during the morning or evening rush hours). They may change their tune if you offer them a decent tip to compensate for their wasted time.

Occasional rogue **unmetred taxis** (often from neighbouring emirates) or other unlicenced cars appear on Dubai's streets. If you use one of these, agree a fare before setting off, although it's unlikely to be to your advantage, unless you bargain very hard. Even worse are the **hotel limousines** which sometimes try to pass themselves off as conventional taxis (hotel doormen may sometimes try to get you into one of these, insisting they're ordinary taxis). These are metred, but usually cost around twice the price of a normal cab. Avoid them unless you're completely stuck. Remember, if it doesn't have a yellow taxi sign on the roof, it's not a proper taxi.

Dubai cab contacts

To book a cab, call any of the companies below:

Dubai Taxi ⓣ04-208 0808

Arabia Taxi ⓣ04-800 272 242 or 285 5111

National Taxi ⓣ04-600 543 322

Cars Taxi ⓣ04-800 269 2900

Metro Taxi ⓣ04-600 566 000 or ⓣ04-267 3222

Ladies Taxis ⓣ04-208 0808

By abra

Despite contemporary Dubai's obsession with modern technology, getting from one side of the Creek to the other in the city centre is still a charmingly old-fashioned experience, involving a trip in one of the hundreds of rickety little boats – or **abras** – which ferry passengers between Deira and Bur Dubai. It's a wonderful, fun journey, offering superb views of the fascinating muddle of creekside buildings.

There are two main abra **routes**: one from the Deira Old Souk Abra Station (next to the Spice Souk) to the Bur Dubai Abra Station (at the north end of the Textile Souk), and another from Al Sabkha Abra Station (at the southern end of the Dhow Wharfage in Deira) to the Bur Dubai Old Souk Abra Station (in the middle of the Textile Souk). There's a third abra route from Al Seef station in Bur Dubai to Baniyas Station in Deira.

The **fare** is a measly 1dh per crossing. Boats leave as soon as full (meaning, in practice, every couple of minutes); the crossing takes a few minutes. Abras run from 6am to midnight, and 24hr on the route from Bur Dubai Old Souk to Al Sabkha (though with a reduced service between midnight and 6am).

By waterbus

A more sedate but much less atmospheric way of getting across the Creek is aboard a **waterbus**. Though launched with the intention of providing a safer and more comfortable means of crossing the water than the traditional abra, they have rather failed to catch on thanks to the relatively high fares, long waiting times between boats and general lack of atmosphere – boats are entirely glassed in behind tinted windows, effectively cutting you off from the views and sea breezes outside. They're worth considering if you might have problems hopping on and off an abra (if you have small children in tow, for instance), but otherwise don't have much to recommend them.

Waterbuses run from 6am to 11pm, with **departures** every 30min (or every 15min during peak morning and evening hours). The **fare** is 4dh per return trip (there are no one-way fares); you'll need a Nol card (see p.22) before you board the boat; tickets aren't sold on board.

There are five different **routes**, mainly using the same "stations" as the city's abras, but following slightly different routings: Line **B1** runs from Bur Dubai to Al Sabkha; **B2** runs from Bur Dubai Old Souk to Baniyas Square; Line **B3/B4** runs from Al Sabkha station to Baniyas, near Baniyas Square in Deira, and Al Seef, at the southern end of Bur Dubai.

There's also a **tourist route**, line **B5**, which shuttles between Al Shindagha Station (on the water outside the Diving Village) and Creek Park, at the far southern end of Bur Dubai, calling in at Bur Dubai, Deira Old Souk and Al Seef en route. If you want to use this line you'll have to purchase a rather expensive **one-day pass** costing 50dh (children 25dh). There are eleven departures daily between 9am and midnight.

By bus

Dubai has a well-developed and efficient network of bus services, though it's mainly designed for the needs of expat Indian and other low-paid workers, rather than tourists, so is only of limited use to visitors. Most services originate or terminate at either the **Gold Souk Bus Station** in Deira or **Al Ghubaiba Bus Station** in Bur Dubai (and many services call at both). The information offices at either should be able to supply you with a useful free map of the network. The only really useful services are #8 and #8A which run from the Gold Souk station to Al Ghubaiba and then head due south, down Jumeirah Road to the *Burj al Arab* and on to Dubai Marina; it takes the best part of an hour to reach the Marina, and buses can also get unbearably hot in summer. Both services run roughly every 20min from early morning till late evening. In general, it makes more sense to cough up the extra cash and take a cab, or alternatively to take the metro and then a cab for the last part of your journey. Buses are included in the **Nol ticket scheme**, meaning that you'll need to be in possession of a paid-up Nol card or ticket before you board; tickets aren't sold on board.

Buses to other emirates

Buses to neighbouring emirates all leave from Al Ghubaiba bus station in Bur Dubai (from the south side of station, opposite the *New Penninsula Hotel*), with regular services to **Sharjah** (every 20–25min; 45min–1hr 15min depending on traffic; services operate 24hr; 5dh), **Abu Dhabi** (every 30min, 5.30am–11.30pm; 2hr–2hr 30min; 20dh) and **Al Ain** (hourly 6.30am–11.30pm; 1hr 30min–2hr; 20dh). These buses aren't covered by the Nol scheme, and you'll need to buy a ticket at the relevant kiosk in the bus station before boarding.

By car

Renting a car is another option, but comes with a couple of major caveats. Driving in Dubai isn't for the faint-hearted: the city's roads are permanently busy and standards of driving somewhat wayward. **Navigational difficulties** are another big problem. Endless construction works, erratic signage, and road layouts and one-way systems of labyrinthine complexity can make getting anywhere a significant challenge. **Outside the city** you're less likely to get lost, although the main highways down to Abu Dhabi and up to Al Ain are notorious for the wildly aggressive driving styles of local Emiratis. Accidents are common, and considerable caution should be exercised.

Driving is on the right-hand side, and there's a 60 or 80kmph **speed limit** in built-up areas, and 100 or 120kmph on main highways (although locals regularly charge down the fast lane at 150km/h or more). **Parking** can be a major headache. Most hotels (apart from city-centre budget establishments) should have spaces available. Elsewhere you'll have to take your chances with finding an on-street space. Many busier streets now have metred parking (from 2dh/hr). On the plus side, **petrol** is a bargain, at around 1.4dh per litre.

There are also four **road toll points**, run under the "Salik" (ⓦwww.salik.ae) scheme. These are located on Maktoum and Garhoud bridges and at two points along Sheikh Zayed Road (near Al Safa Park, and at Al Barsha, next to the Mall of the Emirates). You don't actually have to stop and pay the toll on the spot – it's automatically charged to your vehicle's account every time you drive through. If you're in a hire car, the rental company will subsequently deduct any toll fees (the basic 4dh toll, plus a 1dh service charge) from your credit card. Taxis are exempt from these tolls.

If you have an **accident**, local law prohibits you from moving your vehicle until the police have been called and the exact circumstances of the crash have been investigated. Note also that **drink-driving** is an absolute no-no. If you're caught behind the wheel with even the slightest trace of alcohol in your system you're facing either a hefty fine, or a spell in prison.

Car rental

All the major international car-rental agencies have offices in Dubai, and there are also dozens of local firms. All the major companies have offices at the airport, and there are also car-hire desks at all major hotels. Alternatively, some of the tour operators listed on p.26 also offer car rental. Drivers will need to be aged 21 (25 for some larger vehicles). Your driving licence from your home country should suffice, although you might want to check in advance. Rates are generally cheap – as little as 75dh (£15) per day for a basic vehicle from a local company, although insurance can push the cost up, especially if you opt for a collision damage waiver. Some agencies will also deliver and collect vehicles from your address in Dubai, saving you the bother of picking up the car in person – check when you book.

Car rental agencies

Alamo ⓦwww.alamo.com.
Auto Europe ⓦwww.autoeurope.com.
Avis ⓦwww.avis.com.
Budget ⓦwww.budget.com.
Dollar ⓦwww.dollar.com.
Enterprise ⓦwww.enterprise.com.
Hertz ⓦwww.hertz.com.
Holiday Autos ⓦwww.holidayautos.co.uk.
National ⓦwww.nationalcar.com.
Rental Car Group ⓦwww.rentalcargroup.com.
Skycars ⓦwww.skycars.com.
SIXT ⓦwww.sixt.com.
Thrifty ⓦwww.thrifty.com.

Tours, cruises and desert safaris

Dubai has dozens of identikit tour operators who pull in a regular supply of punters in search of the instant "Arabian" experience. The emphasis is firmly on stereotypical desert safaris and touristy dhow dinner cruises, although a few operators offer more unusual activities ranging from falconry displays to helicopter rides.

Top of most visitors' wishlists is the chance to get out into the **desert** – although it's worth bearing in mind the sandy hinterlands of Dubai are regarded more as a kind of enormous adventure playground rather than as a natural spectacle, and the emphasis is usually on petrol- and adrenalin-fuelled activities rather than on the quiet contemplation of the untamed sands.

Creek cruises of various types are also perennially popular, with most visitors opting for one of the many dhow dinner cruises offered by operators around the city. There are also numerous **city tours** available, as well as trips to neighbouring emirates. Some operators also offer various **watersports**, as well as **snorkelling** and **diving** (although for diving it's better to contact one of the two specialist dive operators listed on p.135).

Prices can vary quite considerably from operator to operator, so it's worth shopping around. Most operators post latest tariffs on their websites. It's usually easiest **to book** by phone, since few places have conveniently located offices, although many hotels have an in-house tour desk.

The one stand-out operator is **Arabian Adventures**, an offshoot of Emirates Airlines. This is easily the biggest tour operator in town, is very professionally run and boasts a larger-than-average range of trips, including walking tours of old Dubai and Sharjah, visits to Ras al Khaimah and so on. They're more expensive than other operators, but it's usually money well spent. They, along with Lama Tours, Travco and Alpha Tours, run tours to the **Dubai Desert Conservation Reserve**, 45km from Dubai itself (see p.156).

Alpha Tours ⓣ04-294 9888, ⓦwww.alphatoursdubai.com.

Arabian Adventures ⓣ04-303 4888, ⓦwww.arabian-adventures.com. Head office at the Emirates Towers, plus counters in the Jumeirah Beach Hotel, One&Only Royal Mirage, Oasis Beach Hotel, Hilton Jumeirah Beach, Grand Hyatt, Mina A'Salam and Al Qasr hotels.

Hormuz Tourism ⓣ04-228 0668, ⓦwww.hormuztourism.com.

Knight Tours ⓣ04-343 7725, ⓦwww.knighttours.co.ae.

Lama Tours ⓣ04-334 4330, ⓦwww.lama.ae.

Net Tours ⓣ04-266 6655, ⓦwww.nettoursdubai.com.

Orient Tours ⓣ04-282 8238, ⓦwww.orienttours.ae.

Right Tourism ⓣ04-396 9308, ⓦwww.righttourism.com.

Sunflower Tours ⓣ04-334 5554, ⓦwww.sunflowerdubai.com.

Travco ⓣ04-336 6643, ⓦwww.travcotravel.com.

City tours

In addition to the two companies listed below, generic city tours are offered by all the tour companies listed above, although the whistlestop approach isn't likely to yield any particularly interesting insights, and you'll do better to follow your own itinerary unless severely pressed for time.

If you've got the cash you might consider an airborne tour of the city, offering peerless views of the Creek and coast. **Seaplane** tours are offered by Seawings (ⓦwww.seawings.ae), while **helicopter** rides around the city can be arranged by several of the operators listed above, including Arabian Adventures. Both start from around 1000dh per person.

The Big Bus Company ⓣ04-324 4187, ⓦwww.bigbustours.com. The Big Bus Company's open-topped London-style double-decker buses ply two routes, one around the city centre and the other travelling all the way down to Dubai Marina. Buses run roughly every 30min from around 9am–7.30pm every day. It's 220/285dh for a 24/48hr ticket (children aged 5–15 100/130dh), which allows you to ride either route, hopping on and off at any of 20 stops.

Other perks include free entrance to a couple of museums and a free dhow cruise and walking tour. They also run two-hour night tours (100dh) leaving from Deira City Centre and Souk Madinat Jumeirah.

Wonder Bus Tours BurJuman Centre ⓣ04-359 5656. This half bus, half boat contraption departs from the BurJuman centre, drives down to Garhoud Bridge, rolls into the water and sails all the way up the Creek to Shindagha. It then emerges back onto land, returning to BurJuman by road. Trips last about 1hr 30min (including 1hr on the Creek) and cost 140dh (95dh for children aged 3–12). There are four or more trips daily, depending on the tide; book a day ahead to make sure of a place and check latest timings.

Boat cruises

Getting out on the waters of the Creek is one of the highlights of a visit to the city, either via the short **abra** ride across the Creek (see p.23) or via longer abra or **dhow** cruises.

Abra cruises

A more leisurely alternative to the standard Creek crossing by abra is to charter your own boat. This costs 100dh for an hour-long ride along the Creek. Starting from somewhere in the city centre, in an hour you can probably get down to the Dubai Creek Golf Club and back. To find an abra for hire, head to the nearest abra station and ask around. The rate is officially set (and posted in writing at all abra stations) and is the same regardless of how many people use the boat, so don't be talked into paying more.

Dinner cruises

A more comfortable alternative to chartering an abra is to go on one of the ever-popular after-dark **dinner cruises**; most of these use traditional old wooden dhows and offer leisurely and beautiful views of nighttime old Dubai. Standard dinner cruises last two hours and cost anything from 120dh up to 350dh, depending on which operator and boat you go with, inclusive of a buffet dinner and on-board entertainment; boats normally leave around 8–8.30pm.

Dinner cruises can be booked through any of the tour operators listed opposite, as well as many of the city's hotels. Independent operators include: **Rikks Cruises** (ⓣ04-357 2200, ⓦwww.rikks.net), with trips for a bargain 145dh; the slightly more upmarket **Al Mansour Dhow**, operated by the *Radisson Blu* hotel (ⓣ04-205 7033), which charges 185dh; and **Bateaux Dubai** (ⓣ04-399 4994, ⓦwww.bateauxdubai.com), which costs 295dh and uses a state-of-the-art glass-sided modern boat rather than a traditional dhow – it offers a touch more luxury than other operators and above-average food.

Desert safaris

One thing that virtually every visitor to Dubai does at some point is go on a **desert safari**. The main attraction of these trips is the chance to see some of the desert scenery surrounding Dubai, and although virtually all tours put the emphasis firmly on cheap thrills and touristy gimmicks most people find the experience enjoyable, in a rather cheesy sort of way.

Sunset safaris

The vast majority of visitors opt for one of the endlessly popular **half-day safaris** (also known as "sunset safaris"). These are offered by every tour operator in town (see the list opposite) and cost from around 165dh up to 330dh. Whoever you decide to go with the basic ingredients remain the same, although staff employed by the cheaper operators are sometimes guilty of shockingly dangerous driving en route to the dunes.

Tours are in large 4WDs holding around eight passengers. You'll be picked up from your hotel between 3 and 4pm and then, once you've driven around town collecting the other passengers in your vehicle, be driven out into the desert. The usual destination is an area 45-minutes drive out of town on the road to Al Ain, opposite the massive dune popularly known as Big Red (see p.167).

After a brief stop, during which your vehicle's tyres will be partially deflated as a preparation for going off-road, you'll be driven out into the dunes on the opposite side of the highway from Big Red for an hour or so to enjoy the traditional Emirati pastime of **dune-bashing**. This involves driving at high speed up and down increasingly precipitous dunes amid great sprays of sand while your vehicle slides, skids, bumps and occasionally takes off completely. Thrills apart, the dunes are magnificent, and very beautiful at sunset, and although it's difficult to see much while you're being bumped around inside the vehicle, your driver will probably stop near the highest point of the dunes so that you can get out, enjoy the scenery and take some photos. You might also be given the chance to try your hand at a brief bit of sand-skiing. Alternatively, some tour operators take you back to the main road, where you can go for a ride across the dunes on a quad bike – or "dune buggy" – generally for an additional fee.

As dusk falls, you'll be driven off to one of the dozens of optimistically named "Bedouin camps", in the desert, usually with various tents rigged up around a sandy enclosure and belly dancing stage. Wherever you're taken you'll find pretty much the same touristy fare on offer, all included in the tour price. These typically include (very short) camel rides, henna painting, dressing up in Gulf national costume, and having your photo taken with an Emirati falcon perched on your arm. A passable international buffet dinner is then served, after which a belly dancer performs for another half hour or so, dragging likely-looking members of the audience up on stage with her (choose your seat carefully). It's all good, cheesy fun, although the belly dancer is more likely to be from Moscow than Muscat, and the floor tends to get rapidly swamped with jolly Indian businessmen. The whole thing winds up at around 9.30pm, after which you'll be driven back to Dubai.

Other desert safaris

If you want to get more of a feel for the desert, some tour operators offer the chance to extend your sunset safari into an **overnight trip**, sleeping out in tents before returning to Dubai after breakfast the following morning. This offers you a much better chance of getting some sense of the emptiness and grandeur of the landscape than during the belly dancing free-for-all.

Some companies also offer **full-day desert safaris**. These usually include a mixture of general sightseeing combined with activities like dune-bashing, camel riding, sand-skiing and dune-buggy riding before returning to Dubai at dusk. These tours are also the best way to experience the popular pastime of wadi-bashing – driving through the rocky, dried-up riverbeds that score the eastern side of the UAE around the Hajar Mountains. Some operators also offer more specifically activity-oriented tours focusing exclusively on things like sand-skiing, camel trekking and dune-buggy riding.

The media

The media in Dubai and elsewhere in the UAE is a classic example of self-censorship in action. Overt government pressure is rarely applied, but the largely expat journalists who work on the country's English-language press are aware that criticism of the government or the discussion of sensitive political or religious issues is likely to result in their publication losing crucial advertising revenue (most of which is likely to come from government-owned companies) or in having their visas cancelled. As a result, Dubai's media is not renowned for its investigative journalism or controversial reportage; for some alternative online news sources, see the websites listed on p.40.

Newspapers and magazines

Easily the best English-language **newspaper** is *The National* (based in Abu Dhabi, but with extensive coverage of Dubai; Ⓦwww.thenational.ae). This has good international reporting and is generally well-written and slightly less cringing in its coverage of UAE affairs than the country's other dailies. Of the two English-language broadsheets printed in Dubai, *Gulf News* (Ⓦwww.gulfnews.com) is usually a bit better than the *Khaleej Times* (Ⓦwww.khaleejtimes.com), though both are a bit turgid, with rather too many pictures of random ruling sheikhs attending official engagements and assorted "news" stories which quite clearly originated in a government press release. Other papers include the free *7 Days* tabloid-style rag (Ⓦwww.7days.ae) and the much more sober *Emirates Business* (Ⓦwww.business24-7.ae).

Television and radio

There are a number of Emirati **television** channels, including the English-language Dubai One (Ⓦwww.dmi.ae/dubaione) and Arabic-language Sama Dubai. The former consists mainly of re-packaged US shows and movies, along with a few local programmes.

There are a couple of local English-language **radio** stations, including Virgin Radio Dubai (104.4 FM; Ⓦwww.virginradiodubai.com) and Dubai 92 (92FM; Ⓦwww.dubai92.com), though both largely subsist on an uninspiring diet of mainstream pop-rock and inane DJ chat.

Festivals

Despite Dubai's popular reputation as the land which culture forgot, the city hosts a number of world-class annual festivals showcasing film, music and the visual arts. Neighbouring Abu Dhabi also stages a number of leading cultural events. Annual sporting events are covered on p.133.

Religious

Ramadan Scheduled to run from approximately 1–29 Aug 2011, 20 July to Aug 18, 2012, 9 July to Aug 7, 2013, 28 June to 27 July 2014; precise dates vary according to local astronomical sightings of the moon. The Islamic holy month of Ramadan is observed with great attention and ceremony in Dubai, and is the one time of the year when you really get the sense of being in an essentially Muslim city. For Muslims, Ramadan represents a period in which to purify mind and body and to reaffirm one's relationship with God. Muslims are required to fast from dawn to dusk, and as a tourist you will be expected to publicly observe these strictures, although you are free to eat and drink in the privacy of your own hotel room, or in any of the carefully screened-off dining areas which are set up in hotels throughout the city (while alcohol is also served discreetly in some places after dark, but not during the day). Eating, drinking, smoking or chewing gum in public, however, is a definite no-no, and will cause considerable offence to local Muslims; singing, dancing and swearing in public are similarly frowned upon. In addition, live music is also completely forbidden during the holy month (though recorded music is allowed), while the city's nightclubs all close for the duration, and many shops scale back their opening hours.

Fasting ends at dusk, at which point the previously comatose city springs to life in a celebratory round of eating, drinking and socializing known as Iftar ("The Breaking of the Fast"). Many of the city's top hotels set up superb "Iftar tents", with lavish Arabian buffets, and the city remains lively until the small hours, when everyone goes off to bed in preparation for another day of abstinence. The atmosphere is particularly exuberant, and the Iftar tents especially lavish, during Eid Al Fitr, the day marking the end of Ramadan, when the entire city erupts in an explosion of celebratory festivity.

Eid al Adha Estimated dates: Nov 6, 2011; Oct 26, 2012; Oct 15, 2013; Oct 4, 2014. Falling approximately 70 days after the end of Ramadan, on the tenth day of the Islamic lunar month of Dhul Hijja, the "Festival of the Sacrifice" celebrates the willingness of Ibrahim to sacrifice his son Ismail at the command of God (although having proved his obedience, he was permitted to sacrifice a ram instead). The festival also marks the end of the traditional pilgrimage season to Mecca. Eid al Adha is celebrated in Dubai with a four-day holiday. During the festival, lambs are sacrificed and the meat divided among the poor. No alcohol is served on the day before the festival day itself.

January/February

Al Dhafra Festival Nine days in late-Jan and early Feb, Ⓦ www.aldhafrafestival.ae/en. Held at the small town of Madinat Zayed in western Abu Dhabi emirate, this lively annual festival is devoted to traditional Bedouin desert culture and heritage. The centrepiece of the festival is a huge camel fair, with races, auctions and even beauty competitions for the best-looking dromedaries. Other events showcase the region's handicrafts, poetry, cooking and traditional date industry.

Dubai Shopping Festival Late Jan–late Feb, Ⓦ www.mydsf.ae. Only Dubai could dream up a festival devoted to shopping – and only in Dubai, one suspects, would it have proved so popular. The festival sees shops city-wide offering all sorts of sales bargains, with discounts of up to 75 percent, while the big malls lay on lots of entertainment and children's events to keep punters' offspring amused during their parents' extended shopping binges. The festival also sees the opening of the Global Village (Ⓦ www.globalvillage.ae) in Dubailand: a range of eye-catching international pavilions showcasing arts and crafts from countries around the world, as well as performances of world music and dance, plus other events. Hotels tend to fill up during the festival, and room rates rise.

Dubai International Jazz Festival First two weeks in Feb, Ⓦ www.dubaijazzfest.com. Top local and international jazz and pop acts perform at Dubai Media City. Previous participants have included the Brand New Heavies, James Morrison and David Gray.

March

Art Dubai mid-March, Ⓦ www.artdubai.ae. The biggest event in the Dubai visual arts calendar, the four-day Art Dubai art fair features exhibits from some 70 galleries from around the world at Madinat Jumeirah.

Bastakiya Art Fair mid-March, Ⓦ www.bastakiyaartfair.com. Held at the same time as Art Dubai (see above), the lively week-long Bastakiya Art Fair offers a kind of fringe alternative to its more mainstream cousin, with shows by local artists spread across venues throughout the historic Bastakiya quarter.

Taste of Dubai mid-March, Dubai Media City, Ⓦ www.tasteofdubaifestival.com. Three days of live cookery exhibitions by local and visiting international celebrity chefs, plus wine-tastings and the chance to sample signature dishes from some of the city's leading restaurants at heavily discounted prices.

April

Perrier Chill Out Festival mid-April. Laidback two-day music festival featuring local and international DJs and bands. The 2010 event was held at the Atlantis resort, although the festival has tended to change venue from year to year. Check *Time Out Dubai* or online for latest details.

Womad Abu Dhabi mid-April, Ⓦ www.womadabudhabi.ae. Abu Dhabi edition of the legendary world music festival, with three days of free concerts on the Abu Dhabi Corniche and at Al Jahili Fort in Al Ain. Previous acts have included Rachid Taha, Tinariwen, Femi Kuti, TV on the Radio and Damian Marley.

June, July and August

Dubai Summer Surprises approximately June 15–Aug 10, Ⓦ www.mydsf.ae. An attempt to lure visitors to Dubai during the blisteringly hot summer months from June to August, Dubai Summer Surprises (DSS) is a mainly mall-based event – really more of a marketing promotion than a genuine festival – with a decent selection of shopping bargains on offer and masses of live children's entertainments presided over by the irritating cartoon figure known as Modhesh, whose crinkly yellow features you'll probably quickly learn to loathe. Great if you've got kids in tow, however.

October

Abu Dhabi Film Festival mid-Oct, Ⓦ www.abudhabifilmfestival.ae. Established in 2007 to encourage the work of Arab film-makers, and serving up a wide-ranging selection of films and documentaries from around the world. The 2009 festival featured 128 films from 49 countries, with guest appearances by assorted Hollywood, Bollywood and Middle Eastern celebrities.

December

Dubai International Film Festival mid-Dec, Ⓦ www.dubaifilmfest.com. This week-long major film festival showcases international art house films, with a particular focus on home-grown work. There are usually a few well known celebs in attendance.

National Day Dec 2. The UAE's independence day is celebrated with a raft of citywide events, including parades, dhow races, and performances of traditional music and dance, while the locals drape their cars with the national flag and drive around tooting their horns.

Culture and etiquette

Given the cultural melting-pot which is contemporary Dubai, it's difficult to generalize about acceptable standards of behaviour and etiquette, which inevitably vary massively between the city's various expat communities, not to mention the hordes of visiting tourists.

If you're lucky enough to have some contact with the city's Emirati population, a few basic rules are worth bearing in mind. Only the right hand should be used for eating and drinking (this rule also applies to Indian establishments), and you should not offer to shake the hand of an Emirati woman unless she extends hers toward you. **Dress** is also a major source of potential cultural embarrassment. All over Dubai you'll see Western (and sometimes expat Arab) women walking around in tiny tops and microscopic skirts, although it's worth remembering that such displays of flesh, although not strictly illegal, cause considerable offence to local Emiratis. Even men who wear shorts can raise eyebrows – to the locals it looks like you're walking around in your underwear.

On a more general note, it's worth remembering Dubai is somewhat less permissive than it would superficially appear, and the emirate's decency laws could conceivably see you locked up for behaviour which would be considered fairly unexceptionable back at home. There are two cardinal rules. The first concerns **drunkenness**. Any public display of drunkenness outside a licenced venue contravenes local law, and could get you locked up. Driving while under any sort of influence is even more of a no-no (see p.25). The second concerns appropriate **public behaviour**. Holding hands or kissing on the cheek is probably just about OK, but any more passionate displays of public affection are severely frowned upon. The case of Michelle Palmer and Vince Acors, who were jailed for three months after allegedly having sex on the beach and assaulting a policeman, received widespread coverage, although far less overt demonstrations of affection can potentially land you in big trouble; in April 2010 two British citizens were sentenced to a month in jail for allegedly kissing one another on the lips in public at a restaurant in Dubai Marina.

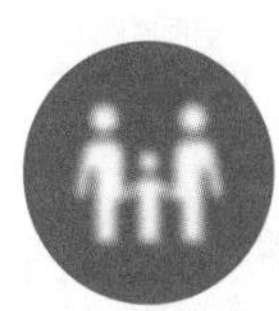

Travelling with children

Dubai has a vast array of attractions children will enjoy, ranging from superb waterparks, dolphinariums, snowdomes and other cutting-edge activities (albeit at generally hefty prices) through to more low-key pleasures including mall-based play areas and hotel kids' clubs, or simply messing around on the beach. Older children will also enjoy the chance to soak up some of the city's traditional Arabian atmosphere, whether taking an abra ride on the Creek or just wandering through the souks.

If you're planning a family holiday to Dubai it's worth noting that all the city's beach hotels have their own in-house **kids' clubs**, providing free childcare while you get on with some serious sunbathing or shopping – a significant perk to offset the usually stratospheric room rates. These clubs usually cater for ages 4 to 12 (under 4s are sometimes admitted, though a parent or guardian will need to stay in attendance), but be sure to check exactly what's included before booking. Most hotels can also arrange **babysitting** services, for a fee.

A number of the city's larger malls have dedicated **kids' play areas** featuring various attractions ranging from soft-play equipment and gentle coin-operated rides for toddlers up to arcade games and other attractions for older kids. Entrance to all these areas is free, although individual attractions within them will cost. The main places are Fun City (BurJuman, Mercato and Ibn Battuta malls), Magic Planet (Mall of the Emirates and Deira City Centre) and the Wafi Encounter Zone at the Wafi mall. The city's malls also host a wide range of **children's events and entertainers** during the Dubai Shopping Festival and Dubai Summer Surprises Citywide (see p.30).

For full coverage of Dubai's **beaches**, see p.93 & p.135.

Dedicated kids' attractions

As well as the various hotel kids' clubs and mall-based play areas covered above, Dubai also boasts several superb dedicated children's attractions aimed at all ages from toddlers to teens.

Children's City Oud Metha ⓦwww.childrencity.ae Occupying a series of brightly coloured red and blue buildings – modelled after children's play bricks – at the southern end of Creekside Park, Children's City is aimed at kids aged 2–15, with a subtle educational slant. A series of galleries with fun interactive exhibits and lots of touchscreens cover subjects including physical science, nature, international culture and space exploration. There's also a play space, while kids aged 2–5 can muck around with sand and water in the toddlers' area. Sat–Thurs 9am–8.30pm, Fri 3–8.30pm; 15dh, children 3–15 years 10dh, under 2s free, family ticket for 2 adults and 2 children 40dh, 5dh park entry fee.

Dubai Dolphinarium Gate #1, Creekside Park, Oud Metha ⓦwww.dubaidolphinarium.ae. Twice-daily shows (Mon–Sat at 11am & 6pm; also Fri & Sat at 3pm; adults 100dh, children 50dh) starring the dolphinarium's three resident bottlenose dolphins and four seals. Alternatively, you can go swimming with the dolphins (advance reservations required; 400dh).

KidZania Dubai Mall, ⓦwww.kidzania.ae. Innovative edu-tainment attraction based on an imaginary, miniaturized city where the kids are in charge. Children get the chance to dress up and role play from 75 different grown-up professions (anything from airline pilot to archeologist), getting involved in the commercial life of the "city" and even earning their own money en route. Under 2s free, ages 2–3 95dh, ages 4–16 125dh, age 17+ 90dh.

Sega Republic Dubai Mall, Level 2 ⓦwww.segarepublic.com. Huge, superb indoor theme park featuring a range of adrenaline-pumping rides and other amusements for kids of all ages, although more likely to appeal to older children. Five themed "zones" cover a range of wildlife, sporting and high-speed rides and activities, including the "Wild Jungle" ride, the Spin Gear indoor horizontal spinning-coaster and the Sonic Hopper drop tower; there's also a big selection of Sega arcade games with prizes. Daily 10am–10pm, Thurs–Sat until midnight. 125dh for one-day pass to the nine main rides, 200dh for one-day pass to nine main rides plus 200dh credit for other attractions; general admission ticket 10dh, with pay as you go from 15–30dh for individual rides.

Top family-friendly hotels

Atlantis Huge beach and a superb range of children's facilities and attractions including Aquaventure, Dolphin Bay and the Lost Chambers. See p.89 and p.106.

Jumeirah Beach Hotel Brilliant kids' facilities, including huge grounds, pools and one of the city's best kids' clubs. See p.83 and p.106.

Le Royal Méridien Vast swathe of beach, gardens and pools, plus good kids' club and watersports centre. See p.108.

Sheraton Jumeirah Beach Low-key and very family-friendly resort, with good kids' facilities and rates which are often significantly lower than those at other beachside hotels. See p.108.

Five top children's shops

Camel Company Cute camels galore – a guaranteed child pleaser. Locations across the city. See p.142.

Al Jabeer The place for kitsch Arabian handicrafts, with locations citywide. See p.142.

Hamley's Branch of the famous London toy store, located in the Dubai Mall.

Toys R Us Head to the Festival Centre for a reliable source of all the latest kiddie crazes.

Toy World Dubai's leading toy shop, with branches in the Mall of the Emirates and Ibn Battuta Mall, offering everything from Teletubbies to Roboraptors.

Other kids' attractions

As well as the dedicated kids' attractions listed above, Dubai also has a wide range of other attractions which are guaranteed child-pleasers. Top of the list are the city's various **waterparks** and other marine attractions, including Wild Wadi (see p.83), Aquaventure and Dolphin Bay (see p.89) and the Dubai Dolphinarium (see opposite), not to mention the various **watersports** offered at the marina hotels (see p.93). Active older kids will also enjoy Dubai Ice Rink (see p.136) and the surreal Ski Dubai (see p.85), while Ferrari World (see p.175) down the road at Yas Island in Abu Dhabi, is another possibility.

In terms of general attractions there are plenty of other **sights** in the city which are likely to amuse the offspring. These include nature-related activities like a visit to the Dubai Aquarium (see p.74), the Lost Chambers at the Atlantis resort (see p.90) and Dubai Zoo (see p.78). A ride on the cable car above Creekside Park (see p.65) is another possibility, as is the spectacular Dubai Fountain (see p.75).

There are also a number of child-friendly **tours** in and around the city. Most kids will enjoy a desert safari (see p.27), while within the city itself there are enjoyable rides with the Big Bus Company (see p.26) and aboard the engaging Wonder Bus (see p.27), not to mention abra rides and cruises across or along the Creek (see p.23 & p.48).

Travel essentials

Costs

Dubai has never been a bargain destination, and although it's possible to get by without spending huge amounts of money, unless you're prepared to splash at least a certain amount of cash you'll miss out on much of what the city has to offer. The biggest basic cost is **accommodation**. At the very bottom end of the scale it's possible to find a double room for the night for around 300dh (£55/$80). For more upmarket hotels you're looking at more like 700dh (£125/$180) per night, while you won't usually get a bed in one of the city's five-stars for less than around 1200dh (£220/$325) per night at the absolute minimum; room rates at the very best places can run into thousands of dirhams. Other costs are more fluid. **Eating** is very much a question of what you want to spend: you can eat well in the budget curry houses or shwarma cafés of Bur Dubai and Karama for around 15dh (£3/$4) per head, although a meal (with drinks) in a more upmarket establishment is likely to set you back around 300dh (£55/$80) per head, and the sky is the limit in the top restaurants. **Tourist attractions** are also likely to put a big dent in your wallet, especially if you're travelling with children: the cost of a family day out at one of the city's waterparks or kids' attractions is likely to set you back at least 600dh (£110/$165). On the plus side, **transport** costs are relatively modest, given the city's inexpensive taxi services (see p.22) and metro system.

Taxes and tipping

Room rates at most of the city's more expensive hotels are subject to a ten percent **service charge** and an additional ten percent **government tax**; these taxes are sometimes included in quoted prices, and sometimes not. Check beforehand, otherwise you may find your bill has suddenly inflated by twenty percent. The prices in most restaurants automatically include a ten percent service charge (though this isn't necessarily passed on to the waiters themselves); whether you wish to leave an additional **tip** is entirely your decision.

Crime, safety and the law

Dubai is an exceptionally safe city. Violent crime is virtually unknown, and even instances of petty theft, pickpocketing and the like are relatively uncommon. The only place you're ever likely to be at risk is while **driving** (see p.24). If you need to **call** the police in an emergency, dial ⓣ999. You can also contact the police's Tourist Security Department toll-free on ⓣ800 4438 if you have an enquiry or complaint which you think the police could help you with. It's also worth having a look at the international government websites listed on p.40 for latest information about safety issues.

Illegal substances and prescription drugs

You should not on any account attempt to enter (or even transit through) Dubai while in possession of any form of **illegal substance**. The death penalty is imposed for drug trafficking, and there's a mandatory four-year sentence for anyone caught in possession of drugs or other proscribed substances. It's vital to note that this doesn't just mean carrying drugs in a conventional sense, but also includes having an illegal substance in your **bloodstream or urine**, or being found in possession of even **microscopic amounts** of banned substance, even if invisible to the naked eye. Previous visitors have been convicted on the basis of minute traces of cannabis and other substances found in the fluff of a pocket or suitcase lining, or even stuck to the sole of a shoe.

Even more contentiously, Dubai's hardline anti-drugs regime also extends to certain **prescription drugs**, including codeine and melatonin, which are also treated as illegal substances. If you're on any form of prescription medicine it's worth either acquiring a doctor's certificate, checking with your local embassy or consulate, or just leaving it at home. A list of prohibited medicines can be found at Ⓦwww.dubaitourism.ae (click on the "Getting to Dubai" then the "Tips for Tourists" tabs and follow the link).

There's clear evidence that customs officials at Dubai airport employ a degree of **racial and/or cultural profiling** in targeting potential "criminals" entering the UAE. Those of African or Afro-Caribbean descent appear to be particularlly at risk, as does anyone dressed in a particularly unusual/alternative manner. The more boringly "respectable" you look, the less hassle you're likely to encounter.

Electricity

UK-style **sockets** with three square pins are the norm (although you might occasionally encounter Indian-style round-pin sockets in budget hotels in Bur Dubai and Deira). The city's **current** runs at 220–240 volts AC, meaning that UK appliances will work without problem directly off the mains supply, although US appliances will probably require a transformer.

Entry requirements

Nationals of most Western European countries including the UK and Ireland, the US, Canada, Australia and New Zealand are issued a **free sixty-day visa** on arrival (renewable for a further thirty days for 500dh). You'll need a passport which will be valid for at least six months after the date of entry. Israeli citizens are not officially permitted to enter the UAE (although exceptions are apparently sometimes made); having an Israeli stamp in your passport should not prevent you entering Dubai. For full details see Ⓦwww.dubaitourism.ae (click on the "Visa" link under the "Getting to Dubai" tab).

Customs regulations allow visitors to bring in up to 400 cigarettes (or 50 cigars or 500g of tobacco), four litres of alcohol (or 2 cartons of beer), and cash and travellers' cheques up to a value of 40,000dh. Prohibited items include drugs (for more on which see opposite), pornographic material, material offensive to Islamic teachings, and goods of Israeli origin or bearing Israeli trademarks or logos. For full details see Ⓦwww.dubaicustoms.gov.ae and click on the "For Travellers" link on the left-hand side of the page.

Consulates

Foreign embassies are mainly located in the UAE's capital, Abu Dhabi, although many countries also maintain consulates in Dubai.

Australia Consulate-General, Level 25, BurJuman Business Tower, Khalifa bin Zayed Rd, Bur Dubai Ⓣ04-5087 100.

Canada Consulate-General, 7th floor, Bank Street Building (behind the BurJuman centre, next to Citibank), Khalid bin al Waleed Rd, Bur Dubai Ⓣ04-314 5555.

Ireland 4th floor, Monarch Hotel Office Tower, 1 Sheikh Zayed Road (opposite the World Trade Centre) Ⓣ0966 1-488 2300.

New Zealand Consulate-General, Suite 1502, 15th Floor, API Tower, Sheikh Zayed Road Ⓣ04-331 7500.

Oman Consulate-General, 6th St, off the north side of Khalid bin al Waleed Rd, Bur Dubai Ⓣ04-397 1000.

South Africa Consulate-General, 3rd Floor, New Sharaf Building, Khaleed bin al Waleed Rd, Bur Dubai Ⓣ04-397 5222.

UK Embassy, Al Seef Rd, Bur Dubai, Ⓣ04-309 4444.

US Consulate-General, World Trade Centre, Sheikh Zayed Rd Ⓣ04-311 6000.

Gay Dubai

Dubai is one of the world's less-friendly gay and lesbian destinations. Homosexuality is illegal under UAE law, with punishments of up to ten years in prison. Despite this, the city boasts a very clandestine gay scene, attracting both foreigners and Arabs from even less-permissive cities around the Gulf, although you'll need to hunt hard to find it without local contacts. Relevant websites (such as Ⓦwww.gaymiddleeast.com) are routinely censored within the UAE, so you'll have to do online research before you arrive.

Health

There are virtually no serious **health risks** in Dubai (unless you include the city's traffic). The

Emergency numbers

Ambulance Ⓣ0999
Police Ⓣ999
Fire Ⓣ997

city is well equipped with modern hospitals, while all four- and five-star hotels have English-speaking **doctors** on call 24 hour. **Tap water** is safe to drink, while even the city's cheapest curry houses and shwarma cafés maintain good standards of **food hygiene**. The only possible health concern is the **heat**. Summer temperatures regularly climb into the mid-forties, making sunburn, heatstroke and acute dehydration a real possibility, especially if combined with excessive alcohol consumption. Stay in the shade, and drink lots of water.

There are **pharmacies** all over the city, including a number run by the BinSina chain which are open 24 hour. These include branches on Mankhool Road just north of the *Ramada* hotel; on the Creek side of Baniyas Square (in the building on the east side of the Deira Tower); in southern Jumeirah at the turn-off to the Majlis Ghorfat um al Sheif; and in Satwa on Al Diyafah Street between the *Al Mallah* and *Beirut* cafés.

Government hospitals

There are three main government hospitals (more details at Ⓦwww.dohms.gov.ae) with emergency departments. You'll need to pay for treatment, though cost should be recoverable through your travel insurance.

Dubai Hospital Between the Corniche and Baraha St, Deira Ⓣ04-271 444 (see map, p.54).
Rashid Hospital Off Oud Metha Rd, near Maktoum Bridge, Oud Metha Ⓣ04-337 4000 (see map, p.63).
Wasl Hospital Oud Metha Rd (just west of Wafi), Oud Metha Ⓣ04-324 1111 (see map, p.63).

Private hospitals

Private hospitals with emergency departments include:

American Hospital Off Oud Metha Rd (opposite the *Mövenpick* hotel), Oud Metha Ⓣ04-336 7777, Ⓦwww.ahdubai.com.
Emirates Hospital Opposite Jumeirah Beach Park, Jumeirah Beach Rd, Jumeirah Ⓣ04-349 6666, Ⓦwww.emirateshospital.ae.

Insurance

There aren't many safety or health risks involved in a visit to Dubai, although it's still strongly recommended that you take out some form of valid **travel insurance** before your trip. At its simplest, this offers some measure of protection against everyday mishaps like cancelled flights and mislaid baggage. More importantly, a valid insurance policy will cover your costs in the (admittedly unlikely) event that you fall ill in Dubai, since otherwise you'll have to pay for all medical treatment. Most insurance policies routinely exclude various "adventure" activities. In Dubai this could mean things like wall-climbing (see p.136) or tackling the black run at Ski Dubai (see p.85). If in doubt, check with your insurer before you leave home.

Internet

Dubai is a very wired city, although getting online can prove frustratingly difficult (or expensive) for casual visitors. All the better **hotels** provide internet access, either via computers in their business centres or via wi-fi or in-room cable connections. This is sometimes provided free, although more often is chargeable, often at extortionate rates (30dh/hr is common in more upmarket hotels).

The major concentration of **internet cafés** is found in Bur Dubai. There are dozens of

Rough Guides travel insurance

Rough Guides has teamed up with WorldNomads.com to offer great **travel insurance** deals. Policies are available to residents of over 150 countries, with cover for a wide range of **adventure sports**, 24-hour emergency assistance, high levels of medical and evacuation cover and a stream of **travel safety information**. Roughguides.com users can take advantage of their policies online 24/7, from anywhere in the world – even if you're already travelling. And since plans often change when you're on the road, you can extend your policy and even claim online. Roughguides.com users who buy travel insurance with WorldNomads.com can also leave a positive footprint and donate to a community development project. For more information go to Ⓦ**www.roughguides.com/shop**.

small places, including many in the small roads and alleyways off Al Fahidi Street, catering to the area's Indian population. Prices are usually cheap – 5dh per hour is typical. One reliable place is the Al Jalssa internet café (10dh/hr; daily 8am–midnight) in the Al Ain centre. Elsewhere, internet cafés are few and far between. The Grano Coffee shop in Wafi (14dh/hr) is one of the few reliable places.

Things are slightly easier if you have **your own wi-fi enabled laptop** or other wi-fi device. There are various free wi-fi hotspots around the city, including the whole of the Dubai Mall. You can also get online on the Dubai Metro for 10dh per hour. Various wi-fi hotspots are also operated by the city's two telecom companies, Eitsalat (Ⓦwww.etisalat.ae) and Du (Ⓦwww.du.ae). Both offer access at numerous places around the city, including most of the city's malls and numerous coffee shops, with various pay-as-you-go packages. Du is currently the cheaper of the two, with rates from 10dh for an hour's one-off surf time. See the websites for full details of charges and hotspot locations.

Internet **censorship** in Dubai is also a major bone of contention. There's a blanket ban on anything remotely pornographic and on any sites considered religiously or politically sensitive, including any sites critical of the UAE government. The axe can fall suddenly and often apparently at random, targetting not just low-grade smut but also mainstream international sites. MySpace, Youtube and Facebook have all been blocked in the past (even the website of the UK's Middlesex University was formerly blocked thanks to its inadvertently suggestive name), while Flickr and certain pages of Wikipedia currently remain inaccessible, and the government has also banned Skype. Useful information about the latest internet censorship can be found at Ⓦwww.dubaifaqs.com/censorship-uae-internet.php.

Mail

The two most convenient **post offices** for visitors are the Al Musalla Post Office at Al Fahidi Roundabout (opposite the Basta Arts Café) in Bur Dubai; and the Deira Post Office on Al Sabkha Road, near the intersection with Baniyas Road. Both are open Sat–Thurs 10am–3pm. Airmail letters to Europe, the US and Australia cost 5dh (postcards 3.5dh); airmail parcels cost 50dh to Europe and 80dh to the US and Australia for parcels weighing 500g to 1kg. Note that there are no **poste restante** facilities in Dubai. If you wish to receive mail it's best to have it addressed to your hotel, clearly marked "guest at hotel", and to forewarn the reception desk of its arrival.

Maps

The best general **city maps** are the pocket-sized *Dubai Mini Map* and the larger *Dubai Map,* (around 40dh/20dh) published by Explorer and widely available from bookshops around the city. Both combine a handy overview map of the city along with more detailed coverage of individual areas, with clear cartography and all relevant tourist attractions and other local landmarks clearly marked. They're also updated on a regular basis, and make a laudable effort to keep pace with the city's constantly changing road layouts and other ongoing developments. The only A–Z style **street atlas** currently available is the *Dubai Street Map* (also published by Explorer; around 80dh); this shows every road in the city, but is frustratingly lacking in other detail and not particularly useful.

For more general coverage, the best source is the *Dubai, UAE, Qatar & Bahrain* (£5.99/$9.99) map (1:470,000), published by Rough Guides. This is easy to read, and printed on virtually indestructible Polyart paper.

Money

The UAE currency is the **dirham** (abbreviated "dh" or "AED"), subdivided into 100 fils. The dirham is pegged against the US dollar at the rate of US$1=3.6725dh; other **exchange rates** at the time of writing were £1=5.47dh, €1=4.75dh. **Notes** come in 5dh, 10dh, 20dh, 50dh, 100dh, 200dh, 500dh and 1000dh denominations; there are also 2dh, 1dh, 50 fils and 25 fils coins. The 5dh, 50dh and 500dh notes are all a confusingly similar shade of brown; take care not to hand over the wrong sort.

There are plenty of **ATMs** all over the city which accept foreign Visa and MasterCards.

All the big shopping malls have at least a few ATMs, as do some large hotels. There are banks everywhere, almost all of which have ATMs. The most common are Mashreqbank, Commercial Bank of Dubai, National Bank of Dubai, National Bank of Abu Dhabi and Emirates Bank. All will also change **travellers' cheques** and **foreign cash**, and there are also plenty of **money-changers** in Bur Dubai (try along and around Al Fahidi St) and Deira (try Sikkat Al Khail Rd, en route to the Gold Souk).

Opening hours and public holidays

Dubai runs on an Islamic rather than a Western schedule, meaning that the city operates according to a basic **five-day working week** running Sunday to Thursday, with Friday as the Islamic holy day (equivalent to the Christian Sunday). Some offices also open on a Saturday, while others close at midday on Thursday. When people talk about the **weekend** in Dubai they mean Friday and Saturday (and perhaps Thursday afternoon/evening as well). The most important fact to note is that many tourist sites and the Dubai Metro are **closed on Friday morning**, while **banks** usually open Sat–Wed 8am–1pm and Thurs 8am–noon (some also re-open in the afternoon from 4.30–6.30pm).

Shops in **malls** generally open daily from 10am to 10pm, and until midnight on Friday and Saturday; shops in **souks** follow a similar pattern, though many places close for a siesta between around 1pm and 4pm depending on the whim of the owner. Most **restaurants** open daily for lunch and dinner – all exceptions are noted in the relevant listings. **Pubs** tend to open daily from around midday until 2am; **bars** from around 6pm until 2/3am.

Phones

The **country code** for the UAE is ⓣ971. The **city code** for Dubai is ⓣ04; Abu Dhabi is ⓣ02; Sharjah is ⓣ06; Al Ain is ⓣ03. To **call abroad from the UAE**, dial ⓣ00, followed by your country code and the number itself (minus its initial zero). To call the UAE from abroad, dial your international access code, then ⓣ9714, followed by the local subscriber number (minus the ⓣ04 city code). Local mobile numbers begin with ⓣ050, 055 or 056 followed by a seven digit number. If you've got a number that's not working, try prefixing it with both ⓣ04 and the various mobile phone prefixes – mobiles are so widely used now that many people don't specify whether a number is a landline or a mobile.

If you're going to be using the phone a lot while you're in Dubai, it might be worth acquiring a **local SIM card**, which will give you cheap local and international calls. The

Public holidays

There are eight public holidays in Dubai: two have fixed dates, while the other six shift annually according to the Islamic calendar (falling around 11 days earlier from year to year).

New Year's Day January 1

National Day (see p.30) December 2

Mouloud (The Prophet's Birthday) Estimated dates: 15 Feb 2011, 4 Feb 2012, 24 Jan 2013.

Leilat al Meiraj (Ascent of the Prophet) Estimated dates: 9 July 2011, 28 June 2012, 17 June 2013.

Eid al Fitr (the end of Ramadan – see p.29) Estimated dates: 31 Aug 2011, 19 Aug 2012, 8 Aug 2013, 29 July 2014.

Eid al Adha (the Festival of the Sacrifice – see p.29). Estimated dates: 6 Nov 2011, 26 Oct 2012, 15 Oct 2013, 4 Oct 2014.

Al Hijra (Islamic New Year) Estimated dates: 26 Nov 2011, 15 Nov 2012, 4 Nov 2013.

Ashura Estimated dates: 5 Dec 2011, 24 Nov 2012, 13 Nov 2013.

Useful phone numbers

Local directory enquiries ⓣ181
International enquiries ⓣ150
Police and ambulance ⓣ999
Airport enquiries ⓣ04-224 5555
Department of Tourism ⓣ04-223 0000

city's two telecoms operators are Etisalat (ⓦwww.etisalat.ae) and Du (ⓦwww.du.ae). The cheapest options are currently the pay-as-you-go Du "Visitor Mobile Line" package (49dh, including 20dh credit) and Etisalat's "Ahlan" package (60dh, including 25dh credit). See the websites for full details. You'll need to present your passport when buying a SIM card.

Photography

Dubai is a very photogenic city, although the often harsh desert light can play havoc with colour and contrast – for the best results head out between around 7am and 9am in the morning, or after 4pm.

It's also worth noting that many upmarket hotels, restaurants and bars are extremely sniffy about people taking photographs of their establishments, particularly if other guests are likely to find their way into your shots – don't be surprised if you're asked to put your camera away. Outside, things are more relaxed, although obviously it's polite to ask before you take photographs of people, and you risk causing considerable offence (or worse) if you shove your lens in the face of a local Emirati (ladies particularly) without permission.

Prostitution

Dubai maintains a bizarrely inconsistent attitude to sexual matters. A couple kissing on the lips in public can potentially face jail, while homosexuality is also illegal. Despite this high-handed moral stance, however, **prostitution** is endemic throughout the city – you won't get round many pubs or bars (particularly in the city centre) without seeing at least a few working girls perched at the bar in unusually short skirts and overbright lipstick. The sex trade is tolerated by the city authorities, it is said, as part of the price to be paid in attracting expat professionals to the emirate, while it also reflects the city's overwhelmingly male demographic (see p.188). Dubai's sex workers come from all over the globe, with a sliding scale of charges to match: Arab girls are the most expensive, followed by Westerners, with Asians and Africans at the bottom of the pile – a snapshot in miniature of the city's traditional social and economic structure. The background of Dubai's working girls is equally varied: many are simply visitors or residents looking to make a bit of extra cash; others are the victims of human trafficking, with girls responding to adverts for "housemaids" and suchlike being sold into the sex trade on arrival. The Dubai government is making efforts to eliminate this illegal trade, although the problem persists.

Smoking

As of late 2007, smoking was banned in Dubai in the vast majority of indoor public places, including offices, malls, cafés and restaurants (although smoking is permitted at most – but not all – outdoor venues). At the time of writing you could still smoke in bars and pubs, although there has also been talk of including these in the ban at a future date. You can still smoke in the majority of **hotels**, though many places now provide non-smoking rooms or non-smoking floors – and a few places have banned smoking completely. During Ramadan, never smoke in public places in daylight hours.

Time

Dubai (and the rest of the UAE) runs on **Gulf Standard Time**. This is 4hr ahead of GMT, 3hr ahead of BST, 9hr ahead of North American Eastern Standard Time, 12hr ahead of North American Western Standard Time, 6hr behind Australian Eastern Standard Time, and 8hr behind New Zealand Standard Time. There is no daylight savings time in Dubai.

Tourist information

Given the importance of tourism to the Dubai economy, there's a frustrating lack of information available about what's on offer in the city. Dubai Tourism runs information desks at Terminal 1 (24hr; ⓣ04-224 5252) and Terminal 3 (24hr; ⓣ04-220 3430) in the airport, as well as at Deira City Centre, BurJuman, Wafi and Ibn Battuta Mall (all open 10am–10pm). Staff have a few leaflets to hand out and will do their best to answer any questions you have, but aren't really trained to deal with anything apart from the most obvious queries – and half the time the kiosks are left unattended anyway. In general, you'll probably be better off consulting the various **websites** listed below.

The best source of local **listings** is the excellent *Time Out Dubai* (7dh), published weekly and readily available at bookshops all over the city. The magazine carries comprehensive listings about pretty much everything going on in Dubai, and is particularly good for information about the constantly changing nightlife scene, including new clubs, club nights and one-off promotions, as well as restaurant and bar promotions and new openings. The glossy *What's On* (monthly; 10dh) is also worth a look, though the listings aren't as detailed.

Websites

Useful websites for visitors include:

ⓦ**www.dubaitourism.ae** Offical website of the Dubai Tourism department. The "Tips for Tourists" section under the "Getting to Dubai" tab is particularly informative.

ⓦ**www.abudhabitourism.ae** Official site of the Abu Dhabi Tourism Authority.

ⓦ**www.timeoutdubai.com** Latest listings and reviews of what's on in the city.

ⓦ**www.thenational.ae** Online home of the UAE's leading English-language newspaper.

ⓦ**www.gulfnews.com** Comprehensive news from the region.

ⓦ**www.dubaifaqs.com** Encyclopedic site with detailed information about pretty much everything you're ever likely to want to know about the city.

ⓦ**www.dubaiforums.com** Leading expat forum, with reams of information.

ⓦ**www.secretdubai.blogspot.com** This irreverent Dubai blog has attained cult status despite – or perhaps because of – being repeatedly blocked by the government.

ⓦ**www.uaeprison.com** Alternative take on the modern UAE, including extensive coverage of Dubai's sometimes murky human-rights record.

Government websites

Australian Department of Foreign Affairs ⓦwww.dfat.gov.au.
British Foreign & Commonwealth Office ⓦwww.fco.gov.uk.
Canadian Department of Foreign Affairs ⓦwww.international.gc.ca.
Irish Department of Foreign Affairs ⓦwww.foreignaffairs.gov.ie.
New Zealand Ministry of Foreign Affairs ⓦwww.mfat.govt.nz.
US State Department ⓦwww.state.gov
South African Department of Foreign Affairs ⓦwww.dfa.gov.za.

Travellers with disabilities

Dubai has made considerable efforts to cater for visitors with disabilities, and ranks as probably the Middle East's most accessible destination. Most of the city's modern **hotels** now make at least some provision for guests with impaired mobility; many of the city's four- and five-stars now have specially adapted rooms, although there's relatively little choice among three-star hotels and below. Quite a few of the city's **malls** also have special facilities, including disabled parking spaces and specially equipped toilets. Inevitably, most of the city's older heritage buildings are not accessible (although the Dubai Museum is).

Transportation is fairly well set up. The Dubai Metro incorporates facilities to assist visually- and mobility-impaired visitors, including tactile guide paths, lifts and ramps, as well as wheelchair spaces in all compartments, while **Dubai Taxi** (ⓣ04-208 0808) has specially designed vehicles equipped with ramps and lifts. The city's **water buses** can also be used by mobility-impaired visitors, and staff will assist you in boarding and disembarking. There are also dedicated facilities at the **airport**.

For more detailed **information** go to ⓦwww.dubaitourism.ae and click on the "Special Needs Tourism" link on the left-hand side of the page.

The City

The City

1

Bur Dubai

Strung out along the southern side of the Creek, the district of **Bur Dubai** is the oldest part of the city, and in many ways still the most interesting. This is where you'll find virtually all the bits of old Dubai which survived the rapid development of the 1960s and 1970s, and parts of Bur Dubai's historic waterfront still retain their engagingly old-fashioned appearance, with a quaint tangle of sand-coloured buildings and a distinctively Arabian skyline, spiked with dozens of wind towers and the occasional minaret.

Away from the Creek the tone of the district is more modern and mercantile, epitomized by the lively Al Fahidi Street and Khalid bin al Waleed Road, lined with neon-clad stores stacked high with phones, watches and all the latest digital knick-knacks. This is also where you'll get the strongest sense of Bur Dubai's status as the city's **Little India**, with dozens of no-frills curry houses, window-displays full of glittery saris, and optimistic touts who periodically emerge from their shops to regale passers-by with offers of fake watches or a "nice pashmina".

Much of the charm of Bur Dubai lies in simply wandering along the waterfront and through the busy backstreets, although there are a number of specific attractions worth exploring. At the heart of the district, the absorbing **Dubai Museum** offers an excellent introduction to the city's history, culture and customs, while the old Iranian quarter of **Bastakiya** nearby is home to the city's most impressive collection of traditional buildings, topped with dozens of wind towers (see p.47). Heading west along the Creek, the old-fashioned **Textile Souk** is the prettiest in the city, while further west along the creekside, the historic old quarter of **Shindagha** is home to another fine cluster of traditional buildings, many of them now converted into low-key museums, including the engaging **Sheikh Saeed al Maktoum House**.

Dubai Museum

The excellent **Dubai Museum** (Sat–Thurs 8.30am–8.30pm, Fri 2.30–8.30pm; 3dh) on Al Fahidi Street makes a logical first stop on any tour of the city, and the perfect place to get up to speed with the history and culture of the emirates. The museum occupies the old **Al Fahidi Fort**, a rough-and-ready little structure whose engagingly lopsided corner turrets – one square and one round – make it look a bit like a giant sandcastle, and offers a welcome contrast to the city's other "old" buildings, most of which have been restored to a state of pristine perfection. Dating from around 1800, the fort is the oldest building in Dubai, having originally been built to defend the town's landward approaches against raids by rival Bedouin tribes; it also served as the residence and office of the ruling sheikh up until the early twentieth century before being converted into a museum in 1971.

Entering the museum you step into the fort's central courtyard, flanked by a few rooms containing exhibits of folklore and weaponry. Assorted wooden boats lie

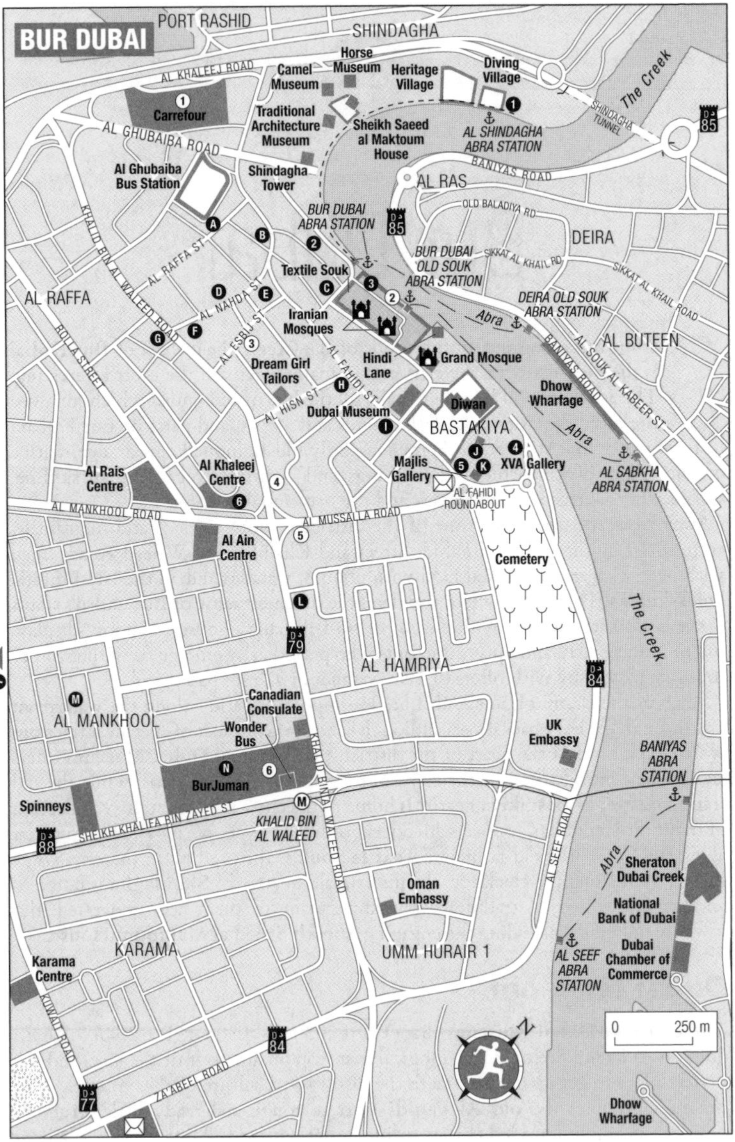

BUR DUBAI

PORT RASHID
SHINDAGHA
AL KHALEEJ ROAD
Horse Museum
Camel Museum
Heritage Village
Diving Village
Carrefour
Traditional Architecture Museum
Sheikh Saeed al Maktoum House
AL SHINDAGHA ABRA STATION
SHINDAGHA TUNNEL
The Creek
AL GHUBAIBA ROAD
BANIYAS ROAD
Al Ghubaiba Bus Station
Shindagha Tower
AL RAS
OLD BALADIYA RD
BUR DUBAI ABRA STATION
DEIRA
KHALID BIN AL WALEED ROAD
AL RAFFA ST
BUR DUBAI OLD SOUK ABRA STATION
SIKKAT AL KHAIL RD
SIKKAT AL KHAIL ROAD
Textile Souk
AL RAFFA
AL NAHDA ST
Iranian Mosques
Abra
DEIRA OLD SOUK ABRA STATION
AL ESBIJ ST
ROLLA STREET
AL BUTEEN
Grand Mosque
BANIYAS ROAD
AL SOUK AL KABEER ST
Dream Girl Tailors
Hindi Lane
AL FAHIDI ST
Dhow Wharfage
AL HISN ST
Diwan
Dubai Museum
BASTAKIYA
Abra
XVA Gallery
Majlis Gallery
AL SABKHA ABRA STATION
Al Rais Centre
Al Khaleej Centre
AL FAHIDI ROUNDABOUT
AL MANKHOOL ROAD
AL MUSSALLA ROAD
Al Ain Centre
Cemetery
The Creek
AL HAMRIYA
Canadian Consulate
AL MANKHOOL
Wonder Bus
UK Embassy
BANIYAS ABRA STATION
BurJuman
Spinneys
SHEIKH KHALIFA BIN ZAYED ST
KHALID BIN AL WALEED
KHALID BIN AL WALEED ROAD
AL SEEF ROAD
Abra
Sheraton Dubai Creek
Oman Embassy
National Bank of Dubai
KARAMA
UMM HURAIR 1
AL SEEF ABRA STATION
Dubai Chamber of Commerce
Karama Centre
KUWAIT ROAD
ZA'ABEEL ROAD
0 250 m
N
Dhow Wharfage

ACCOMMODATION

Ambassador	B
Arabian Courtyard	I
Astoria	E
BurJuman Arjaan Rotana	N
Dallas Hotel	F
Dubai Nova	H
Four Points Sheraton	L
Golden Sands	M
New Penninsula	A
Orient Guest House	K
Royal Ascot	G
Time Palace	C
Vasantan	D
XVA	J

EATING & DRINKING ⓿

Aangan	7
Antique Bazaar	L
Automatic	6
Basta Arts Café	5
Bastakiah Nights	4
Bayt Al Wakeel	3
George & Dragon	B
Kan Zaman	1
Saravanaa Bhavan	2
Sherlock Holmes	I
Vasanta Bhavan	D
Viceroy Bar	L
XVA Café	J
Yakitori	G

SHOPPING ⓪

Ajmal	6
Al Mansoor Video	3 & 5
Al Orooba Oriental Carpets	6
Bateel Dates	6
BurJuman	6
Carrefour	1
International Aladdin Shoes	2
Khaled Bin Al Waleed St.	4
Virgin Megastore	6

The Creek

Cutting a broad, salty swathe through the middle of the city centre, the Creek (Al Khor in Arabic) lies physically and historically at the very heart of Dubai, all that now remains of a river which some believe once flowed inland all the way to Al Ain. The Creek was the location of the earliest settlements in the area – first on the Bur Dubai side of the water, and subsequently in Deira – and also played a **crucial role** in the recent history of the city. One of the first acts of the visionary Sheikh Rashid – the so-called father of modern Dubai – on coming to power in 1958 was to have the Creek **dredged** and made navigable to larger shipping, thus diverting trade from the then far wealthier neighbouring emirate of Sharjah (whose own harbour was allowed to silt up, with disastrous consequences). With its enhanced shipping facilities, Dubai quickly established itself as one of the Gulf's most important **commercial centres**. Indeed in hindsight it's possible to see Sheikh Rashid's opening up of the Creek, just as much as the later discovery of oil, as the key factor in the city's subsequent prosperity.

Although the Creek's economic importance has dwindled in recent decades following the opening of the enormous new docks at Port Rashid and the free-trade zone at Jebel Ali, it continues to sees plenty of small-scale commerce. Almost all of this is transported on the innumerable old-fashioned wooden **dhows** which run between Dubai and neighbouring countries, and which moor up along the Deira side of the water at the Dhow Wharfage (see p.58). Commerce aside, the Creek remains the centrepiece of Dubai and its finest natural feature; a broad, serene stretch of water which is as essential a part of the fabric and texture of the city as the Thames is to London or the Seine to Paris.

marooned around the courtyard, showing the different types of vessel used in old Dubai, including a traditional abra, not so very different from those still in service on the Creek today. In one corner stands a traditional *barasti* (or *areesh*) hut, topped by a basic burlap wind tower – the sort of building most people in Dubai lived in right up until the 1960s. The hut's walls are made out of neatly cut palm branches, spaced so that breezes are able to blow right through the hut, which remains surprisingly cool even in the heat of the day. It's also worth having a look at the rough walls of the courtyard itself, made from horizontal layers of coral held together with powdered gypsum – the standard building technique in old Dubai, but which is usually hidden underneath layers of plaster.

The museum's real attraction, however, is its sprawling **underground section**, a buried wonderland which offers as comprehensive an overview of the traditional life, crafts and culture of Dubai as you'll find anywhere. A sequence of rooms – full of the sound effects and life-size mannequins without which no Dubai museum would be complete – cover every significant aspect of traditional Dubaian life, including Islam, local architecture and wind towers, traditional dress and games, camels and falconry. Many rooms also feature interesting short films on various subjects, including fascinating historic footage of pearl divers at work. There's also a line of shops featuring various traditional trades and crafts – carpenters, blacksmiths, potters, tailors, spice merchants and so on – kitsch but undeniably engaging, populated with colourful mannequins in traditional dress, although the old black-and-white video clips of artisans at work add a slightly spooky touch.

Bastakiya

A couple of minute's walk east of the Dubai Museum, the meticulously restored **Bastakiya** (or Bastakia – with the stress on the *i*) quarter is far and away the best preserved and most complete traditional district in the city. This entire quarter of wind-towered houses and narrow lanes was originally built in the early 1900s by merchants from Bandar Lengeh and other ports just over the Gulf in southern Iran, who had been lured to Dubai by the promise of low taxes and free land, and who in turn helped transform the commercial fortunes of their host city; they named their new suburb Bastakiya after their ancestral home, the Iranian town of Bastak. At a time when virtually the entire population of Dubai was living in palm-thatch huts, the houses of Bastakiya were notably solid and sophisticated, with the added luxury of primitive air conditioning provided by the wind towers which rise up from virtually every rooftop in the district.

By the 1980s, Bastakiya had become increasingly rundown. Many of its old houses turned into warehouses as the wealthy Iranian families who had previously lived there began to move out to more spacious houses in the new suburbs. The entire area was threatened by demolition, but in the end around two-thirds of the original quarter was rescued from the developers and restored – indeed, probably to something quite a lot neater than its original condition. To see what 1970s Bastakiya looked like, seek out the widely available *Windtower: Houses of the Bastaki* by Anne Coles and Peter Jackson, which has dozens of superb old photographs of the district.

You can reach Bastakiya either via the waterfront promenade, on the far side of the Diwan, or from Al Fahidi Street next to the *Basta Arts Café*. It's a nice place for an aimless wander, with a disorienting rabbit-warren of tiny alleyways – built deliberately narrow in order to provide pedestrians with welcome shade – and twisting between the high, bare walls of dozens of fine old traditional houses capped with beautiful wind towers, each one carved in its own unique pattern. Unfortunately, the entire quarter remains rather empty and under-used, despite the presence of a couple of good cafés and two of the city's best galleries.

A number of old Bastakiya houses have now been reopened to the public as small **museums** or government offices. Most boast only a few sparse and

▲ Traditional buildings, Bastakiya quarter

Wind towers

Often described as the world's oldest form of air conditioning, the distinctive rectangular **wind towers** (*barjeel*) that top many old Dubai buildings (as well as numerous modern buildings constructed in faux-Arabian style) formerly offered an ingeniously simple way of countering the Gulf's searing temperatures in a pre-electrical age – as well as solving the problem of ventilating houses in a country where windows (where they existed) were almost always kept closed to protect the occupants' privacy. Traditionally the largest and most highly decorated wind tower was placed over the bedroom, with smaller ones over other rooms. They're built up to about 6m high, are open on all four sides and channel any available breezes down into the building via four triangular flues. Of course, wind towers don't produce the arctic blast of icy air conditioning which nowadays seems *de rigueur* in Dubai's smarter establishments, but stand next to one and you'll notice a slight but significant drop in temperature – particularly welcome in summer, and doubtless a life-saver back in the city's pre-air-con days.

Although the wind tower has become one of the iconic architectural symbols of Dubai and the UAE, it was actually introduced to the city by **Iranian merchants** who settled in the city in the early twentieth century. Many built houses in Bastakiya, whose collection of wind towers is the largest and finest in the city, with subtle variations in design from tower to tower, meaning that no two are ever exactly alike.

uninteresting exhibits, although they do give you the chance to nose around inside and have a look at the various houses' often surprisingly ornate internal courtyards; all are free to enter. The only one with any half-decent exhibits is the **Coins House** (Sat–Thurs 8am–8pm), with a well-presented collection of Ummayad, Sassanian, Abbasid and later Islamic coins through to the Ottoman era, backed up by explanatory touchscreens (which may or may not be working). Other museums and houses open to the public include the **Philately House** (Sat–Thurs 9am–1pm & 5–9pm), **Dar al Nadwa** (Sun–Thurs 8am–2pm), the **Architectural Heritage Society** (Sat–Wed 8am–1pm & 5–8pm) and the **Architectural Heritage Department** (Sun–Thurs 8am–2pm) – the courtyard inside the last is particularly fine, and in a number of these places you can also get up onto the rooftop for fine views over Bastakiya and the Creek. All these places are grouped together on the northern side of Bastakiya, near the Creek, and clearly signed between *Bastakiah Nights* restaurant and the Diwan (see p.49).

Close by is the **Sheikh Mohammed Centre for Cultural Understanding**, or SMCCU (Bastakiya office daily 8am–3pm; Ⓣ04 353 6666, Ⓦwww.cultures.ae), which was set up in the laudable attempt to break down barriers between local Emiratis and Dubai's legion of expats. The latter can spend years in the city without having any meaningful contact with their hosts, while the Emiratis, in turn, tend largely to keep within their own circles (Emiratis are now a minority in their own hometown – less than 20 percent and falling). The SMCCU runs popular tours of Jumeirah Mosque (see p.77) and a number of activities in Bastakiya itself, including walking tours, "cultural" breakfasts and lunches, during which you get the chance to sample some traditional food while chatting to the centre's Emirati staff, plus Gulf Arabic classes.

Bastakiya is also home to two of the city's oldest and most reputable galleries: the **Majlis Gallery** and **XVA** (both covered on p.132) – the latter is also a good place for a long cool drink in the gallery's courtyard café (see p.111).

The Textile Souk and around

At the heart of Bur Dubai, the **Textile Souk** (also sometimes referred to as the "Old Souk") is easily the prettiest in the city, occupying an immaculately restored traditional Emirati bazaar, its long line of sand-coloured stone buildings shaded by a fine arched wooden roof, keeping things pleasantly cool even in the heat of the day. This was once the most important bazaar in the city, though its commercial importance has long since faded; almost all the shops have now been taken over by Indian traders flogging reams of sari cloth, cheap pashminas and fluorescent blankets, alongside other assorted tourist tat.

At the western end of the souk, near the main entrance, the **Bayt al Wakeel** ("Agent's House"), originally known as the Mackenzie House, was the first office in Dubai when it opened in 1935 as the headquarters of local shipping agents, Gray Mackenzie and Company. The house is now a low-key restaurant (see p.111), and it's worth taking a peek inside at the attractively restored ground floor, which once housed the company office (the manager lived upstairs).

A few metres west, just outside the main entrance to the souk, a huddle of boats and people announces **Bur Dubai Abra Station** (for more on abra practicalities, see p.23). This is one of the city's four main abra stations, from where these old-fashioned little wooden boats shuttle back and forth across the Creek, operated by boatmen from India, Bangladesh, Pakistan and Iran. The boats' basic design has changed little for at least a century, apart from the addition of a diesel engine (abras were formerly rowed) and an awning to provide passengers with shade. Up until the opening of Al Maktoum Bridge in 1963, abras provided the only means of getting from one side of the Creek to the other, and despite the fact that they are now effectively floating antiques, they still play a crucial role in the city's transport infrastructure, carrying a staggering twenty million passengers per year for a modest 1dh per trip.

It's also worth exploring the lanes which run inland from the Textile Souk, parallel to the main souk. These hold further examples of traditional (albeit heavily restored) local architecture, as well as a fine pair of **Iranian Shia mosques**, which stand close to one another at the western end of the souk on 11C St, close to the *Time Palace Hotel*. The first mosque boasts a superb facade and dome covered in a lustrous mosaic of predominantly blue tiling decorated with geometrical floral motifs. The second, about 50m west towards the *Time Palace Hotel*, is a contrastingly plain, sand-coloured building, its rooftop enlivened by four tightly packed little egg-shaped domes.

Hindi Lane

Hidden away at the far end of the Textile Souk, the colourful little alleyway popularly known as **Hindi Lane** is one of Dubai's most curious and appealing little ethnic enclaves. Walk to the far (eastern) end of the Textile Souk, turn right by T. Singh Trading and then left by Mohammadi Textiles and you'll find yourself in a tiny alleyway lined with picturesque little Indian shops selling an array of bangles, bindis, coconuts, flowers, bells, almanacs and other religious paraphernalia. On the left-hand side of the lane sits a tiny hybridized Hindu-cum-Sikh temple, sometimes referred to as the **Sikh Gurudaba**. Go up the stairs (leaving your shoes in the lockers at the bottom) to reach the improvised temple; its diminutive size and obscure location give it a charmingly secretive, almost clandestine air. The first floor is home to various Hindu shrines, decorated with images of Shiva, Hanuman and Ganesh, along with the revered South Indian guru Sai Baba and a few swastikas. From here, further stairs (cover your head with a piece of cloth from the box at the top) lead up to a miniature Sikh temple, adorned with pictures of the ten Sikh gurus, with the Sikh mantra "Satnam Waheguru" ("Oh God your name is true") painted on the walls. Visitors are allowed, but photos aren't permitted.

Continue along Hindi Lane and you'll shortly come out at the back of the Grand Mosque (see below). Turn right at the end of the lane and you'll find a second Hindu temple, the **Shri Nathje Jayate Temple** dedicated jointly to Shiva and Krishna. It's not signed, but just look for the piles of shoes and follow the crowds upstairs, where you'll find yourself in a marbled hall decorated with emblems of Shiva (including tridents and peacocks) and images of Krishna in the form of Shri Nathji. In the latter, the black-skinned god is shown lifting Mount Goverdhan above his head in order to protect the people of Vrindavan from a devastating deluge unleashed by the jealous Indra, king of the gods.

Both temples **open** for *puja* (worship) according to a rather complicated timetable – basically from 6am to noon, and then again in the evening from around 5pm until late.

The Grand Mosque and Diwan

Immediately south of the Shri Nathje Jayate temple lies the altogether more visible and imposing **Grand Mosque**, the biggest in Dubai: a large, though rather plain, sand-coloured building topped by eighteen tiny domes and the city's tallest minaret, rising elegantly above Bur Dubai's skyline. The original Grand Mosque was built around 1900 but demolished in the 1960s; the current edifice dates only from the 1990s. Non-Muslims are not allowed inside.

On the other side of the Grand Mosque (go back across the end of the Textile Souk, then turn right along the Creek), protected by ostentatiously high black railings, is the **Diwan**, or Ruler's Court. This houses the offices of various senior government officials, although most of the real power in the city is wielded by Sheikh Mohammed's Executive Office and Executive Council, who preside over Dubai's development from their offices near the summit of the Emirates Towers on Sheikh Zayed Road.The Diwan building itself is a large but uninspiring modern edifice – a big white box topped by a few oversized wind towers. Rather more eye-catching is the attached **mosque**, topped by an unusually flattened onion dome and a slender white minaret which rivals that of the nearby Grand Mosque in height. There are also fine views from here back across the Creek to the Dhow Wharfage at Deira, with the wind towers of the Spice Souk in the background.

Al Fahidi Street and Khalid bin al Waleed Road

South of the Textile Souk lies **Al Fahidi Street**, Bur Dubai's de facto high street, bisecting the area from east to west and lined with a mix of shops selling Indian-style clothing, shoes and jewellery, along with other places stacked high with mobile phones and posh watches (not necessarily genuine). The alleyways to either side are dotted with innumerable downmarket curry houses catering to the area's predominantly Indian community. The strip is particularly vibrant after dark, when the neon comes on and locals come out to eat and shop.

A couple of blocks south of Al Fahidi Street, the dual-carriageway **Khalid bin al Waleed Road** (also known as "Computer Street", and occasionally by its old colonial name of Bank Street) marks the edge of Bur Dubai proper. There's a distinct change of pace here from the narrow streets and souks of the old city centre to the more modern districts beyond, epitomized by the huge **BurJuman**

mall (see p.143), which nestles on a corner near the road's eastern end. The strip is best known for its plethora of computer and electronics shops, concentrated around the junction with Al Mankhool Road – a good place to pick up cheap digital stuff or simply to enjoy the after-dark atmosphere, when it's lit up in a long blaze of neon, and locals emerge to haggle over the laptops, phones and mysterious bits of cable.

Shindagha

Although now effectively swallowed up by Bur Dubai, the historic creekside district of **Shindagha** was, until fifty years ago, a quite separate and self-contained area occupying its own spit of land, and frequently cut off from Bur Dubai proper during high tides. This was also once the most exclusive address in town, home to the ruling family and other local elites, who occupied a series of relatively large and well-built coral-walled and wind-towered houses at a time when most of the population still lived in palm-thatch huts. Many of these old houses, now sprucely restored, have survived, making this part of town – along with Bastakiya – the only place in the city where you can still get a real idea of what old Dubai looked like.

The edge of the district is marked by the distinctive waterfront **Shindagha Tower**, one of only two of the city's original defensive watchtowers to survive (the other is the Burj Nahar – see p.60) and instantly recognizable thanks to the slit windows and protruding buttress on each side, arranged to resemble a human face.

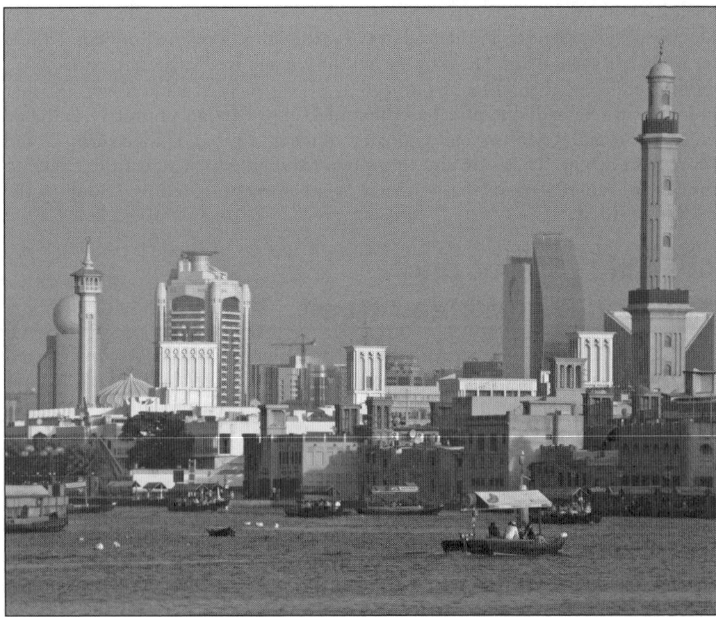

▲ View of the Creek from Shindagha

A walk along the Creek

The walk along the Bur Dubai **waterfront** is far and away the nicest in the city, pedestrianized throughout, and with cooling breezes and wonderful views of the city down the Creek – particularly beautiful towards sunset. For the best views, begin in Shindagha and head south; it takes about 20–25 minutes to walk as far as Bastakiya.

Starting outside the Diving Village, a spacious promenade stretches all the way down the Shindagha waterfront as far as Shindagha Tower, from where a narrow walkway extends to the Bur Dubai Abra Station and Textile Souk. Walk through the souk, exiting it via Hindi Lane (see p.48 for directions) to emerge by the Grand Mosque. Head left from here to regain the waterfront by the high black railings of the Diwan, from where the creekside promenade continues to the edge of Bastakiya and beyond, past the old Bur Dubai cemetery flanking Al Seef Road.

Sheikh Saeed al Maktoum House

Several of the old Shindagha palaces have now been converted into museums. Easily the most interesting is the **Sheikh Saeed al Maktoum House** (Sat–Thurs 8am–8.30pm, Fri 3–9.30pm; 2dh), the principal residence of Dubai's ruling family from 1896 to 1958. Work on the house was begun in 1896 – making it one of the oldest buildings in Dubai – by Sheikh Maktoum bin Hasher al Maktoum, and three further wings were added by subsequent members of the Maktoum family, including Sheikh Saeed bin Maktoum al Maktoum, former ruler of Dubai, who lived here until his death in 1958. Dubai's current ruler, Sheikh Mohammed (grandson of Sheikh Saeed), himself spent the early years of his life in the house, sharing living space with a hundred-odd people and assorted animals, including guards, family slaves, goats, dogs and the occasional camel – basic living conditions for someone who would go on to become one of the world's richest men.

The house is now home to one of the city's most interesting museums, featuring assorted exhibits relating to the history of Dubai. Pride of place goes to the superb collection of old **photographs**, with images of the city from the 1940s through to the late 1960s, showing its amazing transformation from a remote Gulf town to global megalopolis. The old shots of Bur Dubai and Shindagha are particularly striking: several show the contrast between the simple *barasti* (palm-thatch) huts of Bur Dubai and the much grander, wind-towered houses of Shindagha, while others show the old tidal causeway which formerly separated the two. There are also fine shots of fishermen at work and old dhows under their distinctive triangular lateen sails, plus a couple of photos showing the rather Biblical-looking swarm of locusts which descended on the town in 1953. (Locusts have played a surprisingly important role in Dubai's history. One theory holds that the town's name derives from a type of local locust, the *daba*, while during the starvation years of World War II, locusts – netted and fried – provided a valuable source of food for impoverished locals.) Another room is devoted to photos of the various craggy-featured Al Maktoum sheikhs – the startling family resemblance makes it surprisingly difficult to tell them apart – including the prescient image of Sheikh Rashid and his son the young Sheikh Mohammed poring over a petroleum brochure which can also be seen in the Al Ahmadiya School (see p.57)

Elsewhere you'll find some interesting wooden models of traditional dhows, colourful colonial-era stamps and an extensive exhibit of local **coins**, featuring a large selection of the East India Company and Indian colonial coins which were used as common currency in Dubai from the late eighteenth century right through until 1966, when Dubai and Qatar introduced a joint currency to replace them.

Upstairs a couple of further rooms are filled with lovely old **maps** of Dubai and the Arabian peninsula, plus some **documents** detailing assorted administrative and commercial dealings between the British and Dubaians during the later colonial period, including the agreement allowing Imperial Airways seaplanes to land on the Creek from 1938, the first commercial service to touch down in Dubai.

Other museums

A cluster of newly opened museums and other attractions lie dotted along the Shindagha waterfront, though none is likely to detain you for long. Immediately behind Sheikh Saeed al Maktoum House, the **Camel Museum** (also signed as "House of the Camel"; Sat–Thurs 8am–8pm, Fri 2–8pm; free) offers a modest attempt to trace the history and cultural significance of this iconic beast in Dubai and the Emirates – although like many of the city's recently opened museums the overall effect is half-hearted and patchy, with plenty of rather didactic displays but precious few actual exhibits, barring an absolutely surreal pair of animatronic dromedaries in the room devoted to camel racing, which the resident caretaker will take great pleasure in firing into life.

Next door to Camel Museum, the **Horse Museum** (or "House of the Horse"; Sun–Thurs 8am–2pm; free) provides a lacklustre overview of the history of the horse in Arabia from 3000 BC through to current Dubai ruler Sheikh Mohammed's own horse-breeding exploits, covered in displays of spectacular incoherence ("The cavalry Sheikh Mohammad has come to fore in this revered sport for he was known of courage, cavalry, and a tooth for horses" is probably the best).

A few steps beyond Sheikh Saeed al Maktoum House, the grandiose **Obaid bin Thani House** of 1916 is one of the largest in Shindagha, with a flamboyantly decorated exterior. You can go inside, though the interior is much less impressive and the displays on Islam are little better than feeble religious propaganda.

Far more interesting is the **Traditional Architecture Museum** (daily except Fri 7am–7pm; free), halfway between Shindagha Tower and Sheikh Saeed al Maktoum House. The museum is located in one of Shindagha's most attractive traditional houses, with the usual sandy courtyard and elaborately carved stone panels, plus informative displays on topics concerning architecture in the Emirates generally and Dubai in particular.

Heritage and Diving villages

A couple of minutes' walk along the Creekside past Sheikh Saeed al Maktoum House, a further cluster of fine old traditional houses line the edge of the Creek. A couple of these buildings have now been converted into restaurants (including *Kan Zaman*; see p.111), while one of the largest is given over to the so-called **Heritage Village** (Sun–Thurs 8.30am–10.30pm, Fri & Sat 4.30–10.30pm; free). The "village" comprises a string of traditional buildings surrounding a large sandy courtyard, with a few shops at the back of the courtyard selling a mix of kitsch souvenirs along with some more interesting antiques. The atmosphere is pretty moribund during the day, but livens up somewhat after dark, especially during Ramadam and the Dubai Shopping Festival, when locals put on cookery and craft displays, occasionally accompanied by performances of Emirati music and dancing.

The adjacent **Diving Village** (same hours) offers more of the same, with another, notably less imposing, string of traditional buildings around a sandy courtyard dotted with a couple of wooden boats and a few *barasti* huts, plus two boat-shaped phone booths – a rather lame tribute to the pearl-diving trade which underpinned the city's economy up until the 1930s.

2

Deira

North of the Creek lies **Deira**, the second of the old city's two principal districts, founded in 1841, when settlers from Bur Dubai crossed the Creek to establish a new village here. Deira rapidly overtook its older neighbour in commercial importance and remains notably more built-up and cosmopolitan than Bur Dubai, with a heady ethnic mix of Emiratis, Gulf Arabs, Iranians, Indians, Pakistanis and Somalis thronging its packed streets, along with a healthy contingent of African gold traders, Russian bargain-hunters and camera-toting Western tourists. Specific tourist attractions are thinner on the ground here than in Bur Dubai, but the district remains the best place in Dubai for aimless wandering and even the shortest exploration will uncover a kaleidoscopic jumble of cultures. Indian curry houses jostle for space with Iranian grocers, Somali shisha-cafes and backstreet mosques – not to mention an endless array of shops selling everything from formal black *abbeya* to belly-dancing costumes.

For the visitor, Deira's main attraction is its myriad souks – most obviously the famous **Gold Souk** and the small but atmospheric **Spice Souk** – although in many ways the entire quarter is one enormous bazaar through which it's possible to wander for mile after mile without ever surfacing. The district is also home to the interesting traditional **Heritage House** and **Al Ahmadiya School** museums, while along the banks of the Creek itself you'll find the atmospheric **Dhow Wharfage**, an authentic taste of Dubai past, plus a clutch of striking modernist buildings centred on the landmark **National Bank of Dubai**, an icon of Dubai's dazzling present.

Gold Souk

Deira's famous **Gold Souk** is usually the first stop for visitors to the district and attracts a cosmopolitan range of customers, from Western tourists to African traders buying up pieces for re-sale at home. The souk itself, centred around a pedestrianized street of small shops sheltered beneath a wooden roof, isn't particularly exotic, but the sheer quantity of gold jewellery lined up in the shop windows is staggering. If you're not buying, it still offers a pleasantly cool and laidback respite from the city outside – even with the constant offers of "cheap copy watch" from roving Indian traders.

Souk opening hours

There are no set opening hours for the shops in Deira's various souks. In practice, most places open at around 10am and close at 10pm or later; many also close during the afternoon from around 1 to 4pm.

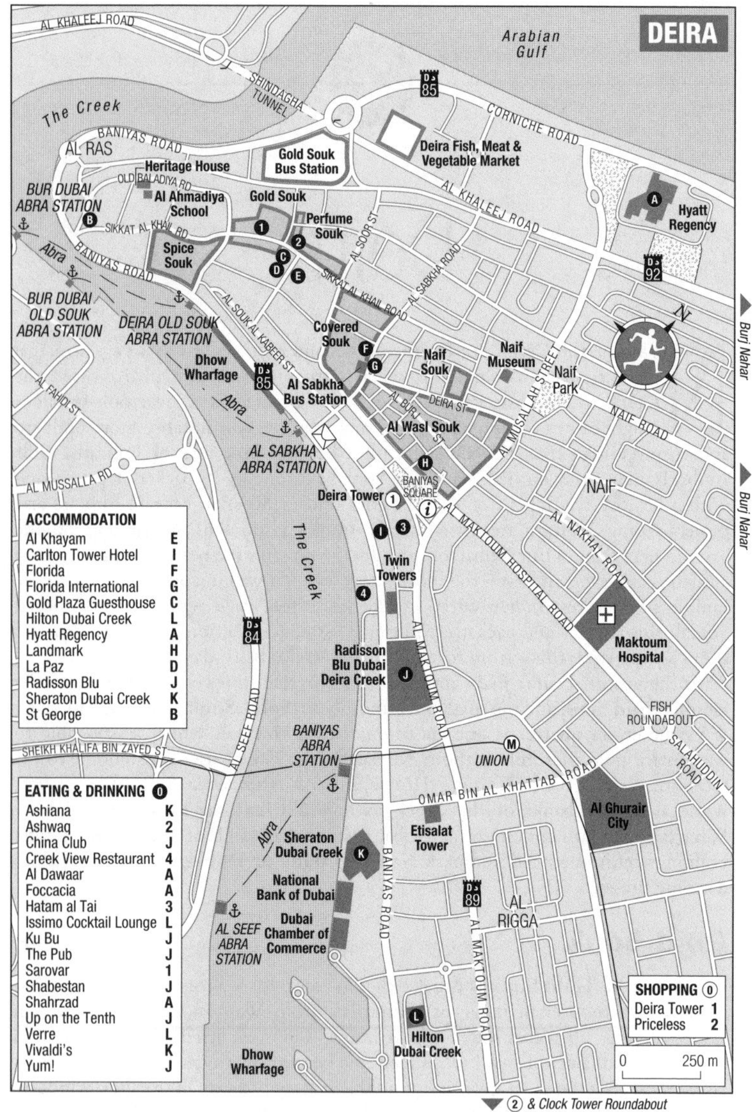

The souk's main attraction is its prices: the gold available here is among the cheapest in the world, and massive competition keeps prices keen. The jewellery on offer ranges from ornate Arabian creations to elegantly restrained pieces aimed at European visitors. Particularly appealing are the traditional Emirati bracelets, fashioned from solid gold (and often exquisitely embellished with white-gold decoration) and hung in long lines in shop windows; these were traditionally used for dowries, as were the heavier and more ornate necklaces also on display. There are also plenty of places selling **precious stones**, including diamonds and a range of other gems.

Shopping in the Gold Souk

The gold industry in Dubai is carefully regulated, so there's no danger of being ripped off with substandard or fake goods, but there are still a few useful basic things to know. First, gold jewellery is **sold by weight** (the quality and detail of the decoration and workmanship, however elaborate, isn't usually factored into the price). Second, the **price** of gold is fixed in all shops city wide (the day's price may be posted up inside) – although the exact figure fluctuates daily depending on the international price of gold. Therefore, if you ask how much a piece of jewellery is, it will first be popped on the scales and weighed, and the cost then calculated according to the day's gold price.

Once you've established this basic price, it's time to start **bargaining**. A request for "best price" or "small discount" (virtually all the Gold Souk shops are run by Indians, who are well versed in the intricacies of barter, not to mention high-pressure salesmanship) should yield an immediate discount of around 20-25 per cent over the basic price; you may be able to lower the price still further depending on how canny you are and how desperate they are for a sale. As ever, it pays to shop around and compare prices; tell the shop you're in that you've found a better deal elsewhere, if necessary. If you're buying multiple items, you should press for further discounts.

If you can't find what you want in the Gold Souk, there are several sizeable malls – Goldland, The Gold Centre and Gold House – with numerous further shops lined up along the Corniche opposite the Gold Souk bus station, a short distance to the north.

Shopping for **precious stones** is more complicated, and it pays to do some research before leaving home. Diamonds are a particularly good buy in Dubai, often selling at up to half the price they would retail for in the West. If you're buying diamonds, it's also well worth visiting the excellent Gold and Diamond Park in southern Jumeirah (see p.143).

The area around the Gold Souk is also one of the major centres of Dubai's flourishing trade in **designer fakes** (see p.145).

▲ Gold Souk, Deira

Heritage House

Exit the rear end of the Gold Souk, then turn right along Old Baladiya Road, following it for a few minutes as it veers around to the left to reach the sprucely restored **Heritage House** (Sat–Thurs 8am–7.30pm, Fri 2.30–7.30pm; free), offering visitors a glimpse into the former lifestyle and traditions of pre-modern Dubai. The house, originally built in 1890, was subsequently enlarged and embellished at various times over the next fifty years, most notably in 1910 by the pearl merchant Sheikh Mohammed bin Ahmed bin Dalmouk, who was also responsible for establishing Al Ahmadiya School next door. The building gives a good idea of the layout of traditional houses in the Gulf, with imposing but largely windowless exterior walls and rooms arranged around a large sandy courtyard – a characteristic feature of inward-looking Arabian houses. There's also a cattle pen on one side and a couple of trees in the middle – a miniature desert at the heart of an urban mansion.

Each of the rooms is enlivened with exhibits evoking aspects of traditional Emirati life. Mannequins loll around on cushions drinking coffee in the main *majlis* (the room in which male guests were traditionally received, business was conducted and news exchanged) by the entrance. In the nearby ladies' *majlis* a child has her hands painted with henna, while others spin thread, work on their embroidery or grind spices. Upstairs, another room has a mildly interesting short film on traditional Emirati children's games, plus a few modest exhibits.

Traditional Emirati houses

The heritage houses in Dubai (and other places around the Emirates) follow a standard pattern – although it's worth remembering that these elaborate stone mansions were far from typical of the living arrangements enjoyed by the population at large, most of whom lived in simple and impermanent palm-thatch huts. Virtually all traditional houses are built around a central **courtyard** (*housh*) and veranda (*liwan*). These provided families with their major living area, and a place where they could cook, play and graze a few animals in complete privacy; some also had a well and a couple of trees. Exterior walls are usually plain and largely windowless in order to protect privacy. Rooms are arranged around the courtyard, the most important being the **majlis** (meeting room), in which the family would receive guests and exchange news (larger houses would have separate *majlis* for men and women). More elaborate houses would also boast one or more **wind towers** (see p.47).

Traditional houses make ingenious use of locally available natural materials. Most coastal houses were constructed using big chunks of coral stone, or *fesht* (look closely and you can make out the delicate outlines of submarine sponges, coral and suchlike on many of the stones). The stones were cemented together using layers of pounded gypsum, while walls were strengthened by the insertion of mangrove poles bound with rope. Mangrove wood was also used as a roofing material along with (in more elaborate houses) planks of Indian teak. Away from the coast, coral was replaced by bricks made from a mixture of mud and straw, or adobe (a word deriving from the Arabic *al tob*, meaning "mud").

Local architecture is remarkably well-adapted to provide shelter from the Gulf's scorching summer: walls were built thick and windows small to keep out the heat, while both coral and adobe have excellent natural insulating properties. Houses were also built close to one another, partly for security, and also to provide shade in the narrow alleyways between. And although most houses look austere, the overall effect of plainness is relieved by richly carved wooden doors and veranda screens, and by floral and geometrical designs around windows, doorways and arches, fashioned from gypsum and coloured with charcoal powder.

Al Ahmadiya School

Tucked away directly behind the Heritage House, the **Al Ahmadiya School** (Sat–Thurs 8am–7.30pm, Fri 2.30–7.30pm; free) is one of the city's finest surviving examples of traditional Emirati architecture, and now houses an interesting museum devoted to the educational history of the emirate. Founded in 1912 by pearl merchant Sheikh Mohammed bin Ahmed bin Dalmouk, Al Ahmadiya was the first public school in UAE, and many of the city's leaders studied here, including Sheikh Rashid (see p.183). The school was also notably egalitarian – only the sons of wealthy families were expected to pay, and education for poorer pupils was free. The curriculum initially focused exclusively on the traditional Islamic disciplines of Koranic study, Arabic calligraphy and mathematics, though the syllabus was later expanded to cover practical subjects such as diving and the pearl trade, as well as more modern disciplines including English, geography and science. After the overcrowded school was relocated in 1962, the original building was allowed to fall into ruin. In 1995 it was meticulously restored by the city authorities – part of a belated attempt to rescue surviving examples of traditional architecture and culture amid the swiftly modernizing city.

The building itself is a simple but attractive two-storey affair arranged around a sandy courtyard and topped by a solitary wind tower; the lower floor is particularly fine, with unusual, richly carved cusped arches surrounding the courtyard, while the rear wall is decorated with a sequence of Koranic inscriptions set into recessed panels. The upper storey is plainer, although one of the rooms still preserves some of the old-fashioned wooden desks used by former pupils. Touchscreens and displays cover the history of the school, along with an interesting ten-minute film containing interviews with former students, plus some intriguing old footage of the school in its heyday showing neatly robed pupils lined up for inspection in the courtyard. The modest exhibits include old photos and the inevitable mannequins, including three tiny pupils being instructed by a rather irritable-looking teacher brandishing a wooden cane. A photograph in the same room shows Dubai's present ruler, Sheikh Mohammed, as a young boy in 1954, sitting with his father, Sheikh Rashid, the pair of them hunched over a book about petroleum – a touching snapshot of the two men most responsible for Dubai's spectacular transformation over the past five decades.

Spice Souk

Just south of the Gold Souk, roughly opposite Deira Old Souk Abra station, the **Spice Souk** is perhaps the most interesting and atmospheric – and certainly the most fragrant – of the city's many bazaars. Run almost exclusively by Iranian traders, the shops here stock a wide variety of culinary, medicinal and cosmetic products, with tubs of merchandise set out in front of a sequence of tiny shops. All the usual spices can be found – cinnamon, cardamom, cumin, coriander – along with more unusual offerings such as dried cucumbers and lemons (a common ingredient in Middle Eastern cuisine), incense and heaps of hibiscus and rose petals, used to make a delicately scented tea. The souk is also famous for its frankincense, sold in various different forms and grades – the most common type looks like a kind of reddish, crumbling crystalline rock; frankincense burners can be bought in the souk for a few dirhams. Most stalls also sell natural cosmetic products such as pumice and *alum*, a clear rock crystal used to soothe the skin after shaving. Male visitors in search of a pick-me-up will also find plentiful supplies of so-called "natural viagra".

Sadly, the Spice Souk is steadily shrinking – most Dubaians nowadays perfer to do their shopping in a supermarket – and the surrounding streets are increasingly being taken over by run of-the-mill shops selling cheap toys and household goods. Despite the humdrum merchandise it's well worth exploring the area north of the Spice Souk, towards the Gold Souk and Al Ahmadiya School, one of the most peaceful and picturesque stretches of souk in the city, with a couple of tiny squares and a spider's web of narrow alleys lined with pretty little green lamps topped with crescent moons.

Dhow Wharfage

Stretching along the Deira Creekside between the Deira Old Souk and Al Sabkha abra stations, the **Dhow Wharfage** offers a fascinating glimpse into the maritime traditions of old Dubai which have survived miraculously intact at the heart of the twenty-first-century city. At any one time, the wharfage is home to dozens of beautiful wooden dhows (some as much as a hundred years old), which berth here to load and unload cargo; hence the great tarpaulin-covered mounds of merchandise – anything from cartons of cigarettes to massive air-conditioning units – that lie stacked up along the waterfront. The dhows themselves range in size from the fairly modest vessels employed for short hops up and down the coast to the large ocean-going craft that are used to transport goods around the Gulf and over to Iran, and even as far afield as Somalia, Pakistan and India. Virtually all of them fly the UAE flag, although they're generally manned by foreign crews who live on board, their lines of washing strung out across the decks and piles of cooking pots giving the boats a quaintly domestic air in the middle of downtown Dubai's hustle and bustle. Hang around long enough and you might be invited to hop on board for a chat (assuming you can find a shared language) and a cup of tea. For more on the Arabian dhow, see p.67.

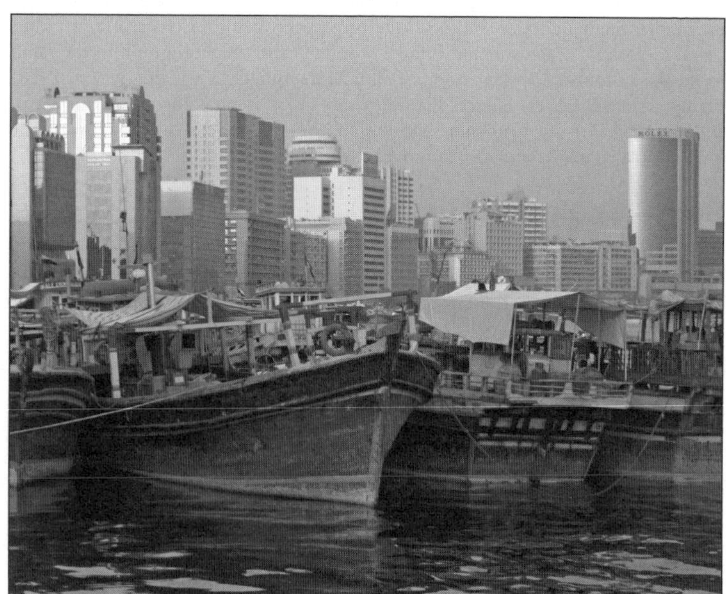

▲ Dhow Wharfage, Deira

Sanctions-busting in old Dubai

Dubai is one of the Middle East's major entrepôts. Huge quantities of goods are imported and then re-exported through the city, with extensive shipping routes stretching up and down the Gulf and beyond to India and East Africa. The city's convenient geographical location and *laissez-faire* trading environment has also made it one of the region's major **smuggling centres**. Dubai's famous gold trade was built on the back of long-established smuggling routes into India, while in recent decades the city has served as an important trans-shipment point for diamonds, hashish, opium and weapons.

A particular bone of international contention – especially with the US – is Dubai's thriving trade with **Iran**, a large part of which is channelled through the dhow wharfage in Deira. Many of the boats here head straight across the Gulf to Iranian ports like Bandar Abbas, just 100km distant, and although most cargoes consist of harmless domestic items, a small but significant proportion do not. Smuggled goods range from simple contraband like American scotch and cigarettes through to more sophisticated items which are exported in contravention of UN sanctions and the long-standing US trade embargo. These include computers, mobile phones and various electronic components, as well as more sophisticated hardware ranging from aeroplane parts to weapons and explosives, as well as items which, it's thought, could potentially be used in Iran's nuclear programme. Dubai has taken significant steps to crack down on illegal trade with Iran in the past few years, although given the number of boats in service and the virtually nonexistent security infrastructure at the wharfage, such efforts are inevitably flawed. "Dubai," as one observer recently put it, "is an absolute sieve."

Perfume Souk

Immediately east of the Gold Souk along Sikkat al Khail Road and up Al Soor Street lies the so-called **Perfume Souk** – although there's no actual souk building, just a line of streetside shops. The biggest concentration is on Al Soor Street, where you'll find places selling a mix of international brands (not necessarily genuine) along with the much heavier and more flowery oil-based *attar* perfumes favoured by local ladies. Keep an eye out for fragrances made with the highly prized oud, derived from agarwood (or aloeswood, as it's called in the west). At many shops you can also create your own scents, mixing and matching from the contents of the big bottles lined up behind the counter before taking them away in chintzy little cut-glass containers, many of which are collectables in their own right.

Deira Fish, Meat and Vegetable Market

Continue north up Al Soor Street and walk across the overpass above Al Khaleej Road to reach the extensive **Deira Fish, Meat and Vegetable Market**. The best time to visit is around 7–8am, when the fish and meat markets are in full swing, though the souk remains busy throughout the day. The fruit and vegetable section features a photogenic array of stalls piled high with all the usual fruit alongside more exotic offerings such as rambutans, mangosteens, coconuts, vast watermelons, yams and big bundles of fresh herbs, as well as a bewildering array of dates in huge, sticky piles. The less colourful – and far more malodorous – fish section is stocked with long lines of sharks, tuna and all sorts of other fish right down to sardines; if you're lucky someone will offer you a prawn. There's also a small but rather gory meat section tucked away at the back.

Covered Souk

South of Sikkat al Khail Road, between Al Soor Street and Al Sabkha Road, the sprawling **Covered Souk** (a misnomer, since it isn't) comprises a rather indeterminate area of small shops stuffed into the narrow streets and alleyways which run south from Naif Road down towards the Creek. Most of the shops here are Indian-run, selling colourful, low-grade cloth for women's clothes, along with large quantities of mass-produced plastic toys and cheap household goods. It's all rather down-at-heel and a bit shabby compared to the Gold and Spice souks, but makes for an interesting stroll, especially in the area at the back of the Al Sabkha bus station, the busiest and densest part of the bazaar, particularly after dark – expect to get lost at least once. The souk then continues, more or less unabated, on the far side of Al Sabkha Road, where it's known variously as the **Naif Souk** and **Al Wasl Souk**, before reaching Al Musallah Street.

Naif Museum and Burj Nahar

North of Al Wasl Souk lies the modest **Naif Museum** (daily except Fri 8am–2pm; free), tucked away in a corner of the eponymous police station, which occupies the imposing Naif Fort (originally built in 1939, but restored to death in 1997). Showcasing the history of the Dubai police force, the museum was created at the behest of Sheikh Mohammed, who himself served as Chief of the Dubai Police for three years from 1968 – his first job, aged just 19 – before graduating to minister of defence in 1971. It's actually a lot less tedious than you might fear, with mildly interesting exhibits on the history of law enforcement in Dubai from the foundation of the police force in 1956 (with just six officers under a British captain) up to the present day. Exhibits include assorted old weapons and uniforms, a trio of short films and various old photos, including a shot of the young, clean-shaven sheikh as Chief of Police.

A ten- to fifteen–minute walk or short taxi ride east from the Naif Museum brings you to the little-visited **Burj Nahar**, marooned next to busy Omar bin al Khattab Road in a pretty little garden studded with palm trees. Built in 1870 to guard the city's landward approaches, it's one of only two of Dubai's original watchtowers which survive (the other is Shindagha Tower; see p.50); the virtually impenetrable round structure is completely devoid of doors and windows in its lower half, with only the narrowest of slits above.

The National Bank of Dubai and around

Another ten minutes' walk south down Omar bin al Khattab Road brings you back to the Creek, right next to the arresting sequence of modern buildings that line the waterfront along Baniyas Road. The most striking is the **National Bank of Dubai** building, designed by Uruguayan architect Carlos Ott, who was also responsible for the equally striking interior of the nearby *Hilton Dubai Creek* and the Bastille Opera House in Paris. The bank's Creek-facing side is covered by an enormous, curved sheet of highly polished glass, modelled on the sail of a traditional dhow, which acts as a kind of huge mirror to the water below and seems positively to catch fire with reflected light towards sunset – although for the best views of the bank you'll need to head over to the opposite side of the Creek.

Next to the bank sits the shorter and squatter **Dubai Chamber of Commerce**, an austerely minimalist glass-clad structure which seems to have been designed using nothing but triangles – a pattern subliminally echoed in the adjacent **Sheraton Dubai Creek**, whose wedge-shaped facade pokes out above the creekside like the prow of some enormous concrete ship. Opposite the Sheraton stands the **Etisalat Tower**, designed by Canadian architect Arthur Erikson and instantly recognizable thanks to the enormous golf ball on its roof. The design proved so catchy it's since been repeated at further Etisalat buildings across the UAE, including the new Etisalat building at the north end of Sheikh Zayed Road and on its two buildings in Abu Dhabi.

There's another large **dhow wharfage** here, just east of the Chamber of Commerce. It's much less visited than central Deira's but just as eye-catching, with the old-fashioned boats superbly framed against the sparkling glass facades of the surrounding modernist high-rises.

3

The inner suburbs

Fringing the southern and eastern edges of the city centre – and separating it from the more modern areas beyond – are a necklace of low-key suburbs: Garhoud, Oud Metha, Karama and Satwa. This whole area of Dubai has a slightly indeterminate, in-between feel, neither properly part of the city centre, but largely lacking the futuristic pizzazz of the southern suburbs, although there are plenty of attractions squirrelled away amid the rather formless concrete expanse. The enjoyably downmarket suburbs of **Karama** and **Satwa** are two of the most interesting parts of the city in which to get off the tourist trail and see something of local life among the city's Indian and Filipina expats, with plenty of lively and inexpensive shops and restaurants for filling up on cheap curry and designer fakes. Beyond Karama, the more upmarket district of **Oud Metha** is home to the Wafi complex, an appealling study in cartoon-Egyptian, complete with assorted stone pharaohs, miniature pyramids, the swanky *Raffles* hotel and the lavish Khan Murjan Souk. On the far side of the Creek and almost within spitting distance of the airport, **Garhoud** is home to the Dubai Creek Golf Club, with its famously futuristic clubhouse, and the adjacent Yacht Club, where you'll find a string of attractive waterside restaurants and the lovely *Park Hyatt* hotel. South of here, the **Festival City** development offers yet another large-scale mall, plus sweeping waterside views.

Satwa

The unpretentious district of **Satwa** is the southernmost outpost of Dubai's predominantly low-rise, low-income inner suburbs before you reach the giant skyscrapers of Sheikh Zayed Road and the beginnings of the supersized modern city beyond. It's also one of the few places in Dubai where the city's different ethnic groups really rub shoulders, with a mix of Arab, Indian, Filipina and even a few European residents, reflected in an unusually eclectic selection of places to

Farewell to Satwa?

Sadly, Satwa's days appear to be numbered. The suburb occupies some of the city's prime real estate, virtually within the shadow of the Emirates Towers and the Dubai International Financial Centre, and in 2007 it was decided to demolish the entire district to make way for an upmarket new development, provisionally named Jumeirah Garden City. Following the credit crunch the project appears to have been put on hold, though some houses have already been knocked down, and Satwa's unfortunate residents – mainly low-income Asian expats, who squeeze into the suburb's overcrowded villas, often five or ten to a room – are already looking for new places to live.

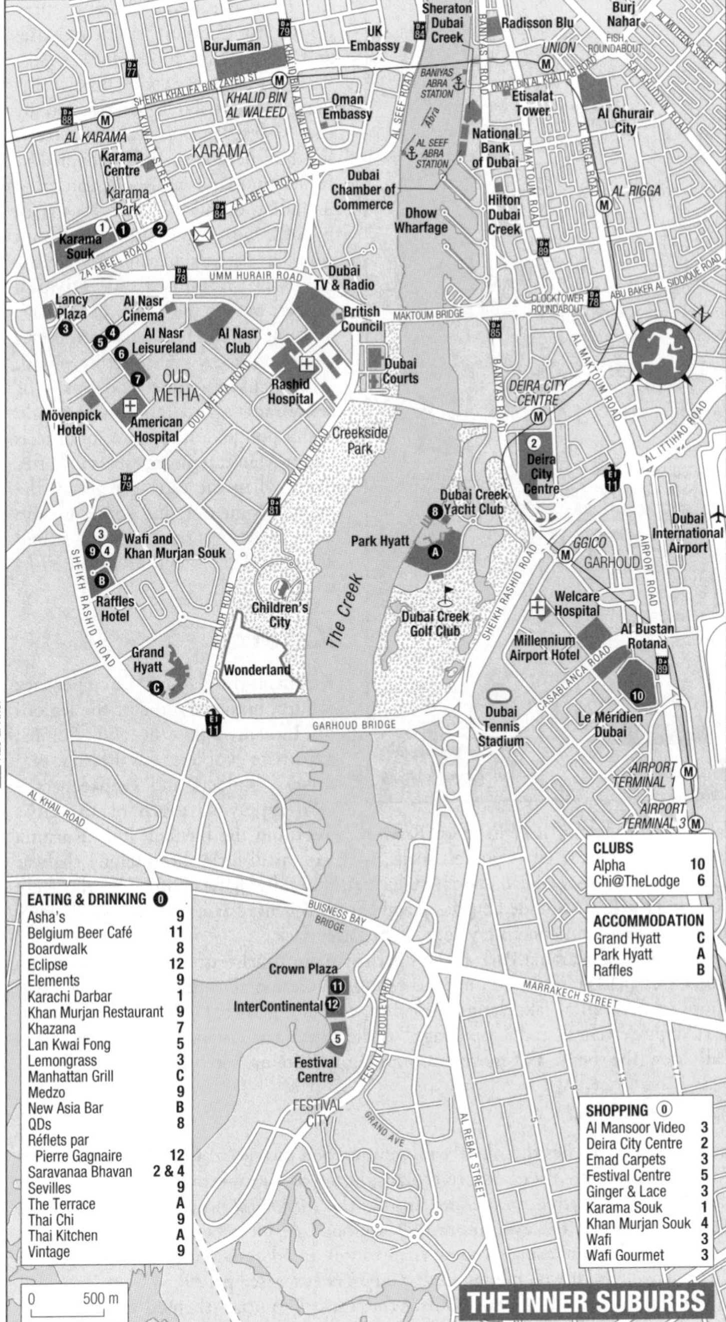

Satwa
Ras al Khor
Sheraton Dubai Creek
Radisson Blu
Burj Nahar
BurJuman
UK Embassy
UNION
FISH ROUNDABOUT
BANIYAS ABRA STATION
Etisalat Tower
Al Ghurair City
KHALID BIN AL WALEED
Oman Embassy
AL KARAMA
KARAMA
Karama Centre
Karama Park
Karama Souk
AL SEEF ABRA STATION
National Bank of Dubai
Dubai Chamber of Commerce
Hilton Dubai Creek
Dhow Wharfage
AL RIGGA
Dubai TV & Radio
Lancy Plaza
Al Nasr Cinema
Al Nasr Leisureland
Al Nasr Club
British Council
CLOCKTOWER ROUNDABOUT
MAKTOUM BRIDGE
Dubai Courts
Rashid Hospital
OUD METHA
Mövenpick Hotel
American Hospital
DEIRA CITY CENTRE
Deira City Centre
Creekside Park
Dubai Creek Yacht Club
Park Hyatt
Wafi and Khan Murjan Souk
Raffles Hotel
Children's City
The Creek
Dubai Creek Golf Club
GGICO
GARHOUD
Dubai International Airport
Welcare Hospital
Millennium Airport Hotel
Al Bustan Rotana
Grand Hyatt
Wonderland
GARHOUD BRIDGE
Dubai Tennis Stadium
Le Méridien Dubai
AIRPORT TERMINAL 1
AIRPORT TERMINAL 3
AL KHAIL ROAD
BUISNESS BAY BRIDGE
MARRAKECH STREET
Crown Plaza
InterContinental
Festival Centre
FESTIVAL CITY
AL REBAT STREET
CLUBS
Alpha 10
Chi@TheLodge 6
ACCOMMODATION
Grand Hyatt C
Park Hyatt A
Raffles B
EATING & DRINKING
Asha's 9
Belgium Beer Café 11
Boardwalk 8
Eclipse 12
Elements 9
Karachi Darbar 1
Khan Murjan Restaurant 9
Khazana 7
Lan Kwai Fong 5
Lemongrass 3
Manhattan Grill C
Medzo 9
New Asia Bar B
QDs 8
Réflets par Pierre Gagnaire 12
Saravanaa Bhavan 2 & 4
Sevilles 9
The Terrace A
Thai Chi 9
Thai Kitchen A
Vintage 9
SHOPPING
Al Mansoor Video 3
Deira City Centre 2
Emad Carpets 3
Festival Centre 5
Ginger & Lace 3
Karama Souk 1
Khan Murjan Souk 4
Wafi 3
Wafi Gourmet 3
0 500 m
THE INNER SUBURBS

eat, from cheap-and-cheerful curry houses to Lebanese shwarma cafés and Western fast-food joints.

At the centre of the district lies Satwa Roundabout, overlooked by the *Rydges Plaza Hotel*. The streets south of here are mainly occupied by Indian and Pakistani shops and cafés, including the well-known *Ravi's* (see p.114). West from the roundabout stretches Satwa's principal thoroughfare, the tree-lined **Al Diyafah Street**, one of the nicest in Dubai – and one of the few outside the city centre with any real streetlife – with wide pavements, dozens of restaurants, and an interestingly cosmopolitan atmosphere; it all feels rather Mediterranean, especially after dark, when the cafés get going, the crowds come out, and young men in expensive cars start driving round and round the block in a vain effort to impress.

Karama

Karama is the classic Dubai inner-city suburb, home to some of the legions of Indian, Pakistani and Filipina expatriate workers – waitresses, taxi drivers, builders and shopkeepers – who supply so much of the city's labour. The district is centred on **Kuwait Street** and the bustling little **Karama Centre**, one of the city's pokiest malls, with colourful little shops selling shalwar kameez and flouncy Indian-style jewellery. At the end of Kuwait Street lies the lively **Karama Park**, surrounded by cheap and cheery Indian restaurants and usually busy with a dozen simultaneous cricket matches after dark.

Just south of Karama Park is the district's main tourist attraction, the **Karama Souk** (see p.145), set in an unprepossessing concrete mall with hundreds of small shops stuffed full of fake designer clothes, watches, glasses, DVDs and other items (or "copy watches" and "copy bags" as the souk's enthusiastic touts euphemistically describe them). For more on shopping in Karama, see p.145.

Oud Metha

South of Karama lies the slightly more upmarket district of **Oud Metha**, a rather formless area dotted with assorted malls, hotels and low-brow leisure attractions. The district is centred on the area around the *Mövenpick* hotel, the old-fashioned Lamcy Plaza and the even more old-fashioned Al Nasr Leisureland amusement park, though there are also some surprisingly good restaurants here (see p.114–115), as well as Dubai's biggest club, *Chi@TheLodge* (see p.129).

The leading attraction hereabouts is the wacky Egyptian-themed **Wafi** complex (see shopping and eating listings, p.145 and p.114–115), a little slice of Vegas in

Dubai, dotted with obelisks, pharaonic statues, random hieroglyphs and assorted miniature pyramids. The Egyptian theme is continued in the opulent **Raffles** hotel next door, built in the form of a vast pyramid, its summit capped with glass – particularly spectacular when it lights up after dark.

Hidden away between Wafi and *Raffles*, **Khan Murjan Souk** is one of Dubai's finest "traditional" developments, allegedly modelled after the fabled fourteenth-century Khan Murjan Souk in Baghdad. The souk is divided into four sections – Egyptian, Syrian, Moroccan and Turkish (not that you can really tell the difference) spread over two underground levels, with a lovely outdoor restaurant (see p.115) at its centre and some 125 shops selling all manner of traditional wares. It's a great (albeit relatively expensive) place to shop, while the faux-Arabian decor is impressively done, with lavish detailing ranging from intricately carved wooden balconies to enormous Moroccan lanterns and colourful tilework. Of course, it's all about as authentic as a Mulberry bag from Karama – indeed if the city authorities are serious about clamping down on the local trade in fakes and forgeries, they could do worse than start here. Still, the whole thing has been done with such enormous panache and at, presumably, such enormous expense that it's hard not to be at least a little bit impressed.

Just south of Wafi next to the main inner city ring road, the vast **Grand Hyatt Hotel** (formerly the largest in the city until the opening of *Atlantis* in late 2008) stands in majestic isolation at Oud Metha's southern end, its curved, interlocking white wings looking like some kind of giant lego toy – although its now been rather upstaged by the dramatic outline of *Raffles*, just down the road.

Immediately west of the *Grand Hyatt*, flanking the Creek between Garhoud and Maktoum bridges, the expansive **Creekside Park** (daily 8am-11pm, Thurs–Sat until 11.30pm; 5dh) serves as one of congested central Dubai's major lungs and is a pleasant place for an idle ramble, with nice views over the Creek towards the golf and yacht clubs and the miniature blue domes of the *Park Hyatt* hotel. The park is nicest towards dusk, when the temperature falls and the place fills up a bit, although it can be eerily deserted during weekdays. It's particularly good for **kids**, with plenty of playgrounds and the fun

▲ Pharaoh statues at the Wafi complex

Children's City (see p.33) to explore, while the Dubai Dolphinarium (see p.33) stands just outside. Children (and, indeed, adults), may also be tempted by the park's **cable car**, which offers half-hour trips (25dh, children 15dh) dangling 30m above the park.

Jaddaf

On the southern edge of Oud Metha, the district of **Jaddaf** is home to a few traditional **dhow-building yards** where you can watch craftsmen at work constructing these magnificent ocean-going vessels using carpenting skills which appear not to have changed for generations. The yard isn't really set up for visitors and is essentially a place of work, rather than a tourist attraction, while there's also a certain degree of pot luck involved depending on how many vessels are under construction at any given time – although the mainly Indian workforce are usually happy to chat to visitors and you're free to explore at will. Unfortunately, finding the yards isn't straightforward, and it's unlikely that taxi drivers will know where to go (or even what you're talking about). Getting there is further complicated by the fact that the whole area is currently in the throes of major development associated with the new metro and the nearby Versace hotel. It may be possible in future to take the metro to Jaddaf station (due to open in Aug 2011, according to latest estimates – see p.22), at the end of the Green Line, and walk from there. Alternatively, you can get a long-distance view of the dhow-building yards from the other side of the Creek, along the waterfront at Festival City.

Ras al Khor Wildlife Sanctuary

South of Jaddaf, the Dubai Creek comes to an impressive end at **Ras al Khor** ("Head of the Creek"), forming an extensive inland lagoon dotted with mangroves and surrounded by intertidal salt- and mud-flats – a unique area of unspoilt nature so close to the city centre. This being Dubai, much of Ras al Khor's rare natural habitat was earmarked for the vast new **The Lagoons** development, featuring seven interconnected artificial islands, along with the usual malls, five-star hotels and the city's first opera house; although as of 2010, the project had been indefinitely suspended after four of the developer's senior executives were arrested on corruption charges.

The southern end of the lagoon, meanwhile, is home to the low-key **Ras al Khor Wildlife Sanctuary** (Sat–Thurs 9am–4pm; free; permit required for more than five visitors; Ⓦwww.wildlife.ae). The sanctuary is an important stopover on winter migratory routes from East Africa to West Asia and almost 70 different species have been spotted here. It's best known for the colourful flocks of bright pink flamingoes which nest here – one of Dubai's most surreal sights when seen perched against the smoggy outlines of the city skyscrapers beyond.

You can't actually go into the sanctuary, but you can birdwatch from one of two **hides** on its edge. Free binoculars are provided, although the roar of the nearby motorways isn't particularly conducive to the relaxed contemplation of nature. The best hide is on the western side of the sanctuary, beside the E66 Highway just north of the junction with the Hatta Road. The second is on the south side of the sanctuary, on the north side of the Hatta Road; to reach it from central Dubai you'll need to do an annoying 8km loop to get back on the correct side of the highway. Signage for both hides is minimal, and don't expect taxi drivers to know where they are.

The Arabian dhow

The inhabitants of the Arabian Peninsula were among the greatest seafarers of medieval times, using innovative shipbuilding techniques and navigational instruments to establish extensive maritime trading connections. Early Arab traders established outposts as far afield as India, Sri Lanka and East Africa; the legacy of these early adventurers can be still be seen in the religious and cultural heritage of places like Lamu in Kenya and Zanzibar in Tanzania, where the distinctive form of the lateen-sailed Arabian **dhow** survives to this day.

The word "**dhow**" itself is simply a generic name used to apply to all boats of Arabian design. Classic designs include the **boom**, a large seafaring dhow, and the **sambuq**, another sizeable ocean-going vessel incorporating Indian and European features, including a square stern which is thought to have been influenced by old Portuguese galleons (traditional Arabian dhows are tapered at both ends). Other smaller dhows still in use around the Gulf include the **shu'ai** and the **jalibut**, both formerly used for trading, pearling and fishing, as well as the **abra**, hundreds of which still ply the Creek today.

Construction

Perhaps the most distinctive feature of the traditional dhow was its so-called **stitched construction** – planks, usually of teak, were literally "sewn" together using coconut rope. Nails were increasingly used after European ships began to visit the region, although stitched boats were made right up until World War II. Traditional dhows are also unusual in being built "outside-in", with exterior planking being nailed together before the internal framework is added (the exact opposite of European boat-building techniques). Dhow hulls are generally left unpainted above the waterline, apart from decorative patterns around cabins, railings and (sometimes) the traditional "thunderbox" overhanging the stern, which serves as the dhow's toilet while at sea.

The traditional dhow's most visually notable feature was its distinctive triangular **lateen** sails, which allows boats to sail closer to the wind when travelling against the monsoon breezes. These have now disappeared on commercial vessels around the Gulf following the introduction of engines, though they can still be seen on local racing dhows (see p.134).

Traditional wooden dhows still play an important part in the local economy, and continue to prove an efficient and cost-effective way of shipping goods up and down the Gulf and, particularly, over to Iran – as well as finding a new lease of life in the local tourist industry. There are still a number of traditional **dhow-building yards** around the UAE: in Dubai at Jaddaf (see opposite), in Abu Dhabi, and also in the neighbouring emirates of Ajman, Umm al Quwain and Ras al Khaimah, although the incredibly labour-intensive production costs and a gradual erosion of the traditional skills required in dhow-construction (local boat-builders are famed for their ability to work entirely without plans, building entirely by eye and experience) may yet lead to an eventual end to dhow-building.

Meydan Racecourse and Godolphin Gallery

Just south of Ras al Khor, the vast new **Meydan Racecourse** (Ⓦwww.meydan.ae/racecourse) opened in early 2010, taking over from the old Nad al Sheba Horse Racecourse as Dubai's premier racetrack and the new home of the **Dubai World Cup**, the world's richest horse race, with a massive $10 million in prize money (though, as with camel-racing, no betting is allowed). The racecourse is also expected to serve as the new home for the **Godolphin Gallery**, formerly located at Nad al Sheba racecourse, but scheduled to reopen at Meydan sometime in 2010; see Ⓦwww.godolphin.com/theGodolphinGallery.aspx). The gallery showcases the history of Godolphin, founded in 1994 by Dubai ruler Sheikh Mohammed and now one of the world's largest and most successful racing stables. Exhibits include some of the innumerable trophies won by Godolphin over the years, along with old photos and films picking out leading moments in its history along with a life-sized model, created by Madame Tussauds, of Dubai Millennium, perhaps the stable's most famous horse, and winner of the 2000 Dubai World Cup.

Festival City

Facing Ras al Khor on the opposite side of the Creek, **Festival City** (Ⓦwww.dubaifestivalcity.com) is one of Dubai's newest and largest purpose-built neighbourhoods – a self-contained city within a city, complete with villas and apartments, offices, golf course, marina, shopping mall and a pair of swanky five-star hotels. The centrepiece of the development is the bright, modern **Festival Centre** shopping mall; there's nothing here that you won't find (and generally done better) at other malls around the city, although the canalside cafés at the Creek end of the centre are pleasant enough, and the ground floor of the new **Gold Market** is one of the sexiest pieces of interior design in Dubai. The development's best physical feature is its creekside location, with sweeping views from the waterfront promenade by the Festival Centre mall and hotels across the water to the dhow-building yard at Jaddaf and the long line of skyscrapers beyond. The panorama is particularly fine towards dusk, when the sun sets behind the Burj Khalifa and towers along Sheikh Zayed Road, turning them a smoky grey, like the outline of some kind of surreal bar-chart.

Garhoud

Covering the area between the airport and the Creek, the suburb of **Garhoud** is an interesting mishmash of up- and down-market attractions. The **Deira City Centre** mall (see p.135) is the suburb's main draw, eternally popular with an eclectic crowd running the gamut from Gulf Arabs and Russian tourists to the many expat Indians and Filipinas who live in the down-at-heel suburbs on the far side of the airport.

On the far side of Baniyas Road lies the **Dubai Creek Golf Club** (see p.135), an impressive swathe of lush fairways and greens centred on the quirky **clubhouse**, built in 1993 and still one of the city's most instantly recognizable modern landmarks – like a Dubai remake of the Sydney Opera House, with its uniquely spiky white roofline echoing the shape of a dhow's sails and masts.

Enclosed within the grounds of the golf club next to the Creek lies another local landmark, the **Dubai Creek Yacht Club**, occupying a full-size replica of a ship's bridge, with dozens of beautiful yachts moored alongside. There are several good restaurants (see p.116) in the golf and yacht club buildings, as well as in the **Park Hyatt** hotel between, whose serene white Moroccan-style buildings, topped with vivid blue-tiled domes, add a further touch of style to the creekside hereabouts.

Sheikh Zayed Road and Downtown Dubai

Around three kilometres south of the Creek, the upwardly mobile suburbs of southern Dubai begin in spectacular style with the massed skyscrapers of **Sheikh Zayed Road**: a vast ten-lane highway flanked by an extraordinary sequence of neck-cricking high-rises which march all the way south to the lavish new **Downtown Dubai** development. This is the modern city at its most futuristic and flamboyant, and perhaps the defining example of Dubai's insatiable desire to offer more luxury, more glitz and more retail opportunities than the competition, with a string of record-breaking attractions which now include the world's highest building, tallest hotel, largest mall and biggest fountain. At the northern end of the strip, the stunning **Emirates Towers** remain one of Dubai's most memorable modern landmarks. At its southern end rises the cloud-capped **Burj Khalifa** – the world's tallest building – the huge new **Dubai Mall** and the kitsch **Old Town** development, arranged around an attractive lake and the **Dubai Fountain**, which shoots spectacularly into life after dark.

Emirates Towers

Opened in 2000, the soaring **Emirates Towers** remain one of the most iconic symbols of modern Dubai, despite increasing competition. The taller office tower (355m) was once the highest in the Middle East and tenth tallest in the world when it was completed, though it's since been outstripped locally by both the Burj Khalifa and Almas Tower. The towers are not just impressively large, but also strikingly beautiful thanks to their unusual triangular groundplan and spiky cutaway summits, while the constantly changing effects of the strong desert light and shadow on the buildings' sharp edges and highly reflective surfaces is equally magical.

The taller tower houses the offices of Emirates airlines, plus the offices of Dubai ruler Sheikh Mohammed and his inner circle of senior advisers; the smaller is occupied by the exclusive *Jumeirah Emirates Towers* hotel (see p.103). One curiosity of the buildings is that the taller office tower, despite its considerable extra height (355m versus 305m), has only two more floors than the hotel tower (53 versus 51); the difference in height is due to the floor-to floor heights. The office tower isn't open to the public, apart from the ground floor, where you'll find the posh **Emirates Towers Boulevard**, one of the city's most exclusive malls (see p.144). There are plenty of opportunities to look around

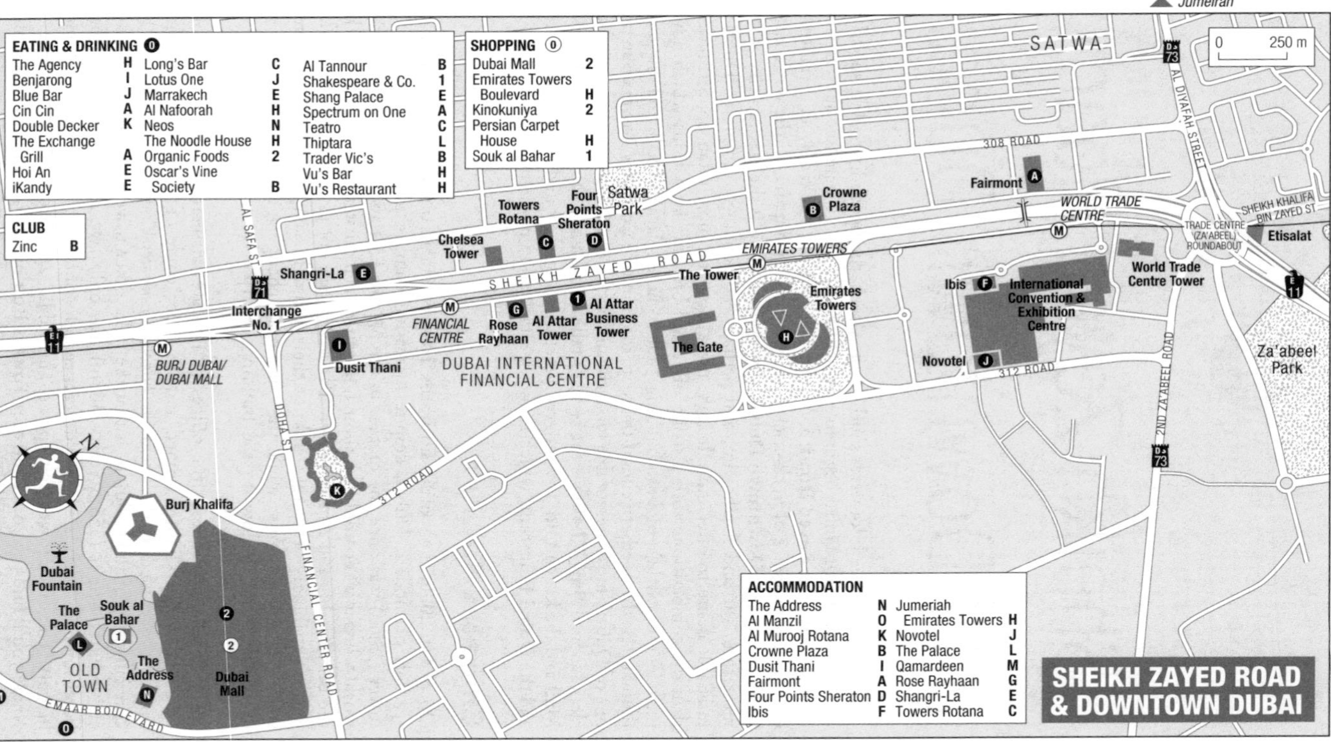
EATING & DRINKING 0
The Agency H
Benjarong I
Blue Bar J
Cin Cin A
Double Decker K
The Exchange Grill A
Hoi An E
iKandy E
Long's Bar C
Lotus One J
Marrakech E
Al Nafoorah H
Neos N
The Noodle House H
Organic Foods 2
Oscar's Vine Society B
Al Tannour B
Shakespeare & Co. 1
Shang Palace E
Spectrum on One A
Teatro C
Thiptara L
Trader Vic's B
Vu's Bar H
Vu's Restaurant H
CLUB
Zinc B
SHOPPING 0
Dubai Mall 2
Emirates Towers Boulevard H
Kinokuniya 2
Persian Carpet House H
Souk al Bahar 1
SATWA
0 250 m
Jumeirah
Bur Dubai
Dubai Marina
AL DIYAFAH STREET
308 ROAD
Fairmont
Crowne Plaza
Satwa Park
Four Points Sheraton
Towers Rotana
Chelsea Tower
WORLD TRADE CENTRE
SHEIKH KHALIFA BIN ZAYED ST
TRADE CENTRE (ZA'ABEEL) ROUNDABOUT
Etisalat
World Trade Centre Tower
International Convention & Exhibition Centre
Ibis
Novotel
312 ROAD
2ND ZA'ABEEL ROAD
Za'abeel Park
EMIRATES TOWERS
Emirates Towers
The Tower
The Gate
SHEIKH ZAYED ROAD
AL SAFA ST
Shangri-La
Interchange No. 1
FINANCIAL CENTRE
Rose Rayhaan
Al Attar Tower
Al Attar Business Tower
BURJ DUBAI/ DUBAI MALL
Dusit Thani
DUBAI INTERNATIONAL FINANCIAL CENTRE
DOHA ST
FINANCIAL CENTER ROAD
Burj Khalifa
Dubai Fountain
The Palace
Souk al Bahar
OLD TOWN
The Address
Dubai Mall
EMAAR BOULEVARD
ACCOMMODATION
The Address N
Al Manzil O
Al Murooj Rotana K
Crowne Plaza B
Dusit Thani I
Fairmont A
Four Points Sheraton D
Ibis F
Jumeirah Emirates Towers H
Novotel J
The Palace L
Qamardeen M
Rose Rayhaan G
Shangri-La E
Towers Rotana C
SHEIKH ZAYED ROAD & DOWNTOWN DUBAI

Sheikh Zayed Road

Technically, Sheikh Zayed Road is the name of the highway which runs all the way from Dubai to Abu Dhabi. In practice, however, when locals refer to "Sheikh Zayed Road" they are usually talking about the section of highway in central Dubai **between Interchange no. 1 and the Trade Centre Roundabout** (also known as Za'abeel Roundabout), ie from the *Dusit Thani* hotel to just north of the Emirates Towers, which is where you'll find most of the road's hotels, restaurants and shops. This is the sense in which the name is used here. Attractions further south along Sheikh Zayed Road past Interchange no. 1 – such as the Mall of the Emirates, Dubai Marina and Ibn Battuta Mall – are covered in later chapters.

the hotel tower though, most spectacularly from the 50th- and 51st-floor *Vu's* bar and restaurant (see p.125 & p.118). It's also worth popping in to have a look at the dramatic atrium, with its little pod-shaped glass elevators shuttling up and down the huge orange wall overhead.

Around the Emirates Towers

The area surrounding the Emirates Towers is Dubai's international commercial and financial heart – the local equivalent of the City of London or Wall Street. Immediately south of the Emirates Towers stretches the **Dubai International Financial Centre**, its northern end marked by **The Gate** building, a rather striking kind of postmodern Arc de Triomphe-cum-office block which now houses the Dubai Stock Exchange.

North of the Emirates Towers stretches the sprawling Dubai International Convention and Exhibition Centre on whose far side rises the venerable old **Dubai World Trade Centre** tower, Dubai's first skyscraper and formerly the tallest building in the Middle East. Commissioned in 1979 by the visionary Sheikh Rashid (see p.183), this 39-storey edifice was widely regarded as a massive white elephant when it was first built, standing as it did in the middle of what was then empty desert far from the old city centre. In fact, history has entirely vindicated Rashid's daring gamble. The centre proved an enormous success with foreign companies and US diplomats, who established a consulate in the tower and used it as a major base for monitoring affairs in nearby Iran; their covert intelligence-gathering vastly aided by the large number of Dubai-based Iranians who arrived at the consulate to apply for US visas. The centre also served as an important anchor of future development along the strip, and it's a measure of Sheikh Rashid's far-sighted ambition that his alleged *folie de grandeur* has been long since overtaken by a string of far more impressive constructions further down the road.

South along Sheikh Zayed Road

South of the Emirates Towers, Sheikh Zayed Road continues in a more or less unbroken line of high-rises, looking like the contestents in some bizarre postmodern architectural beauty parade. Heading down the strip brings you immediately to **The Tower**, one of the prettiest buildings along the strip: a slender edifice rising to a neat pyramidal summit, with three tiers of stylized leaf-shaped metal protuberances sprouting from its sides. Further south lies the eye-catching **Al Attar Tower** (not to be confused with the nearby Al Attar Business Tower), which appears to have been constructed entirely out of plate glass and enormous gold coins, while close by rises the graceful new **Rose Rayhaan**, at 333m the world's tallest hotel. The latter is a beautifully slender and delicate structure,

▲ Sheikh Zayed Road

topped by a small globe which is illuminated prettily after dark. More or less opposite stands the soaring **Chelsea Tower**, topped by what looks like an enormous toothpick. A short walk further south the strip reaches a suitably dramatic end with the iconic **Dusit Thani** hotel, a towering glass-and-metal edifice inspired by the traditional Thai *wai*, a prayer-like gesture of welcome, though it looks more like a huge upended tuning fork thrust into the ground.

Looking south from here, you'll see yet another dense forest of cranes and the outlines of dozens of further high-rises emerging out of the desert alongside Sheikh Zayed Road. These will eventually form the huge new **Business Bay** development, centred on a 12km extension of the Dubai Creek and scheduled to start coming into service from 2012 onwards.

Downtown Dubai

Flanking the east side of Sheikh Zayed Road immediately south of Interchange no. 1 lies the massive **Downtown Dubai** development (formerly known as Downtown Burj Dubai, as some signs still have it), built between 2004 and 2010 at an estimated cost of around $20 billion. The centrepiece of the development is the record-breaking **Burj Khalifa**, in whose shadow sit a string of other landmark attractions including the **Dubai Mall**, **Dubai Fountain** and the Arabian-style **Old Town**.

Burj Khalifa

Rising imperiously skywards at the southern end of Sheikh Zayed Road stands the needle-thin **Burj Khalifa**, the world's tallest building, which finally opened in early 2010 after five years' intensive construction, having topped out at a staggering 828m. The Burj Khalifa – or Burj Dubai, as it was formerly known (see box opposite) – has comprehensively smashed all existing records for the world's tallest man-made structures, past and present, overtaking previous record holders Taipei 101 in Taiwan (formerly the world's tallest building at 509m), the KVLY-TV mast in North Dakota (the world's tallest extant man-made structure at 629m), and the Warsaw Radio Mast, at Gabin in Poland (previously the tallest man-made structure ever erected, at 646m, before it collapsed in 1991). The Burj also returned the record for the world's tallest structure to the Middle East for the first time since 1311, when the towers of Lincoln Cathedral surpassed the Great Pyramid of Giza, which had previously reigned supreme for almost 4000 years. The tower also accumulated a host of other superlatives en route, including the building with the most floors (160), the world's highest and fastest elevators, plus highest mosque (158th floor) and swimming pool (76th floor).

The tower was designed by Chicago high-rise specialists Skidmore, Owings and Merrill, whose other credits include the Willis Tower, formerly the Sears Tower, in Chicago, and New York's 1 World Trade Center. The building consists of a slender central square core, surrounded by three tiers arranged in a Y-shaped plan. These tiers are gradually stepped back as the building rises, forming a series of 27 terraces, before the central core emerges to form the culminating spire – a plan which makes the optimum use of available natural light, as well as providing the best outward views. The shape of the tower has often been compared to that for Frank Lloyd Wright's visionary (but unrealized) plans for The Illinois, a mile-high skyscraper designed for Chicago. Chief architect Adrian Smith has said that the tower's Y-shaped footprint was inspired by the flower *Hymenocallis*; various Islamic architectural precedents have also been invoked, although with no particular conviction.

The astonishing scale of the Burj is difficult to fully comprehend – the building is best appreciated at a distance, from where you can properly appreciate the tower's jaw-dropping height and the degree to which it reduces even the elevated high-rises which surround it to the status of under-nourished pygmies. Distance also emphasizes the Burj's slender, elegantly tapering outline, which has been variously compared to a shard of glass, a latter-day Tower of Babel and, according to Germaine Greer, "a needle stuck in the buttock of the Almighty". Close up the building is less satisfying, with endless tier upon tier of uniform grey glass and aluminium cladding which creates an impression of monumental monotony, and which seems to swallow up the light, making the whole thing look like a monochrome cardboard cut out.

Most of the tower is occupied by some 900 residential apartments (these allegedly sold out within eight hours of launch, and subsequently changed hands, at the height of the Dubai property market, for a cool $3500/sq ft), while fifteen floors will be given over to the world's first **Armani hotel** (Ⓦ www.armanihotels.com), due to open sometime in 2010, with presumably stratospheric prices.

Burj Dubai or Burj Khalifa?

The biggest surprise at the Burj's spectacular opening party in January 2010 was the announcement that the tower, previously known as the Burj Dubai, was to be **renamed** the Burj Khalifa, in honour of Khalifa bin Zayed al Nahyan, ruler of Abu Dhabi and president of the UAE. Announcing the name change, Dubai ruler Sheikh Mohammed stated: "This great project deserves to carry the name of a great man" – although the naming-rights to the world's tallest building may owe less to Sheikh Khalifa's personal qualities and more to the $15-billion-plus bailout which Abu Dhabi provided to cash-strapped Dubai following recent financial difficulties. Oddly enough, Sheikh Khalifa himself didn't bother showing up to the unveiling of the building which will now make his name familiar to millions.

Visiting Burj Khalifa

Until the opening of the *Armani Hotel*, visitors' only access to the tower is by taking the expensive trip up to the misleadingly named **"At the Top"** observation deck (on floor 124, although there are actually 160 floors in total) for sensational views over the city. Tours depart from the ticket desk in the lower-ground floor of the Dubai Mall. **Tickets** cost a hefty 100dh if pre-booked, or a sky-high 400dh for immediate, unreserved access. Reserved tickets can be booked online at Ⓦwww.burjkhalifa.ae or purchased from the ticket desk (daily 10am–10pm, Thurs–Sat until midnight) in the Dubai Mall. Immediate entry tickets must be purchased in person from the ticket office. Make sure you book well in advance – at the time of writing the popularity of the newly opened Burj meant that there was at least a week's waiting time for reserved tickets, although the situation may have eased since.

Dubai Mall

Right next to the Burj Khalifa, the supersized **Dubai Mall** (daily 10am–10pm, Thurs–Sat until midnight; Ⓦwww.thedubaimall.com) is the absolute mother of all malls, with over 1200 shops spread across four floors and covering a total area of 12 million square feet – making it easily the largest mall in the world measured by total area (although other malls contain more shopping space). Just about every retail chain in the city has an outlet here, with flagship names including Galleries Lafayette, Bloomingdales, an offshoot of London's famous Hamley's toy store and a superb branch of the Japanese bookseller Kinokuniya. There are also lashings of upmarket designer stores, mainly concentrated along the section of the mall called **Fashion Avenue** – a positive encyclopedia of labels, complete with its own catwalk and Armani café – as well as a self-contained **Gold Souk**, with attractive contemporary Arabian design and a further 220 shops. Other amenities include some 120 **cafés and restaurants**, divided between various interior foodcourts and the peaceful waterside terrace at the back of the mall overlooking the Dubai Fountain. There are also further places to eat in **The Grove**, a pleasant "outdoor" streetscape under a retractable roof, bounded at one end by eye-catching **The Waterfall**, complete with life-size statues of fibreglass divers, which cascades from the top of the mall down to the bottom, four storeys below.

And that's only the beginning. Add in a glut of other attractions including a five-star hotel (see p.104), 22-screen multiplex, the state-of-the-art SEGA Republic theme park (see p.33), the KidZania "edu-tainment" centre (see p.33), an Olympic-size ice rink (see p.136) and the Dubai Aquarium and Underwater Zoo (see below) and you'll get a sense of the mall's stated ambition to serve as one of the city's leading all-in-one leisure destinations, rather than simply a place to shop (and that's not counting neighbouring attractions like the Souk al Bahar, Dubai Fountain and Burj Khalifa). Not surprisingly, even a casual shopping visit to the mall can be a somewhat overwhelming and exhausting experience – expect to walk several miles at minimum, even if you're just looking for the nearest toilet.

Dubai Aquarium

Assuming you come in the mall's main entrance, one of the first things you'll see is the spectacular viewing panel of the **Dubai Aquarium and Underwater Zoo** (Sun–Weds 10am–10pm, Thurs–Sat 10am–midnight; Ⓦwww.thedubaiaquarium.com; 50dh, including underwater tunnel): a huge transparent floor-to-ceiling aquarium filled to the brim with fish large and small, including sand-tiger sharks, stingrays, colourful shoals of tropical fish and some large and spectacularly ugly grouper. The viewing window holds the record for the world's largest acrylic

Getting to Dubai Mall on the metro

Despite its name, the **Burj Khalifa/Dubai Mall metro station** isn't actually at the Dubai Mall. To get from station to mall is either a short bus ride or a ten-minute walk (assuming you don't get lost). Head towards the Burj Khalifa and you'll see the large, vaguely orange-coloured mall building ahead of you. It's easiest to walk in through the underground car park rather than trudging all the way around to the front.

panel: around 8m high and over 30m wide, with 33,000 fish, 70 species and 10 million litres of water – effectively the largest fish tank on the planet. You can also ride a glass-bottom boat (25dh) across the top of the tank, walk through the underwater tunnel (25dh, children 20dh) which leads through the middle, or even go diving in it (by prior arrangment only), although you won't see anything you can't already see from the mall, and for free.

The **Underwater Zoo** upstairs is relatively unexciting compared to the enormous tank, and more likely to appeal to children than to adults. Displays are arranged according to different marine habitats like freshwater, "rocky shore" and rainforest, with representative fauna from each, ranging from tiny cichlids, poison-dart frogs and soapfish through to otters, penguins and seals.

Dubai Fountain and Souk al Bahar

Exiting the rear entrance of the Dubai Mall via the lower-ground (LG) floor from Star Atrium brings you out onto the large **lake** which forms the centrepiece of the Downtown Dubai development, with waterfront promenades stretching away in various directions and the Burj Khalifa towering above you on your right.

The section of the lake closest to the Dubai Mall doubles as the spectacular 275m-long **Dubai Fountain**, the world's biggest, capable of shooting jets of water up to 150m high, and illuminated with over 6000 lights and 25 colour projectors. The fountain comes to life after dark, spouting carefully choreographed watery flourishes which "dance" elegantly in time to a range of Arabic, Hindi and classical songs. "Performances" are staged every 20min between 6pm and 10pm in the evening (until 11pm Thurs–Sat) and can be watched for free from anywhere around the lake.

Cross the small bridge at the exit from the Dubai Mall's Star Atrium to reach Old Town Island, part of the **Old Town** development, and consisting of low-rise, sand-coloured buildings with traditional Moorish styling. The overall concept, with a soaring futuristic tower placed next to cod-Arabian village with waterways, is effectively a blatant copy of the Madinat Jumeirah/Burj Al Arab concept (see p.84), except not quite as impressively done. The centrepiece of Old Town Island is the **Souk al Bahar** ("Souk of the Sailor"; Sat–Thurs 10am–10pm, Fri 2–10pm), a small, Arabian-themed mall specializing in traditional handicrafts and independent fashion, though it feels rather underpowered after the excesses of the neighbouring Dubai Mall. A string of restaurants line the waterfront terrace outside, offering peerless views of Burj Khalifa – although they tend to get absolutely rammed after dark, and none is of any particular culinary distinction. On the far side of the Souk al Bahar stands the Old Town's opulent showpiece, **The Palace** hotel (see p.104), its rich Moorish facade offering a surreal but quintessentially Dubaiian contrast with the needle-thin outline of the Burj Khalifa rising imperiously behind.

Jumeirah

A couple of kilometres south of the Creek, the beachside suburb of **Jumeirah** marks the beginning of southern Dubai's endless suburban sprawl. The area's swathes of chintzy low-rise villas are home to many of the city's European expats and their wives – immortalized in Dubai legend as the so-called "Jumeirah Janes" who (so the stereotype runs) spend their days in an endless round of luncheons and beach parties, while their hard-working spouses slave away to keep them in the style to which they have very rapidly become accustomed.

The suburb is strung out along the Jumeirah Road, which arrows straight down the coast and provides the area with its principal focus, lined with a long string of shopping malls and cafés, most of them fairly low key, apart from the bizarre, Italian-themed **Mercato** mall. The suburb also offers a handful of low-key attractions. These include the traditional **Jumeirah Mosque**, the only mosque in Dubai currently accessible to non-Muslims thanks to the rewarding tours run by the SMCCU, and the old-fashioned **Majlis Ghorfat um al Sheif**, the former summer retreat of Dubai's erstwhile ruler Sheikh Rashid. More hedonistic attractions can be found at **Jumeirah Beach Park**, the city's most attractive public beach.

Jumeirah: a note on names

Area names in Dubai are often used with a certain vagueness – Bur Dubai and Deira, for example, are both used in varying ways, while no one seems entirely certain yet whether Dubai Marina should be called Dubai Marina, or New Dubai, or perhaps something else entirely. None, however, has proved as enduringly slippery as Jumeirah. Strictly speaking, **Jumeirah proper** covers the area from roughly around the *Dubai Marine Beach Resort* in the north down to around the Majlis Ghorfat um al Sheif in the south. In practice, however, the name is often used loosely to describe the whole of coastal Dubai south of the Creek down to the *Burj al Arab*, and sometimes even beyond; further confusion is added by the fact that Jumeirah has been adopted as the name of the city's leading luxury hotel chain. The **Jumeirah Beach Hotel** and **Madinat Jumeirah**, for instance, aren't strictly speaking in Jumeirah, but in the adjacent suburb of Umm Suqeim (although both are owned by the Jumeirah chain – as is the *Jumeirah Emirates Tower* hotel, which is actually on Sheikh Zayed Road). Further south the J-word crops up again at the *Sheraton Jumeirah Beach* hotel and *Hilton Dubai Jumeirah Resort*, both in what is now the Marina, while it has also wandered off and attached itself to the **Palm Jumeirah** artificial island. And that's not the end of it: thanks to the Jumeirah group the name can now be found attached to properties as far afield as London, New York and Shanghai – an impressive feat of global colonization for the name of what was, until fifty years ago, little more than a humble fishing village.

▲ Jumeirah Mosque

Jumeirah Mosque

Rising proudly above the northern end of the Jumeirah Road, the stately **Jumeirah Mosque** is one of the largest and most attractive in the city. Built in quasi-Fatimid (Egyptian) style, it's reminiscent in appearance, if not quite in size, of the great mosques of Cairo, with a pair of soaring minarets, a roofline embellished with delicately carved miniature domes and richly decorated windows set in elaborate rectangular recesses. As with many of Dubai's more venerable-looking buildings though, appearances are deceptive – the mosque was actually built in 1979.

It also has the added attraction of being the only mosque in Dubai which non-Muslims can visit, owing to the thrice-weekly **tours** run by the Sheikh Mohammed Centre for Cultural Understanding (Tues, Thurs, Sat & Sun 10–11am; 10dh; ⓣ04-353 6666, ⓦwww.cultures.ae; under-5s not allowed; no pre-booking required). These offer a good opportunity to get a look at the mosque's rather chintzy interior, with its distinctive green-and-orange colour scheme and delicately painted arches. The real draw, however, are the entertaining and informative guides, who explain some of the basic precepts and practices of Islam before throwing the floor open for questions – a rare chance to settle some of those perplexing local conundrums, whether it be a description of the workings of the Islamic calendar or an explanation of exactly what Emirati men wear under their robes.

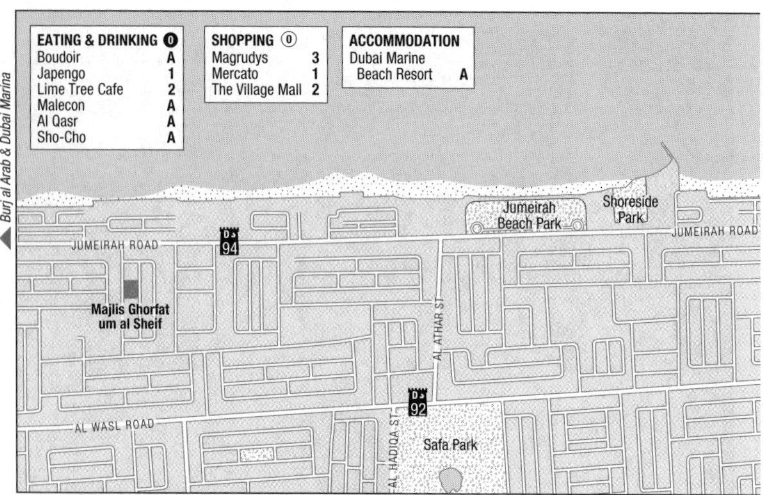

Iranian Hospital and Mosque

Standing on either side of Al Wasl Road, a ten-minute walk inland from the Jumeirah Mosque, the striking **Iranian Hospital** and nearby **Imam Hossein Mosque** (also just known as the "Iranian Mosque") add a welcome splash of colour to the pasty concrete hues which rule in this part of the city. The hospital is a large and rather functional-looking modern building improbably covered in vast quantities of superb, blue-green tiling in the elaborate abstract floral patterns beloved of Persian artists. The mosque is even finer, its sumptuously tiled dome and two minarets particularly magical, especially in low light early or late in the day. Unfortunately the mosque is walled off and you can only see it from a certain distance – the best view is from the small residential side street which runs around the back of it, rather than from Al Wasl Road itself.

Dubai Zoo

The first zoo on the Arabian peninsula when it was founded in 1967, **Dubai Zoo** (daily except Tues 10am–6pm; 2dh), midway down Jumeirah Road, serves as the overcrowded and rather unappealing home to a wide range of animals, almost all of whom arrived at the zoo having been taken from smugglers apprehended by UAE customs officials. The resultant mishmash of haphazardly acquired animals includes giraffes, tigers, lions, chimps, brown bears, Arabian wolves and oryx, plus assorted birds, though it's difficult to see very much thanks to the ugly cages, covered in thick wire-mesh (installed, ironically, to protect the animals from visitors; when the zoo first opened, locals would turn up armed with sticks to prod depressed animals into action, and sadly the behaviour of many of today's visitors is little better).

Mercato mall

About halfway down Jumeirah Road, the eye-popping **Mercato** mall (daily 10am–10pm, Thurs–Sat until midnight; Ⓦ www.mercatoshoppingmall.com) ranks as one of Jumeirah's leading tourist attractions and is well worth a visit

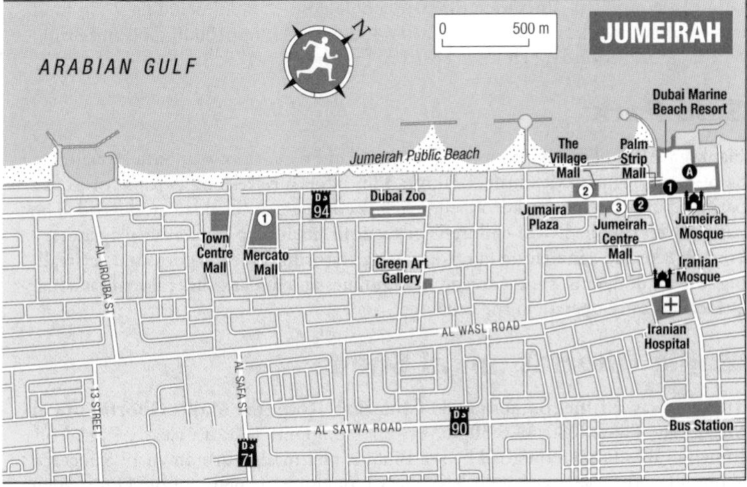

even if you've no intention of actually buying anything. Looking like a kind of miniature medieval Italian city rebuilt by the Disney Corporation, the mall comprises a series of brightly coloured quasi-Venetian-cum-Tuscan palazzi arranged around a huge central atrium overlooked by panoramic balconies, while side passages lead to miniature piazzas on either side – a memorable example of the sort of brazen but entertaining kitsch that Dubai seems to do so well. Not surprisingly, it's all proved immensely popular, and the fake-Florentine thoroughfares are thronged most hours of the day and night by a very eclectic crowd, with Jumeirah Janes ducking in and out of the mall's designer boutiques and crowds of white-robed Emirati men lounging over coffee in the ground-floor Starbucks while their veiled wives and Filipina maids take the kids upstairs for burgers and fries at McDonalds – a picture-perfect example of the multicultural madness of modern Dubai. For more on the mall's shops, see p.145.

Jumeirah Beach Park and Shoreside

Squeezed in between the sea and Jumeirah Road near the suburb's southern end, **Jumeirah Beach Park** (daily 7am–10.30pm, Thurs–Sat until 11pm; Mon ladies and boys aged up to 4 only; 5dh) is easily the nicest park and public beach in Dubai – wildly popular both with city residents and with sand-starved tourists staying in city-centre hotels. The beach itself is large enough to soak up the crowds, with a fine wide swathe of white sand manned with lifeguards and equipped with loungers and parasols, while the pleasantly wooded strip of park behind has lots of shaded grass for picnics, barbecue facilities, a couple of cafés and a well-equipped play area for kids.

There's a further stretch of beach open to the public at the new **Shoreside** complex (Ⓦwww.shoreside.ae), just north of Jumeirah Beach Park. This is an altogether more upmarket offering than its neighbour – more like a resort than a public beach – with a beautifully manicured strip of white sand, comfy loungers and parasols and an attractive modern restaurant. There's also a range of water-sports available, as well as children's activities like face-painting, balloon modelling, sand castle building. **Entrance** for two people costs 250dh (including 75dh food and drink) on weekdays, or a rather hefty 450dh (including 100dh food and drink) on Friday and Saturday; children cost 100dh (Fri & Sat 175dh).

Safa Park

Flanking Al Wasl Road a couple of blocks inland from the coast, **Safa Park** (daily 8am–11pm, Thurs–Sat until 11.30pm; 3dh) offers a refreshing expanse of grassy parkland impressively backdropped by the skyscrapers of Sheikh Zayed Road. The park is well supplied with children's attractions, including numerous play areas, a boating lake and a miniature fairground area featuring a merry-go-round, a (small) big wheel, dodgems, games arcade, trampolines and a giant slide; note that some attractions only operate in the evenings.

Majlis Ghorfat um al Sheif

Tucked away off the southern end of Jumeirah Road, the **Majlis Ghorfat um al Sheif** (Sat–Thurs 8.30am–8.30pm, Fri 2.30–8.30pm; 1dh; it's clearly signed off Jumeirah Road down the road by the BinSina pharmacy; turn down 17 Street for about 50m; the *majlis* is on your left) offers a touching memento of old Dubai, now incongruously marooned amid a sea of chintzy modern villas. Built in 1955 when Jumeirah was no more than a small fishing village, this modest traditional house was used by Sheikh Rashid, the inspiration behind modern Dubai's spectacular development, as a summer retreat and hosted many of the discussions about the city's future, which in turn led to its dramatic economic explosion during the 1960s and 1970s.

The two-storey building serves as a fetching reminder of earlier and simpler times: a sturdy coral-and-gypsum structure embellished with fine doors and window shutters made of solid teak, the whole of it enclosed in an old-fashioned Arabian garden complete with date palms and *falaj* (irrigation) channels. The *majlis* itself is on the upper floor, with cushions laid out around its edges and the walls and floor adorned with a modest selection of household objects, including an old-fashioned European radio and clock, rifles, oil lamps and coffee pots which in 1950s Dubai were considered all the luxury necessary, even in a residence of the ruling sheikh – a far cry from the seven-star amenities enjoyed by today's Emiratis.

6

The Burj al Arab and around

Some 10km south of the Creek, the district of **Umm Suqeim** marks the beginning of Dubai's spectacular modern beachside developments, announced with a flourish by three of Dubai's most famous landmarks: the **Madinat Jumeirah** complex, the rollercoaster **Jumeirah Beach Hotel** and the iconic sail-shaped **Burj al Arab** hotel. There are further attractions at the thrills-and-spills **Wild Wadi** waterpark, next to the *Jumeirah Beach* hotel, and at **Ski Dubai**, the Middle East's first ski-slope. More sedentary pleasures can be found at the vast new **Mall of the Emirates**, next to Ski Dubai, of whose snowy pistes it offers superbly surreal views. Close to the Mall of the Emirates on the far side of Sheikh Zayed Road, the industrial area of Al Quoz provides an unlikely home to a number of Dubai's leading **art galleries**, covered on p.131.

The Burj al Arab

Rising majestically from its own man-made island just off the coast of Umm Suqeim is the peerless **Burj al Arab** ("Tower of the Arabs"), one of the world's most luxurious hotels and *de facto* symbol of the city. Commissioned by Dubai's ruler, Sheikh Mohammed, the aim of the *Burj al Arab* was simple: to serve as a global icon which would put Dubai on the international map. Money was no object. The total cost of the hotel was perhaps as much as $2 billion, and it's been estimated that even if every room in it remains full for the next hundred years, the *Burj* still won't pay back its original investment.

As a modern icon, however, the *Burj* is unmatched. Although little more than a decade old, the building's instantly recognizable outline has already established itself as a global symbol of Dubai to rival the Eiffel Tower, Big Ben and the Sydney Opera House. Even the top-floor helipad has acquired celebrity status: Agassi and Federer were filmed playing tennis on it, while Tiger Woods used it as a makeshift driving range, punting shots into the sea (before ringing room service for more balls).

The *Burj* is home to the world's first so-called **seven-star hotel**, an expression coined by a visiting journalist to emphasize the unique levels of style and luxury offered within (officially, of course, such a category doesn't exist). Staying here is a very expensive pleasure, and even visiting it presents certain financial and practical challenges (see box, p.83 for more). Fortunately the exterior of the building can be enjoyed for free from numerous vantage points nearby.

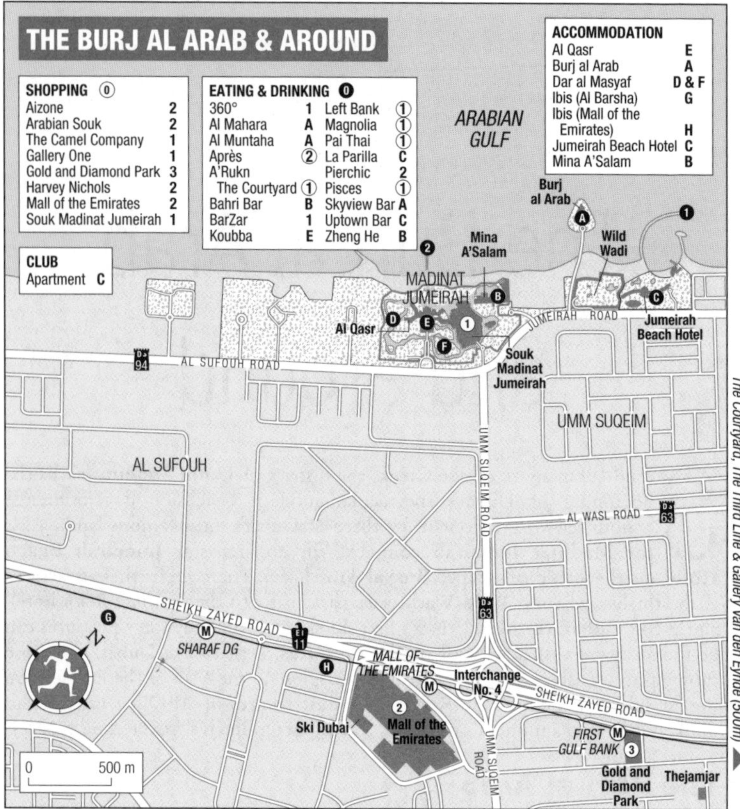

The building

Designed to echo the shape of a dhow's sail, the *Burj* forms a kind of maritime counterpart to the adjacent *Jumeirah Beach* hotel's "breaking wave" (see opposite), offering a contemporary tribute to Dubai's historic seafaring traditions, its sail-like shape (not to mention its very exclusive aura) enhanced by its location on a specially reclaimed island some 300m offshore. The building was constructed between 1993 and 1999 by UK engineering and architectural firm W.S. Atkins under lead designer Tom Wright. The statistics alone are impressive. At 321m, the *Burj* is the second tallest dedicated hotel in the world (only recently surpassed by the nearby *Rose Rayhaan* on Sheikh Zayed Road) and the 34th-highest building full stop. The spire-like superstructure alone, incredibly, is taller than the entire *Jumeirah Beach* hotel, while the atrium (180m) is also the world's loftiest – and capacious enough to swallow up the entire Statue of Liberty or, for that matter, the 38-storey Dubai World Trade Centre (see p.71).

The sheer scale of the *Burj* is overwhelming, and only really appreciated in the flesh, since photographs of the building, perhaps inevitably, always seem to diminish it to the size of an expensive toy. The *Burj*'s scale is tempered by its extraordinary grace and the sinuous simplicity of its basic design, broken only by the celebrated cantilevered helipad and (on the building's seafacing side) the

Traditional Dubai

Contrary to popular perception, Dubai wasn't built yesterday. Many of its old buildings and other sights still provide a living connection with the city's mercantile and maritime past, before the era of oil, malls and mega-projects. These include traditional wind-towered houses, old-fashioned souks, beautiful mosques and temples, plus the hundreds of quaint wooden dhows and abras which continue to ply the breezy waters of the Creek.

Wind tower, Bastakiya ▲

Gold Souk ▼

Traditional houses and wind towers

Despite the city's rapid development during the 1970s and 1980s, a surprisingly large number of Dubai's traditional old dwellings survive amid the city-centre concrete. The biggest concentrations are in Bur Dubai, where you'll find the old Iranian quarter of Bastakiya, with its wonderful array of wind-towered houses clustered among a labyrinthine tangle of narrow alleyways. One of Dubai's most iconic sights, the wind towers are designed to provide cooling breezes in the searing Gulf heat; subtle variations in design mean no two are exactly alike. Closer to the mouth of the Creek lies Shindagha where a fine sequence of homes, once occupied by the city's sheikhs, line the waterway.

Souks

For an authentic taste of Dubai's traditional atmosphere, you can't beat a visit to the city's souks. Large parts of the old city centre, Deira in particular, preserve the classical bazaar layout, with different areas devoted to different goods and trades.

The souks served as the commercial lifeblood of the city (as malls do today), and although the architecture may be uninspiring, the old-style ambience remains largely unchanged, with hundreds of tiny shops packed in around narrow alleyways, thronged with crowds of shoppers – particularly busy after dark. Architecturally, the best preserved is the Textile Souk although there's more commercial buzz in the various souks in Deira, including the glittering Gold Souk and the fragrant Spice Souk, the city's most appealling old-fashioned bazaar.

Dhows and abras

Few sights in Dubai are as evocative as the long lines of wooden dhows moored up alongside the Creek, or the flotillas of diminutive **abras** which scuttle across the waters between Deira and Bur Dubai. These boats are essentially floating antiques, their designs little changed in a century save for the replacement of their customary lateen sails with modern diesel engines.

A ride across the Creek by abra is still one of the most enjoyable things you can do in the city, while dinner **cruises** aboard a traditional dhow are also enduringly popular. Boats are still painstakingly handcrafted at the **dhow-building yard** in Jaddaf (see p.66).

Mosques

To get a sense of Dubai's traditional religious outlook go for a wander around the streets of Bur Dubai, Deira or Jumeirah. The city's mosques spring into life at prayer time, when the air is filled with the sound of the *muezzin*'s call and crowds of worshippers converge to pay their respects. Unfortunately, all Dubai's mosques are off-limits to non-Muslims, except for **Jumeirah Mosque**, which runs informative tours for visitors and is an essential stop if you're interested in Dubai's long-established religion and culture. Other major places of worship include the huge **Grand Mosque**, the largest in the city, whose soaring minaret towers over the creekside in Bur Dubai, and the nearby **Iranian Mosque** in Jumeirah, its exterior decorated in a spectacular array of multi-coloured floral tilework.

Further afield in neighbouring Abu Dhabi is the spectacular **Sheikh Zayed Mosque**, one of the world's largest, and well worth a day trip in its own right.

▲ Abras moored at the creekside

▼ Tilework at Iranian Mosque

Products on display at the Spice Souk ▲

Shindagha Tower ▼

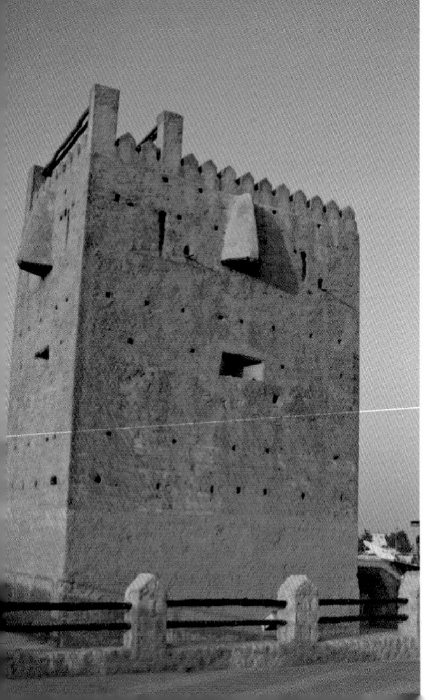

Dubai's top ten traditional sights

▸▸ **Dhow wharfage** See hundreds of traditional wooden dhows moored beside the Creek, with great piles of merchandise stacked up alongside the waterfront. See p.57

▸▸ **Abras** Cross the Creek in classic style aboard one of the city's old abras – easily the most fun you can have in Dubai for a dirham. See p.48

▸▸ **Spice Souk** The city's most atmospheric souk, with fragrant sacks of spices piled up outside a string of shoebox shops. See p.57

▸▸ **Textile Souk**. The best preserved souk in the city, with a long line of old-fashioned buildings sheltered beneath an arching wooden roof. See p.48

▸▸ **Gold Souk** Browse the bling-filled windows of Dubai's most famous souk. It all glitters, and it *is* gold. See p.53

▸▸ **Bastakiya** The marvellously atmospheric old Iranian quarter, with dozens of traditional houses grouped around a labyrinth of tiny alleyways. See p.45

▸▸ **Al Ahmadiya School** The city's first school, in perhaps its most attractive heritage building, now converted into a low-key museum. See p.57

▸▸ **Sheikh Saeed al Maktoum House** One of the finest of Shindagha's clutch of heritage houses, now home to an absorbing museum showcasing a fascinating collection of photographs of old Dubai. See p.51

▸▸ **Shindagha Tower** Quaint little watchtower from which locals would formerly have guarded the approaches to the city. See p.50

▸▸ **Majlis Ghorfat um al Sheif** One-time summer house of the ruling Sheikh Rashid, buried away amid the suburban sprawl of southern Jumeirah. See p.80

projecting *Al Muntaha* ("The Highest") restaurant. The hotel's shore-facing side mainly comprises a huge sheet of white Teflon-coated fibreglass cloth – a symbolic sail which is spectacularly illuminated from within by night, turning the entire building into a magically glowing beacon. Less universally admired is the building's rear elevation, in the shape of a huge cross, a feature that caused considerable controversy among Muslims at the time of construction, though it's only visible from the sea, and is almost never photographed.

Most of the **interior** is actually hollow, comprising an enormous atrium vibrantly coloured in great swathes of red, blue, green and gold. The original design comprised a far more restrained composition of whites and soft blues, but was significantly altered at the insistence of Sheikh Mohammed, who called in interior designer Khuan Chew (responsible for the colourful lobby at the adjacent *Jumeirah Beach Hotel*) to jazz things up. The contrast with the classically simple exterior could hardly be greater, and the atrium and public areas look something between a Vegas casino and a James Bond movie set, the casual extravagance of it all encapsulated by enormous fish tanks flanking the entrance staircase and which are so deep that cleaners have to put on diving suits to scrub them out (a performance you can witness daily from 2–4pm). For many visitors, the whole thing is simply a classic example of Middle Eastern bling gone mad (that's not gold paint on the walls, incidentally, but genuine 22ct gold leaf). Still, there's something undeniably impressive about both the sheer size of the thing, and Chew's slightly psychedelic decor, with huge expanses of vibrant primary colours and endless balconied floors rising far overhead, supported by massive bulbous golden piers – like a "modern-day pirate galleon full of treasure", as Wright himself neatly described it.

Jumeirah Beach Hotel and Wild Wadi

On the beach right next to the *Burj* sits the second of the area's landmark buildings, the huge **Jumeirah Beach Hotel**, or "JBH" as it's often abbreviated. Designed to resemble an enormous breaking wave (although it looks more like an enormous roller coaster), and rising to a height of over 100m, the hotel was considered the most spectacular and luxurious in the city when it opened in 1997, although it has since been overtaken on both counts. It remains a fine sight, however, especially when seen from a distance in combination with the *Burj*, against whose slender sail it appears (with a little imagination) to be about to crash.

Directly behind the JBH, the massively popular **Wild Wadi** waterpark (daily: Nov–Feb 10am–6pm; March–May 10am–7pm; June–Aug 10am–8pm; Sept &

Visiting the Burj

Non-guests are only allowed into the *Burj* with a prior reservation at one of the hotel's bars, cafés or restaurants. The cheapest option is to come for a cocktail at the 27th-floor **Skyview Bar** (see p.127; minimum spend 275dh/person), perhaps the best way of getting a good look at the hotel without going bankrupt. Alternatively, a visit for one of the *Burj*'s sumptuous afternoon teas (around 400dh) in either the *Skyview Bar* or at the **Sahn Eddar** atrium lounge is another possibility. If you want to go the whole hog, the *Burj* boasts two of the city's most spectacular (and pricey) restaurants: **Al Muntaha** and **Al Mahara** (see p.120). There are also two cheaper but significantly less appealing buffet restaurants: the Arabian-style **Al Iwan** (lunch/dinner 395/425dh), or the slighty nicer pan-Asian **Junsui** (lunch/dinner 325/375dh) – although you'd be better off taking afternoon tea or a drink.

For **reservations** call ⓣ04-301 7600 or email BAArestaurants@jumeirah.com. For more on staying at the *Burj*, see p.105.

Oct 10am–7pm; all-day admission 200dh, children under 1.1m 165dh, locker and towel rental 25dh each; ⓣ04-348 4444, ⓦwww.wildwadi.com) offers a variety of attractions to suit everyone from small kids to physically fit adrenalin junkies. The park is modelled on a Sinbad-inspired fantasy tropical lagoon, with cascading waterfalls, whitewater rapids, hanging bridges and big piles of rocks. Get oriented with a circuit of the Whitewater Wadi (MasterBlaster) ride, which runs around the edge of the park, during which you're squirted on powerful jets of water up and down eleven long, twisting slides before being catapaulted down the darkened Tunnel of Doom. Dedicated thrill-seekers should try the Wipeout and Riptide Flowriders, simulating powerful surfing waves, and the park's stellar attraction, the **Jumeirah Sceirah**, the tallest and fastest speed slide outside North America, during which you're likely to hit around 80kmph and experience temporary weightlessness. There are also less demanding attractions such as gentle tube-rides down Lazy River, family-oriented water games in Juha's Dhow and Lagoon or the chance to bob up and down in the big simulated waves of Breaker's Bay. Many people make a day of it, and you can buy food and drinks inside the park using money stored on an ingenious waterproof wristband.

Madinat Jumeirah

Just south of the Burj al Arab lies the huge **Madinat Jumeirah** (ⓦwww.madinatjumeirah.com), a vast mass of faux-Moorish-style buildings rising high above the coastal highway. Opened in 2005, the Madinat is one of Dubai's most spectacular modern developments: a self-contained miniature "Arabian" city comprising a vast sprawl of sand-coloured buildings topped by an extraordinary quantity of wind towers (best viewed from the entrance to the *Al Qasr* hotel), the whole thing arranged around a sequence of meandering waterways along which visitors are chauffeured in replica abras. The complex is home to a trio of ultra-luxurious five-star hotels (see p.105–106), the labyrinthine Souk Madinat Jumeirah bazaar (see p.146), a vast spread of restaurants and bars (see pp.119–120 & pp.126–127), and one of the city's best spas (see p.138).

▲ View of the *Burj al Arab* from the Al Qasr hotel at Souk Madinat Jumeirah

Admittedly, there's an undeniable whiff of Disneyland about the entire complex. The vision, according to the developers, was "to recreate life as it used to be for residents along Dubai Creek, complete with waterways, abras, wind towers and a bustling souk", although in truth Madinat Jumeirah bears about as much relation to old Dubai as Big Ben does to your average grandfather clock. Even so, the sheer scale of the place, with its relentlessly picturesque array of wind towers, wood-framed souks and palm-fringed waterways, is strangely compelling, and a perfect example of the kind of thing – mixing unbridled extravagance with a significant dose of sugar-coated kitsch – which Dubai seems to do so well. The Madinat also offers some of the most eye-boggling views in Dubai, with the futuristic outlines of the *Burj Al Arab* surreally framed between medieval-looking wind towers and Moorish arcading. The fact that the fake olde-worlde city is actually newer than the ultra-modern *Burj* is, by Dubai's standards, exactly what one would expect.

The obvious place from which to explore the complex is the Souk Madinat Jumeirah, though it's well worth investigating some of the superb restaurants and bars in the *Al Qasr* and *Mina A'Salam* hotels (see listings on p.120 & pp.126–127), several of which offer superlative views over the Madinat itself, the *Burj al Arab* and coastline. Thirty-minute **abra cruises** (50dh) around the Madinat's waterways depart from the kiosk outside *Left Bank* bar-restaurant on the waterfront.

Mall of the Emirates and Ski Dubai

The second largest mall in Dubai (outdone only by the Dubai Mall), the swanky **Mall of the Emirates** (daily 10am–10pm, Thurs–Sat until midnight; Ⓦwww.malloftheemirates.com) is one of the most popular in the city, packed with some five hundred shops and crowds of locals and tourists alike. Centred around a huge, glass-roofed central atrium, the mall is spread over three levels, crisscrossed by escalators and little wrought-iron bridges, and topped by the pink, five-star *Kempinski Hotel*. For dedicated shopaholics it's arguably the best place in Dubai to splash some cash (for shopping listings, see p.144). There's also the added bonus of surreal views of the snow-covered slopes of Ski Dubai through huge glass walls at the western end of the mall, or from one of the various restaurants and bars overlooking the slopes, such as *Après* (see p.119).

Attached to the mall, the huge indoor ski resort of **Ski Dubai** (daily: Sun–Wed 10am–11pm, Thurs 10am–midnight, Fri 9am–midnight, Sat 9am–11pm; 2hr ski slope session adult 180dh, children 150dh, ski slope day pass 300/240dh, snow park 100/90dh. Prices include clothing, boots and equipment for both slope and snowpark, but not hats and gloves; Ⓣ04-409 4000, Ⓦwww.skidxb.com) is unquestionably one of the city's weirder ideas. The sight of a huge indoor snow-covered ski slope (the first in the Middle East) complete with regular snowfall is strange enough amid the sultry heat of the Gulf – while the sight of robed Emiratis skiing, snowboarding or just chucking snowballs at one another adds a decidedly surreal touch to the already unlikely proceedings. You can take in the whole spectacle for free from the viewing areas at the attached Mall of the Emirates. The complex contains the world's largest indoor snow park, comprising a huge 3000-square-metres of snow-covered faux-Alpine mountainside, complete with chair lift. Accredited skiiers and snowboarders (you'll need to undergo a brief personal assessment to prove you possess the necessary basic skills to use the main slope) can use five runs of varying height, steepness and difficulty, ranging from a beginners' track through to the world's first indoor black run, as well as a "freestyle zone" for show-off winter sports aficionados. There's also a Snow School ski academy for beginners and improvers (both adults and kids, from 120dh/hour), as well as a twin-track bobsled ride, a snowball-throwing gallery, snow cavern, adventure trail, tobogganing and snowman-building opportunities.

The Palm Jumeirah and Dubai Marina

Nowhere is the scale of Dubai's explosive growth as staggeringly obvious as in the far south of the city, home to the **Palm Jumeirah** man-made island and the vast new **Dubai Marina** development (or "New Dubai" as it's sometimes called) – evidence of the city's apparently magical ability to raise entire new city districts up out of the waves and turn sand into skyscrapers.

Around 3km south of the *Burj Al Arab*, roads lead out to the immense new **Palm Jumeirah**, stretching four kilometres out into the waters of the Arabian Gulf. The world's largest man-made island, the Palm is one of Dubai's most astonishing feats of engineering, although it's not especially impressive to look at – at least until you reach its far end and the gigantic **Atlantis** resort, standing huge and solitary above the waters of the Gulf.

New Dubai: what you won't see

Dubai Marina and the Palm Jumeirah were at the epicentre of the accelerating megalomania which engulfed Dubai developers before the credit crunch brought the emirate back to its financial senses – resulting in the cancellation or indefinite postponement of a string of widely publicized world-breaking initiatives, most of which now seem unlikely ever to be realized. Headline schemes included a project to build the world's first luxury **underwater hotel** (the "ten-star" Hydropolis), although this never managed to get off the seabed, while plans to redevelop the retired **QE2** cruise liner as a floating hotel off Palm Jumeirah also appear to have been at least temporarily scuppered (at the time of writing, the historic liner, which arrived in Dubai amid great fanfare in 2008, had been sent off to South Africa to provide accommodation during the 2010 Word Cup). **The Universe** archipelago (see p.88) has been another casualty of Dubai's reduced circumstances, as has the futuristic **Trump Tower**, which was meant to provide the Palm Jumeirah with one of its two key landmarks.

Even more extravagant were plans for the **Nakheel Tower** (previously known as Al Burj), which was intended to reach a height of over 1km high, smashing the current record held by the nearby Burj Khalifa as the world's tallest building. Slated for construction at various points around the southern city, the tower was finally cancelled in late 2009, although at the time of writing the last metro station in the far south of the city was still going under the name of Nakheel Tower and Harbour – a sad tribute to vanished ambitions.

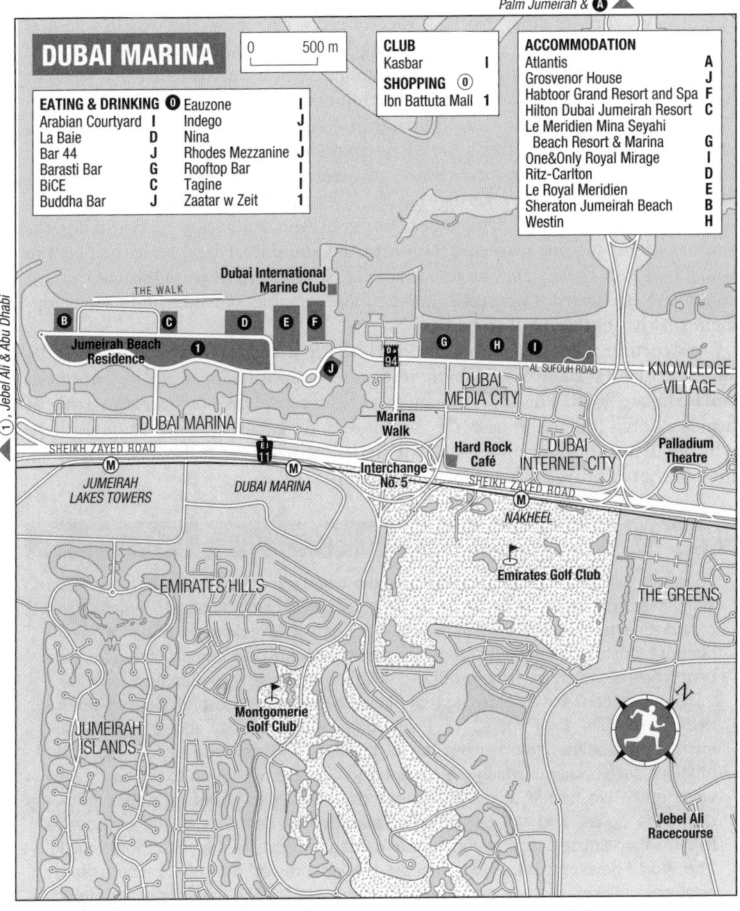

Continuing south down the mainland, the skyline is dominated by the massed high-rises of the huge new **Dubai Marina** development. Barely ten years ago the lower reaches of the emirate beyond the *Burj al Arab* were more or less desert, untouched apart from a discreet string of luxury hotels lining the coast. Then the developers moved in. By 2006 the area had turned into the largest building site on the planet, 10km long and home to an astonishing thirty thousand construction cranes, a quarter of the world's total. Five years on and most of the cranes and work crews have gone, leaving a brand new city in their wake, with a forest of densely packed skyscrapers lined up along either side of Sheikh Zayed Road.

The Palm Jumeirah

Lying off the coast around 2km south of the Burj al Arab, **The Palm Jumeirah** is far and away the largest example of modern Dubai's desire, not just to master its unpromising natural environment, but to transform it entirely. Billed as the

"Eighth Wonder of the World", the Palm is currently the world's largest man-made island, and has doubled the length of the Dubai coastline at a total cost of over $12 billion (although even this grandiose feat is only the first in a series of four artificial islands currently under development; see box below).

As its name suggests, the Palm Jumeirah is designed in the shape of a palm tree, with a central "trunk" and a series of sixteen radiating "fronds", the whole enclosed in an 11km-long breakwater, or "crescent". The design (dreamt up by New Zealander Warren Pickering) has the twin merits of providing an elegantly stylized homage to the city's desert environment while also maximizing the amount of oceanfront space in relation to the amount of land reclaimed (as Jim Krane puts it in *Dubai: The Story of the World's Fastest City*, "It was Dubai at its most cunning. Since seafront properties are the most valuable, why not build a development that has nothing but seafront?")

Construction work began in 2001, with the first apartments opening in 2006, and the island's landmark *Atlantis* resort (see opposite) opening to enormous fanfare in late 2008. The development is far from complete, however: the string of five-star hotels (including new *Taj*, *Kempinski* and *Fairmont* resorts, among others) which will line the crescent were all still under construction at the time of writing, though should probably have opened by 2011/2012.

Dubai's artificial islands

For a city with aspirations of taking over the world's tourism industry, Dubai has a serious lack of one thing: **coast**. In its natural state, the emirate boasts a mere 70km of shoreline, totally insufficient to service the needs of its rocketing number of beach-hungry tourists and residents (currently, the city boasts only around fifteen genuine beach hotels, which are usually booked solid more or less year-round).

Dubai's response to its pressing lack of beach has been characteristically bold: it's decided to build some more. The Palm Jumeirah has already added 68km to the emirate's coastline, although this is just the first (and smallest) of four proposed offshore developments which are intended to create anything up to 500km of new waterfront. Two further palm-shaped islands – the **Palm Jebel Ali**, 20km further down the coast, and the gargantuan **Palm Deira**, right next to the city centre (Ⓦ www.thepalm.ae) – are already under construction, as is the even more fanciful **The World** development. Lying a couple of kilometres off the coast (accessible by boat only, unlike the three palm developments, all of which are connected directly to the mainland), this vast complex of artificial islands has been constructed in the shape of a map of the world (not that you'll notice from ground level, although it's weirdly impressive when seen from the air). Many of the world's nations are represented by their own islands within the map (although the state of Israel is notably absent), while larger countries have been subdivided into several islands. It's been suggested that developers might buy up individual islands and create themed tourist developments, perhaps based on the island they occupy. Plans for a fifth island complex, **The Universe** (with a design based on the solar system) were announced in 2008, but were put on hold soon afterwards and now seem highly unlikely ever to leave the drawing board.

The exact status of the Palm Jebel Ali, Palm Deira and The World also remains unclear following recent economic difficulties, although significant reclamation work has already taken place, as a glance at Google Earth (or out of your aeroplane window) will confirm. The Palm Jebel Ali and The World appear to be largely complete, while large amounts of reclamation work have also been completed at the Palm Deira. Despite this, development on all three appears to be largely stalled at the time of writing, and it is likely to be at least a few more years before any of Dubai's record-breaking new islands are open to the public.

Despite the size and ambition of the development, however, the Palm feels disappointingly botched (the "Eighth Blunder of the World", as local wags put it). The elegant palm-shaped layout remains largely invisible at ground level – although it looks terrific from a plane – and the architecture is deeply undistinguished, with a string of featureless high-rises lining the main trunk road and endless rows of densely packed Legoland villas strung out along the waterside "fronds". The developer, Nakheel, was allegedly forced to almost double the number of villas on the island to cover spiralling construction costs, resulting in the overcrowded suburban crush you see today – much to the chagrin of those who had bought properties off-plan at launch, only to move in and discover that they were virtually living in their neighbours' kitchens. Only towards the far end of the island does the Palm acquire a modest quotient of drama, as the main trunk road dips through a tunnel before emerging in front of the vast *Atlantis* resort – although by then, one feels, it's probably too late.

The best way to see the Palm is from the 5km-long **Palm Jumeirah Monorail** (daily 8am–10pm; trains every 3–20min; 15dh one way, 25dh return) which shuttles between *Atlantis* and the mainland, taking five minutes to complete the trip. Unfortunately, the monorail doesn't connect with the Dubai Metro, while the inflated fares are a further turn-off. It's probably cheaper to take a taxi.

Atlantis

At the furthest end of the Palm, sitting in solitary splendour on the oceanfront crescent, the vast **Atlantis** resort (Ⓦ www.atlantisthepalm.com) is the island's major landmark and a focal point for the entire development. It's a near carbon-copy of its sister establishment, the Atlantis, Paradise Island resort in the Bahamas: a blowsy pink colossus, undeniably huge, vaguely outlandish, and just a little bit camp ("like the tomb of Liberace," as the UK's *Sun* newspaper aptly put it). In fact it's probably the only one of Dubai's recent mega-developments to really live up to the city's widespread reputation for tasteless extravagance and shameless bling – slightly ironic, given that it actually had nothing to do with the Dubai government, being entirely the creation of Jewish South African billionaire Sol Kerzner. Like many of Dubai's newer landmarks it looks best from a distance, especially after dark and from the mainland, when its vast illuminated outline looks like some kind of weird triumphal archway twinkling far out to sea.

Inside, the **hotel** itself is as satisfyingly over-the-top as one would hope, featuring all manner of gold columns, crystal chandeliers and random twinkly bits, not to mention Dale Chihuly's extraordinary sculptural installation in the lobby – a 10m-high study in glass of what looks like a waterfall of deep-frozen spaghetti. There's also the vast in-house aquarium, whose resident marine life one can ogle for free from the public areas (or, for around 30,000dh, from the hotel's "Neptune" suite). Other attractions include a string of top-notch restaurants, including Japanese-American chef Nobuyuki Matsuhisa's *Nobu*, Italian culinary maestro Giorgio Locatelli's *Ronda Locatelli*, and *Ossiano*, by triple-Michelin-starred Catalan chef Santi Santamaria.

Aquaventure, Dolphin Bay and the Lost Chambers

Atlantis boasts a heap of in-house activities – but they come with a steep price tag. Best is the spectacular **Aquaventure** waterpark (200dh, or 165dh for children under 1.2m; or 250/200dh adults/children including The Lost Chambers; free to in-house guests; locker rental 40dh). This features an adrenaline-charged array of master-blasters, water-coasters, speedslides, inner-tube

The Palm Jumeirah: the new Atlantis?

Dubai has never exactly been known for its green credentials (for more on which, see p.191), but no single development has raised the environmental hackles of green activists as much as the Palm Jumeirah. Many concerns have been raised about the Palm's probable adverse effect on local **marine life** (the Palm's developer, Nakheel, has responded by saying that the Palm will in fact eventually *improve* the local marine environment by creating new underwater environments and encouraging biodiversity). Fingers have also been pointed at the Palm's long-range environmental impact: in order to create foundations for the new land some **seven million tons of rock** were piled up on the seabed, most of which was blasted out of the Hajar Mountains in the eastern UAE, with as yet unknown long-term environmental consequences.

As if to prove all the nay-sayers right, in late 2009 the *New York Times* ran an article claiming that the Palm was actually **sinking** at a rate of 5mm a year, and would soon be in danger of flooding or worse, a situation exacerbated by rising sea levels as the result of global warming (which, Dubai is doing more than its fair share to accelerate). In fact, although the continual subsidence of reclaimed land presented major difficulties during the early stages of construction, there seems to be no hard evidence that ongoing land sinkage is a problem – and certainly none of the above-water destruction to property that such dramatic levels of subsidence would inevitably cause. Even so, the image of Dubai's biggest mega-project sinking quietly back into the tranquil waters of the Arabian Gulf offers a compelling symbol of the emirate's subsiding fortunes – and one which is oddly appropriate, too, given that the Palm's major attraction, the Atlantis resort, is based on a similarly dramatic story of a once-great city disappearing beneath the waves.

rides and power-jets; it's all centred on the dramatic "Ziggurat", where'll you'll find the park's headline Leap of Faith waterslide, 27.5m tall and 61m long, which catapults you at stomach-churning speed down into a transparent tunnel and runs through a lagoon full of sharks. There are also various gentler rivers and rapids, plus a children's play area, and you can also use the impressive stretch of adjacent private beach.

There are further watery attractions at the attached **Dolphin Bay**, which offers the chance to swim with the hotel's troupe of resident bottlenose dolphins. Shallow-water "interactions" cost 790dh, deep-water interactions (over 12s only) 975dh, plus observer passes (300dh; only available to visitors accompanying those taking part in full interactions). The hefty price tag also includes same-day admission to Aquaventure and the private beach – although note that you can swim with dolphins far more cheaply at the Dubai Dolphinarium (see p.33).

For a slice of pure historical hocus-pocus, head to **The Lost Chambers** (daily 10am–11pm; 100dh, or 70dh children under 12), a sequence of halls and tunnels running through the hotel's vast underground aquarium, dotted with assorted "ruins". Hotel publicity and wide-eyed guides will attempt to convince you that these are the remains of the legendary city of Atlantis, which vanished (according to Plato) in the western Mediterranean around 10,000 BC, but which has now fortuitously turned up in the waters underneath Dubai's largest hotel. It's all nonsense, of course, and the real reason for visiting is to get a better look at the spectacular aquarium and its colourful array of 65,000-odd tropical fish. Unfortunately, the po-faced cynicism with which this shameless piece of theme-park "historical" bunkum is presented is more or less guaranteed to insult the intelligence of anyone aged over five, while the racked-up admission prices are a further turn-off. And you can, in any case, see parts of the aquarium from the public areas for free.

Dubai Marina

A kilometre further south along the coastal road beyond the Palm Jumeirah, a vast phalanx of tightly packed high-rises signals the appearance of **Dubai Marina**, Dubai's brand new city-within-a-city, built at lightning speed over the past five years. Building continues in certain places, though much of the project is now complete. There's no real precedent anywhere in the world for urban growth on this scale or at this speed, and the area's huge new residential developments and commercial and tourist facilities have already shifted the focus of the entire emirate decisively southwards, and may in time perhaps even eclipse the old city centre itself.

Like much of modern Dubai, the marina is a mish-mash of the good, the bad and the downright ugly. Many of the high-rises are of minimal architectural distinction, and all are packed so closely together that the overall effect is of hyperactive urban development gone completely mad – the result of unregulated construction during the massive real-estate boom in Dubai, which coincided with the marina's creation. The whole area feels oddly piecemeal and under-planned, while the lack of pedestrian facilities (excepting the pleasant oceanfront promenade and Marina Walk) means that you're unlikely to see much more of it than can be glimpsed while speeding down Sheikh Zayed Road by car or metro. Even reaching certain major landmarks like the Marina Mall on foot can present significant orienteering challenges.

It's weirdly impressive, even so, especially by night, when darkness hides the worst examples of gimcrack design and the whole area lights up into a fabulous display of airy neon (or, if you prefer, a display of high-rise ecological catastrophe

▲ Dubai Marina

waiting to happen). Notable structures include the vast **Almas Tower**, the second tallest building in Dubai (and fifteenth tallest in the world) at 363m, rising imposingly above the architectural melee on the east side of Sheikh Zayed Road, and the soaring **Al Kazim Towers**, right next to Sheikh Zayed Road, styled after New York's iconic Chrysler Building – postmodern Dubai at its most unforgettably silly.

Dubai Marina beach

Most of Dubai Marina's tourist development is focused on the string of luxurious **beachside hotels** which established themselves here when the coast was entirely undeveloped, but now find themselves rather tragically hemmed-in by densely packed high-rises on all sides. Much of the area is now dominated by the unlovely **Jumeirah Beach Residence** (JBR), the world's largest single-phase residential complex, comprising a 1.7km-long sprawl of forty high-rises with living space for ten thousand people. The development was widely touted as Dubai's latest thing in luxury beachside living when it was launched, although the massive apartment complexes actually look a bit like some kind of low-grade housing project out of Soviet Russia, their towers packed so closely together that you fancy flat-dwellers could open their windows and shake hands with people in neighbouring blocks.

The JBR's one redeeming feature is **The Walk**, an attractive promenade, lined with (admittedly, rather humdrum) cafés and restaurants, which stretches along the seafront between the *Sheraton* and *Royal Meridien* hotels. It's one of the very few places south of the old city centre which actually encourages people to get out of their cars, and boasts a modicum of street life including, during the winter months, the pleasant **Covent Garden Market** (Weds & Thurs 5pm–midnight, Fri & Sat 10am–9pm; Ⓦwww.coventgardenmarket.ae), with around fifty stalls selling clothes, jewellery and other collectables by local and expat craftsmen, designers and artists.

The **beach** itself comprises a fine wide swathe of white sand. For details of how to get onto it if you're not staying at one of the local hotels, see box opposite.

The Marina and Marina Walk

The **marina** itself is actually a man-made sea inlet, around 1.5km long and lined with luxury yachts and fancy speedboats, which snakes inland behind the JBR, running parallel with the coast. The eastern end of the marina is encircled by the attractive **Marina Walk**, a pleasant pedestrianized promenade lined with waterfront cafés and restaurants, and one of the few places designed on a human scale amid the thrusting high-rises of the marina. It's proved particularly popular with local Emiratis and expat Arabs, and is best after dark, when the cafés fill up, the air mists over with fragrant clouds of shisha smoke and the surrounding towers light up in a modest blaze of neon – an appealing (and blessedly traffic-free) blend of traditional and futuristic Dubai. There are various access points to Marina Walk; the easiest (at least if you're approaching on foot) is to go down the side of the *Marriott* hotel, opposite the *Grosvenor House* hotel, which brings you directly onto the far end of the waterfront promenade.

Dubai Internet and Media cities

At the north end of Dubai Marina lie the twin business areas known as **Dubai Internet City** and **Dubai Media City**. These two districts were the first and most successful in a string of similar initiatives undertaken by the government to encourage foreign firms to set up offices in designated areas of the city under

Marina beaches and watersports

All Dubai's **beach hotels** apart from the *Royal Méridien* and *Westin* allow non-guests to use their beaches, swimming pools and other facilities for a (usually hefty) fee – the best deal is usually at the *Sheraton*. Some places close to outsiders when occupancy levels rise above a certain percentage – it's always best to ring in advance to check the latest situation wherever you're planning to go, since individual hotel policies and charges change frequently. Given the wallet-emptying amounts of money involved, many people prefer to head to the stretch of **free beach** between the *Sheraton* and *Hilton* hotels, which has plenty of white sand to loll about on, but no facilities (although the restaurants and cafés of The Walk – see opposite – are just over the road). For more on the city's free and cheap beaches, see p.135.

There are **watersports centres** at all the marina beach hotels (apart from the *Ritz-Carlton*, which uses the centre at the *Royal Méridien*), offering a wide range of activities including windsurfing, sailing, kayaking, water-skiing, wake-boarding and parasailing (but not jet-skiing, which the authorities have banned).

Jumeirah Beach Hotel (ⓣ04-301 0000) Daily 250dh (children 150dh)

Habtoor Grand (ⓣ04-399 5000) Sun–Wed 200dh (children 150dh), Thurs–Sat 225dh (175dh)

Hilton Dubai Jumeirah Resort (ⓣ04-399 1111) Sun–Wed 180dh, Thurs–Sat 250dh, under 12s free.

Meridien Mina Seyahi (ⓣ04-399 3333) Fri & Sat 250dh, Sun–Thurs 150dh.

One & Only Royal Mirage (ⓣ04-399 9999) Daily 250dh; advance reservations required.

Ritz-Carlton (ⓣ04-399 4000) A painfully expensive 500dh, and even then depending on availability; call in advance to check.

Sheraton Jumeirah Beach (ⓣ04-399 5533) Sun–Thurs 100dh (children 60dh), Fri & Sat 180dh (100dh).

preferential commercial terms (including no income or corporate tax), obviating the bundles of red tape and restrictive local legislation which have traditionally stood in the way of foreign investment in the Gulf. The schemes were so successful that they have now been repeatedly copied in Dubai (Studio City, Sports City, Maritime City and Healthcare City among others) and in neighbouring countries. There's nothing really to see here, though travelling down the coastal road you'll notice a number of large signs advertising the offices of international corporate heavyweights such as Microsoft, CNN and Reuters.

Ibn Battuta Mall

Situated way down along Sheikh Zayed Road south of the Marina, the outlandish, mile-long **Ibn Battuta Mall** (daily 10am–10pm, Wed–Fri until midnight; ⓦwww.ibnbattutamall.com) is worth the trip out to the furthest reaches of the city suburbs to sample what is undoubtedly Dubai's wackiest shopping experience (which is saying something). The mall is themed in six different sections after some of the countries – Morocco, Andalusia, Tunisia, Persia, India and China – visited by the famous Arab traveller Ibn Battuta, with all the architectural kitsch and caprice you'd expect. Highlights include a life-size elephant complete with mechanical *mahout* (rider), a twilit Tunisian village and a full-size Chinese junk, while the lavishness of some of the decoration would seem more appropriate on a Rajput palace or a Persian grand mosque than a motorway mall. As so often in Dubai, the underlying concept may be naff, but it's carried

Dubailand

The vast new **Dubailand** development (www.dubailand.ae) has become the major symbol of Dubai's over-reaching ambition – and current financial difficulties. Occupying a huge swathe of land on the eastern side of the city, Dubailand was originally slated (according to plans announced at the launch in 2003) to become the planet's largest and most spectacular tourist development, with an extraordinary mix of theme parks and sporting and leisure facilities, covering a staggering 280 square kilometres – twice the size of the Walt Disney World Resort in Florida. Major attractions were to have included a massive waterpark and snowdome; the **Great Dubai Wheel**, the Gulf's answer to the London Eye (although, naturally, quite a lot bigger); the **Restless Planet** dinosaur theme park featuring over a hundred animatronic dinosaurs; and the **Falcon City of Wonders**, comprising full-scale replicas of the seven wonders of the world. Other mega-projects within Dubailand were to have included the **Mall of Arabia** (the world's largest) and the **Bawadi** development, with over thirty hotels including – it goes almost without saying – the **world's largest hotel**, *Asia-Asia* (6500 rooms), plus reams of other leisure and residential facilities.

Parts of the complex are already open, including the Dubai Autodrome and Dubai Sports City (see p.134), complete with international cricket stadium and Ernie Els golf course, as well as the *Al Sahra Desert Resort*, where you'll find nightly open-air performances of *Jumana: Secret of the Desert* – a cheesy Arabian-themed theatrical extravaganza with assorted dancers, acrobats and camels, backed up by fancy sound and laser effects (although the name of the so-called "resort" is a misnomer, since you can't actually stay here). Unfortunately, despite all the publicity, the remainder of the development now appears to be stalled – perhaps permanently – and whether any of Dubailand's more ambitious features ever succeed in seeing the light of day is anyone's guess.

through with such extravagance, and on such a scale, that it's difficult not to be at least slightly impressed – or appalled. In addition, the walk from one end of the elongated mall to the other is the most pleasant stroll you can have in Dubai's pedestrian-hating suburbs, especially in the heat of summer. For more on the mall's shopping opportunities, see p.144.

Listings

Listings

8

Accommodation

Dubai has a vast range of **accommodation**, much of it is aimed squarely at big spenders. There's also a decent selection of mid-range places, although travellers on a tight budget will struggle to find inexpensive accommodation.

At the **top end** of the market, Dubai has some of the most stunning hotels on the planet, from the futuristic *Burj al Arab* – the world's first "seven-star" hotel – to traditional Arabian-themed palaces such as *Al Qasr* and the *One&Only Royal Mirage*, and suave modern city hotels like *Raffles* and *Grosvenor House*. When it comes to creature comforts, all the city's top hotels do outrageous luxury as standard, with sumptuous suites, indulgent spa treatments, spectacular bars and gorgeous private beaches. The size and style of the very best places makes them virtually tourist attractions in their own right – self-contained islands of indulgence in which it's possible to spend day after day without ever feeling the need to leave.

Many of the top hotels are ranged **along the beach** in Jumeirah and Dubai Marina, but note that the overall shortage of oceanfront accommodation means these places tend to get booked solid way in advance, especially during the winter months (even in the stifling summer months, occupancy levels remain high). There are also several superb top-end places dotted around the **city centre** and along **Sheikh Zayed Road**.

Hotel apartments

A good alternative in Dubai to a conventional hotel is to book into one of the city's myriad **hotel apartments**. These can often provide significantly better value than hotels, assuming you don't mind doing without some of usual hotel facilities (although some apartments do have pools, and a basic café/restaurant).

Most of the city's **budget** hotel apartments are in Bur Dubai – in fact the entire city block south of the BurJuman centre is pretty much entirely taken up with them. The main operator is Golden Sands (ⓦwww.goldensandsdubai.com; doubles from around 300dh), which has about ten huge apartment blocks scattered across the area. Other places at a similar price include Al Faris (ⓦwww.alfarisdubai.com), Savoy (ⓦwww.savoydubai.com) and Winchester (ⓦwww.winchest.com).

There are also some good **upmarket** apartments, including three run by Arjaan Rotana: the *BurJuman Arjaan*, behind the BurJuman centre in Bur Dubai; the Arjaan in Dubai Media City, opposite the *One&Only Royal Mirage*; and the *Amwaj Rotana* on the beach at the Dubai Marina (ⓦwww.rotana.com; around 700dh). The last two are particularly good for families looking for beachside accommodation but who can't afford the often stratospheric price of rooms in the city's beach hotels; the apartments' kitchen and laundry facilities are another bonus. The nearby *Oasis Beach Tower* (ⓦwww.jebelali-international.com) on the marina beachfront is also worth a look.

Armani, Versace and other new hotels

The roller coaster of glitzy new Dubai hotel openings has slowed somewhat following the credit crunch (the idea for the world's first luxury underwater hotel, for instance, has now sunk without a trace – see p.86) but there are still a number of eye-catching new places slated to open between 2010 and 2012. These include the world's first **Armani Hotel** (Ⓦwww.armanihotels.com; opening late 2010), which will occupy the 1st to 39th floors of the Burj Khalifa, while another leading Italian designer will be wading into Dubai with the 217-room **Palazzo Versace** (Ⓦwww.palazzoversace.ae; opening late 2010), on the waterfront in Jaddaf, featuring the world's first "refrigerated beach". In addition, a string of new five-star beachfront hotels should also begin opening on the **Palm Jumeirah crescent** during 2011 and 2012 (see p.87), including new Taj, Fairmont, Kempinski and One&Only properties.

Mid-range options are more limited; the city as a whole suffers from a distinct lack of really appealing three- and four-star options. Still, there are plenty of comfortable, reasonably priced places scattered around Bur Dubai and Deira – though don't expect any frills or particular character.

You won't find a double room anywhere in the city for much less than about 300dh. The good news is that stringent government regulations and inspections mean standards are good even at the cheapest hotels – all are scrupulously clean and fairly well maintained, and come with en-suite bathroom, plenty of hot water, satellite TV and fridge – although noise from the street or from in-house nightclubs can be a problem in some places.

Room rates

Hotels in all price ranges chop and change their **room rates** constantly according to the time of year and demand, so a hotel may be brilliant value one week, and a rip-off the next. The rates given in the reviews below are only a very rough guide to average prices; actual prices may sometimes be significantly lower or higher, with price fluctuations of up to 100 percent at the same property quite common. Prices usually (but not always) depend on the **season**. In general, prices are highest during the cool winter months from November to February (especially during the Dubai Shopping Festival) and cheapest in high summer (June to Aug), when rates at some places, especially away from the beach) can tumble by fifty percent or more. **Taxes** (a ten percent service charge and a ten percent municipality tax) are sometimes included in the quoted price, but not always, so check when booking or you might find yourself suddenly having to cough up an extra twenty percent.

All the prices given in the reviews below are for the **cheapest double room in high season**, inclusive of all taxes.

Bur Dubai

Central Bur Dubai is, along with Deira, the city's main source of **budget** accommodation – although it's worth looking out for in-house nightclubs, which can make some of the district's cheap hotels unbearably noisy. More upmarket places are strung out along Khalid bin al Waleed Road, though the majority are fairly uninspiring, with a couple of honourable exceptions. The listings below are shown on the **map** on p.44.

Ambassador **Al Falah St ⓣ04-393 9444, ⓦwww.astamb.com.** Claiming to be the oldest hotel in the city (opened 1968), this pleasant three-star occupies a very central location close to the Textile Souk. Rooms are functional but well maintained, while facilities include a swimming pool, a couple of in-house restaurants (Indian and international) and the cosy English-style *George & Dragon* pub. Overpriced at published rates, though discounts may be available. The *Ambassador's* sister hotel, the *Astoria*, around the corner on Al Fahidi St (ⓣ04-353 4300, ⓦwww.astamb.com; 800dh), is similar but a lot less peaceful. 750dh.

Arabian Courtyard **Al Fahidi St ⓣ04-351 9111, ⓦwww.arabiancourtyard.com.** In a brilliantly central location opposite the Dubai Museum, this newish four-star is a distinct cut above the other mid-range places in Bur Dubai – and often excellent value too. Decor features a nice mix of modern and Arabian styles, including attractive wood-furnished rooms, while facilities include a jacuzzi, a small gym, health club and spa – though the pool is disappointingly tiny. There's also a couple of passable in-house restaurants (Indian and Asian) plus the convivial *Sherlock Holmes Pub* (see p.123). Around 650dh.

Dallas Hotel **Al Nahda St ⓣ04-351 1223, ⓦwww.dallashotel-dubai.com.** This passable two-star is one of the more reliable cheapies in Bur Dubai, although can be slightly more expensive than similar places nearby. There's an in-house restaurant, but no bars or nightclubs, so it's all reasonably peaceful. 400dh.

Dubai Nova **Al Fahidi St ⓣ04-355 9000, ⓦwww.dubainovahotel.com.** Well-run modern hotel in a very central location, with comfortable rooms and attentive service. A bit expensive at published rates, although doubles can sometimes go for as little as 300dh.

Four Points Sheraton **Khalid bin al Waleed Rd ⓣ04-397 7444, ⓦwww.fourpoints.com/burdubai.** One of the classiest hotels in Bur Dubai, this understated but very comfortable four-star is a cut above most of the local competition. Rooms are nicely furnished in simple international style, and there's also a gym, sauna, beauty salon, a (smallish) swimming pool, plus the excellent *Antique Bazaar* restaurant (see p.111) and the cosy *Viceroy Bar* (see p.123). Rates fluctuate considerably, but are usually surprisingly good value given the quality. Around 600–800dh.

New Penninsula Hotel **Al Raffa St ⓣ04-393 9111, ⓦwww.newpenninsula.com.** This slightly dog-eared old hotel was one of the cheapest in town at the time of writing. Rooms, set around a cool white atrium, are old-fashioned but comfortable and well maintained, although noise from in-house Indian clubs may be a problem on lower floors. Around 300dh.

Orient Guest House **Bastakiya ⓣ04-351 9111, ⓦwww.orientguesthouse.com.** One of only two heritage hotels in the city (albeit not quite as atmospheric as the nearby *XVA Hotel*), occupying an old Bastakiya house arranged around a pair of pretty little courtyards – although the Starbucks sign on the exterior wall ruins some of the Arabian charm. There are ten rooms, attractively decorated with old wooden furniture and four-poster beds. Guests have free use of the pool and gym at the *Arabian Courtyard* hotel just over the road. Around 600–800dh.

Royal Ascot Hotel & Ascot Hotel **Khalid bin al Waleed Rd ⓣ04-355 8500, ⓦwww.royalascothotel-dubai.com.** This swanky faux-Georgian-style establishment is one of the classiest places in Bur Dubai, with plush and decidedly chintzy rooms. Alternatively there are a few plainer and significently cheaper rooms in the older *Ascot* hotel next door. Facilities comprise a couple of decent in-house restaurants, including the excellent *Yakitori* (see p.112), plus pool, spa and gym. New wing around 600–900dh, old wing 500–750dh.

Time Palace Hotel **Just off Al Fahidi St ⓣ04-353 2111, ⓦwww.time-palace.com.** The most consistently reliable and best-value budget hotel in Bur Dubai, in an unbeatable location just 50m up from the main entrance to the Textile Souk, though it's surprisingly quiet given how central it is (only the local mosque disturbs the peace). Rooms are unusually spacious, and there's a simple in-house Indian restaurant, but no other facilities. Often gets booked up well in advance, so reserve early. Around 300dh.

Vasantan **Al Nahda St (around back of the Astoria hotel) ⓣ04-393 8006, ⓦwww.thevasantabhavan.com.** This simple hotel is one of the cheapest options in Bur Dubai – old-fashioned and looking a bit worn around edges, but perfectly clean, comfy

and peaceful. The excellent in-house *Vasanta Bhavan* restaurant (see p.112) is a bonus. 250–300dh.

XVA Bastakiya ⓣ04-353 5383, ⓦwww.xvahotel.com. One of Dubai's very few genuine heritage hotels, this atmospheric gallery-cum-café (see p.132 and p.111) has seven guest rooms tucked away around the back of a fine old Bastakiya house. Rooms are on the small side but brimming with character, featuring Arabian furnishings, slatted windows and four-poster beds, plus captivating views over the surrounding wind towers. 650dh–750dh.

Deira

Deira has easily the city's biggest selection of **budget** hotels, with literally dozens of places around the Gold Souk and elsewhere, particularly along Sikkat al Khail Road, as well as plenty of mid-range options and a few top-end establishments located along the side of the Creek. Staying in Deira puts you right in the heart of the city-centre action, but, equally, means that you're a longish taxi ride from other parts of the city and the beach. The listings below are shown on the **map** on p.54.

Carlton Tower Hotel Baniyas St ⓣ04-222 7111, ⓦwww.carltontower.net. Pleasantly old-fashioned four-star, enjoying an excellent location right in the thick of the city. Rooms are comfortable, if dated; some boast fine Creek views though road noise can be slightly intrusive on lower floors. Facilities include a second-floor pool and health club, plus Greek, Russian and international restaurants. There's also a free shuttle to the public beach at either Jumeirah Beach Park or Al Mamzar Park. Around 600dh.

Florida International Opposite Al Sabkha Bus Station, Al Sabkha Rd ⓣ04-224 7777, ⓦwww.florahospitality.com. One of Deira's more upmarket budget hotels, right in the heart of the downtown action. Rooms (all with wi-fi) are nicely furnished for the price, while decent soundproofing means they're reasonably quiet despite the location on a busy main road, although you might prefer to sacrifice the street views for a more peaceful room around the back. The sister *Florida* hotel (ⓣ04-226 8888, ⓦwww.florahospitality.com; around 350dh) just down the road is a good alternative and usually slightly cheaper, although not quite as nice. Around 400dh.

Gold Plaza Guesthouse Gold Souk ⓣ04-225 0240, ⓔgoldplaza@asteco.com. Long-standing cheapie almost next door to the Gold Souk entrance, and popular with visiting African gold traders. Rooms are functional but inexpensive and reasonably quiet. A few cheap singles (around 175dh) are available, though you'll probably need to book in advance. Around 250–300dh.

Hilton Dubai Creek Baniyas Rd ⓣ04-227 1111, ⓦwww.hilton.com. The most striking hotel in the city centre, the *Hilton Dubai Creek* is all about slick contemporary style, from the Carlos Ott interior designs to the in-house Gordon Ramsay restaurant, *Verre* (see p.113). The striking decor mixes industrial-chic with designer-Zen, from the in-your-face foyer, twinkling with huge quantities of reflective metal fittings, to the mirrored lifts and soothing wood-panelled corridors with blue floor lights. Rooms are exceptionally well equipped (foot massagers and DVD players come as standard) and stylishly decorated in minimalist whites and creams; most also have grand Creek views, framed by floor-to-ceiling windows. The health club and a small rooftop pool with spectacular views are an added bonus. Around 900–1300dh.

Hyatt Regency ⓣ04-209 1234, ⓦwww.dubai.regency.hyatt.com. This gargantuan five-star stands in monolithic splendour on the northern side of Deira, conveniently close to the Gold Souk and city centre. Inside, it's a very polished offering – literally so, in the case of the shiny white marbled atrium – with spacious rooms attractively decorated in pine-and-white minimalist style. All have views (those from the higher floors are spectacular) and come with five-star mod-cons, while facilities include the attractive Club Olympus spa (see p.137) and a good selection of in-house restaurants (see p.113). Around 900–1000dh.

Al Khayam Hotel Gold Souk ⓣ04-226 4211, ⓔkhayamh@emirates.net.ae. Friendly two-star with a mix of averagely furnished and priced "modern" rooms and a few "old" (slightly shabby) singles and twins. There's also an attractive little first-floor café overlooking the street. A bit expensive at published rates, though worth checking latest prices if you're looking for something in the area. 300–350dh.

Landmark Hotel Baniyas Square ⓣ04-228 6666, ⓦwww.lmhotelgroup.com. Perhaps the best of the options along the north side of Baniyas Square, and a good place if you want a reasonably inexpensive hotel in the thick of Deira but don't fancy the real cheapies nearer the Gold Souk. Rooms are comfy and reasonably spacious, while facilities include a small rooftop pool, health club and a couple of restaurants. Popular with Russians. Around 500dh.

La Paz Gold Souk ⓣ04-226 8800, ⓔhotellapaz@hotmail.com. This "family hotel" (so no alcohol or disreputable ladies) is perhaps the quietest of the guesthouses clustered around the entrance to the Gold Souk. Rooms are a bit old-fashioned, but perfectly clean and comfortable, and rates are often among the cheapest in the city (including bargain singles). 250–300dh.

Radisson Blu Dubai Deira Creek Baniyas Rd ⓣ04-222 7171, ⓦwww.radissonblu.com. The oldest five-star in the city, this grand dame of the Dubai hotel world still has plenty going for it: an extremely central location, an outstanding array of restaurants (see pp.113–114) and a scenic position right on the Creek, of which all rooms have a view. The style is engagingly old-fashioned and European, with rather chintzy public areas and plush rooms (but small bathrooms) and a certain understated swankiness. There's also a pool and a good range of health and fitness facilities. Generally excellent value, and the cheapest of the Deira five-stars at around 600–800dh.

St George ⓣ04-225 1122, ⓦwww.stgeorgedubai.com. Set on the Creek near the tip of the Deira peninsula, this biggish three-star offers rather old-fashioned but spacious rooms, some with good Creek views, and an unbeatable location very close to the souks and abras. The only minus points are the lack of a pool, while the Iranian and Arabian nightclubs and bar on the top floor can be noisy if you're in a room nearby. Around 500–600dh.

Sheraton Dubai Creek Baniyas Rd ⓣ04-228 1111, ⓦwww.sheraton.com/dubai. This old-fashioned five-star enjoys a good central location, a scenic creekside setting, opulent public areas with lots of shiny white marble and an unusual wedge-shaped atrium dotted with palm trees. Roughly half the rooms have Creek views (the higher the better), though the decor is rather dated and dull, and bathrooms are small. Leisure facilities include a sauna, well-equipped gym, health club and small pool, plus a trio of good in-house restaurants (including *Ashiana* and *Vivaldi's* – see pp.113–114), although rates are often poor value compared to other nearby five-stars. Around 1500dh.

The inner suburbs

There aren't many stand-out places to stay in the inner suburbs, although the area does boast Dubai's two finest city hotels – the opulent *Raffles* and the idyllic *Park Hyatt*. The listings below are shown on the **map** on p.63.

Grand Hyatt Sheikh Rashid Rd, Oud Metha ⓣ04-317 1234, ⓦwww.dubai.grand.hyatt.com. This colossus of a hotel – the second biggest in Dubai, with 674 rooms spread over sixteen floors – is grand in every sense. The vast atrium alone could easily swallow two or three smaller establishments and is home to a big array of shops, cafés and restaurants, plus a substantial patch of fake tropical rainforest, with the wooden hulls of four large boats poking out of the ceiling. Rooms are larger than average and have grand views through big picture windows, either towards the Creek or Sheikh Zayed Road, though the decor itself is uninspiring. The range of facilities is vast: four pools (including a nice indoor one with underwater music), spa, jacuzzi, steam bath, sauna, kids' club, a large gym and several good restaurants (see pp.113–114). The only real drawback of the whole place is its middle-of-nowhere location, although its proximity to the Garhoud Bridge and assorted major highways puts it within a fairly short taxi ride of pretty much anywhere in the northern half of the city. Rates are on the high side at around 1200–1500dh.

▲ *Park Hyatt*

Park Hyatt Dubai Creek Golf and Yacht Club, Garhoud ⓣ04-602 1234, ⓦwww.dubai.park.hyatt.com. One of Dubai's most appealing city-centre hotels, this alluring five-star occupies a beautiful complex of white-walled, blue-domed buildings in quasi-Moroccan style, surrounded by extensive grounds and plenty of palm trees – a beguiling mixture of golf and Gulf. Rooms (some with beautiful Creek views) are unusually large, with cool white and cream decor and spacious bathrooms. Facilities include a large pool and the superb Amara spa (see p.137), plus the innovative *Thai Kitchen* restaurant (see p.116) and attractive *The Terrace* (see p.124) marina-side bar. Around 2300dh.

Raffles Sheikh Rashid Rd, Oud Metha ⓣ04-324 8888, ⓦwww.raffles.com. Rivalling the *Park Hyatt* for the title of Dubai's finest city-centre hotel, the spectacular new *Raffles* takes its cue from the Egyptian theme of the Wafi complex next door and pushes it to new levels of opulence. The hotel is designed in the form of an enormous postmodern pyramid, with a beautifully executed blend of Egyptian and Asian styling (the lobby, with huge columns covered in hieroglyphs and enormous hanging lanterns, is particularly dramatic). Rooms feature silky-smooth contemporary decor and fine city views, while facilities include a range of very upmarket eating and drinking establishments plus the appealing Amrita spa. Outside there's a big pool and surprisingly extensive grounds complete with their own botanical garden, stuffed with some 130,000 plants. Despite all the style, rates remain relatively affordable. Around 1300–1600dh.

Rydges Plaza Al Diyafah St, Satwa ⓣ04-398 2222, ⓦwww.rydges.com. If you want to stay in Satwa, this unpretentious and very good-value four-star deluxe overlooking the roundabout is the place to be. Rooms are comfortable (although those with a view of the roundabout suffer from slight road noise) and facilities include an attractive outdoor pool area, gym and health club, plus the in-house *Il Rustico* and *Coconut Grove* restaurants (see p.114). Around 350–550dh.

Sheikh Zayed Road

Sheikh Zayed Road is lined with a long sequence of upmarket hotels aimed mainly at visiting businessmen, with superb views and classy facilities – although, of course, no beach. Rates are on the high side, though often fall over weekends. The listings below are shown on the **map** on p.70.

Crowne Plaza ⓣ04-331 1111, ⓦwww.crowneplaza.com. One of the cheaper five-stars on the strip, the *Crowne Plaza* is a haven of old-world chintz amid the modernist establishments lining Sheikh Zayed Road. It's all rather dated but still engaging, with a distinctly European-style ambience, from the cluttered but convivial foyer and public areas to the cosy rooms, complete with abundant quantities of plush fabrics and slightly naff furnishings, as well as all the usual five-star mod-cons. There's also a decent range of in-house eating and drinking establishments (including the *Al Tannour* and *Trader Vic's* restaurants – see p.118), plus a passable range of leisure facilities including pool and gym – though they don't compare with other places along the road. 800–1000dh.

Dusit Thani ⓣ**04-343 3333,** ⓦ**www.dusit.com.** This *wai*-shaped Sheikh Zayed Road landmark (see p.72) is one of the nicest five-stars hereabouts. Thai-owned and -styled, the whole place has a distinctive ambience which combines serene interior design and ultra-attentive service. Rooms are stylishly decorated in soothing creams and browns (and cleverly designed so that you can even watch TV from the bath), and there are all the usual upmarket facilities, including the excellent *Benjarong* restaurant (see p.117). Average rates are around 1000dh, but prices fluctuate widely.

Fairmont ⓣ**04-332 5555,** ⓦ**www.fairmont.com.** Designed to resemble an enormous wind tower, this Sheikh Zayed Road landmark is instantly recognizable after dark thanks to its four luridly spotlit turrets. Inside, the hotel is one of the most stylish on the road, huddled around a soaring glass-and-steel atrium illuminated with multi-coloured splashes of changing light. Rooms are beautifully furnished, with soothing cream decor, huge TVs and all the usual mod-cons, plus larger-than-average bathrooms. The whole of the ninth floor is given over to leisure facilities, including the sumptuous Willow Stream Spa (see p.138) and sunset and sunrise pools on opposite corners of the building. 1500dh.

Four Points Sheraton ⓣ**04-323 0333,** ⓦ**www.fourpoints.com/sheikhzayedroad.** This smart new business hotel lacks the facilities and panache of other places along the strip – although if you just want a place to sleep it does fine and rates are usually significantly cheaper than those at other places nearby. Facilities include Moroccan and Italian in-house restaurants, a smallish rooftop pool with spectacular views, plus a gym and sauna. 700–900dh.

Ibis World Trade Centre ⓣ**04-332 4444,** ⓦ**www.ibishotel.com.** The only mid-range option in this part of town, and usually one of the modern city's best bargains during periods of low demand. Rooms are small but comfortable, and the higher ones have nice views. In-house facilities are limited to the Italian *Cubo* restaurant and a pleasant bar, but guests can use the fitness centre and two pools at the adjacent *Novotel* for a modest 20dh. Rates can fluctuate widely depending on whether there's a big event on in the attached World Trade Centre. Around 500dh.

Jumeirah Emirates Towers ⓣ**04-319 8760,** ⓦ**www.jumeirahemiratestowers.com.** Occupying the smaller of the two iconic Emirates Towers, this exclusive establishment is generally rated the top business hotel in the city, catering mainly to senior execs on very generous expense accounts. Rooms are tailored to match, with rather austere decor and severe grey furnishings – if you're not here to work, you might find the set-up a bit spartan. Out-of-office hours can be spent in the larger-than-average swimming pool, health club or the men-only H20 spa (see p.137), while the shops, restaurants and bars of the posh Emirates Boulevard mall are virtually on your doorstep. Around 1250–1750dh.

Al Murooj Rotana Doha St ⓣ**04-321 1111,** ⓦ**www.rotana.com.** In a handy location between Sheikh Zayed Road and the Dubai Mall, this sprawling establishment feels more like a traditional resort than a business hotel. Outside, the extensive, attractively landscaped gardens are dotted with lively restaurants and bars, including the ever-popular *Double Decker* pub (see p.125). Inside there's plenty of contemporary style, with spacious and attractively furnished rooms (some with excellent Burj Khalifa views), plus a well-equipped health club and fitness centre. Around 1500dh.

Novotel World Trade Centre ⓣ**04-318 7000,** ⓦ**www.novotel.com.** Tucked away at the back of the Dubai International Convention and Exhibition Centre, this business-oriented five-star has a surprising dash of understated style, from the chic minimalist foyer to the attractively designed rooms with cool cream and pine decor. Its direct connections to the World Trade Centre guarantee a steady flow of business visitors, but there's also a decent-sized pool, plus gym and spa. It's also the (slightly unlikely) home of two of the area's best bars: *Blue Bar* (see p.124) and *Lotus One* (p.125). 700–1000dh.

Rose Rayhaan ⓣ**04-323 0111,** ⓦ**www.rotana.com.** Rising elegantly above Sheikh Zayed Road, this delicate, pencil-thin skyscraper is notable mainly for its status as the world's tallest hotel, at 333m (having snatched the record from the nearby *Burj al Arab*). It's part of Rotana's alcohol-free "Rayhaan" brand, which has made it popular among visitors from neighbouring Gulf countries – although there are plenty of bars within a short stagger if you feel the need for a tipple. Rooms are attractively furnished in contemporary style with dark wood finishes and white walls; higher rooms have predictably superb views. Somewhat bizarrely, no attempt has been made to open the uppermost floors of this record-breaking hotel to the public; all facilities, including the pool and the modest selection of places to eat, are located at the bottom, meaning if you want to see the top of the world's tallest hotel, you'll have to book a room there. 700dh–900dh.

Shangri-La ⓣ **04-343 8888,** ⓦ **www.shangri-la.com.** The most stylish hotel on Sheikh Zayed Road, the *Shangri-La* is pure contemporary class – a beguiling mix of Zen-chic and Scandinavian-cool. Rooms come with smooth pine finishes, beautiful artwork on the wall and mirrors everywhere, while leisure facilities include a spa, an unusually large and well-equipped gym, and one of the biggest pools in this part of town. There are also several excellent restaurants (see pp.117–118), plus the very chilled-out *iKandy* poolside bar (see p.125). Around 1300–1500dh.

Towers Rotana ⓣ **04-312 2320,** ⓦ **www.rotana.com.** This no-fuss four-star is one of the cheapest Shekih Zayed Road options. It's a bit run-of-the-mill compared to other places in the area, but benefits from a good central location and a decent range of leisure amenities, with a pool, well-equipped gym, sauna, steambath and massage rooms. There are also a couple of decent in-house restaurants, including the excellent, multi-cuisine *Teatro* (see p.118) and the popular *Long's Bar* (see p.125). Around 700–900dh.

Downtown Dubai

There are several places to stay dotted around the **Downtown Dubai** district, including a trio of new establishments tucked away in the attractive "Old Town" development. The area will also host the world's first Armani hotel (see p.73), which was scheduled to open by late 2010. The listings below are shown on the **map** on p.70.

The Address Downtown Dubai Emaar Blvd, ⓣ **04-436 8888,** ⓦ **www.theaddress.com.** Occupying an eye-catching modern high-rise virtually in the shadow of the Burj Khalifa, this sleek new five-star is one of the most lavish in Dubai. The spectacular interior design features lots of dark wood, moody lighting and huge quantities of dangling braided screens, giving the whole place the look of some kind of weird futuristic bordello. Facilities include a good range of in-house eating and drinking options, including the signature *Hukama* Chinese restaurant and the spectacular *Neos* bar, the highest in Dubai (see p.125), on the 63rd floor. There's also a lavish spa, kid's club and a lovely infinity pool with superb views of the Burj Khalifa. Around 1800–2000dh.

Al Manzil Emaar Blvd, The Old Town ⓣ **04-428 5888,** ⓦ **www.southernsunme.com.** Stylish little modern hotel in the Downtown Dubai Old Town development, with an engaging mix of traditional Arabian styling and quirky contemporary touches – including walls made out of what looks like petrified vanilla and chocolate ice cream. Rooms are on the small side, although there's a decent spread of amenities including a reasonable-sized pool and gym, an attractive outdoor restaurant-cum-shisha café and the pleasant *Nezesaussi* sports-themed pub-restaurant, featuring dishes from New Zealand, South Africa and Australia (hence the unpronounceable name). The nearby *Qamardeen* hotel (ⓣ04-428 6888, ⓦwww.southernsunme.com), run by the same company, is very similar. Around 1000dh.

The Palace Emaar Blvd, The Old Town Island ⓣ **04-428 7888,** ⓦ **www.thepalace-dubai.com.** One of the flagship properties of the vast Downtown Dubai development, this opulent, Arabian-themed "city-resort" offers a surreal contrast to the nearby Burj Khalifa. It's all beautifully done, with lavish, quasi-Moroccan styling and a perfect lakeside view of the Dubai Fountain and Burj (best enjoyed from the fine in-house *Thiptara* restaurant; see p.118). There's also a superb spa (see p.138) and large lakeside pool – although for real Arabian romance it's not a patch on beachside places like the *One&Only Royal Mirage* or *Al Qasr*. Around 1500–1700dh.

Jumeirah and Umm Suqeim

The suburbs of Jumeirah and Umm Suqeim are home to some of Dubai's most memorable beachfront hotels, ranging from the party-atmosphere *Dubai Marine Beach Resort* to the world-famous *Burj al Arab* – though not surprisingly, none of them come cheap. The listings below are shown on the **map** on p.82, unless otherwise stated.

Burj al Arab Ⓣ**04-301 7777,** Ⓦ**www.burj-al-arab.com.** A stay in this staggering hotel (see p.81) is the ultimate Dubaian luxury. The "seven-star" facilities include fabulous split-level deluxe suites (the lowest category of accommodation – there are no ordinary rooms here), arrival in a chauffeur-driven Rolls and your own butler, while a paltry 80,000dh per night gets you the royal suite, complete with private elevator and cinema, rotating four-poster bed and your own Arabian *majlis*. Whatever form of suite you stay in there's pretty much every business and leisure facility you could imagine, including the superlative Assawan Spa, a handful of spectacular restaurants and bars (see p.120 & p.127) and a fabulous stretch of beach. For unbridled luxury it all takes some beating, and offers the perfect playground for image-conscious wannabes, although the overwhelming atmosphere of super-heated opulence isn't necessarily conducive to a particularly peaceful or romantic stay; if that's what you're after, try the less attention-grabbing (but still pricey) beachside hotels along the coast nearby. Around 6500–9000dh.

▲ *Burj al Arab*

Dar al Masyaf Madinat Jumeirah Ⓣ**04-366 8888,** Ⓦ**www.madinatjumeirah.com.** A more intimate alternative to the Madinat Jumeirah's big two hotels, *Dar al Masyaf* consists of a chain of modest, low-rise villa-style buildings scattered around the edges of the Madinat complex within extensive, palm-studded gardens. Each building contains a small number of rooms, sharing an exclusive pool and decorated in the deluxe Arabian manner of *Al Qasr* and *Mina A'Salam*, whose myriad facilities they share. Around 2500dh.

Dubai Marine Beach Resort Jumeirah Rd, near Jumeirah Mosque Ⓣ**04-346 1111,** Ⓦ**www.dxbmarine.com. See Jumeirah map, p.78.** This attractive resort is best known for its superb array of bars and restaurants (see p.119 & p.126) – a major draw for most visitors, although things can get quite lively after dark, so it's not really the place for a quiet beach holiday and early nights. The location also makes it the only five-star in Dubai where you can be on the beach but also within easy striking distance of the city centre. Rooms are attractively decorated and set in pleasingly simple modern white "villas" amid lush gardens stuffed with tropical greenery. There's also a small stretch of white-sand beach, two medium-sized pools and a spa. Around 1000–1200dh.

Ibis Mall of the Emirates, 2A St Ⓣ**04-382 3000,** Ⓦ**www.ibishotel.com.** This cheery little no-frills hotel is usually the best bargain in southern Dubai, with superb-value rooms and a decent location on the south side of the Mall of the Emirates. There's another Ibis nearby at Al Barsha (Ⓣ04-399 6699) about 1.5km further south next to Sheikh Zayed Road, which is usually even cheaper (around 350dh), though the location is unappealing. Around 400dh.

Jumeirah Beach Hotel ⓣ04-301 0000, ⓦwww.jumeirahbeachhotel.com. The most luxurious and stylish place in town when it opened a decade ago, this iconic hotel (see p.83) has come down in the world slightly since then, and now caters to a more low-brow crowd of (mainly UK) families and couples. The facilities are among the best in the city, including over twenty restaurants, several top nightspots (see p.126), seven pools, six tennis courts, a golf driving range and the Pavilion PADI diving centre (see p.135). It's particularly good for children, with a newly renovated kids' club, spacious grounds and a large and lovely stretch of beach with plenty of watersports available and jaw-dropping *Burj* views; guests also get unlimited access to the Wild Wadi waterpark next door. The hotel is also home to *Beit al Bahar* (ⓦwww.beitalbahar.com), nineteen freestanding villas, set in lush gardens with beautiful Arabian decor and their own private plunge pools. Around 1500–2500dh.

Mina A'Salam Madinat Jumeirah ⓣ04-366 8888, ⓦwww.madinatjumeirah.com. Part of the stunning Madinat Jumeirah complex (see p.84), *Mina A'Salam* ("Harbour of Peace") shares the Madinat's Arabian theming, with wind tower-topped buildings and quasi-Moroccan decorative touches, although the sheer size of the place lends it a faint package-resort atmosphere which sits incongruously with its refined traditional Middle Eastern styling. Rooms are beautifully furnished with traditional Arabian wooden furniture and fabrics, and the public areas are full of character. That said, the whole place can seem like a slightly watered-down version of the rather more extravagant (and often only fractionally more expensive) *Al Qasr* hotel on the opposite side of the Madinat – although you might possibly prefer *Mina A'Salam*'s less ostentatious and more homely style. Facilities include a nice-looking stretch of private beach, three pools, plus the forty-odd restaurants and bars (and myriad shops) of the Madinat complex outside. Around 1500–2500dh.

Al Qasr Madinat Jumeirah ⓣ04-366 8888, ⓦwww.madinatjumeirah.com. This extravagantly opulent Arabian-themed hotel looks like something out of a film set, from the statues of rearing horses and jaw-dropping views over the Madinat which greet you on arrival, to the many-pillared foyer with cascading fountains and vast chandeliers inside. Rooms are similarly dramatic, with show-stopping views over the surrounding attractions and sumptuous oriental decor featuring reproduction antique wooden furniture, plus copious quantities of colourful drapes, cushions and carpets – and pretty much every luxury and mod-con you can imagine. There's also a huge pool and all the facilities of the Madinat complex on your doorstep. Around 2500dh.

Dubai Marina and the Palm Jumeirah

Dubai Marina is where you'll find the majority of the city's big **beachside resorts**, lined up in a long row along the seafront. There's also a growing number of more business-oriented hotels slightly inland, like the suave *Grosvenor House*, wedged in amid the skyscrapers of the Marina proper. Close by, Palm Jumeirah island is home to the mighty *Atlantis* resort, the largest hotel in the city. The listings below are shown on the **map** on p.87.

Atlantis Palm Jumeirah ⓣ04-426 2000, ⓦwww.atlantisthepalm.com. This vast new mega-resort (see p.89) is one of the most spectacular places to stay in Dubai, and literally has everything: in-house waterpark, dolphinarium, celebrity-chef restaurants, luxurious spa and vast swathes of sand. One of the main reasons to stay is to get free or discounted admission to the otherwise rather expensive ream of on-site attractions (see p.89), although room rates are on the high side, going on stratospheric. It's also not the most peaceful place in town and more suited to an up-tempo family holiday than a romantic break. There's also an excellent array of kids' activities, including a top-notch kids club (4–12yrs) and the teen-only nightclub, *Club Rush*. Around 2500dh.

Grosvenor House ⓣ04-399 8888, ⓦwww.grosvenorhouse-dubai.com. Set slightly away from the seafront, this elegantly tapering 45-storey high-rise (spectacularly illuminated at night) is more Sheikh Zayed Road urban chic than bucket-and-spade beach resort. The entire hotel is a model of contemporary cool, from the suave public areas right through to the elegantly furnished rooms, decorated in muted whites, creams and cottons, and with big picture windows affording sweeping views over the marina and coast. There's also a pool, gym, massage centre, health club and the excellent Retreat Spa (see p.137), and guests also have free use of the beach and pools at the nearby *Royal Méridien*. The hotel's very select array of restaurants and bars (see p.121 & p.127) is a further attraction. It's all surprisingly affordable, even so. 1000–1500dh.

Habtoor Grand Resort and Spa ⓣ**04-399 5000,** ⓦ**www.habtoorhotels.com.** This rather overblown five-star resort mixes city high-rise and beachside styles to rather mishmash effect, with a pair of huge towers overlooking the hotel's busy gardens, pools and beach. The whole place often feels a bit manic, the grounds are unattractively cluttered and the beach is nothing to write home about. Still, rooms (either in the two towers or in the slighty cheaper "cottages" in the beachside grounds) are comfortable and cheery, with bright colours, attractive decor and, from higher levels, huge views over the marina, sea and Palm Jumeirah. The extensive facilities include thirteen bars and restaurants, spa, watersports centre, tennis and squash courts and children's club, plus three pools. Around 1200dh.

Hilton Dubai Jumeirah Resort ⓣ**04-399 1111,** ⓦ**www.hilton.com/worldwideresorts.** This glitzy Hilton boasts lots of shiny metal and an air of cosmopolitan chic – it's more of a city-slicker's beach bolthole than family seaside resort, and the place tends to attract a young and stylish local crowd. Rooms are bright and cheerfully decorated, but facilities are relatively limited compared to nearby places, although you do get a health club, a gym and a passable range of restaurants and bars, including the attractive *BiCE* Italian restaurant (see p.120). Outside there's a medium-sized pool and lovely terraced gardens running down to the sea, though the hotel beach itself is smaller than at neighbouring establishments, and the sunloungers are rather packed in. There's also a range of watersports available and a kids' club, playground. Around 1500dh.

Le Méridien Mina Seyahi ⓣ**04-399 3333,** ⓦ**www.lemeridien-minaseyahi.com.** This rather humdrum five-star is perhaps the least impressive of the marina hotels to look at, with dull public areas, dated rooms and all the atmosphere of a railway station buffet. The real selling points are the superb grounds and big swathe of beach, one of the largest of any of the marina hotels – good for families on vacation, but not the place for a romantic break. The excellent *Barasti* beachside bar (see p.127) is also worth a visit. Around 1200dh.

One&Only Royal Mirage ⓣ**04-399 9999,** ⓦ**www.oneandonlyresorts.com.** The finest Arabian-themed hotel in town (only *Al Qasr* – see opposite – comes close), this dreamy resort is the perfect 1001 Nights fantasy made flesh, with a superb sequence of quasi-Moroccan-style buildings scattered amid extensive, palm-filled grounds. It's particularly stunning at night, when the labyrinthine sequence of beautifully sculpted and tiled courtyards, hallways and corridors – and the thousands of palms – are illuminated. The whole complex is actually three hotels in one: *The Palace*, the *Arabian Court*, and the *Residence & Spa*, each a little bit more sumptuous (and expensive) than the last. Rooms are attractively appointed, with

▲ *One&Only Royal Mirage*

Arabian decor, reproduction antique wooden furniture and colourful rugs, while facilities include a one-kilometre stretch of private beach, four pools, the delectable Oriental Hammam-style spa and some of the best restaurants and bars in town (see p.121 & p.127). From around 2500–3000dh.

Ritz-Carlton ⓣ **04-399 4000,** ⓦ **www.ritzcarlton.com.** Set in a low-rise, Tuscan-style ochre building this very stylish establishment is one of the classiest and most expensive in the city, and makes for a refreshing change from the in-your-face high-rises surrounding it. Rooms are spacious, with slightly chintzy European-style decor, while public areas boast all the charm of a luxurious old country house, especially in the sumptuous lobby lounge and the flagship *La Baie* restaurant (see p.120). There's also a big and very quiet stretch of private beach and gardens, while children are surprisingly well catered for, with a big kids' club, covered outdoor play area and their own pool. Other facilities include tennis and squash courts, a small golf course, attractive spa (see p.137) and one of the smartest gyms in town. Around 2000–3000dh.

Le Royal Méridien ⓣ **04-399 5555,** ⓦ **www.leroyalmeridien-dubai.com.** This large and slightly pretentious five-star is comfortable enough, but lacks the style or charm of some other places along the beach. The five hundred plush but unexciting rooms are split between three different – though all equally uninspiring – parts of the hotel. The best features are the extensive grounds and beach, complete with three larger-than-average pools, perhaps the most attractive of any of the marina hotels. Facilities include the ostentatious, Roman-themed Caracalla Spa (see p.137), a smart gym, tennis and squash courts, a kids' club and a decent selection of restaurants. Around 1250–1750dh.

Sheraton Jumeirah Beach ⓣ **04-399 5533,** ⓦ **www.sheraton.com/jumeirahbeach.** At the southern end of the marina, this is the area's most low-key and flash-free five-star – and usually a bit cheaper than the competition. Rooms are passable, if unexciting, but the hotel's real attraction is its laidback, family-friendly atmosphere, and its extensive palm-studded gardens and beach; kids get their own pool, shaded playground and the Pirates day-care club. There's also a range of watersports available, plus squash courts, a gym, wellness centre and a trio of low-key restaurants. Around 1000–1200dh.

Westin Dubai ⓣ **04-399 3333,** ⓦ **www.westinminaseyahi.com.** The newest of the beachside marina hotels, the *Westin* is a strong contender for the fiercely contested prize of Dubai's tackiest hotel. Outside, it's a pompous neo-Georgian eyesore – with wind towers. Inside, it's a study in interior undesign, with brightly coloured furniture and fluorescent potted trees failing to distract attention from public areas which have all the style of an international airport lounge. Where the hotel scores highly, however, is for its huge and attractive grounds, enormous pool and attractive spa, while the rooms themselves are surprisingly tasteful compared to what lies outside. It's best for families, although there are plenty of more stylish places to hang out in this part of town for this price. Around 1500–2000dh.

Around Dubai

If you want to get away from the city proper, a couple of resorts offer visitors the chance to enjoy the emirate's unspoilt desert hinterlands. For **Abu Dhabi** hotels see p.170; for **Al Ain** see p.157; for **east coast** resorts see p.165; and for **Hatta** see p.167. The listings below feature on the Eastern UAE colour map at the end of the book.

Desert Palm ⓣ **04-323 8888,** ⓦ **http://desertpalm.peraquum.com.** On the edge of Dubai, around twenty minutes' drive from the city centre, the *Desert Palm* is a pleasantly laidback suburban bolthole, surrounded by polo fields, with distant views of the skyscrapers along Sheikh Zayed Road. The suites and villas (there are no rooms) are beautifully designed and equipped with fancy mod-cons like pre-loaded iPods and espresso machines; villas come with private pool and indoor and outdoor rain showers. Facilities include the excellent *Rare* steakhouse and the superb in-house Lime Spa (see p.137). 1500–2500dh.

Jumeirah Bab Al Shams Desert Resort and Spa ⓣ **04-832 6699,** ⓦ **www.jumeirahbabalshams.com.** Hidden out in the desert a 45-minute drive from the airport, this gorgeous resort occupies a wonderfully atmospheric replica Arabian fort and offers a complete change of pace and style from the city five-stars, with desert camel- and horse-riding or falconry displays the order of the day, rather than lounging on the beach. Rooms are decorated in traditional Gulf style, with rustic ochre walls and Bedouin-style fabrics, while facilities include a magnificent infinity pool and an unusual "rain room" where you can take a dip in a temperature-controlled waterfall. There's also a good selection of restaurants, including *Al Hadheerah* – Dubai's first traditional Arabian open-air desert restaurant, complete with belly dancers and live band. Around 1500–1750dh.

Kempinski Hotel Ajman ⓣ **06-714 5555,** ⓦ **www.kempinski.com.** Very chilled-out beachside resort hotel in the sleepy emirate of Ajman, around an hour's drive north of Dubai, but feeling a million miles away from the big city. The hotel's main attraction is its blissful strip of beach and attractive gardens, backed up by the usual five-star amenities including a spa and fitness centre. Around 1200dh.

Al Maha Desert Resort and Spa Dubai Desert Conservation Reserve, Al Ain Rd ⓣ **04-303 4222,** ⓦ **www.al-maha.com.** Some 60km from Dubai, this very exclusive, very expensive resort occupies a picture-perfect setting amid the pristine Dubai Desert Conservation Reserve (see p.156) – gazelles and rare Arabian oryx can often been seen wandering through the grounds. The resort is styled like a Bedouin encampment, with stunning views of the surrounding dunes and accommodation in tented suites with handcrafted furnishings and artefacts, plus small private pools. Activities include falconry, camel treks, horseriding, archery, 4WD desert drives and guided nature walks; or you can just relax in the resort's serene spa. Around 5000dh.

9

Eating

It's almost impossible not to eat well in Dubai, whatever your budget. The city serves up a vast array of food, ranging from inexpensive local curry houses and shwarma stands through to a string of fine-dining restaurants overseen by some of the world's leading celebrity chefs.

If you've got cash to burn, Dubai offers a superb spread of top-quality **international restaurants**, with gourmet food served up in some of the city's most magical locations, whether atop the soaring skyscrapers of Sheikh Zayed Road, alongside the tranquil waters of the Creek, or amid the idyllic palm-studded grounds of the southern city's beachside hotels. Italian, Thai, Japanese and Chinese are all popular, while there's a particularly good spread of **Indian** restaurants catering to Dubai's large subcontinental population. There's also an outstanding clutch of **European fine-dining** establishments including an increasing number of places overseen by internationally famous celebrity chefs such as Gordon Ramsay, Gary Rhodes and Pierre Gagnaire, to name just three. The city is also a brilliant place to sample the many different types of **Middle Eastern** (aka "Lebanese") cuisine. Restaurants all over the city – from streetside shwarma stalls to fancy hotel establishments complete with live bands and belly dancers – offer varying takes on the classic dishes of the region, usually featuring a big range of tasty mezze through to delicately grilled kebabs, often with a good selection of shisha (tobacco smoked through a waterpipe) on the side. **Iranian** food is also popular, while the cooking of North Africa is represented by a small but excellent selection of **Moroccan** places serving up sumptuous tajines and helpings of traditional pigeon pie. There are also plenty of good **cheap eats** to be had, with budget **Indian curry houses** scattered all over the city centre, often with surprisingly good food, plus plenty of shwarma stands for instant, inexpensive culinary gratification.

Unless otherwise stated, all the places in the reviews below are **open daily** for lunch and dinner. We've also given phone numbers for places where **reservations** are advised. Only hotel restaurants and a very small number of mall-based establishments have **alcohol** licences. You won't find booze at independent restaurants and cafés.

Friday brunch

The Dubai Friday brunch is a highlight of the weekly calendar among the city's Western community – a bit like the British Sunday lunch, only with a lot more booze. Restaurants across the city open for brunch from around midday, often with all-you-can-eat (and sometimes drink) offers which attract crowds of partying expats letting off steam at the end of the long working week. Check *Time Out Dubai* (Ⓦwww.timeoutdubai.com) for the latest offers.

Bur Dubai

The listings below are marked on the **map** on p.44.

Cafés

Automatic Al Khaleej Centre, Al Mankhool Rd. Part of a Gulf-wide chain offering Middle Eastern meals in its string of comfortable and fuss-free outlets. Not much atmosphere, but prices are reasonably cheap and food is usually pretty good, with a decent range of mezze (from 12dh) plus grills and kebabs (from 28h) and some more expensive seafood options. There are other branches on Sheikh Zayed Road and on the upper level of The Walk at Jumeirah Beach Residence (see p.92) in Dubai Marina, roughly opposite the *Ritz Carlton*.

Basta Arts Café Al Fahidi St, next to the main entrance to Bastakiya. Set in the idyllic garden of a traditional old Bastakiya house, this lovely little courtyard café offers a serene retreat from the modern city outside. The menu features a good range of light meals (from 20dh) including pasta, quiches, jacket potatoes, sandwiches and salads, plus speciality teas, smoothies and juices.

Bayt Al Wakeel Mackenzie House, near the main entrance of the Textile Souk. The small menu of rather pedestrian Arabian food, plus a few Chinese options, won't win any awards, but the convenient location near the entrance to the Textile Souk and the setting – either on an attractive terrace jutting out into the Creek or inside the historic old Mackenzie House (see p.48) itself – more than compensate. Mains from around 30dh.

Kan Zaman Heritage Village, Shindagha. Occupying a beautiful Creekside location in the historic Shindagha area, this large Middle Eastern restaurant is one of the best places in the city for a blast of authentic Arabian atmosphere, usually full of local Emiratis and expat Arabs puffing on shishas, while old-style Arabic music wails in the background. There's a big selection of food, including good hot and cold mezze (15–30dh) plus meat and seafood grills, as well as an excellent shisha selection. Mains from around 35dh. Open daily for dinner only.

XVA Café Bastakiya. Tucked away in an alley at the back of Bastakiya, the shady courtyard café of this lovely gallery-cum-guesthouse serves up good Middle Eastern-style vegetarian food (from around 25dh), including flavoursome salads (think tuna, burgul, bean, fattoush), tasty sandwiches and assorted mezze. Daily except Fri 9am–9pm.

Restaurants

Aangan Dhow Palace Hotel, Kuwait St. This is the place to come if you want really good mainstream Indian food but aren't too fussed about atmosphere or ambience. The decor is dated and boring and the atmosphere is often borderline chaos – usually with half-a-dozen extended Indian families trying to make themselves heard over the (admittedly, rather good) in-house Indian band. The food, however, is top-notch, with richly flavoured renditions of classic North Indian meat and veg tandooris and curries, served up in big portions and with a fair helping of spice. Mains from around 40dh (veg) and 50dh (meat).

Antique Bazaar Four Points Sheraton, Khalid bin al Waleed Rd ☎04-397 7444. This pretty little Indian restaurant looks like a forgotten corner of a Rajput palace, littered with carved wooden pillars, antique tables and assorted Indian artefacts. The menu covers all the basic North Indian and Mughlai favourites – tandooris, biriyani, chicken and veg curries – with reasonable aplomb, and there's the added incentive of a very passable

▲ *Kan Zaman*

Dhow dinner cruises

A dinner cruise aboard a traditional wooden dhow is often touted as one of the obligatory Dubai tourist "experiences", offering the chance to wine and dine on the water as your boat sails sedately up and down the Creek. The experience is undeniably romantic, and the views are wonderful, although food usually comprises a lame Arabian-style buffet at inflated prices, and you may feel that you can get a better (and much cheaper) sense of Dubai's maritime past simply by going for a ride on an abra.

Dinner cruises are offered by pretty much every tour operator in the city (see p.26 for listings). One of the more reliable options is the **Al Mansour Dhow**, operated by the *Radisson Blu* hotel (ⓣ04-205 7333; nightly cruises 185dh). Alternatively, **Bateaux Dubai** (ⓣ04-399 4994, ⓦwww.jebelali-international.com; 295dh) is another decent option, using a state-of-the-art modern boat (it looks a bit like a floating greenhouse) rather than a traditional dhow and offering a touch more luxury than other operators, plus above-average food.

resident band (nightly from 9pm) churning out Bollywood tunes, plus a couple of female dancers twirling around in gauzy costumes. Not the place for a quiet romantic dinner, but good fun otherwise. Mains from around 40dh (veg), 50dh (meat). Closed Fri lunchtime.

Bastakiah Nights Bastakiya ⓣ04-353 7772. This Middle Eastern restaurant is one of the most beautiful places to eat in central Dubai, occupying a superbly restored old house in Bastakiya – the perfect place to indulge in a few orientalist fantasies while sitting in the courtyard. The menu runs the usual gamut of Middle Eastern favourites, including a small range of mezze (18–25dh), plus Lebanese and Iranian kebabs, stews and biriyanis, including a couple of vegetarian options – all competent rather than outstanding. Mains cost a fairly reasonable 55–75dh, although they'll sting you an extra 45dh for a simple plate of rice.

Saravanaa Bhavan Kahlifa bin Saeed Building, about 100m east of the Bur Dubai Abra Station, between the HSBC and Bank of Baroda buildings. One of several Dubai branches of the much-loved South Indian vegetarian restaurant chain from Chennai. The menu features an encyclopedic array of favourites, ranging from South Indian dosas, *iddlis* and *uppuma* through to classic North Indian veg curries, plus a few Chinese dishes. Given the rock-bottom prices (mains 5–15dh), quality is astonishingly high. There are other branches in Oud Metha (a few doors down from *Lan Kwai Fong* – see p.115), and in Karama on the opposite side of the square across from *Karachi Darbar* (see p.114).

Yakitori Ascot Hotel, Khalid bin al Waleed Rd ⓣ04-352 0900. Hidden away on the fifth floor of the *Ascot Hotel*, this unpretentious little Japanese restaurant is like an unexpected slice of downtown Tokyo in the middle of Bur Dubai, with Japanese sushi and teppanyaki chefs, NHK TV playing in the background and a regular crowd of Japanese businessmen who sit around calmly flaunting Dubai's no-smoking regulations. The big menu covers all the usual bases: stir-fries, sushi, sashimi, maki, yakitori, curries and bento boxes, plus regional specialities like fried octopus balls and Korean fish stomach. It's all quite reasonably priced, and there's beer or jugs of draught saki to wash it down with.

Vasanta Bhavan Vasantam Hotel, Al Nahda St (around the back of the Astoria Hotel). Of the hundreds of little curry houses dotted around Bur Dubai, this cosy little vegetarian establishment is one of the best. Food is served upstairs in a comfortable and peaceful dining room, with an excellent range of North and South Indian veg standards (plus a few Chinese options), delicately spiced and at giveaway prices. Mains 6–11dh.

Deira

The listings below are marked on the **map** on p.54.

Cafés

Ashwaq Sikkat al Khail Rd, just outside the entrance to the Gold Souk. Conveniently close to the bustling Gold Souk, this is one of the busiest and best of Deira's innumerable shwarma stands, with succulent cuts of meat and big fruit juices. The perfect place for a cheap lunch, especially if you can snag a seat at one of the pavement tables – brilliant for people-watching.

Creek View Restaurant Baniyas Rd. This convivial little open-air café scores highly for its breezy creekside location and lively late-night atmosphere, when it's usually busy with shisha-smoking locals and expat Arabs. It's a good place for an after-dinner smoke and coffee, although the food (mainly mezze and kebabs) is mediocre; you're better off eating somewhere else.

Hatam al Tai Just off Baniyas Rd, near Al Sabkha Abra Station. Bustling, no-frills café serving meaty and filling Iranian food – kebabs, stews, shwarma plates and biriyanis – at bargain prices (30–35dh). If there's no space, *Shiraz Nights* next door makes a very acceptable alternative.

Sarovar 45 Sikka, Gold Souk. Tucked away down a side alley off the Gold Souk, this tiny little café is a good place for a quick and inexpensive refuelling stop during a visit to the shops. The juices are fresh and the South Indian snacks and meals cheap, but you'll struggle to find a seat at lunchtime, when it gets packed out with local workers.

Restaurants

Ashiana Sheraton Dubai Creek, Baniyas Rd ⓣ04-228 1111. Pleasantly sedate and old-fashioned restaurant specializing in hearty North Indian cuisine served up in rich and flavoursome sauces, with meat and seafood options, plus a better-than-average vegetarian selection. There's a singer and band nightly from 9pm, performing anything from ghazals to Bollywood hits. Mains from 40dh (veg), 65dh (meat). Open for dinner daily, plus Friday brunch.

China Club Radisson Blu, Baniyas Rd ⓣ04-222 7171. The best Chinese restaurant in central Dubai, with tastefully simple modern decor and some seating in cosily intimate, high-backed booths. There's a daily "Yum Cha" dim sum buffet (95dh/person) at lunchtimes, and à la carte in the evening, with well-prepared standards – live seafood, stir-fries and noodles – along with the restaurant's signature dim sum (32–42dh) and Peking duck. Mains from 60dh.

Al Dawaar Hyatt Regency, Deira Corniche ⓣ04-317 2222. Dubai's only revolving restaurant, balanced atop the gargantuan *Hyatt Regency* and offering superlative city views – each revolution takes 1hr 45min, so you should get to see the whole 360-degree panorama if you don't eat too fast. Food is buffet only (165dh at lunch, 230dh at dinner, excluding drinks), featuring a mix of Mediterranean, Arabian, Asian and Japanese dishes plus US steaks – not the city's greatest culinary experience, but a decent accompaniment to the head-turning vistas outside.

Focaccia Hyatt Regency, Deira Corniche ⓣ04-317 2222. This rambling Italian restaurant feels more like a rather smart country club than a city-centre restaurant, with a casual ambience, soothing Gulf views and attentive but unobtrusive service. Food features a mix of traditional and modern Italian cuisine, with a seasonally changing menu and a mix of pasta and risottos, plus meat and fish. Mains from around 60dh.

Shabestan Radisson Blu, Baniyas Rd ⓣ04-222 7171. This posh but rather plain Iranian restaurant retains a loyal following among local Arabs and Iranians thanks to its huge *chelo* kebabs, fish stews and other Persian specialities like *baghalah polo* (slow-cooked lamb) and *zereshk polo* (baked chicken with wild berries). There's also a resident three-piece band of violin, drum and *santour* (nightly except Sat) plus lovely creekside views if you can get a seat near the window. Mains from around 70dh.

Shahrzad Hyatt Regency, Deira Corniche ⓣ04-317 2222. This picture-perfect little Iranian restaurant looks like it's leapt straight out of an illustration for the *1001 Nights* (after whose narrator it takes its name). It also dishes up some of the best traditional Persian food in the city, with mainly chicken and lamb dishes, plus a few seafood options; mains include delicately spiced *chelo* kebabs and classic *polos* (rice stews) such as *zareshk polo ba morgh* (baked chicken covered with rice mixed with barberries and saffron). There's also live Iranian music and a bellydancer nightly. Mains from around 90dh. Open daily for dinner only.

Verre Hilton Dubai Creek, Baniyas Rd ⓣ04-212 7551. Under the management of Gordon Ramsay (who visits twice a year), *Verre* makes a strong case to be considered the best restaurant in Dubai, constantly wowing diners with its superb modern European cuisine, featuring a range of artfully crafted meat, fish and seafood dishes. Even if you're utterly cynical about the whole celebrity chef industry, it's difficult not to be impressed by the heavenly flavours and subtle culinary combinations which most other restaurants don't even begin to imagine, let alone reach. The smooth but unfussy modern decor and muted music make sure that attention is firmly focused where it should be – on the food – while an extensive but relatively affordable wine list provides an appropriate accompaniment. And although it's not cheap, it's significantly less wallet-emptying than other top restaurants in town (starters 80–140dh; mains 180–225dh; seven-course "Menu Prestige" 615dh), especially when you factor in all the additional between-courses *amuses-bouches* which are dished up as part of a meal. The only negative is the complete lack of vegetarian options. Reserve as far in advance as possible. Open dinner only; closed Sat.

Vivaldi's Sheraton Dubai Creek, Baniyas Rd ☎04-228 1111. This cosy and unpretentious Italian restaurant seems to have been around for ever, but continues to pull in the punters thanks to its reasonably priced and well-prepared selection of pizzas, pastas and risottos, plus hearty meat and seafood mains. Arrive early (or book) to secure a table overlooking the Creek. Mains from around 60dh. Open daily for dinner only.

Yum! Radisson Blu, Baniyas Rd ☎04-222 7171. Sleek modern café-restaurant with cool minimalist lines and glassed-in open-plan kitchen. The menu is Southeast and East Asian (mainly Thai, with some Chinese, Malay, Indonesian and Singaporean dishes), with a good range of tasty offerings, briskly served, including soups, noodles, rice dishes, Thai curries and vegetarian selections. It all comes at very reasonable prices and is backed up by a surprisingly extensive wine list. Mains 50–65dh.

Satwa and Karama

The listings below are marked on the **maps** on p.63 & p.64.

Coconut Grove Rydges Plaza Hotel, Satwa Roundabout ☎04-398 3800. This slightly shabby little restaurant on the ninth floor of the *Rydges Plaza* hotel doesn't look like much, but remains enduringly popular thanks to its excellent range of Goan, Keralan, Tamil Nadu and Sri Lankan regional specialities, with authentically fiery chilli-infused coconut sauces. Offerings include numerous spicy seafood options, plus a decent range of meat and veg dishes – from Sri Lankan Negombo prawns to Goan-style chicken xacutty – at affordable prices, with mains from 40dh. There's a decent drinks list and good views of the Satwa sprawl from the window seats.

Karachi Darbar In front of the Karama Souk, Karama. Long-established, no-frills Indo-Pakistani restaurant specializing in tasty chicken and mutton dishes prepared in a range of styles (Mughlai, Kashmiri, Baghdadi, Afghani, Shahjahani), with big portions, giveaway prices and pleasant outdoor seating overlooking Karama Park. There's another branch in Bur Dubai opposite the *Ambassador Hotel*, though it's less appealing.

Al Mallah Al Diyafah St. A classic slice of Satwa nightlife, this no-frills Lebanese café churns out good shwarmas, grills and other Middle Eastern food at bargain prices to a lively local crowd; the pavement terrace is a great place to people watch. If there's no space here, *Beirut*, just down the road, is very similar and almost as good.

Pars Satwa Roundabout, just behind Rydges Plaza Hotel. Attractive garden restaurant offering big portions of well-prepared Iranian food, including the usual meat kebabs and stews, plus a smattering of seafood. Mains from 40dh. Open daily for dinner only.

Ravi's Satwa Rd, just south of Satwa Roundabout, between the copycat Ravi Palace and Rawi Palace restaurants. This famous little Pakistani café attracts a loyal local and expat clientele thanks to its tasty array of subcontinental standards – veg, chicken and mutton curries, biriyanis and breads. Most mains are a measly 8dh, though if you go for all the trimmings you might be able to push the bill up to 20dh. The interior is usually packed, and it's more fun, despite the traffic, to sit out on the pavement and watch the street life of Satwa drift by.

Il Rustico Rydges Plaza Hotel, Satwa Roundabout, Satwa ☎04-398 2222. The homeliest little trattoria in Dubai, with rustic wooden furniture, delicious garlicky smells wafting out of the kitchen and a reasonably priced selection of pizzas, pastas and risottos (from 50dh), along with meat and seafood mains (from 65dh). It doesn't make the city's greatest Italian food, but is still a pleasant place for an inexpensive and romantic tete-a-tete.

Oud Metha

The listings below are marked on the **map** on p.63.

Asha's Wafi ☎04-324 4100. Named after legendary Bollywood chanteuse

Asha Bhosle, *Asha's* is a far cry from your average curry house, with sleek modern orange decor, colourful artwork on the walls and the voice of the great lady herself warbling discreetly in the background. The interesting menu features a good selection of traditional North Indian classics – tandooris, biriyanis and curries – along with more unusual offerings from Bhosle's own family recipe book, including unusual regional and local specialities like Goan brown cashew chicken curry or Khandesh brinjals in peanut sauce. Mains from 65dh.

Elements Wafi. With its mix of experimental artwork on the walls and huge metal pipes overhead, this funky café looks like an avant-garde gallery inserted into an oil refinery. The very eclectic menu includes a decent range of sandwiches, salads, dim sum, sushi, pasta and pizza (from around 40dh), plus more substantial meat and fish mains and a bizarre range of so-called "tapas" – meaning anything from chicken yakitori to vol au vents. There's also a good selection of shisha available in the pretty little tented terrace outside (open from 4pm). Mains from 70dh.

Khan Murjan Restaurant Souk Khan Murjan, Wafi. The centrepiece of the spectacular new Souk Khan Murjan (see p.65), this beautiful courtyard restaurant boasts plenty of local colour and has proved a big hit with the city's Emiratis and expat Arabs, thanks to the traditional atmosphere and unusually wide-ranging menu, featuring tempting selections from assorted Middle Eastern cuisines. All the usual Lebanese favourites are present and correct, alongside more unusual Egyptian, Moroccan and Turkish dishes. The restaurant also offers a rare chance to try local Gulf dishes like *fouga* (a kind of Emirati-style chicken biriyani) and *goboli* (rice cooked with lamb, spices, onions and raisins). Mains from around 70dh. Unlicensed.

Khazana Al Nasr Leisureland ☎04-336 0061. Run by leading Indian chef Sanjeev Kapoor, this pretty little garden-style establishment is one of Dubai's most appealing but unexpected Indian restaurants, tucked away in a low-key setting next to the entrance of the Al Nasr Leisureland entertainment complex. The menu offers a good range of North Indian and Mughlai classics, including kebabs, curries and Lucknow-style slow-cooked *dum pukht,* a selection of feisty Goan and Mangalorean seafood curries and a few intriguing Anglo–Indian dishes like "railway mutton curry". Given the quality, prices are remarkably restrained, with mains from around 50dh.

Lan Kwai Fong 10th St, diagonally opposite the Mövenpick Hotel. This cheery establishment is one of the best budget Chinese restaurants in the city, and has a loyal following among the city's expat Chinese community, who come for the Hong Kong-style food (an eclectic offshoot of Cantonese cooking) and more-ish Peking Duck. The big menu also features plenty of meat and veg options along with seafood, dim sum and claypot sizzlers. Mains from 30dh.

Lemongrass Opposite Lamcy Plaza. This cosy modern restaurant dishes up what is generally reckoned to be the best cheap Thai food in the city. Expect a good range of authentically spicy curries, stir-fries, soups and salads, plus a decent selection of seafood, all backed up with smooth and attentive service. Mains from 40dh.

Manhattan Grill Grand Hyatt ☎04-317 222. One of the city's top steak houses, with big hunks of beautifully cooked prime Wagyu and Nebraska beef served with a variety of sauces and accompanied by a huge wine list. There's also a small selection of seafood dishes for non-carnivores. Mains from around 200dh.

Medzo Wafi ☎04-324 4100. This suave little restaurant offers top-notch Italian-cum-Mediterranean cuisine in a stylish but laidback setting with lots of black leather and white linen – although it feels more like a place for a business lunch than a romantic dinner. Food ranges from pastas, pizzas and risottos through to more substantial meat and seafood mains, all bursting with sunny southern flavours. Mains around 80dh.

Sevilles Wafi ☎04-324 4777. One of the city's few Spanish restaurants, with an authentically rustic wood-and-brick interior and an outdoor terrace. The menu offers a decent spread of traditional tapas (*calamares fritos* and *patatas bravas* among them), meat and fish mains, including five kinds of paella, and assorted regional specialities. There's a good selection of Iberian wines to wash it all down with too. Mains from 70dh.

Thai Chi Wafi ☎04-324 4100. This schizophrenic restaurant offers a mix of contemporary Chinese and traditional Thai cooking, with two kitchens and two dining areas; one a pleasantly rustic Chinese-themed space, the other a more formal Thai room (you can mix and match cuisines regardless of where you sit). Dishes include solidly prepared takes on all the classic Thai dishes and a slightly smaller range of Chinese offerings with the emphasis on seafood. Mains from 70dh. Open daily for lunch and dinner (Fri & Sat lunchtime is buffet food only).

Garhoud

The listings below are marked on the **map** on p.63.

Boardwalk Dubai Creek Yacht Club, Garhoud. Seemingly always packed, this unpretentious restaurant occupies a spectacular perch on the yacht club's creekside boardwalk, with stunning city views. The international menu ranges from pastas and seafood to curries and stir-fries (most mains around 60–90dh). Reservations aren't accepted, so arrive early or be prepared to wait. Alternatively, head for the slightly more sedate and upmarket *Aquarium* upstairs (ⓣ04-295 6000; mains from around 90dh), which has similar creekside views, a spectacular fish tank and a menu of international and Pacific-rim meat and seafood fusion dishes.

QDs Dubai Creek Yacht Club, Garhoud. Fun and good-value restaurant/bar/shisha café in a superb location athwart a large open-air terrace overlooking the Creek. Watch the city lights and the boats plying to and fro while working your way through one of the cheap and well-prepared pizzas, assorted snacks and other light meals, from Lebanese kebabs to fish and chips (mains from around 50dh); there's also a big selection of shisha and a well-stocked bar. It can get surprisingly lively later on, with live DJs occasionally provoking spontaneous outbreaks of dancing. Open daily for dinner only; no reservations.

Thai Kitchen Park Hyatt, Garhoud ⓣ04-602 1234. Occupying part of the *Park Hyatt*'s lovely creekside terrace, this superb restaurant specializes in the little-known cooking of northeast Thailand, with a mix of mainly meat and seafood dishes including unusual offerings like roast duck curry and banana blossom salad with chicken. Food is served in small, tapas-sized portions, meaning that you can work your way through a much wider range of dishes and flavours than you'd normally be able to – although three dishes per person will probably suffice, whatever the waiters may tell you. Dishes from around 30dh. Open daily for dinner only.

Festival City

The listings below are marked on the **map** on p.63.

Belgium Beer Café Crowne Plaza Hotel. This convivial Belgian-style pub-cum-restaurant (also see p.124) serves mainly as a drinking venue, but is also a good place for a nourishing helping of traditional Belgium cuisine, usually featuring Flemish classics like *waterzooi*, braised rabbit in Gueuze beer, and the inevitable mussels. Mains around 70dh.

Reflets par Pierre Gagnaire InterContinental hotel ⓣ04-701 1111. Opened in 2008 by multiple Michelin-starred French chef Pierre Gagnaire, *Reflets* has rapidly established itself as one of the city's top European fine-dining experiences, showcasing Gagnaire's innovative and superbly crafted modern French cuisine. The short menu features a mix of regularly changing meat and seafood creations – anything from blue Atlantic lobster to wild pigeon – backed up by heaps of luscious little *amuses-bouches*. The service is super-smooth, there's a

▲ *Thai Kitchen*

spectacularly expensive wine list and the over-the-top purple decor with pink chandeliers adds a further flourish – although the floor-to-ceiling mirrored toilets aren't to everyone's taste. It's seriously expensive though, with mains from 320–480dh; expect to pay around 2000dh/person total once you've factored in drinks. Open daily for dinner only except Sat.

Sheikh Zayed Road and Downtown Dubai

The listings below are on Sheikh Zayed Road, unless otherwise stated, and are marked on the **map** on p.70.

Cafés

Organic Foods Dubai Mall. Despite its size and profusion of food outlets, the Dubai Mall isn't overly blessed with good places to eat, and this is one of the best. The café itself (which doubles as an organic food store) is spacious and blessedly peaceful compared to most other cafés in the mall. The menu features a good and very reasonably priced selection of additive-free offerings, including soups, sandwiches and salads, and an eclectic selection of mains stretching from burgers, fish 'n' chips and pasta through to steaks, stir-fries and laksa (although surprisingly few vegetarian options). Mains from 25dh.

Shakespeare & Co south side of Al Attar Business Tower on 37th St, off Sheikh Zayed Rd ⓣ04-329 1040, ⓦwww.shakespeareandco.ae. One of the most appealing of the numerous shisha cafés dotted along Sheikh Zayed Road (it's by the southernmost of the two HSBC ATMs), with pleasantly chintzy European decor. The menu has a wide selection of soups, salads, saj, sandwiches and crêpes (from 35dh), plus more substantial mains. There's also a shisha tent outside if you're hankering for a puff.

Restaurants

Benjarong Dusit Thani Hotel ⓣ04-317 4515. No surprises that the signature restaurant at this excellent Thai-owned hotel offers some of the best Royal Thai cooking in Dubai. Set in a delicately painted wooden pavilion on the 24th floor, it covers pretty much every aspect of the country's cuisine. There's a particularly good selection of fish and seafood, plus the usual meat stir-fries and red and yellow curries, although disappointingly few vegetarian offerings. It also does a lively Friday brunch. Mains from 55dh.

The Exchange Grill Fairmont Hotel ⓣ04-311 8559. This small and rather exclusive steakhouse feels more like a room in a private gentlemen's club than a public restaurant, with just fourteen tables surrounded by huge leather armchairs. Sink back and choose from a range of Premium Gold Angus and Wagyu cuts, browse the extensive wine list and then enjoy the views of the crazy traffic on Sheikh Zayed Road through the big windows. Mains from 200dh. Open Sun–Thurs for dinner only.

Hoi An Shangri-La Hotel ⓣ04-343 8888. One of the *Shangri-La*'s collection of small but perfectly formed dining establishments, the *Hoi An* specializes in hybrid Vietnamese-French cuisine served in an elegant wood-panelled restaurant framed with French-colonial-style latticed windows. The unusual menu combines traditional Asian dishes and ingredients with modern Continental cooking techniques to produce a delicate and aromatic range of fusion creations; think rice paper crêpes stuffed with chicken and shrimps and scallops, or grilled five-spice marinated tournedos of beef with crusted garlic yam mushroom sauce. Mains from 115dh. Open daily for dinner only.

Marrakech Shangri-La Hotel ⓣ04-343 8888. Vies with *Tagine* (see p.121) for the title of Dubai's best Moroccan restaurant. The decor – a subtle melange of pale green tiles and Moorish cusped arches – is lovely, while the menu includes a good spread of authentic Moroccan cooking, including couscous dishes and tagines alongside traditional favourites like *harira*, *pastilla* and *tangia*. Mains from 70dh. Open daily for dinner only.

Al Nafoorah Emirates Towers Boulevard shopping complex. One of the city's best Middle Eastern restaurants, this place looks more like a slightly starchy Parisian establishment than a traditional Lebanese restaurant, with floor-length white tablecloths, flouncy chandeliers and tasteful old black-and-white photos on walls. The food is the real deal, however, from the superb array of mezze (from 30dh) through to the perfectly cooked selection of fish, meat grills and kebabs. Mains from 60dh.

The Noodle House Emirates Towers Boulevard shopping complex. A Dubai institution, this cheapish and very cheerful noodle bar caters to an endless stream of diners who huddle up on long communal tables to refuel on excellent South East and East Asian food, with a mix of Thai, Chinese, Malay, Singaporean, Indonesian and Japanese dishes. Reservations aren't accepted, so you might have to queue at busy times. There are other branches at Madinat Jumeirah and the BurJuman Centre, though neither has yet quite managed to recreate the atmosphere of the original. Mains 50–60dh.

Shang Palace Shangri-La Hotel ⑦04-343 8888. This intimate circular restaurant specializes in top-notch traditional Cantonese and Szechuan cooking – with a particularly good selection of seafood ranging from hammour to lobster and mudcrab, plus meat and veg claypots. Mains from 80dh.

Spectrum on One Fairmont Hotel ⑦04-311 8101. This good-looking modern restaurant would be a nice place to eat whatever was on the menu, but it also boasts a unique selling point: there are no fewer than seven separate kitchens, each specializing in a different cuisine, so you can mix and match from Arabian, Indian, Chinese, Japanese, Thai, European and seafood menus as you fancy. The whole concept is typical of Dubai's more-is-more approach to life, and the food is actually pretty good – and where else could you experience a meal of sashimi, chicken tikka masala and creme brule, followed by a pot of English breakfast tea accompanied by chocolate-coated dates? Mains from 100dh, but the "Early Bird" deal gets you 41 percent off the bill if you eat between 6.30 and 8.30pm. Also hosts one of the city's most opulent Friday brunches (550dh; bookings strongly recommended). Open daily for dinner, plus Friday brunch.

Al Tannour Crowne Plaza Hotel ⑦04-331 1111. This large and slightly barn-like restaurant is nothing much to look at, but the atmosphere is comfortable and unpretentious and the food offers a good, if predictable, survey of Middle Eastern standards running through the usual mezze to fragrant fish dishes and kebabs. The place only really gets going late at night, however, when the live music and belly-dancing kicks in (nightly 11pm–2am). Earlier in the evening, the nearby *Al Nafoorah* (see p.117) has a better atmosphere. Mains from around 80dh. Open daily for dinner only.

Teatro Towers Rotana Hotel ⑦04-343 8000. This long-running Sheikh Zayed Road favourite is one of the strip's livelier and less exclusive offerings, with theatrically themed decor and a mix-and-match menu featuring a range of Thai, Chinese, Italian and Indian, plus sushi and sashimi, all well prepared and affordably priced. Mains from around 60dh. Open daily for dinner only.

Thiptara The Palace Hotel, Old Town, Downtown Dubai ⑦04-428 7961. This beautiful Thai restaurant, set in a traditional wooden pavilion jutting out into the waters of the lake behind the Dubai Mall, offers probably the best nightime view of the Burj Khalifa and Dubai Fountain. The menu concentrates on sumptuous "Bangkok-style" seafood, but also offers a fair spread of meat dishes, plus a few veg options. Mains from 130dh. Reservations recommended. Open daily for dinner only.

Trader Vic's Crowne Plaza Hotel ⑦04-305 6399. This lively Polynesian-themed restaurant is best known for its kick-ass cocktails, party atmosphere and live music (a Cuban band plays from 9.20pm till late). The food is an eclectic mixture of grills, seafood and Asian dishes, with filling portions and bright flavours, although it's rather pricey for what you get, with mains from 90dh. There's another branch at the Souk Madinat Jumeirah. Open daily for dinner only; happy hour 6–8pm.

Vu's Restaurant Jumeirah Emirates Towers Hotel ⑦04-319 8088. Perched within the 50th floor of the *Jumeirah Emirates Towers* hotel, this smart and rather formal restaurant is the highest in the city. The view, of course, is a major draw, but the restaurant itself is one of the city's top fine-dining venues, offering modern European food with a touch of Asian influence – slow-roasted pork belly with seared scallops and pineapple chutney, for example, or the signature trio of foie gras and raspberry served three ways. Visit either for the brisk three-course business lunch (165dh) or for a more relaxed evening a la carte experience. Mains from 200dh. Open daily for lunch except Fri & Sat; open daily for dinner except Fri.

Jumeirah

The listings below are marked on the **map** on p.78.

Japengo Palm Strip Mall, Jumeirah Rd. The original branch of this lively Dubai chain of café-restaurants, with chic decor, jazzy music and a fun atmosphere. The menu is the most shamelessly eclectic in town, based around a longish list of Japanese standards (sushi, sashimi, noodles) spliced together with Middle Eastern mezze, Southeast Asian stir-fries, Italian pizzas and pastas, plus sandwiches, salads and a range of Japengo "specials" (meaning anything from yakitori to lamb chops). The end result of this culinary free-for-all is much tastier and more consistent than you might expect, and prices are reasonable too, with mains from 50dh. There are other branches in Wafi, BurJuman, the Oasis Tower on Sheikh Zayed Road, Madinat Jumeirah and Ibn Battuta Mall.

Lime Tree Café Jumeirah Rd ⓣ04-349 8498, ⓦwww.thelimetreecafe.com. Eternally popular with Jumeirah's large community of expat wives and ladies-who-lunch, this cheery little establishment feels more like a neighbourhood café in some upwardly mobile suburb of London or Melbourne than anything remotely Arabian. It's a great place to people watch, while the food's pretty good too, with moreish wraps, focaccias, paninis, quiches, salads, fat cakes and a good selection of tasty fruit juices. Open daily 7.30am–6pm.

Al Qasr Dubai Marine Beach Resort ⓣ04-346 1111. One of the city's better Middle Eastern restaurants, churning out good Lebanese mezze and grills, while the setting on a balcony above the floodlit hotel pool and palms is lovely, too – albeit rather more Barbados than Beirut. It's a better deal at lunch, when you can choose from the extensive a la carte menu with mains from 50dh; in the evenings you're stuck with the obligatory 250dh set menu. There's also a bellydancer and live music nightly from 11pm.

Malecon Dubai Marine Beach Resort ⓣ04-346 1111. This lively bar-restaurant specializes in contemporary Latino food (mains from around 80dh), with a mix of seafood and meat dishes, plus the famous "Cuban Smokeless Cigar", a cigar-shaped chocolate mousse complete with ice-cream ashtray. It's also a good place just for a drink, with live Latin bands nightly from 9–11pm, followed by a late-night DJ; the drinks list includes plenty of mojitos and rum-based cocktails to help bring out your inner *salsero*. Open daily for dinner only.

Sho-Cho Dubai Marine Beach Resort ⓣ04-346 1111. This very chic bar-restaurant dishes up a reasonably priced and prepared list of Japanese standards (mains from 40dh), though it's best known for its cool little outside terrace bar, one of the posiest spots to sup a cocktail in Dubai (see p.126).

▲ *Lime Tree Café*

Burj al Arab and around

The listings below are marked on the **map** on p.82.

Après Mall of the Emirates ⓣ04-341 2575. This cool bar-restaurant offers a good lunch or dinner stop during a visit to the Mall of the Emirates, with wonderful views over the slopes of Ski Dubai through big picture windows. The range of international food includes boeuf bourguignon, coq au vin, Australian rib-eye steak and fish & chips, plus excellent thin-crust pizzas (from 60dh). It's also a good place for a drink, with its long mirrored bar, from whose vast array of backlit bottles staff conjure up some of the city's best classic and contemporary cocktails, plus draught and bottled beers. Mains from 70dh.

Magnolia Madinat Jumeirah ⓣ04-366 6730. Dubai's only upmarket vegetarian restaurant, occupying a blissfully tranquil location in the sprawling gardens of the Madinat Jumeirah near the Talisse Spa. There's a tempting selection of innovative vegetarian cuisine on offer, featuring an eclectic range of international flavours and ingredients – anything from ricotta-stuffed kamut cannelloni to miso-glazed beetroot with leek potato mash and green asparagus. Mains around 75dh. Open for dinner only; closed Tues.

Al Mahara Burj al Arab ☏04-301 7600. Perhaps the more appealing of the Burj al Arab's two signature restaurants, *Al Mahara* looks like some kind of fantastic underwater grotto, entered through a huge golden arch and with seats arranged around a giant fish tank. There's a range of gourmet international seafood to choose from – Dover sole Grenoblaise, Atlantic seabass, Omani lobster and so on – although you'll get equally good food and better views at nearby *Pierchic* and *Pisces* (see below) at around half the price. Mains around 370dh. Open daily for dinner only.

Al Muntaha Burj al Arab ☏04-301 7600. For the ultimate splurge in the *Burj*, head to *Al Muntaha*, ("The Highest"), referring to the restaurant's stunning location at the summit of the famed hotel, although it does equally well to describe the prices. The menu features fine international dining – anything from Wagyu fillet Rossini to pan-fried barramundi – and the views are spectacular, although some visitors find the psychedelic decor unappealing. If you just want to have a quick look it's much cheaper to come for a drink at the attached Skyview Bar (see p.127). Mains around 385dh. Friday brunch 495dh. Open daily for dinner only, plus Friday brunch.

Pai Tai Al Qasr Hotel, Madinat Jumeirah ☏04-366 6730. This beautiful Thai restaurant is one of the city's most romantic places to eat, with stunning *Burj al Arab* views from the candlelit terrace and live music murmuring gently in the background. The menu features all the usual Thai classics, including spicy salads and meat and seafood curries. It's not the most original menu in town, although given the setting you probably won't care. Mains around 110dh. Open daily for dinner only.

La Parilla Jumeirah Beach Hotel ☏04-406 8999. Perched atop the *Jumeirah Beach Hotel*, this Argentinian-themed steakhouse boasts superb views of the *Burj al Arab,* excellent Argentinian, Australian and Wagyu steaks and an appealing splash of Latin atmosphere, with live music and tango dancers nightly – ask nicely and the manager might even sing you a song. Mains around 170dh. Open daily for dinner only.

Pierchic Al Qasr Hotel, Madinat Jumeirah ☏04-366 6730. One of the city's most spectacularly situated restaurants, perched at the end of a breezy pier jutting out in front of the grandiose *Al Qasr* hotel, and with unbeatable views of the nearby *Burj Al Arab*, *Jumeirah Beach Hotel* and Madinat Jumeirah. The mainly seafood menu has prices to match the location, with a selection of international-style fine-dining fish and seafood offerings, ranging from Chilean seabass to Norwegian king crab, plus a few meat and a couple of token vegetarian choices. Mains around 165dh.

Pisces Madinat Jumeirah ☏04-366 6730. One of top seafood restaurants in town, with cool blue-ish decor and a lovely outdoor terrace overlooking the Madinat Jumeirah. The menu focuses on international seafood done with a contemporary twist – confit grey snapper with seafood dumplings and king crab risotto, for example. It's all very inventive but equally expensive, with mains around 190dh. Open daily for dinner only.

Zheng He Mina A'Salam ☏04-366 6730. This classy Chinese restaurant – generally reckoned one of the best in the city – offers a range of "progressive" Chinese fine-dining, sometimes using unexpected ingredients and flavour-combinations (sauteed Dover sole with celery and sambol sauce, for example), along with excellent dim sum. Seating is either inside the svelte restaurant itself or outside on the beautiful *Burj*-facing terrace. Mains from 80dh.

Dubai Marina

The listings below are marked on the **map** on p.87.

La Baie Ritz Carlton Hotel ☏04-399 4000. This decidedly formal, old-school French-style restaurant would feel very odd in most parts of Dubai, but works well in the context of the *Ritz Carlton*'s rather patrician setting. The menu features a very small range of so-called "progressive" European meat and fish dishes (but no vegetarian options), meaning things like cider-braised pork belly with butter-poached Normandy crayfish, Asian pear and salsa verde. Mains from 130dh. Open for dinner only; closed Sun.

BiCE Hilton Jumeirah Beach Hotel ☏04-399 1111. This smooth modern Italian restaurant is generally reckoned the best in the southern city (it's pronounced "Bee-Chay" –

the nickname of Beatrice Ruggeri, who founded the original BiCE restaurant in Milan in 1926). Food includes tasty pizzas and pastas (from 80dh) bursting with fresh ingredients and flavours, plus a mix of meat and seafood mains including regional classics like Sicilian rigatoni and more contemporary creations like lobster carpaccio. A second Dubai branch, *BiCE Mare*, specializing in seafood, has recently opened at Souk al Bahar. Mains from 150dh.

Buddha Bar Grosvenor House Hotel ☎04-317 6000. Modelled after the famous Parisian joint, this superb bar-restaurant is a sight in its own right: a huge, sepulchral space hung with dozens of red-lantern chandeliers and presided over by an enormous golden Buddha, with classic Buddha Bar soundtracks murmuring away in the background. The menu features a fine array of Japanese and pan-Asian cooking, with sushi, maki and sashimi plates alongside Thai- and Chinese-inspired meat, seafood and vegetarian mains. It's a bit pricey for what you get, with mains from 155dh, but the setting is superb. Alternatively, just pop in for a drink to sample the atmosphere and try one of the bar's long, minty cocktails. It's wildly popular, so advance reservations are essential. Open daily for dinner only.

Eauzone Arabian Courtyard, One&Only Royal Mirage ☎04-399 9999. Regularly voted the most romantic restaurant in Dubai, with seating within little Arabian tents set up amid the beautifully floodlit waters of one of the hotel's swimming pools – which seems to transform by night into a luminous, palm-studded lagoon. It's also open for lunch, but doesn't look nearly as beautiful. The food consists of a decent, if rather pricey, array of European cuisine with an Asian twist, largely a mix of meat and seafood dishes. The only problem is getting a reservation; if you can't, console yourself with a drink at the beautiful attached bar – just make sure you don't fall into the water on your way out. Mains from 120dh, or from 75dh at lunch.

Indego Grosvenor House Hotel ☎04-317 6000. Overseen by Vineet Bhatia, India's first Michelin-starred chef, this stylish restaurant showcases his distinctive style of "contemporary Indian" cooking, blending subcontinental and international ingredients and techniques to unusual effect – think lamb chop biriyani or hammour poached in raw mango-flavoured coastal gravy. Mains 110–280dh. Open for dinner only; closed Sat.

Nina Arabian Courtyard, One&Only Royal Mirage ☎04-399 9999. Along with *Indego* (see above), this is Dubai's most innovative Indian restaurant, combining Indian spices and flavours with international ingredients and cooking techniques – anything from traditional butter chicken through to tandoori salmon steak with yellow mustard sauce, or frogs' legs and rambutan in pickling five spices. The sumptuous orange decor, complete with oddly mismatched chandeliers, red Chinese lanterns and quasi-Moroccan arches, adds its own curious touch of hybrid magic. Mains from 85dh. Open daily for dinner only; closed Sun.

Rhodes Mezzanine Grosvenor House Hotel ☎04-317 6000. Dubai outpost of UK celebrity chef Gary Rhodes, with a short but inventive menu showcasing the chef's distinctive brand of modern European cuisine, accompanied by classic British puddings like jam rolypoly and bread-and-butter pudding. The decor – a pure-white space dotted with brightly-coloured armchairs – has its own slightly Alice-in-Wonderland appeal. Mains 150–240dh. Open for dinner only; closed Sun.

Tagine The Palace, One&Only Royal Mirage ☎04-399 9999. This sumptuous little Moroccan restaurant is a feast for both the eye and taste buds. The beautiful Moorish decor is complemented by rich cooking, including spicy harira soup, lamb's brain and pigeon pie, a delicious selection of tagines (sweetly flavoured with ingredients like honey, crushed almonds, lemon, red olives, raisins and apricot), plus a few kebabs and seafood options. There's also good live music, and friendly service. Mains from around 80dh. Open for dinner daily except Mon.

Zaatar w Zeit The Walk at Jumeirah Beach Residence. One of the best of the disappointingly average string of cafés which line The Walk. Cheap fast-food with a Lebanese twist is the focus here, with salads, wraps and pizzas alongside various kinds of *manakish* (a kind of Middle Eastern-style pizza served with thyme, yoghurt and cheese) and other Lebanese-style snacks. Mains 14–32dh. There are other branches on Sheikh Zayed Road next to the *Shangri-La* hotel and in the Dubai Mall.

10

Drinking

You won't go thirsty in Dubai, and the huge number of drinking holes tucked away all over the city attests to the extraordinary degree to which this Muslim city has gone in accommodating western tastes. The best **bars** encapsulate Dubai at its most beguiling and opulent, whether your taste is for lounging on cushions in alfresco Arabian-themed venues or sipping champagne in cool contemporary cocktail bars – and there are often superlative views thrown in for good measure too. Many hotels also have English-style **pubs**, with obligatory faux-wooden decor and banks of TVs showing the latest sporting events – these are a lot less stylish than the city's bars, but usually a bit cheaper.

Not surprisingly, boozing in Dubai comes at a **price**, thanks to high government taxes. A pint of beer will usually set you back around 30dh, a glass of wine around 35–40dh and a basic cocktail around 50dh. Costs in the city's pubs can be cut (slightly) by looking out for happy hours and special promotions, usually chalked up on a blackboard behind the bar.

Alcohol is only served in hotel restaurants, bars and pubs, along with a small number of mall-based restaurants. It's not served in independent restaurants, and is not available over the counter in any shop or supermarket in the city. The only exception to this is if you're a resident expat in possession of an **official liquor licence**, in which case you can buy alcohol from one of the city's two authorized off-licence chains. Still, visitors can bring in alcohol up to the limits outlined on p.35. In addition, note that alcohol is not served anywhere until after sundown during Ramadan (see p.29). Most bars **open** at 6pm or 7pm and stay open till around 1–3am; pubs generally open from around noon until 2am. Most of the city's more upmarket drinking holes accept **reservations** (phone numbers for relevant places are listed), although a few of the more club-style DJ bars sometimes require a certain minimum spend in return for booking you a table.

Although Dubai is extremely liberal in its provision of alcohol, be aware that any form of **public drunkenness** is strongly frowned upon, and may even get you arrested, particularly if accompanied by any form of lewd behaviour, which can be

Ladies nights

Ladies Nights are something of a Dubai institution. These are basically an attempt to drum up custom during the quieter midweek evenings, and are usually held on Wednesday, Thursday or, most commonly, Tuesday nights, with various places around the city offering all sorts of deals, ranging from a couple of free cocktails up to complimentary champagne all night. Yet the free booze sometimes comes at a price – unaccompanied ladies may spend half their time fighting off the attentions of the would-be amorous blokes who tend to congregate on such occasions. Pick up a copy of *Time Out Dubai* for latest listings.

Booze with views

Dubai has a wonderful collection of **high-rise bars** with superlative city views, and prices in many places aren't quite as sky-high as you might imagine. Some of the best places include:

Neos 63rd floor, *The Address*, Downtown Dubai. Wonderful views over the Burj Khalifa and Downtown Dubai. See p.125.

Vu's 51st floor, *Emirates Tower*, Sheikh Zayed Rd. Chic modern bar atop the landmark Emirates Towers. See p.125.

Bar 44 44th floor, *Grosvenor House*, Dubai Marina. Glitzy cocktail bar with stunning marina views. See p.127.

Skyview Bar 27th floor, *Burj al Arab*. Swanky cocktail bar at the top of the iconic hotel. See p.127.

Eclipse 26th floor, *InterContinental*, Festival City. Funky contemporary bar with birds' eye view of Festival City and the Creek. See p.124.

Uptown Bar 24th floor, *Jumeirah Beach Hotel*. At the top of the JBH, with superb views of the *Burj al Arab* and southern Dubai. See p.127.

New Asia Bar 18th floor, *Raffles*, Oud Metha. Very cool contemporary bar at the summit of this spectacular pyramidal hotel. See p.124.

Up on the Tenth 10th floor *Radisson Blu Dubai Deira Creek*, Deira. Fusty old hotel bar, but with unbeatable views of the Creek by night. See p.124.

taken to include even fairly innocuous acts like kissing in public (see p.31); wait until you get back to your room. The city also has a zero-tolerance policy towards **drink-driving** – worth remembering if you get behind the wheel on the morning after a heavy night, since even the faintest trace of alcohol in your system is likely to land you in jail.

Bur Dubai

The listings below are marked on the **map** on p.44.

Pubs

George & Dragon Ambassador Hotel, Al Falah St. This simple but pleasantly cosy little pub won't win any style awards but has the important distinction of serving up the cheapest beer in the city; at the time of writing it was the only place in Dubai where you could reliably pick up a pint for 20dh.

Sherlock Holmes Arabian Courtyard Hotel, Al Fahidi St. One of the nicer English pubs in Bur Dubai, with a relaxed atmosphere, flock wallpaper, leatherette chairs and glass cases full of vaguely Sherlock Holmes-related memorabilia. It does decent pub food, and regular beer promotions keep things busy.

Viceroy Bar Four Points Sheraton Hotel, Khalid bin al Waleed Rd. This traditional English-style pub is the nicest in Bur Dubai, complete with fake oak-beamed ceiling, authentic wooden bar and oodles of comfy leather armchairs. There's a decent range of draught beers and other drinks, plus assorted sports on the overhead TVs, and it's also a conveniently short stagger to the excellent *Antique Bazaar* Indian restaurant (see p.111).

Deira

The listings below are marked on the **map** on p.54.

Issimo Cocktail Lounge Hilton Dubai Creek Hotel, Baniyas Rd ⓣ04-227 1111. Occupying a corner of the *Hilton*'s ultra-modern, chrome-obsessed ground floor, this chic little cocktail bar has a cute boat-shaped bar and a refreshingly unposey atmosphere. A good spot for an aperitif or digestif before or after a meal at *Verre* (see p.113) upstairs. Daily noon–4pm & 6am–2am.

Ku Bu Radisson Blu Dubai Deira Creek Hotel, Baniyas Rd ⓣ04-205 7033. Intimate little drinking hole with a fancy backlit bar, moody lighting and big comfy sofas and barside perches. It's usually pleasantly chilled early in the evening, though things can get livelier later on when the beautiful people of Deira arrive for cocktails and the resident DJ (nightly except Fri 9pm–3am) cranks up the volume. The drinks menu majors on champagnes, cocktails and shooters, though there's a passable wine list and draught beer. Best of all, however, is the view from the gents' loos, where one-way mirrors allow you look into the bar while going about your business.

The Pub Radisson Blu Dubai Deira Creek Hotel, Baniyas Rd. Spacious and usually fairly peaceful English-style pub, complete with the usual fake wooden bar and dozens of TVs screening global sports.

Up on the Tenth 10th floor, Radisson Blu Dubai Deira Creek Hotel, Baniyas Rd ☎04-205 7033. Not the most stylish venue in Dubai – the 80s'-style mirrored Manhattan skyline-effect behind the bar is so dated it's almost an antique, the drinks list is feeble and the whole place is poky and usually stinks of cigars. On the upside, it also offers just about the best Creek views to be had in the city centre, with memorable vistas of the water and twinkling lights on either side. Arrive early (the bar opens at 6.30pm), grab a window seat and watch the city light up. A jazz singer and pianist perform daily (except Fri) from 10pm.

The inner suburbs

The listings below are marked on the **map** on p.63.

Belgium Beer Café Crowne Plaza Hotel, Festival City. This convivial Belgian-style pub-cum-restaurant is one of the highlights of the new Festival City development, with an eye-catching traditional wooden interior and an excellent range of speciality beers on tap or by the bottle, including draught Hoegaarden, Leffe and Kriek. There's also good traditional Belgian cuisine (see p.116).

Eclipse InterContinental Hotel, Festival City ☎04-701 1111. Swanky modern bar at the top of this fancy new hotel, offering huge views over Sheikh Zayed Road and the Creek, plus a good range of beers, wines and cocktails at surprisingly average prices.

New Asia Bar Raffles, Wafi ☎04-314 9888. Occupying the spectacular glass-walled pyramid at the summit of the *Raffles* hotel, this slick and very upmarket bar boasts beautiful city views, sleek contemporary Asian styling – complete with an enormous quasi-Polynesian ebony statue looming over the entrance – plus a cocktail list as long as your arm. Try the "Dubai Sling", the local remake of the classic "Singapore Sling" cocktail, invented in the original *Raffles* hotel in Singapore sometime in the early 1900s. Dress code is "smart-elegant".

The Terrace Park Hyatt Hotel, Garhoud ☎04-602 1234. Seductive waterside bar, with seating either indoors or outside on the terrace overlooking the Creek and the numerous fancy yachts parked at the adjacent marina. It's all very romantic and mellow, the mood helped along by smooth chill-out music and a nice selection of cocktails and other tipples. It also has a good selection of superior bar snacks and meals if you get peckish and can't be bothered to wander over to the adjacent *Thai Kitchen*.

Vintage Wafi, Oud Metha ☎04-324 4100. This cosy little wine bar is perhaps the nicest in the city, with a good spread of international vintages, including a decent selection by the glass, and a convivial atmosphere. There's also champagnes, beers, spirits and soft drinks, plus a few superior bar snacks and a cheese board should you get peckish.

Sheikh Zayed Road and Downtown Dubai

The listings below are all located on or just off Sheikh Zayed Road, except where noted, and are marked on the **map** on p.70.

The Agency Emirates Towers Boulevard shopping complex ☎04-319 8088. A rather sedate-looking wood-panelled wine bar, quiet enough during the daytime, though it often gets packed out with a noisy expat crowd in the evenings, especially over the weekend. There's a huge wine list with vintages from all the world's major wine-producing countries by the glass or bottle, plus tasting selections, assorted champagnes and a small menu of fancy bar snacks.

Blue Bar Novotel, World Trade Centre ☎04-332 0000. This stylish little bar is a pleasant spot for a mellow drink earlier in the evening, with a sedate crowd and a good selection of speciality Belgian beers, plus cocktails, wines, premium whiskeys and superior bar meals. It can get lively later on in the evening, particularly Weds–Fri, when there's live music (mainly blues and soul) from around 9.30pm until 1am.

Cin Cin **Fairmont Hotel ⓣ04-311 8316.** One of the most exclusive and expensive bars in the city; more a superior gentleman's club than party venue, attracting a sedate older crowd of monied bon viveurs. Wine-buffs can choose from around 450 vintages, including a few bottles of the classic 1989 Château Petrus, selling for a cool 68,000dh; there's also a well-stocked selection of vodkas and rare whiskeys to browse, as well as a special "cigar bar" with walk-in humidor. A discreet live DJ supplies an ambient soundtrack Tues–Thurs from 9.30pm. Dress code is smart-casual/formal.

Double Decker **Al Murooj Rotana Hotel.** One of the liveliest pubs in town, with quirky decor themed after the old London Routemaster buses and usually busy with a more-than-averagely tanked-up crowd of expats and Western tourists. There's also a live DJ most evenings (Mon–Thurs from 9pm, Fri from 5pm).

iKandy **Shangri-La Hotel ⓣ04-343 8888.** Ibiza-style chill-out venue set around the pool-side terrace on the fourth floor of the *Shangri-La*, with big white sofas to recline on and ambient music in the background. Closed during summer.

Long's Bar **Towers Rotana Hotel.** Proud home to the the longest bar in the Middle East, this English-style pub offers one of the strip's more convivial and downmarket drinking holes. There are all the usual tipples, pop-rock soundtrack, TV sports and other Dubai pub essentials, plus a separate dining area serving up basic pub grub. The small dance area sees action during the intermittent DJ and live music nights, and – in a slightly more spontaneous fashion – towards closing time during the bar's innumerable drinks promotions.

Lotus One **World Trade Centre, next to the Novotel lobby ⓣ04-329 3200, ⓦwww.lotusonedubai.com.** Very glam bar with a kind of retro-chic decor (think fluffy cushions, furry poufs, lotus-shaped candles and a couple of swinging chairs) and a very modish crowd. The place really kicks off during its regular weekend DJ nights, though at other times the atmosphere is fairly laidback, with discreet modern jazz/chill-out sounds.

Neos **The Address Hotel, Emaar Blvd, Downtown Dubai ⓣ04-436 8888.** The highest bar in Dubai at the time of writing, with great 63rd floor views over the surrounding Downtown Dubai and Burj Khalifa – although the overblown decor may leave you shaken rather than stirred. Drinks include a decent range of wines (from 40dh) and cocktails (from 60dh), at slightly less elevated prices than you might fear, but no beer.

Oscar's Vine Society **Crowne Plaza Hotel ⓣ04-331 1111.** If you like your wine bars rustic and with an overwhelming smell of cheese, you'll love *Oscar's*, which manages a fair impression of a Provençale wine cellar in the unlikely setting of the fourth floor of the *Crowne Plaza*. Tipples include a modest spread of international wines, with assorted French-style light meals and snacks to accompany.

Vu's Bar **Jumeirah Emirates Towers Hotel ⓣ04-319 8088.** On the 51st floor of Dubai's top business hotel, this is one of the highest licensed perches in Dubai. The small, capsule-like bar itself, with floor-to-ceiling windows on one side, feels like the business end of a space rocket, and the muted music, dark decor, dim lighting and rather subdued ambience means there's not much to distract one from wide-eyed contemplation of the endless city lights below. Tipples from the vast drinks list run the gamut of cocktails, mocktails, shorts, beers, wines and champagnes, all at slightly less stratospheric prices than one might expect. Dress is smart-casual. Daily 6pm–3am.

▲ *Vu's Bar*

Jumeirah

The listings below are marked on the **map** on p.78.

Boudoir Dubai Marine Beach Resort ⓣ04-345 5995 or 346-1111, ⓦwww.myboudoir.com. This sultry bar-cum-nightclub looks like the apartment of an upper-class nineteenth-century Parisian courtesan, with plush red drapes, chintzy chandeliers and an indecent number of mirrors. The whole place can feel oddly sleazy (think Emile Zola with tequila slammers) and is a good place to catch up with the city's Lebanese party crowd drowning in cocktails and champagne. Music features a mix of hip-hop and house, with occasional visiting international DJs. At the time of writing, the ladies night deal included free champagne all night on Tues, Fri and Sun; otherwise, it's couples only. Open 9pm–3am nightly.

Malecon Dubai Marine Beach Resort ⓣ04-346 1111. This popular restaurant (see p.119) turns into more of a bar-cum-live music venue later in the evening, with live Latin bands nightly 9am–11am, followed by a DJ.

Sho-Cho Dubai Marine Beach Resort ⓣ04-346 1111. Very chic, very posey little bar-cum-Japanese restaurant (see p.119), eternally popular among the city's Lebanese and Bollywood party set and still one of *the* places to be seen. Most nights see a cast of confirmed fashionistas ranging from freshly tanned tourists to Lebanese pop stars slumming around in expensive scraps of Armani and Chanel. Dress to impress (or alternatively go and buy some fake labels in Karama), though you'll have to arrive unfashionably early if you want to get a seat. Live DJs (nightly from 11pm except Sun; retro at weekends; House the rest of the week) add to the very cool ambience. Open daily for dinner only (kitchen closes at midnight, bar stays open till 2am or later).

Burj al Arab and around

The listings below are marked on the **map** on p.82.

360° Jumeirah Beach Hotel ⓣ04-406 8769. The ultimate Dubaian chill-out bar, spectacularly located at the end of a long breakwater which arcs out into the Gulf opposite the *Jumeirah Beach Hotel* and *Burj al Arab*, and offering sublime after-dark views of both. White sofas and beanbags lie scattered around the circular open-air terrace, filled most nights with a very mellow crowd of tanned tourists and expat Arabs who lounge in attitudes of fashionable insensibility over cocktails, beers and shishas, while resident and visiting DJs pump hypnotic house out into the night. Closed June–August. Occasional entrance charge when visiting DJs are in residence.

Bahri Bar Mina A'Salam ⓣ04-366 6730. This superb little Arabian-style outdoor terrace is deservedly popular, liberally scattered with canopied sofas, Moorish artefacts and Persian carpets, and offering drop-dead gorgeous views of the *Burj* and Madinat Jumeirah. It's particularly lovely towards sunset, though once you've got stuck into the long list of cocktails and wines, plus relatively affordable draught beer, you might find the time passing quicker than you anticipated.

BarZar Souk Madinat Jumeirah. The bar here is busy and unappealing, but the big outdoor terrace is one of the Madinat's best chill-out spaces, with views of the fake Arabian wind towers and waterways and lots of beanbags to crash out on over drinks, plus a good range of shisha.

▲ *Bahri Bar*

Koubba **Al Qasr** ☎ **04-366 6730.** One of the most memorable of the many idyllic drinking holes scattered about the Madinat Jumeirah complex, this superb Arabian-themed bar offers jaw-dropping views over *Al Qasr* and the *Burj al Arab* from its spacious terrace and can prove remarkably difficult to leave once you've settled down on one of its comfy sofas scattered with piles of brightly coloured cushions. There's a good list of classic and contemporary cocktails, a small wine list and reasonably priced draught pints.

Left Bank **Souk Madinat Jumeirah.** Jostling for elbow room among the string of incredibly popular eating and drinking spots along the Souk Madinat Jumeirah waterfront, this cool but unpretentious modern bar offers a good spot to watch the passing scene if you can bag a table on the outside terrace; the indoor section is convivial as well. There's a big selection of wine, beer and cocktails, plus rather superior international bar food (from 80dh) and cheaper sandwiches. Noon–2am daily. No reservations.

Skyview Bar **Burj al Arab** ☎ **04-301 7600 or** Ⓔ BAArestaurants@jumeirah.com for required reservations. Landmark bar perched near the summit of the *Burj al Arab*, with colourful, slightly psychedelic decor pus vast sea and city views – coming for a drink here is currently the cheapest way to see the inside of this fabulous hotel (for more on which see p.81). The huge drinks list majors in cocktails (from 100dh), but also sports a decent spread of wines, spirits, mocktails and even a few beers. There's a minimum spend of 275dh per person.

Uptown Bar **Jumeirah Beach Hotel** ☎ **04-406 8769.** Superb views of the *Burj al Arab* and southern Dubai are the main draw at this place, located on the 24th floor of the *Jumeirah Beach Hotel*. There's indoor and outdoor seating, plus a reasonable drinks list, although the decor is disappointingly humdrum for such a fine perch.

Dubai Marina

The listings below are marked on the **map** on p.87.

Bar 44 **Grosvenor House** ☎ **04-399 8888.** On the hotel's 44th floor, this svelte contemporary bar offers peerless views of the entire marina development, with twinkling high-rises stretching away in every direction – as memorable a view of the southern city as you're likely to get, short of climbing in a helicopter. The drinks list is as upmarket as the setting, with a big selection of wallet-emptying champagnes alongside cool cocktails and other designer beverages.

Barasti Bar **Le Méridien Mina Sehayi.** One of southern Dubai's most consistently popular nightspots, this fun, two-level beachside bar is more or less always packed with an eclectic crowd of tourists and expats. Downstairs is usually more Ibiza chill-out, with cool ambient music and beautiful people slumped over shisha, while upstairs is generally noisier, with live DJs and more of a party atmosphere.

Rooftop Bar **Arabian Courtyard, One&Only Royal Mirage** ☎ **04-399 9999.** The most romantic bar in the southern city, this seductive, Arabian-themed rooftop establishment offers one of Dubai's ultimate orientalist fantasies, with Moroccan-style pavilions scattered with cushions, silver-tray tables and other assorted ethnic artefacts; vaguely psychedelic lighting and a smooth live DJ add to the *1001 Nights* ambience. The downstairs bar-cum-pub area is also attractive, with a nice outdoor terrace, although inside the Arabian style is slightly neutered by the banks of TVs dotted about the place showing wall-to-wall sports.

11

Nightlife, entertainment and the arts

Like pretty much everywhere else in the Gulf, Dubai only really gets going after dark. As dusk falls, the streets light up in a blaze of neon and the pavements begin to fill up with cosmopolitan crowds of Emiratis, Arabs, Westerners, Indians and Filipinos. The city's vibrant **nightlife** takes many forms. Western expats and tourists tend to head out to the city's restaurants, bars and clubs, while locals and expat Arabs can be found relaxing in the city's myriad shisha cafés, and shopping malls and souks across the city fill up with crowds of consumers from all walks of Dubai society. Most places stay open until around midnight, while bars and clubs kick on until the small hours.

In terms of more **cultural** diversions, there's significantly less on offer. Dubai is widely derided as the city which culture forgot – and in many ways the stereotype is richly deserved. The city has five-star hotels, luxury spas, celebrity chefs and shopping malls aplenty, but until a few years back lacked even a single functioning theatre. Even now, Dubai's musical life is largely limited to Filipino cover bands and the occasional big-name visiting rock act.

Yet things are changing – abeit slowly. The city now hosts a decent range of cultural festivals, including good film and jazz events (see p.30), although outside festival time the city's cultural calendar can feel decidedly undernourished. Where Dubai has scored a major success, however, is in establishing itself as the Gulf's **art capital**, boasting a remarkable number of independent galleries; many of these are set up in unlikely places around the city by expats from around the Arab world and showcase a healthy spread of cutting-edge work by a range of international artists.

Clubs

Dubai has a reasonably busy **clubbing** scene, driven by a mix of Western expats and tourists along with the city's large expat Arab (particularly Lebanese) community. Venues come and go on an annual basis, so it's worth checking the latest listings in *Time Out Dubai* or visit Ⓦwww.platinumlist.ae to find out what's new and happening. Music tends to be a fairly mainstream selection of house, hip-hop and r'n'b (perhaps with a splash of Arabic pop), although a healthy number of visiting international DJs help keep things fresh. The emphasis at more upmarket places still tends to be on posing and pouting – expect to see lots of beautiful young things from Beirut or Bombay quaffing champagne and inspecting their make-up – although there's more fashion-free and egalitarian clubbing to be had at places like *Zinc* and *Chi@TheLodge*, the latter being Dubai's nearest equivalent to an Ibiza-style super-club. Most clubs don't get going until at least midnight or 1am and close promptly at 3am. Entrance **charges** generally vary depending on who's playing; occasionally it's free, but more usually expect to pay 50–100dh. Most places also have a **couples-only policy** and rather sniffy doormen. Dress to impress, or prepare to be turned away.

Alpha Le Méridien Village, Le Méridien, Garhoud ⓣ04-702 2640, ⓦwww.alphaclub.ae; see Inner Suburbs map, p.63. Dubai's leading alternative club, an intimate little venue with quirky Neoclassical decor – remnants of its former incarnation as a Greek restaurant. Hosts a wide range of DJs and bands, including emerging local acts spinning or playing an eclectic range of music.

Apartment Jumeirah Beach Hotel ⓣ04 406 8999; see Burj al Arab & around map, p.82. Long-running club tucked away around the back of the *Jumeirah Beach Hotel*. It's divided into two sections: a larger club area with dancefloor and the more chilled-out lounge, with a mix of r'n'b, house, plus salsa nights.

Chi@The Lodge Al Nasr Leisureland, Oud Metha ⓣ04-337 9471, ⓦwww.lodgedubai.com; see Inner Suburbs map, p.63. Chi has space for about 3500 and an eclectic music policy. There are five different areas (each with its own soundtrack) ranging from the snooty VIP lounge to the main garden, hosting regular big-name international DJs and occasional bands. Entrance charges vary, depending on what's on. Expect to queue later at night, especially over the weekend.

Kasbar The Palace, One&Only Royal Mirage; see Dubai Marina map, p.87. This very superior-looking club shares the opulent Moroccan styling of the rest of the *Royal Mirage* complex and is spread over three large floors, with the resident DJ serving up a mixed menu of Arabian and international tunes. It's sometimes lively, but at other times there's more of a crowd and a better atmosphere at the hotel's *Rooftop Bar* (see p.127). Open daily except Sun 9pm–3am. Hotel guests free. Non-guests couples only 70dh/person.

Zinc Crowne Plaza Hotel; see Sheikh Zayed Road & around map, p.70. One of the longest running and most enduringly popular clubs in Dubai, thanks to an eclectic soundtrack, unposey atmosphere and the off-duty air crews that frequent it. Music features a mix of retro, r'n'b, hip-hop and house depending on the night, plus Saturday salsa sessions. Couples only. 100dh entrance Thurs–Sun, 50dh rest of week. Nightly 10pm–3am.

Shisha cafés

For an authentic Arabian alternative to the pub, club or bar, nothing beats a visit to one of Dubai's **shisha cafés**. These are the places where local Emiratis and expat Arabs tend to head when they want to kick back, lounging around over endless cups of coffee while puffing away on a shisha (also known as waterpipe), filling the air with aromatic clouds of perfumed smoke – far more fragrant than your average smoke-filled pub. Many of Dubai's Arabian restaurants also do a good line in shisha, and the best places will have twenty or more varieties to choose from, with all sorts of fruit-scented flavours, plus a house special or two.

Along with the two places listed below, **other good places for shisha** include bars such as *Barzar* at Souk Madinat Jumeirah (p.84) and *360°* at the *Jumeirah Beach Hotel* (p.83), along with cafes such as the *Creek View Restaurant* (see p.113), *Elements* (p.115), *Kan Zaman* in Bur Dubai (p.111), *QD's* in Garhoud (p.116), and *Shakespeare & Co.* on Sheikh Zayed Road (p.117).

A'Rukn The Courtyard Souk Madinat Jumeirah; see Burj al Arab & around map, p.82. The picturesque central courtyard of the Madinat Jumeirah offers a captivating place to kick back over a pricey shisha (65–85dh) and watch the engaging night-time life of the souk – from sunburnt tourists to robed Emiratis and their *abbeya*-clad wives – roll past. There's also mezze and Lebanese grills to snack on, plus a decent drinks list, making this one of the few places in the city where you can enjoy a shisha and a tipple at the same time. Daily from 6pm.

Arabian Courtyard Arabian Courtyard, One&Only Royal Mirage; see Dubai Marina map, p.87. This beautiful Moroccan-style courtyard, with fairy-lit palms and seating in pretty little open-side tented pavilions, provides the magical setting for one of Dubai's most romantic shisha venues. Choose from sixteen varieties of shisha (40dh), plus assorted mezze, Lebanese grills and a big list of beers, wines and cocktails. *The Palace Courtyard*, in the same hotel's Palace wing, is similar. Daily 7pm–12.30am.

Live music

Dubai's regular live music scene is limited to a small number of venues, usually featuring local bands bashing out cover-versions of classic rock tracks, although occasional big-name international acts drop by from time to time, and things look up considerably during the Dubai Jazz Festival (see p.30), not to mention the Womad festival down the road at Abu Dhabi (see p.30).

Dubai Media City Amphitheatre Dubai Media City; see Dubai Marina map, p.87. This spacious outdoor arena, in the heart of Dubai Media City and with a capacity of 15,000, is the city's main venue for big shows by visiting international music acts, and also hosts the annual Dubai Jazz Festival (see p.30). Check *Time Out Dubai* (Ⓦwww.timeoutdubai.com) for details of forthcoming events.

Jambase Souk Madinat Jumeirah; see Burj al Arab & around map, p.82. Popular live-music bar in the Souk Madinat Jumeirah, hosting a variety of enthusiastic local cover bands. Not the most original music you'll ever hear, but the cracking party atmosphere generally compensates. Open nightly except Sun & Mon.

The Music Room Majestic Hotel, Mankhool Road; see Bur Dubai map, p.44. This dimly lit hotel pub serves up a classic slice of offbeat Bur Dubai nightlife, hosting the legendary Rock Spiders (daily except Mon 9.45pm–2.15am), a heavy-metal Filipino cover band with huge amps and plenty of attitude, who draw a loyal crowd of tanked-up tourists and expats singing along to Bon Jovi classics, plus lots of Thai working girls touting for custom from their barside stools.

Peanut Butter Jam Wafi; see Inner Suburbs map, p.63. Popular informal music evenings held on the open-air rooftop terrace of the Wafi complex, with local jazz and rock musicians belting out a mix of cover versions and assorted original tunes to a chilled-out audience reclining on bean bags under the stars. Fridays from Oct–May 8pm–midnight.

Cinema

Dubai is well equipped with a string of modern multiplexes serving up all the latest Hollywood blockbusters, plus a few Bollywood flicks and the occasional Arabic film – although screenings of alternative and art-house cinema are rare outside the excellent Dubai International Film Festival (see p.30). It's worth bearing in mind that the authorities **censor** any scenes featuring nudity, sex, drugs and homosexuality, as well as anything of a sensitive religious or political nature. In addition, **audiences** are generally less well behaved than in western cinemas, with noisy teenagers and out-of-control kids the norm, usually accompanied by assorted mobile phone conversations and much noisy cracking of popcorn.

Tickets cost around 30–50dh, while some cinemas have also introduced so-called "Gold" and "Grand" class screenings in their smaller auditoriums (tickets around 100dh) complete with luxurious reclining seats and personal table service.

CineStar Ⓦ**www.cinestarcinemas.com.** Two large modern multiplexes, at Deira City Centre, Garhoud and the Mall of the Emirates.

Grand Cinemas Ⓦ**www.grandcinemas.com.** The city's largest cinema chain, with a range of multiplexes including the Grand Cineplex at Wafi in Garhoud, the Grand in the Mercato mall in Jumeirah, the Megaplex at Ibn Battuta Mall, and the Grand Festival at Festival City.

Lamcy Plaza Cinema Lamcy Plaza, Oud Metha Ⓣ**04-336 8808.** For something a bit different from the usual Hollywood fare, head to the no-frills Lamcy Plaza Cinema, which caters to the local Indian community with regular screenings of Bollywood, Tamil and Malayalam films – particularly lively on a Friday.

Movies Under the Stars Rooftop Gardens, Wafi, Oud Metha Ⓦ**www.wafi.com.** Free open-air cinematic double-bills, screened every Sunday evening (starting at 8pm) from October to May, with seating on beanbags and an enjoyably informal and chilled-out atmosphere.

Theatre

Dubai's theatrical scene remains decidedly moribund. The good news is that the city now possesses a couple of decent theatres, although the bad news is that neither of them is yet staging anything particularly worth seeing, unless you're lucky enough to time your visit to coincide with the arrival of one of the international productions which occasionally stop by. In the meantime it's left largely to the ground-breaking DUCTAC to keep the cultural fires burning.

Dubai Community and Arts Centre (DUCTAC) Mall of the Emirates Ⓦ**www.ductac.org;** **see Burj al Arab & around map, p.82.** A rare and refreshing burst of alternative creative spirit, DUCTAC is home to the excellent little Centrepoint Threatre, Kilachand Studio Theatre and Manu Chhabria Arts Centre which collectively host an engaging and eclectic array of productions, including film, music and theatre, with the emphasis on local and community-based projects.

Madinat Theatre Madinat Jumeirah Ⓦ**www.madinattheatre.com;** **see Burj al Arab & around map, p.82.** Squirrelled away in the depths of the Madinat Jumeirah, this was Dubai's first proper theatre when it opened a few years back, although the pedestrian programme of events – featuring an uninspiring mix of mainstream musicals, theatrical performances and other assorted low-brow crowd-pleasers – hasn't yet done much to invigorate Dubai's flagging cultural credentials.

The Palladium Dubai Media City Ⓦ**www.thepalladiumdubai.com;** **see Dubai Marina map, p.87.** State-of-the-art new cultural venue, opened in 2009 and currently hosting a rather mishmash range of events – anything from stand-up comedy and live music performances to international seminars and awards ceremonies.

Art galleries

Art galleries have positively mushroomed over Dubai during the past few years – the places below are just a few of the better-known venues. For comprehensive listings, consult the excellent *Art Map*, available free from many galleries, or check out Ⓦwww.artinthecity.com, which also covers galleries in Sharjah and Abu Dhabi.

The (unlikely) hub of the city's art scene is the rundown industrial area of **Al Quoz**, off Sheikh Zayed Road (between interchanges 3 and 4), where low rents have attracted a string of gallery owners from across the Arab world. Exhibitions at all the places below tend to change every month or so. The city also hosts two big annual arts **festivals** in mid-March, when Art Dubai and the Bastakiya Art Fair hit town – see p.30 for more details.

Artspace The Gate Village Building 3, Podium Level, Dubai International Financial Centre ⓦwww.artspace-dubai.com. Upmarket gallery specializing in painting and sculpture by established Middle Eastern artists.

Courtyard Gallery Sheikh Zayed Rd, off interchange 3 (exit 43), Al Quoz ⓦwww.courtyardgallerydubai.com; see Burj al Arab & around map, p.82. One of the city's largest galleries, hosting local Arab and Iranian artists alongside big European names. Part of a quaint and colourful little complex which also includes its own café and a couple of handicraft shops.

Gallery Isabelle van den Eynde (formerly the B21 Gallery) Sheikh Zayed Rd, off interchange 3 (exit 43), Al Quoz ⓦwww.ivde.net; see Burj al Arab & around map, p.82. One of the city's more cutting-edge venues, priding itself on nurturing and showcasing the talents of the young Arab artists.

Green Art Gallery Villa 23, 51 St, just off Jumeirah Rd by Dubai Zoo, Jumeirah ⓦwww.gagallery.com; see Jumeirah map, p.78. One of the longest-established galleries in the city, particularly known for its role in promoting the work of Arab artists.

thejamjar Sheikh Zayed Rd, off Interchange 4 (exit 39), Al Quoz ⓦwww.thejamjardubai.com; see Burj al Arab & around map, p.82. Part gallery, part community project, thejamjar exhibits work by local and international artists and also provides a range of other facilities and events including art classes for children and adults and a "DIY Painting Studio" where you can have a crack at painting; all materials are provided free.

Majlis Gallery on Al Fahidi Roundabout, next to the main entrance into Bastakiya, Bur Dubai ⓦwww.majlisgallery.com; see Bur Dubai map, p.44. Set in a pretty old Bastakiya house, this is the oldest gallery in the city, founded in 1976 by English interior designer Alison Collins (who still co-owns it), and hosting monthly exhibitions showcasing the work of Emirati and international artists.

The Third Line Sheikh Zayed Rd, off interchange 3 (exit 43), Al Quoz ⓦwww.thethirdline.com; see Burj al Arab & around map, p.82. Focusing on the work of Arab artists, this is one of Dubai's most experimental venues, with engaging displays of painting, photography and assorted installations.

XVA Gallery Bastakiya ⓦwww.xvagallery.com; see Bur Dubai map, p.44. One of Dubai's most attractive galleries, hidden in a traditional house at the back of Bastakiya. The main focus here is on Middle Eastern artists, though the old building is a work of art in its own right, and well worth a look over a long cool drink in the gallery's courtyard café (see p.111).

12

Sport, outdoor and leisure activities

Despite the sometimes punishing climate, Dubai (and neighbouring Abu Dhabi) boast a top-notch calendar of annual **sporting events**, including leading tennis, golf and rugby touraments, as well as the Dubai World Cup, the world's richest horse race, and the season-ending Abu Dhabi Formula 1 Grand Prix. There are also more traditional Arabian pursuits on offer including traditional dhow and camel races.

If you want to get active, there's a fair range of **outdoor** pursuits on offer, including world-class diving, plenty of watersports, assorted desert activities, plus a spectacular selection of golf courses. If you need a break from the heat head **indoors**, where you can hit the slopes at Ski Dubai (see p.85) or glide about on the Dubai Ice Rink (see p.136). If all the activity proves too much, then head straight for one of Dubai's numerous **spas** for some pampering.

Annual sporting events

Abu Dhabi Desert Challenge (formerly the UAE Desert Challenge) ⓦ www.abudhabidesertchallenge.com. Five days in March. Rally drivers, bikers and quad-bikers race each other across the desert regions of Abu Dhabi emirate in one of the Middle East's leading motorsports events (and the opening round of the FIA Cross Country Rally World Cup).

Abu Dhabi F1 Grand Prix Yas Marina Circuit ⓦ www.yasmarinacircuit.com. Mid-Nov. The crown jewel in the Middle Eastern sporting calendar, this is the last race in the Formula 1 championship. It was held at the spectacular new Yas Marina Circuit for the first time in 2009, when it was won by Sebastian Vettel. Tickets from around 1500dh.

Dubai Desert Classic Emirates Golf Club ⓦ www.dubaidesertclassic.com. Four days in Nov. Established in 1993, the Dubai Desert Classic has established itself as an important – and very lucrative – event in the PGA European Tour. Past winners feature a virtual who's who of the game's leading players, including Ernie Els, Tiger Woods, Colin Montgomerie and Seve Ballesteros. Tickets from around 200dh.

Dubai Marathon ⓦ www.dubaimarathon.org. Mid-Jan. A leading international marathon that attracts top distance runners like three-time champion Haile Gebrselassie, who run from the city centre all the way down the coast to Dubai Media City, and back again.

Dubai Rugby Sevens The Sevens stadium, Al Ain Road ⓦ www.dubairugby7s.com. Late Nov/early Dec. This annual IRB Sevens World Series tournament is one of the highlights of the international rugby sevens calendar, featuring top national teams from around the globe, with recent winners including England, South Africa and New Zealand. Also provides the excuse for some of the city's most raucous partying. Tickets from 170–230dh; check website for latest details.

▲ Dubai Tennis Championships

Dubai Tennis Championships Dubai Tennis Stadium, Garhoud ⓦwww.dubaitennischampionships.com. Two weeks in late Feb/early March. Well-established fixture on the international ATP and WTA calendar, attracting many of the world's leading players. Recent winners include Rafael Nadal, Venus Williams, Andy Roddick, Novak Djokovic and four-time champion Roger Federer. Tickets from 30–200dh.

Dubai World Championship Earth course, Jumeirah Golf Estates ⓦwww.dubaiworldchampionship.com. Four days in Nov. This is now the world's richest golfing event and marks the end of the European Tour's season-long "Race to Dubai" (formerly known as the Order of Merit). Sixty top players battlle it out for $7.5 million in prize money at the spectacular new Greg Norman-designed "Earth" course. Entrance is free.

Dubai World Cup Meydan Racecourse ⓦwww.dubaiworldcup.com. March. The world's richest horse race, and the climax of the city's annual racing calendar, with a massive $10 million in prize money. Tickets from 350dh.

Traditional dhow racing Dubai International Marine Club ⓦwww.dimc.ae. May. A rare opportunity to see the Gulf's traditional wooden dhows under sail, with races held on weekends throughout May starting at the Dubai International Marine Club in Dubai Marina.

Other spectator sports

Racing of various types is wildly popular in Dubai. Traditional **camel races** are held at **Al Lisaili Race Track**, around 40km from Dubai off exit 37 of the Al Ain Road – one of Dubai's most evocative sights, as dozens of camels gallop across the sands to the enthusiastic cheers of local dromedary fanciers. Races are held from September to May, usually very early in the morning at around 6am (there are also sometimes afternoon races at around 4pm). For details of forthcoming meets call the race track on ⓣ050-658 8528 (Sun–Thurs 8am–1.30pm). Dubai's extensive programme of **horse racing** is held nearby at the spectacular new Meydan Racecourse (ⓦwww.meydan.ae/racecourse; see p.67). The racing season runs from November to March; details can be found on ⓦwww.emiratesracing.com. Just don't expect to make any money at the bookies – betting is illegal in the UAE.

Various sporting events are also held at the vast new **Dubai Sports City** (ⓦwww.dubaisportscity.ae) in Dubailand; this was still under construction at the time of writing but should eventually comprise a 60,000-seat multi-purpose stadium, along with a 25,000-seat cricket ground, plus a hockey stadium and an indoor arena. The **cricket** stadium has already hosted a number of one-day internationals and Twenty20 matches featuring England, Australia, New Zealand and Pakistan, while the hockey stadium served as the venue for the 2009 Asia Cup hockey tournament.

Motorsports enthusiasts should head to the nearby **Dubai Autodrome** (ⓦwww.dubaiautodrome.com), a FIA-approved circuit which hosts various events including FIA GT3 European Championship and GP2 Asia Series races. You can also have a drive yourself in a variety of cars either on the main circuit or on the Kartdrome karting track; check the website for details.

Diving and watersports

Dubai itself has only limited **diving** opportunities: the offshore marine environment has been significantly damaged by development and there are no natural reefs, although a number of wreck dives lie reasonably close to shore. Dubai does, however, lie within easy striking distance of outstanding dive sites off the UAE's east coast in Fujairah, and off the Musandam Peninsula in Oman (see p.166), both of which are only a couple of hours' drive away.

There are a couple of reputable diving **operators** in Dubai. The Pavilion Dive Centre at the *Jumeirah Beach Hotel* (see p.83) offers a range of on-site PADI courses and introductory dives, plus dives to nearby wrecks and one- to three-day excursions to Musandam. Al Boom Diving (Ⓦwww.alboomdiving.com) operates dive centres at the Jebel Ali Golf Resort and Spa in the far south of the city, and at the *Al Aqah Méridien* hotel in Fujairah (see p.165), offering a range of PADI courses and dives, plus Musandam excursions. For more detailed information about the region's dive sites, pick up a copy of the *UAE Underwater Explorer* guidebook, available at bookshops throughout the city.

Watersports facilities are available at all the beachside hotels (see p.93). Typical offerings include sailing, windsurfing, kayaking, banana-boating, wakeboarding and deep-sea fishing. The city also boasts several **waterparks**, including Wild Wadi (see p.83) and Aquaventure (see p.89).

Golf

Golf is big business in Dubai, and the city has an outstanding selection of international-standard courses. Prices are sky-high though, and you'll be lucky to get a round anywhere for less than 500dh.

Al Badia Golf Course Festival City Ⓦwww.albadiagolfclub.ae. Attractive Creekside course in the southern city centre designed by Robert Trent Jones II. The oasis-style theme holds lots of water features and a variety of teeing angles and hole lengths to suit both serious and recreational players.

Desert Course Arabian Ranches Dubailand Ⓦwww.thedesertcoursedubai.com. Striking modern course (created by Ian Baker-Finch and Nicklaus Design) consisting of a links-style grass course set in the middle of natural desert.

Dubai Creek Golf Club Garhoud Ⓦwww.dubaigolf.com/dcgyc. Famous for its

Free (or almost free) beaches

If you want some sand but don't fancy stumping up the punishing prices levied by the various five-star hotels (see p.93) there are other options. Easily the nicest is the lovely **Jumeirah Beach Park** (see p.79). Another option is the spacious **Mamzar Park** (daily 8am–11pm, Thurs–Sat until 11.30; 5dh) at the far eastern edge of Deira, close to the border with Sharjah, surrounded by a fringe of golden sand dotted with palm trees and parasols. It also boasts good facilities, including a children's playground and amusement arcades, swimming pool, spacious palm-shaded lawns and impressive views of Sharjah.

There's also a nice stretch of free sand (but no facilities) at Umm Suqeim beach, immediately north of the *Burj al Arab*; a bit further north at Kite Beach; and at the rather cheerless Russian Beach, immediately south of the *Dubai Marine Beach Resort* at the north end of Jumeirah. The latter is somewhat bare and windswept, as well as being rather too close to the cranes and gantries of Port Rashid for aesthetic comfort.

spiky-roofed club house (see p.68), this Thomas Bjorn-designed course enjoys a superb creekside setting, and there's also a floodlit nine-hole par-3 course for after-dark swingers. It's also one of the most affordable clubs for visitors.

The Els Club Dubai Sports City, Dubailand ⓦwww.elsclubdubai.com. Spectacular "desert links" course, with greens and fairways surrounded by rolling dunes and untouched desert scenery, and with a range of tees and hole lengths to suit ability.

Emirates Golf Club Dubai Marina ⓦwww.dubaigolf.com/egc. The oldest all-grass championship course in the Gulf, and probably still the most prestigious, centred around a striking Bedouin tent-style clubhouse. Current home of the Dubai Desert Classic (see p.133).

Jumeirah Golf Estates Dubai Marina ⓦwww.jumeirahgolfestates.com. Huge, dedicated golfing "community" boasting four separate state-of-the-art courses – "Fire", "Earth", "Water" and "Wind" (designed by Greg Norman, Vijay Singh, Sergio Garcia and Pete Dye) – set amid dramatic desert scenery. Only partially open at the time of writing, and access to casual visitors may be limited.

The Montgomerie Dubai Dubai Marina ⓦwww.themontgomerie.com. Links-style course designed by the eponymous Scotsman, featuring the world's largest green (playable from a 360-degree teeing ground), as well as many other unusual features and top-notch facilities.

Indoor activities

If you're fed up with the heat there are a couple of good places to cool down and burn off some energy, as well as a pair of climbing walls if you want to work up a head for heights.

Dubai Ice Rink Dubai Mall ⓦwww.dubaiicerink.com. Olympic-sized ice rink offering a range of open-to-all public sessions (50dh including skate rental), plus "disco sessions" and learn-to-skate classes. Check the website for the latest schedule.

Ski Dubai Mall of the Emirates, ⓦwww.skidxb.com. Go skiing in the middle of the desert. See p.85 for full details.

The Wall Dubai World Trade Centre ⓦwww.climbingdubai.com/wall.html. Open-air climbing wall, the highest in the UAE, with a range of routes for different abilities, including some challenging overhangs for more advanced climbers. There's also a special "speedwall" on which two climbers can race one another over identical routes, and climbing lessons are also available. Daily 1.30–10pm, Fri & Sat closes at 6.30pm; 50dh. Another (slightly smaller) possibility is the Pharaohs' Club Climbing Wall at the Pharoah's Club in Wafi (ⓣ04-324 0000; 40dh/2hr).

Desert activities

A range of desert excursions and "safaris" are offered by the city's various tour operators (for full details, see p.26) – although by and large the selection of activities is disappointingly stereotypical, and most trips involve being sat in the back of a vehicle while someone drives you across the desert or through the mountains. Slightly more active alternatives (offered by most local tour operators) include **camel safaris**, often featuring a bit of sand-boarding en route, while adrenaline junkies will enjoy the chance to try their hand at riding a **dune-buggy** or **quad-bike** across the dunes, and a couple of operators like Arabian Adventures (see p.26) also offer courses in **off-road desert driving**. Drivers with off-road experience and a 4WD should pick up a copy of the *UAE Off-Road Explorer* by Shelley Frost, available at bookshops around the city, which lists twenty off-road routes with maps and GPS coordinates. Trips featuring the traditional Arabian pursuit of **falconry** are also sometimes offered by tour operators; alternatively, contact specialist operator Shaheen Xtreme (ⓦwww.shaheenxtreme.com).

There are also myriad **trekking** possibilities in the craggy Hajar mountains in the east and north of the UAE, although at present no tour operators are offering guided walks to these areas, meaning that they remain the preserve of independent and adventurous travellers with local knowledge.

Spas

Dubai has a gorgeous array of excellent spas, most (but not all) of which are in the city's various five-star **hotels**. A huge choice of treatments are on offer, from conventional facials, massages and beauty treatments through to everything from colour therapy rituals to traditional Ayurvedic remedies. All the following hotel spas are open to non-guests, though it's always best to reserve in advance. **Prices** are predictably steep: count on a minimum of around 250dh or more for a half-hour treatment, or 500dh for an hour.

Amara Park Hyatt Hotel (see p.102) ⓣ04-602 1234. One of the most idyllic spas in the city, with eight private treatment rooms in the hotel grounds, all with private walled garden and rain shower. Treatments are based around the "ancient healing philosophies of diamond, emerald, ruby and sapphire", featuring Thai, Swedish and Indian head massages, phyto-aromatic facials, marine-inspired scrubs and baths, aromatherapy, reflexology, ear candling and volcanic hot stone treatments.

Caracalla Spa Le Royal Méridien Hotel (see p.108) ⓣ04-399 5555 x 5322/5543 or ⓔcaracallaspa@lrm-gh-dubai.com for bookings. Swanky Roman-themed spa specializing in Elemis-brand body treatments, including Balinese and Swedish massages, reflexology and algae body wraps. They also do a series of "Himalayan" treatments, using natural mountain herbs.

Cleopatra's Wafi (see p.64) ⓣ04-324 7700, ⓦwww.waficity.com. Set in the upmarket Wafi complex, with separate male and female spas. Treatments include Elemis facials, a range of Thai, Balinese, Chinese and other massages, and an extensive selection of Ayurvedic treatments.

Club Olympus Hyatt Regency Hotel (see p.100) ⓣ04-209 1234. The nicest spa in the old city, offering a range of Eminence facials, Thai, Swedish and Ayurvedic massages along with invigorating body scrubs featuring ingredients ranging from papaya, jasmine and seaweed through to coffee and chocolate.

H20 Jumeirah Emirates Towers (see p.103) ⓣ04-319 8181, ⓔJETh2o@jumeirah.com for bookings. Exclusive men-only spa, buried away in the basement of the *Emirates Towers* hotel and aimed squarely at the cashed-up, stressed-out executives staying in the tower above. The muted lighting and hushed atmosphere is guaranteed to calm frayed nerves.

Lime Spa Desert Palm (see p.108) ⓣ04-323 8888. Sumptuous Per Aquum spa in the chilled-out *Desert Palm* resort on the edge of the city. Treatments use an exclusive range of Anne Semonin products and feature personalized, holistic treatments like the Lime "Intuitive Massage", using a mix of Swedish, Thai, shiatsu, aromatherapy and Balinese massage techniques, as well as reiki, reflexology and ear candling.

One&Only Spa and Oriental Hammam One&Only Royal Mirage (see p.107) ⓣ04-399 9999. Classy spa offering a range of wraps, scrubs, massages and facials (including special men's treatments). Alternatively, check out the picture-perfect Oriental Hammam, a marvellous little traditional steam bath with Arabian massages by experts from Morocco, Tunisia and Turkey, performed while you lie supine on a heated marble slab.

Retreat Spa Grosvenor House Hotel (see p.106) ⓣ04-399 8888. Suave modern spa specializing in marine-based Phytomer products and treatments, including body wraps, sea essential hydro baths, and the Rasul skin ceremony using natural muds.

Ritz-Carlton Spa Ritz-Carlton Hotel (see p.108) ⓣ04-399 4000. Upmarket hotel spa specializing in Balinese massages, Carita Paris facials, and a range of signature fruity treatments ranging from "ginger-cocoon" body rituals to "raspberry-ripple" hydrotherapy baths.

The Spa at The Palace The Palace Hotel (see p.104) ⓣ04-428 7805, ⓔspawomen@thepalace-dubai.com or spamen@thepalace-dubai.com for bookings. Male and female spas, with opulent Moorish styling and a menu featuring unusual Arabian-inspired treatments, including the oriental hammam scrub, the desert sand scrub (using desert sand and sea salt) and the Moroccan-inspired "One Desert Journey" sand scrub and massage.

Talise Madinat Jumeirah (see p.84) ⓣ04-366 6818, ⓦhttp://talise.jumeirah.com. Set in the beautiful grounds of the Madinat Jumeirah, Talise is more of a miniature health resort than a simple spa, with 26 villa-cum-treatment rooms scattered around verdant gardens and a huge range of traditional spa treatments along with other therapies, wellness treatments and activities ranging from Chinese medicine to yoga.

Willow Stream Fairmont Hotel (see p.103) ⓣ04-332-5555. Fancy, upmarket spa with Roman-style decor, separate male and female spas, Hammam-style steam rooms and a pair of pools outside on the fourth floor.

Shopping

Dubai is shopaholic heaven. This is the city which boasts the world's largest shopping mall, whose major annual event is the Dubai Shopping Festival (see p.30), and whose name even sounds like "do buy!" In fact, the general obsession with retail therapy is often used as a stick to beat Dubai with by people who like to make out the whole place is nothing but a vacuous consumerist fleshpot – to which one might reply that Dubai has always lived off trade and commerce, and that the modern shopping mall is nothing more than a contemporary version of the traditional Middle Eastern bazaar.

Where to shop

There are two sides to shopping in Dubai. First, there are the old-fashioned **souks** of Bur Dubai and, especially, Deira (see pp.53–60). This is shopping old-style, good for traditional items like gold, perfume and spices, with **bargaining** the norm and shops opening and closing as the owner sees fit. Then there are the city's modern **malls**, with fixed prices and set opening times. In many ways, the modern Dubai mall is just the contemporary equivalent of the traditional Arabian café and souk; the city's malls act as a magnet for local Emiratis, who cruise the shops and chew the fat with friends over coffee just as they have for centuries – even if it's now Starbucks rather than shisha that's king. The seriousness with which Dubai takes its shopping is also evident in the lavishness of many of its malls, some of which are tourist attractions in their own right.

Opening hours for mall shops are usually 10am to 10pm; some stay open until midnight between Thursday and Saturday, while some remain closed on Fridays until 2pm. Opening hours in souks are more variable, although in general most places open from 10am to 10pm, although many close in the afternoon from around 1 to 4pm.

What to buy

Almost everything, is the answer. **Gold**, **diamonds** and other precious stones are cheaper here than just about anywhere else in the world. Dubai is also good for cheap **spices** and Middle Eastern **food**, bought either in the Deira souks or a local supermarket; dates are a particularly good buy. Other bargains are local **perfumes**, **clothes** and **shoes**, including pretty little Arabian-style embroidered slippers – or you could go the whole hog and kit yourself out in a traditional

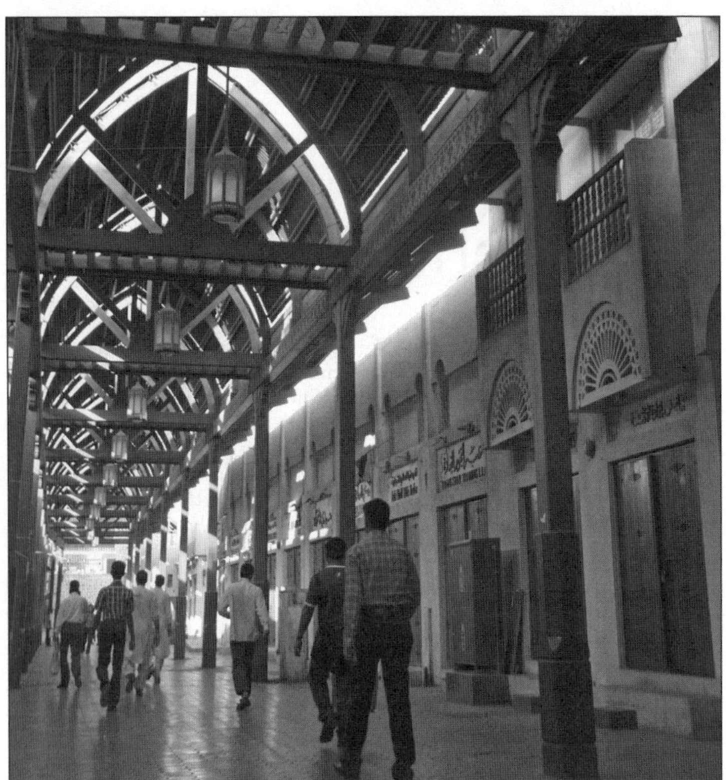

▲ Textile Souk, Bur Dubai

dishdasha or *abbeya*. The city also has a thriving **carpet** trade (though you might want to check the Blue Souk in Sharjah too) ranging from inexpensive kilims to heirloom-quality Persian rugs. Arabian **souvenirs** are another obvious choice and there are heaps of collectable antiques such as old coffee pots, khanjars, wooden boxes and antique Bedouin jewellery, along with shisha pipes andfrankincense, not to mention plenty of memorably awful toy camels, mosque alarm clocks and *Burj al Arab* paperweights. Arabian **music** is another inter-esting buy (try Virgin or Al Mansoor for a good selection of CDs), althoughfor a quintessentially Dubaian memento, check out some of the vast array of **fake designer** stuff on offer in Karama and Bur Dubai (see p.145).

For (genuine) contemporary **fashion**, all the world's top brands are represented in Dubai's malls. In fact, label-fatigue sets in pretty rapidly during any shopping tour of the city and you might prefer to forego looking at yet more Armani in favour of searching out some of the city's small number of more interesting independent boutiques like S★uce or Ginger & Lace (see opposite) – or just take your revenge on the dominant brands by buying a pile of fakes from Karama. Most major labels have their own stores; alternatively, check out what's available at one of the city's increasing number of flagship international **department stores**, which now include Harvey Nichols, Galleries Lafayette, Bloomingdales, Saks Fifth Avenue and Marks & Spencer.

Books and music

Kinokuniya (Book World) Dubai Mall. This local outpost of the famous Japanese chain is far and away Dubai's best bookshop – a vast emporium stuffed with a simply massive array of titles, ranging from mainstream novels, travel guides and magazines through to graphic novels, works in French and German and a brilliant manga selection.

Magrudy's Branches citywide **Ⓦwww.magrudy.com.** The leading local bookstore chain, now with branches in most large malls in the city, although the well-stocked original branch in Jumeirah (on the north side of the Jumeirah Centre Mall) is still the best.

Al Mansoor Video Wafi, Lamcy Plaza and two in Bur Dubai, on Al Esbij St (near the Astoria Hotel) and Al Mussalla St. Good place to stock up on cheap music and films, with heaps of Arabian, Indian and Western cassettes, CDs and DVDs, usually including a fair selection of discounted items; the cheap cassettes (from as little as 10dh) are particularly good for neophytes exploring the vast wealth of Arabian music for the first time. The Bur Dubai branches sell mainly Bollywood films and CDs.

Virgin Megastore BurJuman, Deira City Centre, Mall of the Emirates and Mercato. Dubai offshoot of the now defunct UK chain, stocking all the usual international CDs and DVDs. The real highlight, though, is the superb collection of Arabic pop and other music from Morocco to Iraq – anything from traditional oud music or Um Kalthoum through to May Hariri and the REG Project, as well as recordings by many Gulf and Emirati musicians. Listening posts allow you to browse before you buy.

Clothes

Aizone Mall of the Emirates. This Dubai branch of the famous Beirut store specializes in very chic, very expensive clothing (mainly ladieswear, but with some stuff for blokes too), with the emphasis on skimpy party frocks, figure-hugging dresses and outrageously tiny tops. It's all essential designer bling for the city's monied Lebanese party crowd, and perfect for very thin people with very fat wallets.

Ginger & Lace Wafi and Ibn Battuta Mall Ⓦwww.gingerandlace.com. There aren't many independent boutiques in Dubai but this is one of the best, selling a range of bright and funky ladieswear sourced from international designers.

Harvey Nichols Mall of the Emirates. The flagship store of one of Dubai's flagship malls, this suave, minimalist three-storey department store offers a vast array of international labels, along with British classics like Gieves & Hawkes, Thomas Pink, Alexander McQueen and Burberry. There's also a selection of superior homeware and the shop's signature range of upmarket food and drink – an essential resource if you're hunting for "gourmet salt" or want to spend 40dh on a bottle of tomato sauce.

Priceless Al Maktoum Rd, near Deira Clock Tower. Worth the schlep down Al Maktoum Road for the excellent spread of top designer menswear and ladieswear, with lashings of Armani, Yves Saint-Laurent, Gucci and the like all sold at phenomenal discounts – 75 per cent or more is standard.

S*uce Village Mall, Jumeirah Ⓦwww.shopatsauce.com. The city's leading independent boutique, stocking a wide range of designs you won't find anywhere else in the city, usually with the emphasis on colourful hippychick chic, plus a good range of funky accessories.

Tailoring in Dubai

Although not as well known for its tailoring industry as places like Hong Kong, Bangkok or India are, Dubai is a decent place to get tailor-made clothes run up at fairly modest prices. A good tailor will be able to copy any existing garment you bring in or, alternatively, make up clothes from a photograph or even a hand-drawn design. The best place to head to is **Al Hisn Street** (off Al Fahidi Street near the Dubai Museum) in Bur Dubai, where you'll find a line of tailors along the west side of the road. One of the best is the reliable Dream Girl Tailors, who'll charge you around 60dh for a shirt or trousers, or from 150dh for a dress (not including material).

Electronics

Khaled bin al Waleed Road Bur Dubai. The massed computer and electronics shops lining Khaled bin al Waleed Road around the junction with Mankhool Road are heaven for technophiles in search of a deal, with everything from cut-price PCs to mobile phone accessories at discount prices; be prepared to shop around. It's also worth checking out the nearby Al Ain Centre on Al Mankhool Road, which is also stuffed with mountains of digital gadgets.

Food

Bateel Dates Dubai Mall, Souk al Bahar, Deira City Center, BurJuman and Festival Centre ⓦwww.bateel.ae. The best dates in the city, grown in Bateel's own plantations in Saudi Arabia and sold either plain, stuffed with ingredients (such as almonds and slices of lemon or orange) or covered in chocolate. Other offerings include date biscuits, juice and jam, along with more outlandish concoctions like date pesto and date mustard, plus a small selection of fine (date-free) chocolates. They also do nice gift boxes if you're looking for a present.

Carrefour Branch near Al Ghubabia Bus Station in Bur Dubai, and in Deira City Centre, Mall of the Emirates and Marina Mall ⓦwww.carrefouruae.com. This vast French hypermarket chain might not be the most atmospheric place to shop in the city, but is one of the best places to pick up just about any kind of Middle Eastern foodstuff you fancy, including dates, sweets like halva and baklava, teas, tropical fruits, nuts, spices, Arabian honey, turkish coffee, saffron, caviar, labneh and olives.

Spice Souk Deira. All sort of spices and other local specialities – see p.57.

Wafi Gourmet Wafi, Oud Metha. The ultimate Dubai deli, this little slice of foodie heaven is piled high with tempting Middle Eastern items, including big buckets of olives, nuts, spices and dried fruits, and trays of date rolls, marzipan fruits, baklava and fine chocolates. If you can't wait to get stuck in, the shop also has its own restaurant, offering instant gratification with a range of tasty kebabs, mezze and seafood.

Handicrafts, carpets and souvenirs

The Camel Company Souk Madinat Jumeirah, Mall of the Emirates, Dubai Mall and Souk al Bahar. This dromedary-obsessed shop stocks Dubai's cutest selection of stuffed toy camels – vastly superior to the usual hump-backed horrors on offer elsewhere in the city – plus camel mugs, camel cards, camel T-shirts and so on.

Deira Tower Baniyas Square. Home to the biggest collection of rug shops in the city, the so-called Deira Tower "Carpet Souk" comprises thirty-odd shops spread over the ground and first floors of this large office block. There's a massive amount of stuff on sale, ranging from huge, museum-quality Persian heirlooms to ghastly framed carpet pictures and other tat, but it's mostly good quality, and likely to work out cheaper than in one of the city's mall-based rug shops.

Emad Carpets Wafi, Khan Murjan, Dubai Mall, Souk Al Bahar, Trade Route Pavilion Festival Centre. A very smart carpet and handicrafts chain with a superb array of (expensive) carpets and kilims from Iran, Pakistan, Turkey and Aghanistan. There's also a classy selection of Arabian and other souvenirs including antique Omani silver, scarves, Pakistani and Kashmiri shawls and unusual jewellery and beaded pashminas.

Gallery One Souk Madinat Jumeirah, Mall of the Emirates, Souk Al Bahar, Dubai Mall, and The Walk in Dubai Marina ⓦwww.g-1.com. Citywide gallery chain selling a good range of superb, limited-edition photographs of Dubai – expensive, but not outrageous – as well as other fine-art photography and superior postcards.

International Aladdin Shoes Next to Bur Dubai Old Souk Abra Station. In a prime position right next to the Bur Dubai Old Souk Abra Station, this eyecatching little stall (no sign) in the midst of the Textile Souk stocks a gorgeous selection of colourful embroidered ladies slippers (40-95dh) – pretty little souvenirs, although they can be a bit tight unless you've got skinny feet – along with lovely embroidered belts.

Al Jaber Gallery Dubai Mall, Mall of the Emirates, Souk Madinat Jumeirah and Trade Route Pavilion Festival Centre. Dubai's leading purveyor of low-grade Arabian "handicrafts"; look hard enough and you might find some half-decent stuff, including attractive old traditional wooden boxes and coffee pots, though the shop is perhaps best regarded as a source of hilarious kitsch – dodgy daggers, constipated camels, fluorescent shisha pipes and the like. Kids will love it.

Al Orooba Oriental Carpets BurJuman. This attractive handicrafts shop sells a good range of carpets from all the main Asian rug-producing centres. There's also a fine range of other decorative items and collectables including tablecloths, pashmina and organza shawls, Islamic silverware, Omani khanjars, walking sticks, coffee pots, frankincense burners and prayer beads. All the stock is new, though some pieces are oxidized to give them a convincing antique appearance. Daily 10am–10pm (Thurs & Fri until 11pm).

Persian Carpet House Dubai Mall, Emirates Towers Boulevard, Mall of the Emirates, Souk Madinat Jumeirah and Trade Route Pavilion Festival Centre ⓦ ww.persiancarpethouse.com. This upmarket chain of carpet shops specializes in superb rugs (plus a few kilims) from Iran, Pakistan, Afghanistan and Kashmir. It also stocks superior arts and crafts, usually including things like richly embroidered organza and pashmina shawls from Kashmir, Arabian, Iranian and Pakistani silver antiques, colourful Turkish hanging lights and other collectables.

Pride of Kashmir Mercato mall, Deira City Centre, Souk Al Bahar and Trade Route Pavilion Festival Centre ⓦ www.prideofkashmir.com. Another of the leading citywide handicrafts chains, more upmarket than Al Jaber Gallery (see above) but still affordable. The stock consists of a range of stuff that usually includes carpets and kilims alongside antiques (and cleverly aged fake antiques), pashminas and traditional-style wooden furniture.

Jewellery and perfume

Ajmal BurJuman, Deira Gold Souk, Deira City Centra, Mall of the Emirates, Khan Murjan and elsewhere ⓦ www.ajmalperfume.com. Dubai's leading parfumiers, offering a wide range of fragrances including traditional *attar*-based Arabian scents. If you don't like any of the ready-made perfumes on offer you can make up your own from the big glass bottles on display behind the counter.

Damas Citywide ⓦ www.damasjewel.com. Dubai's leading chain of jewellery shops, the ubiquitous Damas has branches in virtually every mall in the city. Gold and diamond jewellery predominate, and designs range from classic Italian to chintzy Arabian.

Gold and Diamond Park Sheikh Zayed Rd between interchanges 3 and 4, ⓦ www.goldanddiamondpark.com. This low-key little mall is the place to come if you want diamonds, which retail here for up to half the price you'd expect to pay back home. The ninety-odd shops are stuffed full of diamond-encrusted jewellery; most is made according to European rather than Arabian designs, with a good range of pieces in classic Italian styles. You'll also find a few other precious stones and platinum jewellery for sale, plus a small amount of gold. Daily 10am–10pm.

Gold Souk Deira Huge selection of gold in Dubai's most famous souk. See p.53 for full details.

Perfume Souk Deira Local and international brands from a string of shops – or mix your own. See p.59 for full details.

Malls

BurJuman Corner of Khalid bin al Waleed and Sheikh Zayed rds ⓦ www.burjuman.com. The best city centre mall, BurJuman remains enduringly popular with tourists and locals alike thanks to its 300-plus shops and convenient location. The older and relatively run-of-the-mill section has branches of Virgin, Ajmal and Bateel Dates, while a posh extension at the mall's south end combines stylish architecture with a chain of upmarket shops, including the flagship Saks Fifth Avenue department store. Daily 10am–10pm (Thurs & Fri until 11pm).

Deira City Centre Garhoud ⓦ www.deiracitycentre.com. Long overtaken in the glamour and glitz stakes by newer shopping centres, this big old mall nevertheless remains one of the most popular in the city among less label-conscious consumers. It also offers a quintessential slice of Dubaian life, attracting everyone from veiled Emirati women to bargain-crazed Russian carpet-baggers – though the crowds can make the whole place rather chaotic and exhausting. The 340-plus outlets here have a largely (though not exclusively) downmarket, bargain-basement emphasis, although it's also worth checking out the "Jewellery Court" on Level 1, featuring an extraordinary collection of jewellery and watch shops selling everything from svelte Italian designs to the most outrageous, gem-encrusted Arabian bling imaginable, at equally fabulous prices. Think diamonds – lots of them. Daily 10am–10pm (Thurs–Sat until midnight).

Dubai Mall Downtown Dubai ⓦ**www.thedubaimall.com.** With a stupendous 1200-odd shops, this mother of all malls (for more see p.74) has pretty much everything you'll ever need to buy, and branches of just about every chain which does business in the city; the few which aren't here can be found in the adjacent Souk Al Bahar (see p.75 & p.146). Highlights include the flagship Bloomingdales and Galleries Lafayette department stores; "Fashion Avenue", home to the biggest array of designer labels in Dubai; and the in-house "Gold Souk", home to a further 120 shops selling gold, jewellery and Arabian perfumes and artefacts. Upstairs you'll find a Dubai branch of Hamleys, the famous London toy shop, plus Kinokuniya, the Japanese mega-store for books, while the basement holds a massive Waitrose supermarket. Daily 10am–10pm, Thurs–Sat until midnight.

Emirates Towers Boulevard Emirates Towers, Sheikh Zayed Rd. On the bottom two floors of the Emirates Towers business tower, this small but very exclusive mall offers the last word in Dubaian ultra-chic. The marbled floor is polished so brightly you could probably fix your make-up in it before sloping off to one of the small but very select number of upmarket outlets, including Jimmy Choo, Prada, Emporio Armani, Bulgari, Cartier, Gucci and Yves Saint-Laurent; there's also an outlet of Egyptian designer Azzha Fahmy, whose jewellery blends Islamic and Western motifs to memorable effect. Sat-Thurs 10am–10pm, Fri 4–10pm.

Festival Centre Festival City ⓦ**www.festivalcentre.com.** The centrepiece of the new Festival City development, this big new mall (see p.68) is nicely designed with attractive waterfront walks and has a big (albeit predictable) range of shops. The best part of the complex is likely to be the assorted crafts and carpets shops in the Trade Routes Pavilion, on the waterfront side of the centre, although many of these had failed to open at the time of writing, even though the rest of the centre had been in operation for well over a year.

Ibn Battuta Mall Between interchanges 5 and 6, Sheikh Zayed Rd ⓦ**www.ibnbattutamall.com.** This Ibn Battuta-inspired mall (see p.93) is worth a visit for its stunning decor alone – which is just as well, since as a shopping experience it's decidedly humdrum (the fact that the Mall of the Emirates down the road has Harvey Nichols as its flagship store, while Ibn Battuta has to make do with Debenhams, should give you an idea). Kids will enjoy the branch of the Toy Store (see p.33) located here, but otherwise there's little to inspire. Daily 10am–10pm, Wed–Fri until midnight.

Mall of the Emirates Interchange 4, Sheikh Zayed Rd ⓦ**www.malloftheemirates.com.** Perhaps the best one-stop shopping destination in the city, with around 500 stores to browse, good places to eat and drink and the surreal snow-covered slopes of Ski Dubai to ogle. Standout shops include Harvey Nichols and the very fashionable Aizone (see above for both). There's also a dedicated "Arabian Souk" housing various handicrafts and carpet sellers (including Al Jaber Gallery, Pride of Kashmir, the Camel Company and Gallery One). Other attractions include a big Borders – one of the few really good bookshops in the city – and the spacious Toy Store, scattered with giant stuffed animals and selling everything from Thomas the Tank Engines to Tamagotchis. Daily 10am–10pm (Thurs–Sat until midnight).

▲ Mall of the Emirates

Shopping for fakes

Despite ongoing government clampdowns, Dubai's vibrant trade in **counterfeit goods** (bags, watches, sunglasses, pens, counterfeit DVDs and so on) is still going strong, and for many visitors, the acquisition of a top-notch fake Chanel bag or Gucci watch at a fraction of the price of the real thing may be the shopping highlight of a visit to the city – although the brands and city authorities won't thank you for saying so. Spend any amount of time in **Karama Souk**, the **Gold Souk** or around **Al Fahidi Street** in Bur Dubai and you'll be repeatedly importuned with offers of "cheap copy watches" or "copy bags". If you decide to investigate further you'll probably be led into a backroom behind a nearby shop – often stuffed with counterfeit watches, bags, sunglasses and other designer accessories. Many fake pieces are still relatively expensive – you're unlikely to find much for under $50, and plenty of items cost double that, although still a lot cheaper than the real thing. Quality is often excellent (it's been suggested some counterfeits are actually manufactured in the same factories which produce the genuine items and aren't really fakes at all, but just seconds or "overmakes"). Longevity varies however; some fakes can fall to pieces within a fortnight, while others last just as long as the original. It's essential to check quality carefully – particularly stitching and zips – and you should also be prepared to shop around and bargain like crazy. Don't be afraid to walk away if you can't get the price you want – you'll have plenty of other offers.

Marina Mall Sheikh Zayed Rd ⓦ **www.marinamall.ae.** Aimed more at local marina residents than visiting tourists, this bright modern mall is worth a visit if you're in the area and fancy a bit of clothes shopping, but not worth a special visit otherwise. Daily 10am–10pm.

Mercato Jumeirah Rd ⓦ **www.mercatoshoppingmall.com.** This kitsch Italian-themed mall (see p.78) is relatively small compared to many others in the city, but packs in a good selection of rather upmarket outlets aimed at the affluent local villa dwellers. It's particularly strong on mainstream designer labels, as well as a couple of independent ladies' boutiques like Fleurt. Daily 10am–10pm (Fri until midnight).

The Village Mall Jumeirah Beach Rd ⓦ **www.thevillagedubai.com.** The best of the various small malls scattered along the northern end of Jumeirah Beach Road, attractively designed and home to the excellent S*uce boutique (see p.141), selling a range of very chic international ladieswear, and the stylish Indian designer Ayesha Depala, plus a homely little branch of *Shakespeare & Co.* (see p.117) and a passable Jashanmal bookshop, although Magrudy's over the road is better. Sat–Thurs 10am–10pm, Fri 4pm–10pm.

Wafi Oud Metha ⓦ **www.waficity.com.** This zany Egyptian-themed mall makes for a pleasantly superior shopping experience, with quirky decor and a refreshingly peaceful atmosphere. There's a good spread of upmarket designer outlets, while the attached Khan Murjan (see p.65 & below) is one of the best places in the city to shop for traditional arts and crafts. Daily 10am–10pm (Thurs & Fri until midnight).

Souks

For information on the Gold and Perfume souks, see p.53 & p.59.

Khan Murjan Wafi, Oud Metha. This eye-catching new development (see p.65) is one of Dubai's most seductive and successful attempts at taking a humble collection of shops and turning them into a full-blown Orientalist fantasy; it's retail therapy masquerading as culture, although in Dubai it's often difficult to separate the two. Whatever you think about the place, it's got probably the city's best and most upmarket array of traditional crafts shops selling just about every kind of Arabian geegaw, artefact and antique, including carpets, perfumes, clothes, musical instruments, paintings, lamps and anything else you can think of (and lots you probably can't). Sat–Wed 10am–10pm, Thurs & Fri 10am–midnight.

Karama Souk Karama. This open-air concrete complex in Karama is the best place to explore Dubai's roaring trade in fake designer gear and offers the perfect opportunity to stock up on anything from dodgy D&G to the latest Manchester United football strip, although sadly the uniquely amateurish forgeries – think 'Adibas' and 'Hugo Bros' – which used to be one of the souk's specialities are no longer seen, following crackdowns by the city authorities. The little shops here have racks full of reasonable-quality imitation designer clothing and sportswear, while there are also plenty of fake designer bags and "genuine fake watches" to be had – if you don't mind the constant low-level hassle. A few low-grade souvenir shops can also be found dotted around the souk selling every kind of desirable and not-so-desirable object, including kitsch classics like mosque-shaped alarm clocks, pictures made from sand and miniature *Burj al Arab*s moulded in glass. The poky little Karama Centre nearby has some nice Indian ladieswear, including pretty shalwar kameez, plus jewellery.

Souk al Bahar Old Town Island. Seemingly an afterthought to the massive Dubai Mall next door, the Arabian-themed Souk al Bahar specializes in local arts and crafts shops. Branches of Pride of Kashmir, Emad Carpets, Al Jaber Gallery and Gallery One, among others, are all here, plus a few independent fashion boutiques, including a store by celebrity Indian designer Manish Malhotra. The underpowered decor, gloomy lighting and bizarrely confusing layout don't encourage you to stay long, however. Sat–Thurs 10am–10pm, Fri 2–10pm.

Souk Madinat Jumeirah Madinat Jumeirah ⓦ www.madinatjumeirah.com. At the heart of the Madinat Jumeirah, this superb recreation of a "traditional" souk serves up a beguiling mix of shopping, eating and drinking opportunities either within its narrow, wood-framed passageways or on the lagoon-facing terraces outside. Like all good bazaars, the layout is mazy and disorienting so pick up a map at the entrance, even though it's more fun to get lost and just wander; the place isn't so big that you'll ever be far from where you want to be. The superb array of shops (including branches of Al Jaber Gallery, Pride of Kashmir, the Persian Carpet House, Camel Company and Gallery One) are mainly concerned with traditional arts and crafts – anything from ouds and embroidered slippers to Moroccan hanging lamps and tagine pots. Daily 10am–10pm.

▲ Slippers at market stall

Futuristic Dubai

Dubai makes a fair claim to being the most futuristic city on the planet. Over the past four decades an entire new megalopolis has sprung up, with skyscrapers, motorways and malls mushrooming out of the sands on a seemingly daily basis. Parts of the city's bristling postmodern skyline look like the deranged scribblings of an architectural convention on speed, with a whimsical array of outlandish high-rises strung out as far as the eye can see. Inevitably the results are mixed, though for sheer urban chutzpah the city has few rivals; its major contemporary landmarks, such as the Burj al Arab and Burj Khalifa, rank among the world's most spectacular modern buildings.

Dubai Marina ▲

The Palm Jumeirah ▼

New cities in the desert

Dubai's modern growth has followed a patchwork system, based around a string of self-contained urban developments – effectively a series of miniature cities within the city. Perhaps the most spectacular example is **Dubai Marina**, a dense forest of tightly packed skyscrapers at the southern edge of the city. Other major developments include the new **Downtown Dubai**, centred on the landmark Burj Khalifa; the Creekside **Festival City**; and the Palm Jumeirah artificial island. Further clusters of high-rises are already well underway at places like Business Bay, not to mention the gargantuan new **Dubailand** project.

Artificial islands

Perhaps the most attention-grabbing of all modern Dubai's mega-projects are the string of vast artificial islands, currently in various stages of completion, which line the coast, designed to provide the city with a staggering 500km of new beachfront property. The **Palm Jumeirah** (see p.87), now the world's largest man-made island, is largely completed, although even this will be dwarfed by the three artificial islands and archipelagos currently beng built, including the **Palm Jebel Ali** and **Palm Deira**, and the huge new **The World** project.

The world's tallest city

Dubai is now officially the tallest city on the planet. At the time of writing the city was home to 25 of the world's 200 highest buildings, compared to sixteen in New York, thirteen apiece in Shanghai and Chicago, and seven in Hong Kong. The landmark example of Dubai's sky-high ambition is provided by the staggering **Burj Khalifa**, the world's tallest building, at 828m. Other high-rise icons include the **Burj al Arab** and the glittering Emirates Towers, as well as less well-known buildings such as the needle-thin **Rose Rayhaan**, the world's tallest hotel.

Towers of Babel

Dubai's contemporary architecture defies categorization, with a polyglot confusion of styles which is occasionally brilliant, frequently bland, and sometimes downright weird – such as the fork-shaped *Dusit Thani* hotel, the golf ball-topped Etisalat Tower or the soaring Al Kazim Towers, a postmodern remake of the New York Chrysler Building. Tradition lurks beneath the surface however, and many of Dubai's finest modern buildings pay homage to the city's maritime past. The *Burj al Arab*, **National Bank of Dubai** and the clubhouse of the Dubai Creek Golf Club, three of the city's finest modern buildings, were all variously inspired by the shape of the **sails** of a traditional dhow. The eye-catchingly original outline of the **Jumeirah Beach Hotel**, meanwhile, was inspired by the shape of a breaking wave.

Dubai Metro

Adding a further splash of modernity to Dubai's twenty-first-century cityscape is the new Metro, one of the world's largest fully automated rail systems. Opened in late 2009, most of the network runs on elevated tracks, with state-of-the-art **driverless trains** shooting to and fro high above the streets. A string of strikingly modern stations resemble enormous metallic pods, the insides of which are modelled on one of the four elements – the water-themed interiors are particularly memorable.

▲ The *Burj al Arab*

▼ A Dubai Metro train

The Burj Khalifa ▼

Top ten modernist landmarks

▶▶ **Burj Khalifa** The world's tallest building: a slender space-rocket of a skyscraper, rising 828m above the streets of Downtown Dubai. See p.72

▶▶ **Burj al Arab** The iconic "seven-star" hotel which put Dubai on the world map, and still the city's most original and instantly recognizable landmark. See p.81

▶▶ **Jumeirah Beach Hotel** Great rollercoaster of a hotel, designed to resemble the shape of a breaking wave. See p.83

▶▶ **Sheikh Zayed Road** Dubai's finest architectural parade, with a cloud-capped line of pencil-thin skyscrapers including some of the city's finest – and silliest – modernist buildings. See p.69

▶▶ **Emirates Towers** Landmark pair of skyscrapers, their distinctive triangular summits rising high above Sheikh Zayed Road's northern end. See p.69

▶▶ **Dubai Creek Golf Club Clubhouse** Dubai's answer to the Sydney Opera House, inspired by the shape of the masts and sails of a traditional Arabian dhow. See p.68

▶▶ **National Bank of Dubai** The city centre's most striking modern building, with a huge, sail-shaped metallic facade rising high above, and providing memorable reflections of, the waters of the Creek. See p.60

▶▶ **Etisalat Tower** Quirky office tower, topped by an enormous golf ball. See p.61

▶▶ **Dubai Marina** The city's most spectacular modern development, with a dense forest of high-rises fighting for space at the city's southern end. See p.91

▶▶ **Al Kazim Towers** Eye-catching pair of skyscrapers, designed to resemble a postmodern remake of New York's famous Chrysler Tower, not once, but twice. See p.92

Out of the City

Out of the City

14

Out of the City

Not until you leave it do you realize how unrepresentative Dubai is of the UAE as a whole, and a visit to any of the neighbouring emirates offers an interesting alternative perspective on life in the Gulf. The easiest day-trip is to the nearby city of **Sharjah**, now virtually a suburb of Dubai, which boasts a fine array of museums devoted to various aspects of the UAE's traditional religion and culture. Slightly further afield, the "garden city" of **Al Ain** offers a pleasantly laidback contrast to life on the coast, with a string of traditional mud-brick forts, souks and a wonderful oasis. Beyond Al Ain, the tranquil **east coast** of the UAE offers dramatic mountain scenery and a string of beautiful – and still largely deserted – beaches; the perfect place to hole up for a few days away from the urban melee. Two hours' drive down the coast from Dubai, **Abu Dhabi**, the capital of the UAE, is now gradually emerging from the shadow of its more famous neighbour, and boasts a growing range of attractions including the opulent *Emirates Palace* hotel and the monumental new Sheikh Zayed Mosque, one of the world's most spectacular places of Islamic worship.

Sharjah

Just 10km north up the coast, the city of **Sharjah** seems at first sight like simply an extension of Dubai, with whose northern suburbs it merges seamlessly in an ugly concrete sprawl. Physically, the two cities may have virtually fused into one, but culturally they remain light years apart. Sharjah has a distinctively different flavour, having clung much more firmly to its traditional Islamic roots, with none of Dubai's freewheeling glitz and tourist fleshpots – and precious few tourists either.

There *are* compensations, however, mainly in the shape of the city's fine array of museums devoted to various aspects of Islamic culture and local Emirati life, all of which offer some compensation for Sharjah's architectural squalor and puritanical regime (see p.150). These include the world-class new **Museum of Islamic Civilization**, the excellent **Sharjah Art Gallery** and the quaint little **Al Hisn Fort**. Slightly more modest, but still interesting, are the exhibits at the **Bait al Naboodah**, the **Calligraphy Museum** and the **Sharjah Heritage Museum**. Further attractions include the massive **Blue Souk**, one of the largest in the UAE, and the **Souq al Arsa**, one of the prettiest.

Arrival and information

Regular **buses** (5dh; every 20–25min; 24hr) run from Bur Dubai's Al Ghubaiba bus station (see p.24) to the main bus terminal in Sharjah a short distance east of the Blue Souk. **Taxis** in Dubai levy a 20dh surcharge to travel to Sharjah; count on around 60–70dh from central Dubai to Sharjah in total. The city's significantly lower rents mean that many people commute daily from Sharjah to Dubai, resulting in the main highway's now-notorious **traffic jams**, at their worst between 7am and 10am when heading into Dubai, and from 5pm to 8pm travelling back towards Sharjah. As a tourist, you'll be travelling in the opposite direction to most of the traffic, but the roads can still be horribly congested so it's worth avoiding the peak hours if possible; the best option may be to travel to Sharjah mid-afternoon and return in the evening. Depending on traffic the journey takes from 45min to well over an hour.

A convenient alternative to travelling under your own steam is to take a **tour** of Sharjah. These are offered by most of the companies listed on p.26 and cost around 150dh, sometimes including a brief visit to the neighbouring emirate of Ajman as well.

Sharjah's Islamic laws

Among the relatively liberal Islamic emirates of the UAE, Sharjah is infamous for its **hardline stance** on matters of dress, alcohol and the relationship between the sexes. These derive from the close financial ties linking Sharjah with Saudi Arabia. In 1989 a Saudi consortium provided a financial rescue package after the emirate's banking system collapsed with debts of over $500 million. Saudi advisers subsequently succeeded in persuading Sharjah's ruler to introduce a version of *sharia*-style law, and Saudi influence remains strong to this day. Many locals bemoan the stultifying effect these laws have had on the the emirate's development – particularly painful given that, up until the 1950s, Sharjah was one of the most developed and cosmopolitan cities in the lower Gulf. **Alcohol is banned**, making it the only dry emirate in the UAE; the wearing of tight or revealing clothing in public areas is likely to get you into trouble with locals or the police; couples "not in a legally acceptable relationship" are, according to the emirate's "decency laws", not even meant to be alone in public together; and in 2009 the authorities revived a traditional Islamic law prohibiting men from wearing silver or gold jewellery (apart from rings) in public. Punishments for more serious offences include imprisonment and flogging.

In practice, unmarried Western couples behaving in a respectable manner are extremely unlikely to experience any hassle. There have, however, been repeated reports of relatively powerless Asian and Arab expat workers being arrested by the city's hardline police and being carted off into detention. Even westerners are not always immune. In 2009, South African expat Roxanne Hillier, who was working as a dive instructor in Sharjah, was accused of having spent time alone in a room with her Emirati boss, technically an offence under Sharjah law. She was imprisoned and subsequently spent 68 days in prison before being "pardoned" by Sharjah's ruler Sheikh Qassimi.

Although it is generally recognized that any sovereign state has the right to impose its own legal codes and cultural standards, the seemingly abitrary manner in which Sharjah has pursued its vision of Islamic law has raised significant concerns among both local expatriates and the international community at large. Given the extent to which the emirate relies on expatriate workers to drive its economic development, its vigorous application of sharia law seems absurd – not to mention a sure-fire disincentive to any future tourist development.

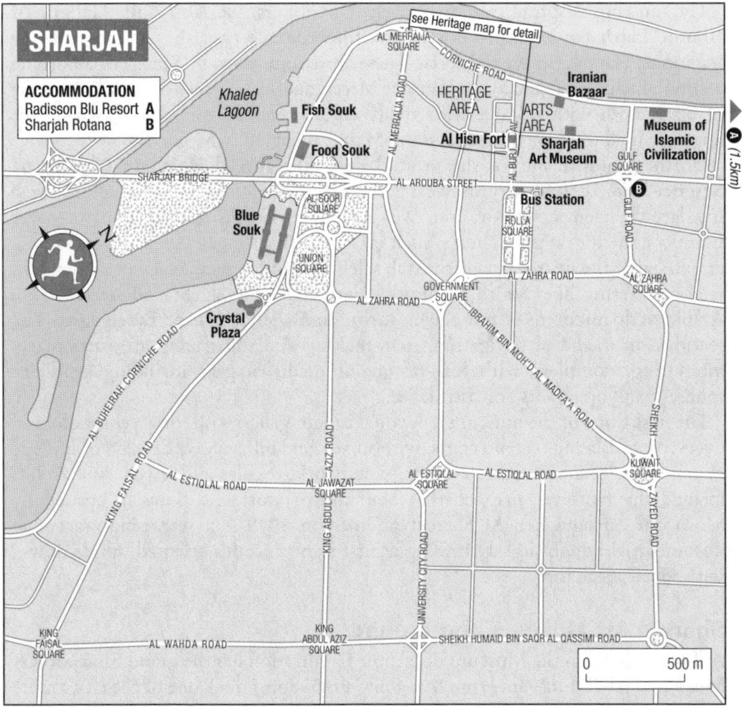

There are plenty of **taxis in Sharjah** for short hops around the city. Most of the city's taxis are now metered, and slightly cheaper than those in Dubai, with a basic flag fare of 2.5dh. A few unmetred taxis remain in service, in which case you'll have to agree a fare before you set off.

The City

Sharjah's appeal is far from obvious. Physically it's the most unattractive place in the UAE, a desperately ugly mass of clumpy high-rises which has all the concrete of Dubai but none of its charm. On the ground the entire city, despite its size, seems oddly lacking in any kind of street life or definite personality, managing somehow to combine the charmlessness of a contemporary urban jungle with the tedium of a backwater provincial town.

Sharjah Museum of Islamic Civilization

The main reason for trekking out to Sharjah is to visit the superb new **Sharjah Museum of Islamic Civilization** (Sat–Thurs 8am–8pm, Fri 4–8pm; 5dh), which occupies the beautifully restored waterfront Souk al Majara, topped with a distinctive golden dome. The museum offers an absorbing overview of the massive – and often unheralded – contributions to the world's culture made by Muslim scientists, artists and architects over the past five hundred years or so, although some of the displays are irritatingly self-congratulatory, and occasionally veer into pure ahistorical propaganda (like the attempt to claim the purely Hindu Jantar Mantar observatory in Jaipur, India, as a work of Islamic provenance).

The museum is spread over two levels. Downstairs, the **Abu Bakr Gallery of Islamic Faith** has extensive displays on the elaborate rituals associated with the traditional Haj pilgrimage to Mecca. These are accompanied by a range of absorbing exhibits, including fascinating photos of Mecca, and a large piece of *kiswah*, the sheet of black cloth with Koranic texts richly embroidered in gold thread, which was formerly used to drape the *kaaba* in the Masjid al Haram in Mecca.

On the opposite side of the ground floor, the **Ibn al Haitham Gallery of Science and Technology** showcases the extensive contributions made by Arab scholars to scientific innovation over the centuries. Absorbing displays cover Islamic contributions to fields such as chemistry, medicine and astronomy, emphasizing the degree to which Arab scientists led the medieval world (standard scientific terms like zenith, azimuth, algorithm and algebra all derive from Arabic, as do hundreds of star names, including Rigel, Algol and Betelgeuse). The sections on medieval navigation, map-making and star-gazing are particularly interesting, complete with lots of quaint medieval gear including armillary spheres, wall quadrants and astrolabes.

The **first floor** of the museum is devoted to four galleries offering a chronological overview of Islamic arts and crafts, with superb and informative displays of historic manuscripts, ceramics, glass, armour, woodwork, textiles and jewellery. Exhibits include the first-ever map of the then known world (ie Eurasia), created by Moroccan cartographer Al Shereef al Idrisi in 1099 – a surprisingly accurate document, although slightly baffling at first sight since it's oriented upside down, with south at the top.

Sharjah Art Museum and around

A short walk from the Museum of Islamic Civilization lies the grand **Sharjah Art Museum** (Sat–Thurs 9am–1pm & 5–8pm, Fri 5–8pm; free), one of the city's more interesting attractions – albeit one which seems totally incongruous in the context of this Islamic-leaning emirate, and given the religion's traditional strictures against the painting of humans and animals. The museum is tucked away in the backstreets east of Al Hisn Fort in a large modern wind-towered building, signed from the waterfront or reachable from Al Burj Avenue, behind the fort.

The ground floor is devoted to temporary exhibitions, usually featuring local and/or Arab artists of varying originality and ability. Much more interesting is the permanent **Orientalist collection** upstairs, devoted to paintings by nineteenth-century European artists depicting life in Islamic lands. The collection is centred on a wonderful selection of lithographs by Scottish artist David Roberts drawn from his celebrated *Sketches in the Holy Land and Syria*, based on a journey through the Middle East in 1838–39. Robert's work remains one of the quintessential pictorial expressions of Orientalism, with canvases showing picturesquely robed natives reclining in carefully staged postures amid even more picturesque mosques, forts and assorted ruins.

The waterfront just west of the Art Museum is home to Sharjah's **dhow wharfage**, similar to the one in Dubai (see p.58), with dozens of traditional old wooden dhows moored up along the edge of the Khaled Lagoon, and great piles of merchandise stacked up along the quayside.

Al Hisn Fort

At the very heart of Sharjah on Al Burj Avenue, the modest little **Al Hisn Fort** (Sat–Thurs 8am–2pm; free) is one of the traditional symbols of old Sharjah, formerly home to the ruling Al Qassimi family and the rallying-point in days gone by for all important city gatherings, although it's now rather ignominiously

▲ Al Hisn Fort

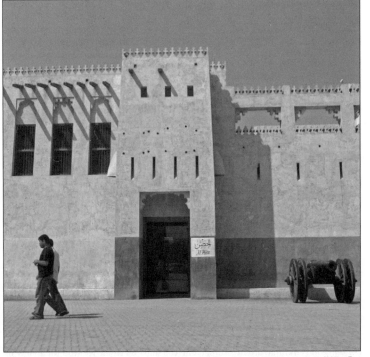

hemmed in by rows of unforgiveably ugly apartment blocks. The fact that it exists at all is entirely due to the current ruler of Sharjah, Sheikh Sultan bin Mohammad al Qassimi. In 1969, the young sheikh (then crown prince) was studying in Cairo when he heard the fort was being demolished. Al Qassimi returned to Sharjah post-haste to halt the destruction, only to discover he had arrived too late to prevent most of the fort from being demolished, apart from a single tower. Undaunted, he ordered the immediate rebuilding of the fort, whose reconstruction he personally supervised, using old photos and plans, and salvaging as much of the material of the razed building – including its fine old wooden doors – as was possible.

The fort now houses an interesting **museum** (closed for renovation at the time of writing) devoted to the history of the emirate, with most exhibits housed in the rooms around the edge of the large central courtyard. These include the usual old coins, rifles and swords, a fascinating sequence of old photographs of Sharjah in the 1930s, dhows and the old fish market – a reminder that, up until World War II, it was Sharjah, rather than Dubai, that was the leading commercial player in this part of the Gulf.

Heritage Area

Heading due west from Al Hisn Fort brings you to the long section of reconstructed old city wall which marks the edge of Sharjah's extensive **Heritage Area**. This is where you'll find several of the city's most interesting museums, dotted around an

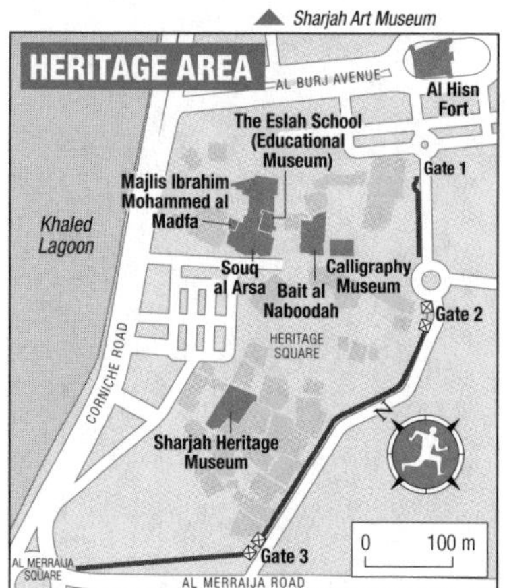

attractively old-fashioned and labyrinthine quarter of traditional Emirati houses. The entire area is nicest towards dusk and after dark; during the day, the lack of shade and wind means it can get oppressively hot.

Bait al Naboodah and the Calligraphy Museum

Situated in an atmospheric old house opposite the Souq al Arsa (see below), the **Bait al Naboodah** (daily 8am–1pm & 5–8pm, Fri 5–8pm only; 5dh) offers an interesting re-creation of traditional family life in Sharjah. The main attraction is the rambling two-storey building itself, one of the most attractive in the UAE, flanking a spacious central courtyard, its exposed coral-brick walls and wooden verandas supported by incongruous Greek-style wooden columns. Only the rooms on the ground floor are open. These include a string of bedrooms furnished in traditional Gulf style, with canopied wooden beds and floor cushions, the walls hung with old rifles, clocks and radios. There are also a couple of rustic kitchens, a small *majlis* (with a few pictures of the Al Naboodah family who once lived here) and a traditional games room with quaint local toys including a cute toy car made out of two old oil cans, with food tins for wheels. A couple of further rooms are devoted to the restoration of the house and another has insightful exhibits on traditional Emirati architecture. For an eyeful of contemporary Emirati architecture, climb the stairs up to the rooftop for a view of Sharjah's uninspiring concrete skyline.

Next door to the Bait al Naboodah, the attractive **Calligraphy Museum** (Sat–Thurs 8am–8pm, Fri 4–8pm; 5dh) houses a huge collection of Arabic calligraphic artworks. Exhibits include an outstanding array of traditional and contemporary calligraphic design, from lines of blocky Kufic script to extravagantly florid rosette patterns and modern renderings in acrylic on canvas, all consumately executed and beautifully displayed.

Souq al Arsa and around

Immediately north of the Bait al Naboodah, the Souq al Arsa is far and away the prettiest in Sharjah, if not the whole of the UAE. The souk is centred around an atmospheric central pillared courtyard, flanked by carpet shops and the quaint little *Al Arsaha Public Coffee Shop* (see opposite), beyond which radiates an intriguing tangle of alleyways. The coral-stone buildings are stuffed with all sorts of colourful local handicrafts, from Persian rugs and Omani silver to Indian textiles and stuffed camels; you'll find more unusual curios, too, including various antiques and Saddam Hussein-era Iraqi banknotes.

Tucked away around the back (north) side of the Souq al Arsa, the **Majlis Ibrahim Mohammed al Madfa** (Sat–Thurs 8am–8pm, Fri 4–8pm; free) is one of the prettiest buildings in the Heritage Area. The building itself is particularly quaint, topped by a diminutive round wind tower, said to be the only one in the UAE. The small interior hosts a few personal effects of the house's former owner, pearl merchant Ibrahim Mohammed al Madfa, including a few items associated with the pearling trade, plus *khanjar* and a bandolier.

Tucked into one side of the Souq Al Arsa is the small and eminently missable **Eslah School Museum** (Sat–Thurs 8am–8pm, Fri 4–10pm; free) – a couple of old classrooms with wooden desks and photographs of former pupils.

Sharjah Heritage Museum

Set amid another warren of alleyways west of the Souq al Arsa, the **Sharjah Heritage Museum** (Sat–Thurs 8am–8pm, Fri 4–8pm; free) offers a comprehensive overview of the emirate's traditional culture and commerce. The museum comprises a sequence of rooms each focusing on a different subject of local interest, and although it's all a bit didactic and school-mistressy compared to other museums in the city, serious students of Gulf history will find much of interest. Exhibits include a display of the coins and banknotes used before the establishment of a unified UAE currency in 1973 (mainly Indian rupees issued under British rule); a big array of unusual and colourful colonial-era stamps (Sharjah didn't issue its own stamps until 1963, and didn't even have a post office until 1965); a room showing the items used in a traditional Gulf classroom; a folk arts room containing drums, ouds (Arabian lutes) and strange wind instruments; plus rooms devoted to popular medicine.

Blue Souk

A kilometre west of the city centre, the huge **Blue Souk** (officially known as the Central Market; most shops open roughly 10am–10pm, although some may close in the afternoon between around 1–4pm) is Sharjah's most visited and photographed attraction, occupying an enormous, eye-catching and ungainly pair of buildings which – despite the myriad wind towers, blue tiling and other Arabian decorative touches – bear an uncanny resemblance to a large railway station. The souk is best known for its numerous carpet shops, which stock a vast range of Persian and other rugs at prices that are generally significantly cheaper than in Dubai. If you're not after rugs, there are plenty of electronics, clothes, jewellery and handicrafts shops to browse, although Souq al Arsa has a better selection of Arabian souvenirs, and the quality and range of goods on offer is fairly underwhelming compared to Dubai.

Eating

Eating in Sharjah is a fairly utilitarian business. There are a fair number of places for a quick spot of lunch or dinner during a visit to the city, but nowhere that really deserves a special visit on account of its food or atmosphere alone, with the exception of the engaging *Al Arsaha Public Coffee Shop*, one of the UAE's most personable little cafés.

Al Arsaha Public Coffee Shop Souq al Arsa. At the heart of the pretty Souq al Arsa, this quaint little café offers a beguiling window on local life, with rattan-covered walls, colourful tables covered in big Lipton's tea logos and a colourful clientele of local Emiratis and expat Arabs. It's a good place to grab a glass of mint tea or a cup of coffee, and there's also a small range of spicy chicken, mutton and fish biriyanis.

Crystal Plaza Corniche Road, immediately south of the Blue Souk. One of Sharjah's fanciest malls, set in eye-catching pyramidal glass-covered towers. There's a range of low-key eating options here, including a ground-floor pizzeria, ice-cream parlour and coffee shop, as well as a rather moribund upstairs food court centred around the *Danial Restaurant*, which offers a mix of Middle Eastern and Iranian dishes. Given that there's nowhere to eat or drink in the Blue Souk itself (bar a few modest coffee stalls), it offers a convenient pit stop, if not much else.

Radisson Blu Resort Corniche Rd. A ten-minute taxi ride east of the city centre, the *Radisson* has Sharjah's best selection of eating outlets, including *Shahzadeh* (Persian and Moroccan), *Canton China* and *Café at the Falls*, located in the hotel's striking, tropical-rainforest-themed atrium.

Sharjah Rotana Al Arouba St. Central Sharjah's leading business hotel is about 500m east of the centre and offers a pleasant retreat from the drab city streets outside. Eating options include the *Al Dar* restaurant, with international buffet and a la carte, plus a peaceful lobby café.

Al Ain

For a complete change of pace and scenery, a day-trip out to the desert city of Al Ain, some 130km inland from Dubai on the border with Oman, offers the perfect antidote to the rip-roaring pace of life on the coast. The UAE's fourth largest city and only major inland settlement, Al Ain – and the twin city of **Buraimi**, on the Omani side of the border – grew up around the string of oases whose densely packed swathes of palms still provide the modern city with one of its most attractive features. The city served as an important staging post on trading routes between Oman and the Gulf, a fact attested to by the numerous forts that dot the town and its hinterland and by the rich archeological remains found in the vicinity, evidence of continuous settlement dating back perhaps as long as four thousand years. Al Ain is actually part of **Abu Dhabi Emirate**, and is also celebrated as the birthplace of Sheikh Zayed bin Sultan al Nahyan (1918–2004), Abu Dhabi's revered former ruler and first president of the UAE; he served as the city's governor before taking over the reins of power in Abu Dhabi in 1966.

Arrival and information

Minibuses (hourly; 1hr 30min–2hr; 20dh) run between Al Ghubaiba bus station in Bur Dubai (see p.24) and Al Ain's bus station. Al Ain is quite spread out, so you're likely to have to use **taxis** to get around; there are plenty on the streets, and you'll probably be hooted at constantly by the drivers of empty cabs. Taxis in Al Ain are painted gold and white, with Islamic-style green pointed signs on top; they're metred (or should be), with a flag fare of 2.5dh.

A convenient alternative is to take a **tour** to Al Ain. These are offered by virtually all the operators listed on p.26 and cost around 200dh.

Dubai Desert Conservation Reserve

Unfortunately, much of the desert around Dubai is a total mess, disfigured by endless building works, pylons, petrol stations and other unforgiveable clutter. For a real taste of unadulterated desert, the best place to head is the superb **Dubai Desert Conservation Reserve** (Ⓦwww.ddcr.org), around 45km from Dubai alongside the main E66 highway to Al Ain. Interestingly, this is not an untouched piece of original desert, but one which has been systematically rehabilitated over the past decade and restored to something approaching its original condition – perhaps offering a model of what could be done elsewhere to rejuvenate Dubai's beautiful but severely damaged natural environment.

The reserve encloses 250km of shifting dunes, dotted with stunted acacia, firebush and indigenous ghaf trees, and serves as a refuge for 33 local mammal and reptile species, including rare and endangered creatures such as the oryx, Arabian gazelle, sand gazelle, Arabian red fox and sand fox. Access to the reserve is carefully controlled. The cheapest option is to come on a visit with one of the small and select group of Dubai operators who are allowed to run tours here (at present: Arabian Adventures, Lama, Travco and Alpha – see p.26). Alternatively, you can stay in the reserve at the idyllic, but wickedly expensive, Al Maha resort (see p.109).

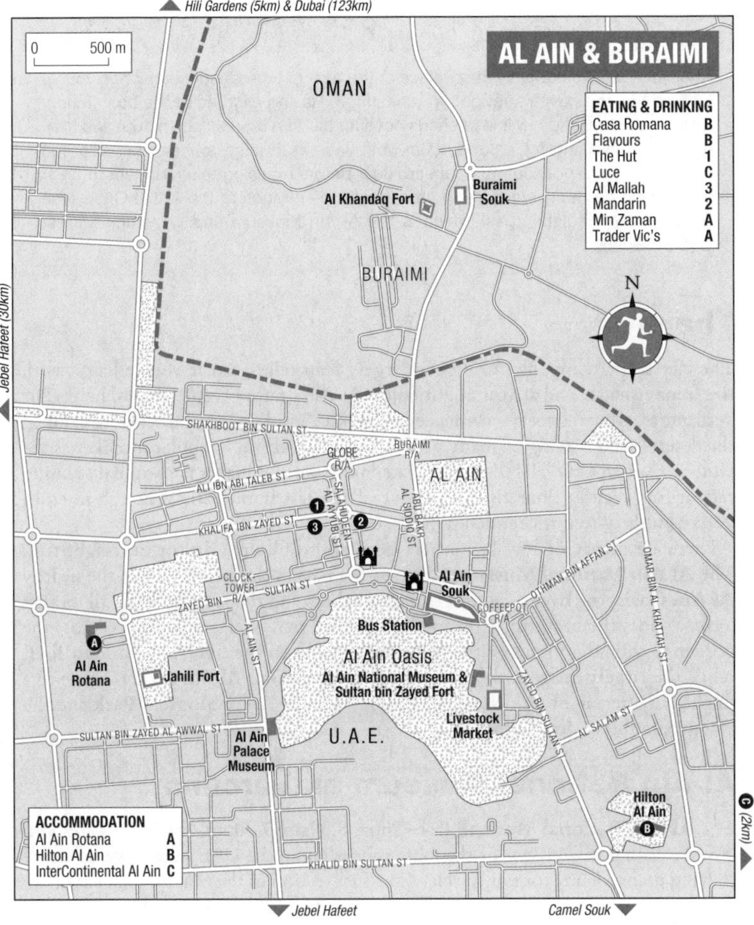

Accommodation

Al Ain isn't exactly overflowing with accommodation options. Apart from the three low-key five-stars listed below there are a few drab and overpriced places dotted around the centre, but no budget options.

Al Ain Rotana ⓣ **03-754 5111** ⓦ **www.rotana.com**. The nicest of the city's three five-star hotels, and conveniently close to the city centre, with pleasantly chintzy Arabian decor. Rooms are very spacious and well appointed, and there are also a few two- and three-bedroom villas, while in-house amenities include a nice pool, gardens and a couple of good restaurants (see above). Around 1500dh.

Hilton Al Ain ⓣ **03-678 6666,** ⓦ **www.hilton.com**. Run-of-the-mill and rather dated hotel, though rates are usually good value and the grounds and pools are spacious and attractive. Around 600–750dh.

Intercontinental Al Ain Resort ⓣ **03-768 6686,** ⓦ **www.intercontinental.com**. Very peaceful hotel on the edge of town, set amid extensive gardens. Rooms are uninspiring, though rates are often the best value in town. Around 500dh.

Getting oriented in Al Ain

Al Ain can be a remarkably mazy place at the best of times, especially when you've just arrived and haven't yet got your bearings. Having alighted at the bus station, turn to face the long low line of sheds housing the Al Ain Souk (see p.160) and then head right, walking for around 100m until you see a large roundabout, adorned with a big coffeepot sculpture, ahead. Just before reaching this roundabout, veer right, across a dusty car parking area, past the entrance to the Al Ain Oasis (see opposite), immediately past which is the Al Ain Museum and Livestock Market (see p.below).

The city

The city is sprawling, confusing and largely featureless, but if you've had it with the frenzy that is Dubai you might enjoy Al Ain's rather sedate atmosphere. The verdant, tree-lined streets – evidence of Sheikh Zayed's obsession with "greening" the desert – and a string of shady oases have led to Al Ain's popular moniker as the Gulf's "Garden City". Its slightly elevated position also makes it a popular summer retreat for wealthy Emiratis on account of the less humid air, although in truth you're unlikely to notice much difference.

There are plenty of low-key attractions here to fill up a day or overnight trip. The **Al Ain National Museum** is one of the best in the region, while the nearby **Al Ain Oasis**, the **livestock and camel markets** and the **Al Ain Souk** all merit a look, as does the beautifully restored **Al Jahili Fort**. You can also hop across the border to visit the Omani city of Buraimi, home to the fine **Al Khandaq fort**, while the largely unspoilt desert scenery that surrounds Al Ain itself is home to a further smattering of attractions, including the **Hili Archeological Park** and the craggy summit of **Jebel Hafeet**.

Al Ain National Museum and around

The **Al Ain National Museum** (Sat–Thurs 8.30am–7.30pm, Fri 3–7.30pm; 3dh. Ⓦwww.aam.gov.ae) is one of the more rewarding in the UAE, and makes a logical starting point for any tour of the city. The first section of the museum has extensive displays covering various aspects of local life. These include unusual exhibits such as implements used during circumcisions and the shoulder bones of cows (which students used as writing slates) alongside old Korans, fine antique silver jewellery and some marvellous photos of Abu Dhabi Emirate in the 1960s. There's also a mishmash of gifts presented by various luminaries to Sheikh Zayed over the years, including Egyptian president Gamal Nasser (a pair of large embossed plates) and the celebrated female Palestinian freedom fighter Lyla Khaled (a bullet).

The second section offers a comprehensive overview of the archeology of the UAE, including extensive artefacts from sites such as Umm an Nar, near Abu Dhabi, and Jebel Hafeet and Hili (see pp.160–161), just outside Al Ain. Most of the exhibits are fairly unexciting – pots, seals, fragments of arrow heads and other stone fragments – but they're well displayed and explained, offering an interesting picture of local cultural and commercial links right back to the Sumerian era.

Sultan bin Zayed Fort and Livestock Market

Right next to the museum, the **Sultan bin Zayed Fort** (or Eastern Fort; same hours and ticket) is one of the eighteen or so forts scattered around Al Ain and the surrounding desert. The picturesque three-towered structure is best known as the birthplace of Sheikh Zayed bin Sultan al Nahyan (ruled 1966–2004), who oversaw the transformation of the emirate from impoverished Arabian backwater into today's oil-rich contemporary city-state. The fort houses a superb collection of 1960s and 1970s black-and-white photos from around the Gulf, while the picturesque little courtyard at its centre is dotted with a trio of trees and a couple of little traditional palm-thatched *barasti* huts – humble beginnings for the sheikh who would subsequently become one of the world's richest men.

Immediately behind the museum lies the city's rough-and-ready **Livestock Market**, an attractively rustic-looking place, with mooing, bleating and clucking livestock penned up in the backs of long lines of collapsed pick-up trucks. It's liveliest in the early morning, up to around 9am, when a colourful crowd of local Emiratis and Omanis come to haggle over anything from chickens to cows. At other times things can be pretty sleepy, though it's still worth a quick look.

Al Ain Oasis

Spreading west of the National Museum, a dusty green wall of palms announces the presence of the beautiful **Al Ain Oasis** (daily sunrise–sunset; free), the largest of the seven oases scattered across the city (the name Al Ain, means, literally, "The Spring"). This is easily the most idyllic spot in the city, with a mazy network of little walled lanes running between densely planted thickets of trees. There are an estimated 150,000-odd date palms here, along with mango, fig, banana and orange trees, their roots watered in the summer months using traditional *falaj* irrigation channels, which bring water down from the mountains over a distance of some 30km. It's a wonderfully peaceful spot, the silence only broken by the calls to prayer from the two mosques nestled amongst the palms, and pleasantly cool as well. There are eight entrances dotted around the perimeter of the oasis, although given the disorienting tangle of roads within you're unlikely to end up coming out where you entered.

▲ Al Ain Oasis

Al Ain Souk

Immediately in front of the bus station, **Al Ain Souk** is home to the city's main meat, fruit and vegetable market. Housed in a long, functional warehouse-style building, the souk is stocked with the usual picturesque piles of produce (along with the dangling carcasses of animals in the meat section), prettiest at the structure's west end, where Indian traders sit enthroned amid huge mounds of fruit and vegetables. The souk attracts a colourful cast of characters, including patrician-looking Omani men with splendid beards and big white turbans, along with heavily veiled local Bedouin women in their distinctive metal face masks.

Al Ain Palace Museum and Jahili Fort

On the western side of Al Ain Oasis stands the recently opened **Al Ain Palace Museum** (Sat–Thurs 8.30am–7.30pm, Fri 3–7.30pm; free), occupying one of the various forts around Al Ain owned by the ruling Nahyan family of Abu Dhabi and hallowed thanks to its associations with Sheikh Zayed. The sprawing complex is pleasant enough, with rambling, orangey-pink buildings arranged around a sequence of five courtyards and small gardens, although the palace's thirty-odd rooms, including assorted bedrooms, *majlis* and a small school, aren't particularly interesting.

Much more rewarding is the nearby **Jahili Fort** (Tues–Thurs, Sat & Sun 9am–5pm, Fri 3pm–5pm; free). Built in 1898, this is one of the finest traditional buildings in the Al Ain area, with an impressively battlemented main tower and a spacious central courtyard. The much-photographed circular tower on the northern side – with four levels of diminishing size, each topped with a line of triangular battlements – probably pre-dates the rest of the fort. The **information desk** here has an extensive selection of booklets and is a good place to pick up details about other attractions around Al Ain.

The fort is also home to the excellent little **Mubarak bin London** exhibition, devoted to the life of legendary explorer **Wilfred Thesiger** (1910–2003). Thesiger – or Mubarak bin London (the "Blessed Son of London") as he was known to his Arab friends – stayed at the fort in the late 1940s at the end of one of the two pioneering journeys across the deserts of the Empty Quarter which later formed the centrepiece of *Arabian Sands*, his classic narrative of Middle Eastern exploration. The exhibition showcases some of Thesiger's superb photography, along with an interesting short film and assorted personal effects, plus a few photographs of Thesiger and his close friend Sheikh Zayed (to whom Thesiger bore an uncanny resemblance).

Around Al Ain

North of the centre, the **Hili Gardens and Archeological Park** (daily 9am–10pm; 1dh), about 8km north of the city, is the site of one of the most important archeological finds in the UAE; many finds from here are displayed in the Al Ain Museum, which also provides a good explanation of their significance. The main surviving building is the so-called Great Hili Tomb (though it may actually have been some kind of temple), a diminutive circular structure dating from the third century BC and decorated with primitive carvings of animals and humans; The adjacent Grand Garden Tomb yielded over two hundred skeletons when excavated.

Al Ain's old-fashioned **Camel Souk** (actually just a series of pens in the open desert) is also worth a visit, despite being a bit tricky to find, attracting a lively crowd of local camel-fanciers haggling over dozens of dromedaries lined up for sale. The souk is busiest in the mornings from around 9–10am, although low-key trading may continue throughout the day. To reach the souk, find the roundabout in front of the *Hilton* hotel and follow the road towards the Oman border at Mazyad. After about three kilometres you'll see the huge new Bawadi mall on your left. Do a U-turn at the next roundabout, a kilometre or so beyond the mall, and start driving back towards Al Ain. The souk is off the road on your right, about 500m before you get back to the Bawadi mall.

If you have your own vehicle or are prepared to stump up the taxi fare, the soaring 1180-metre **Jebel Hafeet** (or Hafit), 30km south of Al Ain on the Omani border is a popular local retreat with Emiratis wanting to escape the heat of the desert plains. The second-highest mountain in the UAE, Jebel Hafeet's distinctively craggy outline (sometimes rather fancifully compared to the tail of a dragon) provides an impressive backdrop to the city and is especially pretty after dark, when the lights lining the road up it seem to hang suspended in mid-air. You can drive to the top in half an hour or less along the excellent road, from where there are peerless views over the surrounding Hajar mountains. The outdoor terrace at the plush *Mercure Grand* hotel, perched just below the summit, makes a memorable – if often surprisingly chilly – spot for a drink.

Into Oman: Buraimi

The border with Oman lies about 1km north of central Al Ain, beyond which lies the contiguous Omani city of **Buraimi** – traditionally the larger and more famous of the two settlements, though now increasingly overshadowed by its upstart neighbour. The border between the two countries, which had always been open, with minimal or nonexistent checks, was closed in late 2006 to all except Gulf Cooperation Council (GCC) citizens, meaning it's no longer possible to walk across the border to visit the fine Al Khandaq Fort and Buraimi Souk on the Oman side. Foreign tourists wanting to cross into Oman must now travel via the border post north of Al Ain at Hili (see above), where full border formalities are in force. Doing so is a fairly pointless exercise if you're only in Al Ain on a short visit, as you might spend an hour crossing the border each way in busy times. If you do intend to cross the border, check the latest visa situation with the Oman embassy in Dubai carefully before travel; regulations have changed with bewildering rapidity over the past few years.

Eating

For simple meals, snacks and drinks, there's a good cluster of places just south of Globe roundabout, on the northern edge of the city centre. These include *Al Mallah*, a simple little shwarma joint which serves up good-sized portions of tasty Lebanese food, and the nearby *Mandarin* coffee shop and *The Hut* café, both cosy spots for a (non-alocholic) drink and a snack or light meal; all these places are open daily for lunch and dinner. Various no-frills cafés around the city centre cater to Al Ain's sizeable Indian and Pakistani community, and serve cheap, basic north Indian staples.

For something a bit smarter you'll need to head out to one of the city's trio of five-star hotels. The **Al Ain Rotana**, about 1km west of the city centre, hosts a branch of the ever-popular *Trader Vic's* (see p.118) and the attractive *Min Zaman* Lebanese restaurant, while the **Hilton Al Ain**, 1km south of the Al Ain Museum, is home to the cheeful *Casa Romana* and the alfresco *Flavours* terrace restaurant. The **InterContinental Al Ain** hotel, about 4km east of the city centre, is home to various restaurants, including the chic Italian *Luce*, probably the most stylish venue in town. All these venues are licenced.

The East Coast

The east coast of the UAE is almost the exact opposite of the west. Compared to the country's heavily developed Arabian Gulf seaboard, the Indian Ocean-facing east is only thinly settled and still relatively untouched, thanks largely to the Hajar Mountains which occupy much of the region. Somnolent and scenic, the east is a popular weekend destination for visitors from Dubai, just two hours' drive away, who come to loll around on the largely deserted beaches dotting the coast. A day-trip around the region is an easy way to get a feel for the UAE's relatively undeveloped hinterlands.

One of the major attractions of a trip out to the east coast is the chance to get a look at the magnificent **Hajar Mountains**, which run down the eastern side of the UAE and on into Oman. Bare and craggy, the UAE section of the Hajar rise to a high point of 1527m at Jebel Yibir, inland from Dibba in the far north of the country, and provide a scenic backdrop to the length of the eastern coast, changing from slate grey to deep red as the light alters through the course of the day and picks out the different red, yellow, grey and green mineral strata.

There are a number of low-key sights scatterd around the east coast, including the old fort at **Fujairah** and the UAE's oldest mosque at **Bidiya**, although for many visitors the main attraction is the trio of attractive beachside resorts which dot the beautiful **Al Aqah Beach**.

Travelling around the east coast

Most of the tour operators listed on p.26 offer **day-tours** of the east, usually costing around 200–250dh. **Vehicle rental** is another possibility, and once you've managed to get out of Dubai, the roads in the east are some of the emptiest and most driver-friendly in the country. **Public transport** around the east is sketchy, however, and won't get you very far in a day.

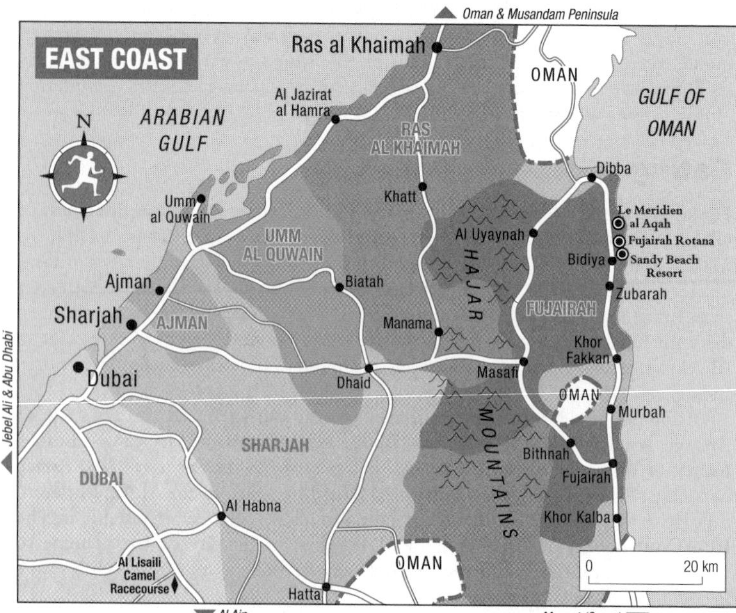

The emirates of the east

The division of the tip of the Arabian peninsula between the seven emirates of the UAE and Oman is a complicated little jigsaw puzzle, with different segments of territory owing allegiance to different emirates. The borders were drawn up by British colonial officials who simply wandered around the peninsula for months enquiring in each village as to which sheikh they owed allegiance to, and drawing up the boundaries accordingly. Most of the area covered here falls within the Emirate of Fujairah, though Masafi belongs to Ras Al Khaimah and Khor Fakkan to Sharjah, while Dibba is divided into three districts: Dibba Muhallab, ruled by Fujairah; Dibba al Hisn, ruled by Sharjah; and Dibba Bayah, which belongs to Oman.

Masafi

Most tours to the east coast stop en route at the small town of **Masafi**, the western gateway to the Hajar Mountains and around 80km from Dubai. Masafi is famous for two things: the first is water – this is where the eponymous mineral water, sold all over the Emirates, is bottled; the second is the town's so-called **Friday Market** (open daily from around 8am–10pm, despite its name). Strung along either side of the busy main road, this heavily visited and decidedly unatmospheric highway bazaar survives largely on the passing coach-party trade. The market is best for carpets, and you can occasionally unearth a few decent items here, and at cheaper prices than Dubai, although most of the stock is kitsch factory-made tat. If you ever wanted a rug embellished with an enormous portrait of Sheikh Zayed, for example, now's your chance.

Dibba to Khor Fakkan

From Masafi, the road heads north to the sleepy coastal town of **Dibba**, pushed right up against the border with Oman. This quiet little spot was the site of one of the major battles of early Islamic history in 633 AD (a year after the Prophet Mohammed's death) when the forces of the caliph Abu Bakr defeated those of a local ruler who had renounced Islam. A large cemetery outside town is traditionally believed to house the remains of the apostates killed in the battle. Despite its illustrious past, there's nothing much to see here apart from the town's fine main mosque, topped by four soaring minarets. Still, the setting on a broad bay backed by dramatic mountains is breezy and scenic, and the town itself is about as pretty as any in the UAE, with low-slung little houses, many of them embellished with the brightly painted metal doors typical of neighbouring Oman.

Dibba is also the jumping-off point for the lovely **Al Aqah Beach**, a fine stretch of golden sand with a trio of upmarket hotels (see p.165) – any of which make a good spot for a meal or an overnight stay. The long swathe of unspoilt coastline hereabouts ranks amongst the UAE's most attractive destinations if you want to get out of Dubai for a few days, and gets busy at weekends with city-dwellers escaping the urban rush. The waters around the curiously shaped rock – popularly known as Snoopy Island on account of its supposed resemblance to the the famous cartoon dog – directly offshore, opposite the *Sandy Beach Motel*, are a popular spot for diving and snorkelling.

A couple of kilometres south of Snoopy Island, the small fishing village of **Bidiya** is famous as the site of the UAE's oldest mosque (and, for once, "old" doesn't mean 1975), dating back to the fifteenth century. It's a rustic little structure made of mud brick and gypsum, topped by four very flat, small domes; visitors are sometimes allowed into the small and dimly lit interior, which is

▲ Bidiya Mosque

supported by a single column. Behind the mosque, steps lead up to the top of the hill behind, studded with a couple of watchtowers and offering superb views over the Hajar mountains.

Around 10km further down the coast, the sizeable town of **Khor Fakkan** sprawls round a superb bay, one of the loveliest in the UAE. The town is part of the booze-free and ultra-conservative Sharjah emirate, and hasn't enjoyed the tourist boom its location would otherwise suggest. It's a pleasant spot for a brief visit though, with a fine seafront corniche complete with fish market, a tempting stretch of beach (although, this being Sharjah, modest beachwear is advised) and views of another popular diving spot, Sharq Island; don't let any mistranslation fool you – *sharq* is Arabic for "east".

Fujairah

Another 20km down the coast brings you to **Fujairah**, the largest settlement on the east coast, although the city itself is fairly unexciting, and its urban sprawl and modest high-rises come as something of a surprise after the unspoilt surrounding countryside. The city has recently enjoyed something of a minor boom, mainly on the back of economic developments in neighbouring emirates, especially Dubai. The focus of much of this is the city's massive oil-refuelling port – the world's third largest after Singapore and Rotterdam – at the southern end of town. This is where most of the UAE's oil is exported from, as its east coast location saves shipping from making a two-day dog-leg around the tip of the Arabian peninsula. There's usually a line of tankers several kilometres long offshore waiting for their turn at the pumps.

Altogether more picturesque is **Fujairah Fort**, one of the most attractive in the UAE, on the northern edge of the city centre. Dating back to the sixteenth century, the fort is unusually well fortified, set atop a large plinth and with high, bare walls rising to a pretty cluster of towers and battlements, dramatically posed

Bull-fighting Fujairah-style

If you happen to be around Fujairah on a Friday afternoon don't miss the chance to watch one of the town's traditional **bull-butting** contests (*mnattah* in Arabic). The sport is said to have been introduced to the Gulf by the Portuguese sometime during the seventeenth or eighteenth centuries; unlike Spanish bull-fighting, the bulls fight one another, rather than a matador. And although there's plenty of bovine testosterone floating around, no blood is spilled – although spectators occasionally have to dash for cover if one of the bulls decides to make a run for it.

The highly prized Brahma bulls which take part in the contests are brought in from across the UAE; the animals are fed up on a diet of milk, honey and butter and weigh around a ton. The bulls are led into the ring by their handlers, after which the "arena master" – a challenging and potentially lethal occupation – takes charge. All being well, the bulls will lock horns and begin to test their strength against the other (although some simply can't be bothered, and will just stand around eyeing up the crowd). Bouts last two or three minutes. The winning bull is that one that suceeds in butting the other one out of the ring, although many contests end in a draw

The bull-butting ground (an open area with tethering posts) is at the southern end of town between the seafont Corniche Road and the main coastal highway. Meetings start around 4.30–5pm on Fridays year-round and last a couple of hours.

against the backdrop of the Hajar Mountains. The fort was closed for restoration at the time of writing but is scheduled to open to the public in the fairly near future (although people have been saying this for years). Immediately south, the rather pedestrian **Fujairah Museum** (Sun–Thurs 8.30am–1.30pm & 4.30–6.30pm, Fri 2–6.30pm; 1dh) houses a run-of-the-mill collection of local weaponry, jewellery and archeological displays. Around 1.5km inland, near Madhab Park just beyond the main bypass, a few of the town's old-fashioned, low-lying mud-brick buildings and *barasti* huts here have been restored as the so-called **Fujairah Heritage Village**.

Accommodation and eating

If you want to spend a night or two on the east coast, the three best **places to stay** are the trio of upmarket hotels on Al Aqah Beach (see p.163). Towering over its northern end is the landmark *Le Méridien Al Aqah Beach Resort* (Ⓣ09-244 900, Ⓦwww.lemeridien-alaqah.com; around 750–1000dh), an impressive high-rise colossus which looks like it's been air-lifted directly from Dubai Marina and plonked down on this sleepy stretch of coast. The hotel serves up plenty of five-star style; facilities include a spa, dive centre and kids' club, plus extensive gardens and private beach. Nearby, the equally large though rather less overpowering *Fujairah Rotana Resort & Spa* (Ⓣ09-244 9888, Ⓦwww.rotana.com; around 600–900dh) offers similar five-star luxury and an equivalent spread of facilities and in-house activities. Slightly further down the beach, the much more low-key *Sandy Beach Hotel & Resort* (Ⓣ09-244 5555, Ⓦwww.sandybm.com; around 800dh) has accommodation in a range of beach chalets and hotel rooms, plus diving and watersports centres.

For **eating**, both the *Fujairah Rotana* and *Le Méridien* have a wide range of all-day cafés and restaurants. Coach parties normally head for the *Sandy Beach Resort* – although the buffet lunches are pretty awful.

Into Oman: the Musandam peninsula

Around two-and-a-half hour's drive north of Dubai lies Oman's **Musandam peninsula**, perhaps the most scenically spectacular area in the entire Gulf, as the towering red-rock Hajar mountains fall precipitously into the blue waters of the Arabian Gulf, creating a labyrinthine system of steep-sided fjords (*khors*), channels and islands. This is one of the region's most pristine natural wildernesses, thinly populated and boasting a magically unspoilt marine environment, including pods of frolicking humpback dolphins and the occasional basking shark. The contrast with Dubai could hardly be greater.

Until the last few decades this was one of the least accessible places in Arabia, and even now there are few roads into or around the peninsula. The easiest way to explore is **by boat**, offering superlative views of the surrounding *khors*, as well as the chance of spotting dolphins and other sealife. Various boat trips, usually aboard a traditional wooden **dhow**, start from Khasab, the peninsula's main town, most of them heading up into Khor Ash Sham, the largest of Musandam's many *khors*, ringed with remote fishing villages.

If you want to see something of Musandam's dramatic **mountainous interior**, a rough road (4WD only) climbs dramatically up towards Jebel Harim ("Mountain of Women"), the peninsula's highest peak, south of Khasab, via the unexpectedly agricultural Sayh Plateau – one of the few flat areas in Musandam, divided into small fields populated with browsing sheep, goats and donkeys.

Visiting Musandam from Dubai

The peninsula is separated from the rest of Oman by a large stretch of UAE territory, and is actually a lot easier to visit from Dubai than from Muscat. Musandam is just about do-able as a **day-trip** from Dubai, if you make a very early start. Leaving at around 6am, you'll have time for a five-hour boat ride or mountain safari before heading back, although you probably won't be back in Dubai anytime much before 10pm. It usually takes about half-an-hour each way to clear the UAE–Oman border post and you should be able to get an Omani visa on the spot. The peninsula also makes a good destination for a longer **two- or three-night** stay. Several of the tour operators listed on p.26 now offer one-day excursions, as well as longer diving and other trips. Alternatively contact one of the two specialist travel agents based in Khasab (although both have representatives also in Dubai). These are Khasab Travel and Tours (in Dubai ⓣ04-266 9950, ⓦwww.khasabtours.com); and Musandam Sea Adventure (in Dubai ⓣ0450-750 3001, ⓦwww.msaoman.com).

Hatta

Another easy day trip from Dubai is to the village of **Hatta**, a small enclave of territory close to the east coast belonging to Dubai Emirate. Built in the shadow of the magnificently craggy Hajar mountains, the village was founded in the sixteenth century and once served as an important staging post on the overland route from Oman to Dubai, as the watchtowers which dot the surrounding hillsides testify. Many people come to visit the **Hatta Heritage Village**, one of the UAE's most appealing museums of traditional life, while the town and surrounding countryside is a popular weekend getaway from Dubai, partly on account of its fractionally cooler temperatures and lower humidity, although things are pretty somnolent during the week.

Arrival and information

Hatta is around 115km from central Dubai, or just over an hour's drive along a fast modern highway. The highway passes through a small section of Oman on

Big Red

Just before you reach the Oman border on the Dubai side you'll notice a huge sand dune off on your left. Known as **Big Red**, this is one of the most popular off-road destinations in the UAE and usually crawling with 4WDs and quad-bikers attempting to make their way to the top, especially over the weekend; many Dubai tour operators use the stretch of less elevated dunes on the other side of the road for dune-bashing excursions during their afternoon desert safaris (see p.27). You can hire your own quad bike from the outlet next to the main road if you fancy a crack at the sands, or just a turn around the flat quad-bike course next to the highway.

route – there are cursory checkpoints entering and leaving Oman territory, but visitors aren't required to produce any paperwork, although note that unless you've made special arrangements, UAE rental cars aren't insured while you're in Oman. **Buses** for Hatta leave from the Gold Souk Bus Station in Deira (6am–9pm; 90min trip; 7dh). The Oman stretch is also notably less developed than the UAE territory on either side, with unspoilt stretches of rocky desert stretching away to the Hajar mountains in the distance.

The Village and around

The main attraction hereabouts is the extensive **Hatta Heritage Village** (Sat–Thurs 8am–8.30pm, Fri 2.30–8.30pm; free). Approaching from Dubai, turn right at the roundabout in front of the *Hatta Fort Hotel*, from where it's about a 3km drive uphill. Scattered across a rugged hillside ringed by craggy mountains, the village comprises a number of low and unusually solid-looking traditional structures with tiny windows and stout teak doors. Restoration here has been relatively light compared to similar heritage sites in the UAE, which adds to the village's rather rustic appeal.

Inside the complex the first building you reach is also the largest, **Al Husen** fort, its rooms filled with the usual displays of dusty weaponry and a *majlis* with unusually tiny windows. There's also a "traditional house" and other smaller buildings with exhibits on traditional folklore, palm tree products and a "poets' *majlis*". The path up through the village eventually climbs up to one of Hatta's two watchtowers, from where there are fine panoramic views. A second **watchtower**, roughly opposite the entrance to the Heritage Village, is reached by a short footpath and worth the climb for the further superb views from the top.

The only other attraction nearby is the **Hatta Rock Pools**, around 20km from Hatta itself and over the border in Oman. The pools sit inside a kind of miniature canyon which has been carved by water erosion out of the rocky floor of the surrounding *wadi*. It's an attractive spot for a dip, although it gets overrun at weekends and has been rather spoilt by the rubbish, graffiti and other junk left by day-trippers; it's strongly recommended to have a 4WD to reach them. There are no border checks but it's worth carrying your passport just in case, and remember UAE rental cars won't be insured while you're in Oman, unless you've made special arrangements. If you're still interested ask for directions locally, as the pools are quite tricky to find.

Accommodation and eating

The only place to **stay and eat** in the village is the *Hatta Fort Hotel* (ⓣ04-809 9333, ⓦwww.jebelali-international.com; around 800dh), an appealing, rather old-fashioned country resort, with fine mountain views, attractive gardens and a spacious pool with its own little rocky waterfall – great for a day or two away from the urban jungle. It's a popular retreat at weekends, when it can get absolutely overrun, but is very peaceful at other times. There's a 50dh per person entrance charge on Fridays and Saturdays, redeemable against food and drink at one of the hotel's trio of restaurants.

Abu Dhabi

The capital of the UAE, **ABU DHABI** is the very model of a modern Gulf petro-city: thoroughly contemporary, shamelessly wealthy and decidedly staid. Abu Dhabi's lightning change from obscure fishing village into modern city-state within the past thirty years is perhaps the most dramatic of all the stories of oil-driven transformation that dot the region. Although the city's endless glass-fronted high-rises and multi-lane highways can seem fairly uninspiring on first aquaintance, locals take understandable pride in the city's remarkable recent metamorphosis.

Arrival and information

Regular **express buses** (5.30am–11.30pm; every 30min; 2hr–2hr 30min trip; 20dh) run from Al Ghubaiba bus station (see p.24) in Bur Dubai to Abu Dhabi's main bus station, about 3km inland from the city centre. A convenient alternative is to take a **tour** from Dubai. Many of the companies listed on p.26 offer Abu Dhabi day-trips, generally costing around 200dh. Abu Dhabi's various attractions are very spread out, but there are plenty of metred **taxis** around town (flag fare 3dh).

Sheikh Zayed and the rise of modern Abu Dhabi

In matters of historical precedence, Abu Dhabi has had the clear advantage over Dubai. The town was established much earlier as an independent settlement and commercial centre, and also struck oil many years before (and in much greater quantities than) Dubai. The city has, however, always lagged behind its neighbour in terms of development. Much of the blame for this can be laid at the door of the insular, old-fashioned and often downright eccentric **Sheikh Shakhbut bin Sultan al Nahyan** (ruled 1926–1966). Despite the sudden wealth of oil revenues, Sheikh Shakhbut signally declined to make any notable improvements to his city, preferring to keep oil revenues locked up in a wooden chest under his bed.

Increasing frustration at the non-existent pace of change (particularly when compared to events in burgeoning Dubai) led to Sheikh Shakhbut's overthrow in a peaceful coup in 1966, and his replacement by his younger brother, **Sheikh Zayed bin Sultan al Nahyan** (ruled 1966–2004). Sheikh Zayed had previously served as governor of Al Ain, proving a resourceful and charismatic leader. On becoming ruler he immediately set about transforming Abu Dhabi. Electricity and telephones were rapidly installed, followed by a new port and airport, schools and a university. Sheikh Zayed also initiated a vast public handout of accumulated oil money to cash-strapped locals and other impoverished families across the neighbouring emirates – an act of fabulous generosity which did much to establish his reputation, and paved the way for his role as leader of the UAE following independence in 1971, when he became the new country's first president.

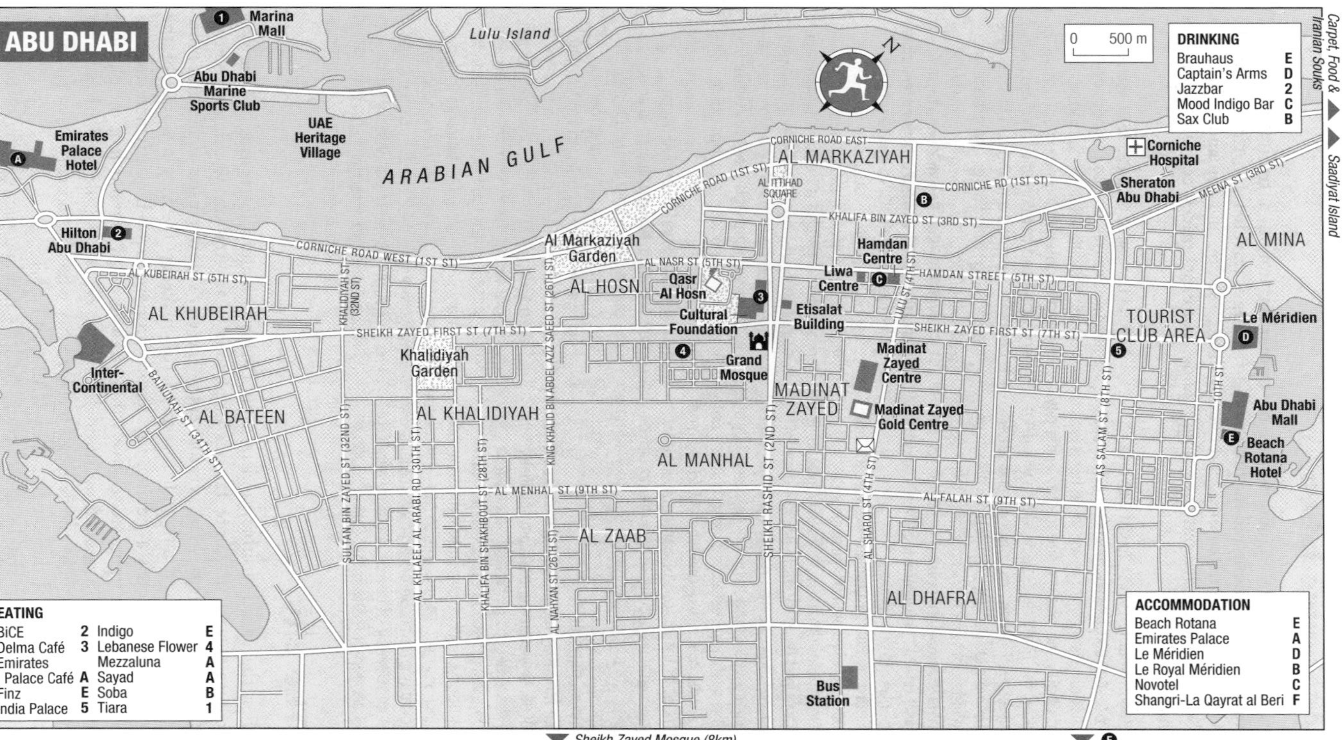

ABU DHABI
Carpet, Food & Iranian Souks
Saadiyat Island
President's Palace
Sheikh Zayed Mosque (8km)
0
500 m
N
DRINKING
Brauhaus E
Captain's Arms D
Jazzbar 2
Mood Indigo Bar C
Sax Club B
ACCOMMODATION
Beach Rotana E
Emirates Palace A
Le Méridien D
Le Royal Méridien B
Novotel C
Shangri-La Qayrat al Beri F
EATING
BiCE 2
Delma Café 3
Emirates Palace Café A
Finz E
India Palace 5
Indigo E
Lebanese Flower 4
Mezzaluna A
Sayad A
Soba B
Tiara 1
ARABIAN GULF
Lulu Island
Marina Mall
Abu Dhabi Marine Sports Club
UAE Heritage Village
Emirates Palace Hotel
Hilton Abu Dhabi
Inter-Continental
AL KHUBEIRAH
AL BATEEN
Khalidiyah Garden
AL KHALIDIYAH
AL ZAAB
AL MANHAL
Al Markaziyah Garden
AL HOSN
Qasr Al Hosn
Cultural Foundation
Grand Mosque
AL MARKAZIYAH
AL ITTIHAD SQUARE
Hamdan Centre
Liwa Centre
Etisalat Building
Madinat Zayed Centre
MADINAT ZAYED
Madinat Zayed Gold Centre
AL DHAFRA
Bus Station
TOURIST CLUB AREA
AL MINA
Le Méridien
Abu Dhabi Mall
Beach Rotana Hotel
Corniche Hospital
Sheraton Abu Dhabi
CORNICHE ROAD EAST
CORNICHE ROAD (1ST ST)
CORNICHE RD (1ST ST)
CORNICHE ROAD WEST (1ST ST)
MEENA ST (3RD ST)
KHALIFA BIN ZAYED ST (3RD ST)
AL NASR ST (5TH ST)
HAMDAN STREET (5TH ST)
AL KUBEIRAH ST (5TH ST)
SHEIKH ZAYED FIRST ST (7TH ST)
AL MENHAL ST (9TH ST)
AL FALAH ST (9TH ST)
KHALIDIYAH ST (32ND ST)
SULTAN BIN ZAYED ST (32ND ST)
AL KHALEEJ AL ARABI RD (30TH ST)
KHALIFA BIN SHAKHBOUT ST (28TH ST)
KING KHALID BIN ABDEL AZIZ SAEED ST (26TH ST)
AL NAHYAN ST (26TH ST)
SHEIKH RASHID ST (2ND ST)
ULLUST (4TH ST)
AL SHARQI ST (4TH ST)
AS SALAM ST (8TH ST)
10TH ST
BAINUNAH ST (34TH ST)

Accommodation

Abu Dhabi has a good spread of **upmarket** hotels, a frustrating lack of **mid-range** options and nothing at all for **budget** travellers. As throughout the UAE, rates fluctuate considerably according to season and demand – the prices below are intended only as a rough guide. For exact prices, consult the various hotel websites.

Beach Rotana **10th St, Tourist Club Area ⓣ02-697 900, ⓦwww.rotana.com.** This smart modern beachfront resort-style hotel is probably the nicest place to stay in the city after the *Emirates Palace*, and a whole lot cheaper. Rooms are spacious and attractively styled, and there's a nice stretch of waterfront beach and gardens to relax on, plus an excellent spread of places to eat and drink. The central location is another bonus. 1200–1500dh.

Emirates Palace **Corniche Rd West ⓣ02-690 9000, ⓦwww.emiratespalace.com.** Abu Dhabi's landmark hotel (see opposite) is the favoured residence of visiting heads of state and assorted celebrities, with every luxury you could think of, including many of the city's top restaurants and a vast swathe of beach. It's expensive as you'd imagine most of the time, but can occasionally become almost affordable during slow periods (especially during the slow summer months). Check the website for offers. 1700–2200dh.

Le Méridien **10th St, Tourist Club Area ⓣ02-644 6666, ⓦwww.lemeridien.com/abudhabi.** Pleasantly old-fashioned hotel with a vaguely old-world European air and attractive rooms decorated in warm reds and oranges. Plus points include the central location, attractive oceanfront gardens with a smallish bit of beach and a pleasant collection of restaurants. 900–1200dh.

Novotel **Hamdan St ⓣ02-633 3555, ⓦwww.novotel.com.** This no-frills business hotel bang in the city centre is nothing to get excited about, although rooms are well-equipped and comfortable, and rates are often as cheap as anywhere in town unless there's a big exhibition or conference on. Around 600dh.

Le Royal Méridien **Sheikh Khalifa St, Al Markaziyah ⓣ02-674 2020, ⓦwww.lemeridien.com/royalabudhabi.** Chic modern hotel catering to a mix of business and tourist visitors, with stylish, rather minimalist, modern rooms and a better-than average selection of in-house eating and drinking venues (see pp.175–176). It's not actually on the beach, though there are attractive walled gardens with a pair of pools. 1000–1250dh.

Shangri-La Qaryat al Beri **Al Maqta ⓣ02-509 8888, ⓦwww.shangri-la.com.** One of the city's most alluring hotels, with gorgeous Arabian-nights decor, huge gardens, four pools, the lovely Chi spa and wonderful views of the Sheikh Zayed Mosque. The main drawback is the location, about 10km from the centre and near Al Maqta Bridge but some distance from anywhere else. Restaurants include the signature *Shang Palace* and *Hoi An* (modelled after their twins in Dubai – see p.117 & p.118), and the chic modern French *Bord Eau*. Around 1700dh.

The city

For the casual visitor, modern Abu Dhabi is mainly interesting for how it contrasts with its more famous neighbour – an Arabian Washington versus Dubai's Las Vegas. Many visitors enjoy the city's slower pace of life and more human scale, and although foreigners still make up the vast majority of the population, there's a significantly higher proportion of Emiratis here than in Dubai. Specific sights are relatively thin on the ground, and much of the pleasure of a visit lies in wandering through the city centre and along the handsome waterfront Corniche and getting a feel for a city which is, in many ways, far more representative of the contemporary UAE than Dubai.

The city's two stand-out attractions (at least pending the opening of Saadiyat Island – see p.175) are the stunning new **Sheikh Zayed Mosque**, one of the world's largest and most extravagant, and the vast **Emirates Palace Hotel**. Other attractions include the city's **Cultural Foundation** and adjacent **Al Hosn Fort**, and the **UAE Heritage Village**, offering superb views of Abu Dhabi's long waterfront **Corniche**.

Emirates Palace Hotel

Standing in solitary splendour at the western end of the city lies the vast **Emirates Palace Hotel** (Ⓦwww.emiratespalace.com). Opened in 2005, it was intended to rival Dubai's *Burj al Arab* and provide Abu Dhabi with a similarly iconic "seven-star" landmark – although in fact the two buildings could hardly be more different. Driveways climb up through the grounds to the main entrance to the hotel, which sits in an elevated position above the sea and surrounding gardens. It's impressively stage-managed, although the only really unusual thing about the building is its sheer size: 1km in length, 114 domes, 140 elevators, 2000 staff and so on. The quasi-Arabian design, meanwhile, is disapointingly pedestrian and much of the exterior looks strangely drab and even a little bit cheap – ironic, really, given that the hotel is believed to have been the most expensive ever built (at a rumoured cost of US$3 billion). All of which means the *Emirates Palace* is as cautiously conservative as the *Burj al Arab* is daringly futuristic and innovative – which may just say something about the contrasting outlooks of the two very different cities which they represent.

The **interior** is far more memorable, centred on a dazzling central dome-cum-atrium, with vast quantities of marble, gold-leaf and huge chandeliers. Cavernous corridors stretch out for what seem like miles towards rooms in the two huge flanking wings – if you're staying here you can keep fit and work up

▲ *Emirates Palace Hotel*

a healthy appetite just walking between your room and the lobby; even staff have been known to get lost. The six "ruler's suites", with gold-plated fittings throughout, are more conveniently situated, but are reserved for visiting heads of state (who have so far included George Bush, Gordon Brown and the Sultan of Brunei). Non-guests can visit for a meal at one of the numerous restaurants (see p.176); alternatively, drop in for one of the sumptuous afternoon teas (see p.175).

UAE Heritage Village and Marina Mall

Dramatically situated on the Corniche-facing side of the Breakwater – a small protuberance of reclaimed land jutting out from the southern end of the corniche – the **UAE Heritage Village** (Sat–Thurs 9am–5pm, Fri 3.30–9pm; free) offers a slice of traditional Abu Dhabi done up for the visiting coach parties who flock here for whistlestop visits. The "village" consists of picturesque *barasti* huts and has spectacular views over the water to the Corniche. There's a decent little **museum** here, housed in a miniature replica fort, with displays of traditional dress and a fine collection of old silver jewellery, along with weaponry, currency, pearling equipment and a few curios, including a camel harness and a stuffed puffer fish. Opposite the museum is a string of **workshops** where local artisans practise traditional skills such as carpentry, glassworking, pottery and brass-working; the so-called "old market", however, is basically just a few ladies flogging cheap handicrafts out of a line of *barasti* huts.

The Heritage Village is right next to the enormous **flagpole**, which can be seen for miles around. At 123m, it was formerly claimed to be the tallest in the world, until topped by one in Jordan in 2003 (which, ironically, was made in Dubai); a flagpole in North Korea actually outstrips both of them by over 30m.

Just over the road from the Heritage Village the large **Marina Mall** (Sat–Thurs 10am–10pm, Fri 2–10pm; Ⓦwww.marinamall.ae), an attractive modern complex built around a series of tented courtyards and fountains, is one of the city's two top shopping destinations, along with the glitzy Abu Dhabi Mall on the opposite side of the city. The mall's main attraction for non-shopping visitors are its views of the long string of glass-faced high-rises lining the Corniche, best appreciated from the soaring **Burj al Marina** tower, located at the back of the mall. This can be accessed either by taking a meal at the *Tiara* revolving restaurant (see p.176) on the tower's 42nd floor, or (rather more cheaply) for the cost of a slightly overpriced drink at the *Colombiano* coffee shop immediately below.

The Corniche

Driving through the modern city's suburban sprawl, it's easy not to notice that Abu Dhabi is built on an island rather than on the mainland itself; it wasn't until the building of the Maqta Bridge in 1966 that the two were connected. The city's location amid the balmy waters of the Gulf is best appreciated from the **Corniche**, the long waterfront road (divided into Corniche Road East and Corniche Road West) which runs for the best part of 5km along Abu Dhabi's western edge. It's flanked by spacious gardens on either side and lined by a long line of glass-clad high-rises and five-star hotels, which encapsulate the modern city's internationalist credentials and provide Abu Dhabi with its most memorable views (although the entire waterfront is perhaps best appreciated from the UAE Heritage Village across the water). The Corniche is also a popular spot with local residents catching (or shooting) the breeze, particularly towards dusk, when its Gulf-side walkways fill up with a diverse crowd of promenading Emiratis, jogging Europeans and picnicking Indians – a perfect snapshot of modern Abu Dhabi in miniature.

Qasr al Hosn and the Cultural Foundation

More or less at the very centre of Abu Dhabi sits **Qasr Al Hosn** ("The Palace Fort"), the oldest building in Abu Dhabi. The fort started life around 1761 as a single round watchtower built to defend the only freshwater well in Abu Dhabi, and was subsequently expanded into a small fort in 1793, becoming the residence of Abu Dhabi's ruling Al Nahyan family. In 1939, Sheikh Shakhbut bin Sultan al Nahyan, the elder brother of Sheikh Zayed, began to significantly enlarge the complex using income raised from the first oil-prospecting concessions granted to foreign companies (the remainder of this and Abu Dhabi's subsequent oil revenues he allegedly hid in a wooden chest under his bed, refusing to trust them to a bank).

The fort continued to serve as the ruler's palace and seat of government until Sheikh Zayed came to power in 1966, when the ruling family decamped and the fort was given over to purely administrative uses. It was eventually renovated, acquiring a bright new covering of white-painted concrete – hence its popular name of the "White Fort". The large and rather plain whitewashed structure you see today is of no particular architectural distinction, although the rambling battlemented walls, dotted with a few watchtowers, are modestly pretty. The fort was being renovated again at the time of writing and is due to reopen in 2011 as a major new museum of Abu Dhabi's historical and cultural heritage.

Right next to Qasr al Hosn sits the city's sleek modern **Cultural Foundation** (Ⓦ www.adach.ae/en). The foundation hosts various collections, including the National Library and Archives, and offers a pleasantly cool and peaceful retreat from the city. Casual visitors will usually find something going on here: regular (free) temporary exhibitions, usually with a local or Islamic theme, are held downstairs, while there are a few other exhibits dotted around the corridors, and artisans can often be found working upstairs by the pleasant *Delma Cafe* (see p.175). There are also regular film screenings and classical music concerts in the evening. The Foundation was closed at the time of writing as part of the Qasr al Hosn redevelopment, but should reopen some time in 2011.

Immediately north of the Cultural Foundation, **Etihad Square** is home to an arresting sequence of oversized sculptures, including a vast cannon, enormous perfume bottle and gargantuan coffee pot – an endearingly quirky contrast to the drab surrounding architecture.

East from Qasr al Hosn

The area to the east of Qasr al Hosn is the heart of downtown Abu Dhabi, and where you'll find the city's liveliest streetlife and densest concentration of cafés and shops. The parallel **Hamdan Street** and **Sheikh Zayed the First Street** are the two major thoroughfares, each lined with identikit office blocks stacked tightly together like Lego bricks. Just south of the latter lies the **Madinat Zayed Gold Centre** (Sat–Thurs 9am–2pm & 4–11pm, Fri 4–11pm; no photography), Abu Dhabi's low-key equivalent to Dubai's Gold Souk, with two floors of shops selling traditional and contemporary jewellery.

A fifteen-minute walk east along Sheikh Zayed the First Street brings you to Abu Dhabi's eastern waterfront, although the actual water is hidden away behind the buildings lining 10th Street. This part of town is known as the **Tourist Club Area**, with landmarks including the large *Le Méridien* and *Beach Rotana* hotels, as well as the flash Abu Dhabi Mall, the smartest in the city.

North of here stretches the workaday **Al Mina** port district, which is where you'll find the nearest thing to a traditional souk in Abu Dhabi. First up is the so-called **Carpet Souk**, a modest square surrounded by small shops. Most of the stock on offer consists of low-grade factory carpet, though some places have more valuable traditional rugs and kilims if you hunt around. A five-minute walk beyond here, the **Food Souk** is aimed largely at the wholesale trade, although there's a colourful line of date merchants at the southern end. A further ten minutes' walk away, the **Iranian Souk** sounds promising, but is mainly devoted to kitchenware and potted plants.

Sheikh Zayed Mosque

Some 10km from central Abu Dhabi, the mighty **Sheikh Zayed Mosque** (Sat–Thurs 9am–9pm, Fri 4–9pm; interior closed for about 30min during prayers at 12.30pm, 3.30pm, 6pm & 7.30pm; free; free guided tours Sat–Thurs at 10am) dominates all landward approaches to the city, its snowy-white mass of domes and minarets visible for miles around, and providing a spectacular symbol of Islamic pride at the entrance to the capital of the UAE.

Completed in 2007, the mosque was commissioned by and named after Sheikh Zayed bin Sultan al Nahyan (see p.168), who lies buried in a modest white marble mausoleum close to the entrance. The mosque is one of the world's biggest – roughly the eighth largest, depending on how you measure it – and certainly the most expensive, having taken twelve years to build at a cost of around $500 million. It's also unusual in being one of only two mosques in the UAE (along with the Jumeirah Mosque in Dubai; see p.77) **open to non-Muslims**. If visiting, you'll be expected to dress conservatively; female visitors not suitably attired will be offered a black *abbeya* robe to wear.

The huge **exterior** is classically plain, framed by four 107m-high minarets and topped with some 80 domes. Entrance to the mosque is through a vast **courtyard** – capable of accommodating some 40,000 worshippers – which is surrounded by an arcade of rather Moorish-looking arches, the columns picked out with pietra dura floral designs and topped with unusual gold capitals resembling bits of palm tree. Flanking one side of the courtyard, the vast **prayer hall** is a spectacular piece of contemporary Islamic design. The hall is home to the world's largest carpet (made in Iran by around twelve hundred artisans, measuring over 5000 square metres, containing some 2.2 million knots and weighing 47 tonnes) and the world's largest chandelier (made in Germany, measuring 10m in diameter, 15m tall and containing a million Swarowski crystals). It's not the world records which impress, however, so much as the extraordinary muted opulence of the design, with every surface richly carved and decorated, and the prayer hall's three massive chandeliers dangling overhead like enormous pieces of very expensive jewellery. Look out, too, for the hand-crafted panels made from Turkish Iznik tiles which decorate the corridors outside, and for the *qibla* wall itself, inscribed with the 99 names (qualities) of Allah in traditional Kufic calligraphy, subtly illuminated using fibreoptic lighting.

A **taxi** to the mosque from the city centre should cost around 10–15dh; if you're driving it's easy enough to find your way, given that the mosque is visible for several miles in all directions.

Desert islands: coming soon to Abu Dhabi

Though it may currently be playing second-fiddle to Dubai in the global tourism stakes, Abu Dhabi is increasingly looking for ways to challenge its upstart neighbour's pre-eminence in the region. This ambition is given added clout because any planned development here is backed by the emirate's apparently bottomless well of petrodollars – unlike credit-crunched Dubai, many of whose most ambitious projects have now been mothballed.

Saadiyat Island

At the centre of Abu Dhabi's strategic vision is the new $27 billion cultural district to be developed on the currently uninhabited island of **Saadiyat** ("Island of Happiness"), a few kilometres from the city centre. The complex, scheduled to be completed by 2018, will comprise a mix of residential and tourist attractions, including a golf course, assorted marinas and a 9km beach lined with luxury hotels. Most exciting, however, are plans for a string of top-notch international **museums** to be located on the island, each in its own landmark building designed by one of the world's top architects. Pride of place will go to the **Louvre Abu Dhabi**, housed in a huge flying saucer-shaped edifice designed by French architect Jean Nouvel, while a new Frank Gehry-designed **Guggenheim Museum** will stand nearby. Other developments will include the new **Sheikh Zayed National Museum** by Foster & Partners, a **Maritime Museum** designed by leading Japanese architect Tadao Ando and a **Performing Arts Centre** by acclaimed Iraqi architect Zaha Hadid. All five museums are expected to open sometime during 2013–2014.

Yas Island

Further massive developments are also currently underway at **Yas Island**, about 20km from central Abu Dhabi, just off the mainland coastal highway to Dubai. The island is home to the **Yas Marina** Circuit, which hosted the first ever Abu Dhabi F1 Grand Prix in 2009 (see p.133), as well as the spectacular new **Ferrari World** theme park (due to open in October 2010), which will include over twenty rides and attractions, including the world's fastest roller coaster. Other forthcoming attractions on the island include a Warner Brothers theme park, a state-of-the-art waterpark and a Kyle Phillips-designed links golf course.

Eating

Even more so than in Dubai, eating in Abu Dhabi revolves around the big hotels – although there are a few cheaper options also worth hunting out if you're on a budget. For instant gratification, there are various cheap fast-food joints scattered along and around Hamdan Street and in the Marina Mall and Abu Dhabi Mall food courts.

BiCE **Hilton Abu Dhabi Hotel, Corniche Rd West ☎02-692 4160.** Abu Dhabi branch of the popular Italian chain, with a similar menu of flavourful Italian meat, fish and pasta dishes to its cousin in Dubai (see p.120).

Delma Café **First floor, Cultural Foundation.** This little flower-filled café offers an excellent, low-key lunch option if you're in the vicinity of the Cultural Foundation. The simple menu features cheap and tasty sandwiches and salads, all at bargain prices (from around 10dh). Popular with Abu Dhabi's older female expat set. Closed at the time of writing as part of the Cultural Foundation/ Qasr al Hosn refurbishment (see p.173).

Emirates Palace Café **Emirates Palace Hotel.** The beautiful foyer café of this opulent hotel makes a memorable setting for one of the Middle East's most sumptuous afternoon teas; choose from either traditional English or Arabian style (225dh).

Finz **Beach Rotana Hotel, Tourist Club Area ☎02-697 9000.** One of the best seafood restaurants in town, occupying an unusual A-frame wooden dining room and terrace overlooking the water. The menu features a wide selection of fish and seafood prepared in a variety of international (particularly Asian) styles, ranging from wok to tandoori, as well as the restaurant's signature Portuguese-style *cataplana* dishes, cooked and served in a large copper pan. There are also a few meat and vegetarian options, plus a good wine list. Mains from 150dh.

India Palace As Salam St, Tourist Club Area. Long-established and pleasantly old-fashioned Indian restaurant, serving up a big spread of tasty and very reasonably priced North Indian meat, seafood and veg offerings, including tandoori dishes, *kadais* and Lucknow-style *dum pukht* biriyanis. Veg mains from 25dh, non-veg from 30dh.

Indigo Beach Rotana Hotel, Tourist Club Area ☎02-697 9000. Good-looking modern Indian restaurant serving well-prepared North Indian meat tandooris and biriyanis, plus a few seafood and veg options. Mains from around 100dh.

Lebanese Flower Off 26th St. One of a line of colourful Lebanese restaurants (which also includes the neighbouring *Beirut Roastery*, *Lebanon Flower Bakery* and *Maatouk* café), this enduringly popular restaurant is the best place in the city to fill up on inexpensive Middle Eastern food, with a big and beautifully cooked range of fish and meat grills, kebabs (35–50dh) and mezze.

Mezzaluna Emirates Palace Hotel ☎02-690 7999. This classy restaurant is the most affordable of the *Emirates Palace*'s string of upmarket eating venues. Food here is traditional Italian and Mediterranean with a fine-dining twist, including a good range of antipasti and pasta dishes, plus lavish meat and seafood mains like *Piccione arrosto* (double-roasted pigeon with wild mushroom risotto and black truffles). Mains from around 150dh.

Royal Orchid Hilton Abu Dhabi Hotel, Corniche Rd West ☎02-681 3883. Tucked away in the *Hilton*, this is one of the oldest restaurants in the city and is still going strong, thanks to its good and reasonably priced range of Thai, Chinese and Mongolian favourites. Mains from around 75dh.

Sayad Emirates Palace Hotel ☎02-690 7999. The hotel's exclusive signature restaurant specializes in top-notch Pacific rim-style seafood (Sayad is Arabic for "fisherman"), served up in a strangely calming dining space which glows softly with muted underwater blues and greens. Mains from around 200dh.

Soba Le Royal Méridien Hotel, Al Markaziyah ☎02-695 0413. Cool contemporary Asian restaurant serving up a mix of Thai, Malaysian and Japanese meat and seafood dishes, including good sushi, maki and sashimi. Mains from around 90dh.

Tiara Burj al Marina, Marina Mall. Revolving restaurant on the 36th floor of the landmark Burj al Marina (see p.172), offering sublime city views, accompanied by a decent selection of international meat and seafood dishes (from 60dh; minimum spend 100dh).

Drinking

Abu Dhabi lacks Dubai's alluring range of swanky cocktail bars and other upscale establishments, although there's still a good range of places to drink, with virtually every hotel in the city hosting some kind of licenced venue. These follow essentially the same formula as in Dubai, with a mix of cheery British-style **pubs** and more upmarket (and expensive) **bars**, sometimes with live music or DJ.

Brauhaus Beach Rotana Hotel, 10th St, Tourist Club Area. This convivial pub-cum-restaurant makes a surprisingly convincing stab at an authentic Bavarian *bierkeller*, with speciality German beers on tap or by the bottle and a good range of food to soak it all up with. Very popular, so arrive early if you want to bag a seat.

Captain's Arms Le Méridien Hotel, 10th St, Tourist Club Area. Cheery British-style pub with attractive outdoor seating overlooking the hotel gardens.

The Jazz Bar Hilton Abu Dhabi Hotel, Corniche Rd West. Long-established after-hours venue, with good live jazz and a rather gentrified atmosphere.

Mood Indigo Bar Novotel, Hamdan St. This under-used hotel bar-cum-pub is one of the best places in the city for a quiet, inexpensive pint. The atmosphere is relaxed, and there's discreet live jazz some evenings.

Sax Restaurant & Club Le Royal Méridien Hotel, Sheikh Khalifa St, Al Markaziyah. Upmarket bar with lots of cocktails and one of the city's more glamorous crowds.

Contexts

Contexts

History

Dubai's history has been shaped by its location at the southern end of the Arabian Gulf, squeezed between sand and sea. There has been some sort of human presence here since the beginning of the Bronze Age or earlier, though the region's harsh desert environment proved an effective barrier to sustained settlement and development until relatively recent times, save for a small and hardy population of itinerant Bedouin, fishermen and pearl divers. Not until the advent of oil and air-conditioning in the 1960s did the city's population rise above 100,000.

Up until the early nineteenth century Dubai remained an obscure Arabian outpost. This all changed following the arrival first of the British and, soon afterwards, of the city's visionary Maktoum rulers. It was the latter who would gradually transform the city's fortunes, establishing it first as one of the region's leading commercial ports and then, more recently, as one of the world's leading tourism and business destinations.

Early Dubai

The history of the Dubai area before the colonial era remains frustratingly vague. There are relatively abundant **Bronze Age** (c.3000–2000 BC) finds and a few later **Ummayad** (see below) remains, but virtually no other archeological or written records until the arrival of the British in the eighteenth century – an accurate reflection of the region's isolation, lack of development and historically low population levels.

Bronze Age-era archeological finds in the Dubai area include the remains of extensive settlements at Al Sufouh and Al Qusais, and inland at Hatta. The region was an important source of copper and appears to have enjoyed extensive trading connections which extended as far as the great Mesopotamian city of Ur (in what is now Iraq). From the third through to the seventh centuries AD, the region was loosely incorporated into the **Sassanians** empire, ruled from Iran. The Sassanians were displaced in the seventh century by the arrival of the **Ummayads** of Damascus, the first great Islamic dynasty. The Ummayads introduced Islam to the region, as well as stimulating local and overseas trade. The extensive remains of an Ummayad-era settlement have been discovered in **Jumeirah**, including a mosque and caravanserai, suggesting that the area was an important staging post on the caravan route between Oman and Iraq.

Very little is known about the history of the Dubai area for the next thousand years. There's a passing reference to Dubai in the *Book of Roads and Kingdoms*, a collection of travellers' anecdotes and legends compiled by Arab–Andalucian geographer Abu Abdullah al-Bakri in around 1095. The first eye-witness account can be found in the *Voyage to Pegu, and Observations There* by **Gaspero Balbi**, describing the Venetian traveller's visit to the area in 1580 en route from Italy to Burma, with a brief mention of the coastal settlement of "Dibei" and its vibrant local pearl industry.

Early Dubai and the Trucial States

Dubai reappears in the historical record in the eighteenth century. During this period the territory which now makes up the UAE was largely controlled by two main tribal groupings. The first, the **Bani Yas**, were ruled by the Al Nahyan family from Abu Dhabi, and controlled the coast from Dubai to Qatar, as well as much of the region's desert hinterland. The second, the seafaring **Qawasim** (or

Al Qasimi), were based further north in Sharjah and Ras al Khaimah, and had also established a significant presence on the far side of the Gulf along the southern coast of Iran.

The first **permanent settlement** around the Dubai Creek appears to have been established sometime during the eighteenth century by the Al Bu Falasah branch of the Bani Yas. This settlement remained, albeit loosely, under the control of the Bani Yas sheikhs in Abu Dhabi, but was regularly threatened by Qawasim incursions from the north.

At around the same time, the Gulf began to enter the mainstream of colonial politics thanks to its strategic location on the increasingly important sea route between Britain and India. By the late eighteenth century, the **British East India Company** had achieved a monopoly on the lucrative sea trade with the Subcontinent, although its commercial interests were increasingly threatened by astute Qawasim sailors, who repeatedly outmanoeuvred and undercut their European rivals. Faced with this competition, the British began to concoct tales (probably ficitious) of Qawasim "piracy" against British and Indian shipping. In 1820, the Royal Navy launched a punitive attack against the Qawasim. Seven thousand troops were landed at Ras al Khaimah and the fort there bombarded. The Qawasim rulers soon surrendered and entered into peace negotiations. Qawasim power and prestige never recovered, and the political landscape of the southern Arabian Gulf had been changed for ever.

Following their suppression of the Qawasim, the British signed a series of "anti-piracy" treaties with the rulers of the various Gulf emirates which now make up the UAE. These henceforth became known as the **Trucial States**, on account of the "truces" agreed with the British. The arrival of the British and the subsequent treaties did much to stabilize the political situation in the region, although by confirming the position of the ruling sheikhs it also had the effect of destroying local traditions of tribal democracy, whereby unpopular or incompetent rulers could be removed from office – an arrangement which was, therefore, very much to the advantage of the ruling families, if not always to their subjects.

The arrival of the Maktoums

For Dubai, the arrival of the British had the welcome result of significantly reducing Qawasim threats. Visiting in the late 1820s, the British Political Resident described a town of some 1200 people, living in simple palm-thatch huts around the governor's small fort (Al Fahidi Fort, which now houses the Dubai Museum), with three watchtowers equipped with old Portuguese cannons guarding the main approaches to the town.

Dubai's subordinate position was about to change, however, thanks to a power struggle amongst the Bani Yas leaders in Abu Dhabi. In 1833, the popular leader of the Bani Yas, Sheikh Tahnun, was assassinated by his half-brother, **Sheikh Khalifa**. Khalifa's *coup d'état* was not well received, and soon afterwards he was forced to supress two uprisings with further bloodshed. By the summer of 1833, popular disgust at Khalifa's repressive regime led to around a thousand Bani Yas tribesmen (perhaps a fifth of the local population) abandoning Abu Dhabi and trekking down the coast to establish a new home in Dubai.

The absconders were led by a certain **Maktoum bin Buti** and his uncle Obaid bin Said al Falasi. Arriving in Dubai (where they instantly doubled the local population), Maktoum and Obaid immediately took over the running of the town. This arrangement lasted until 1836, when Obaid died and Maktoum became sole leader – thus establishing the Maktoum family dynasty which endures to this day.

The initial position of Maktoum and his followers was precarious, however. Not surprisingly, the fratricidal Sheikh Khalifa was less than impressed by the mass defection, although following a series of clever diplomatic manoeuvres Maktoum bin Buti succeeded in establishing Dubai's independence from Abu Dhabi with the support of his powerful Qawasim neighbours to the north, who were naturally delighted to see their rivals in Abu Dhabi lose a significant slice of territory. Dubai was thus established as a buffer zone between Abu Dhabi and Qawasim territories – a small and relatively powerless enclave wedged between powerful and potentially hostile neighbours.

Despite their precarious situation, the new Maktoum rulers began quickly to establish Dubai as a local force in the lower Gulf. In 1835 the British signed a further round of treaties with the various Gulf emirates, now including Dubai, thus granting the newly independent settlement a measure of official recognition and British protection. Dubai's commercial life also flourished (a foretaste of things to come), and within a few years of Maktoum's arrival the town's souk had grown exponentially to include around a hundred shops. Dubai's standing was further enhanced in 1845, when it helped to remove the perennially unpopular Sheikh Khalifa from power, ushering in a new period of close and cordial relations between Abu Dhabi and its breakaway neighbour.

Maktoum bin Buti died in 1852, and was succeeded in turn by his youngest brother Sheikh Said (ruled 1852–59), by Maktoum's eldest son, Sheikh Hasher (1859–1886), and by Sheikh Hasher's brother Sheikh Rashid (1886–1894). This stable succession of Maktoum rulers followed a consistent policy of forging strategic alliances with their more powerful neighbours while achieving a modest level of economic prosperity. This was based largely on the city's flourishing **pearling industry**, which yielded some of the world's finest pearls, exported to London, Bombay and elsewhere. Meanwhile, the town was also establishing itself as an increasingly important local entrepot, challenging the supremacy of both Abu Dhabi and neighbouring Sharjah.

British influence, meanwhile, continued to rise, thanks to the ongoing stategic importance of the Gulf on sea routes to India and increasing competition from Britain's colonial rivals such as France and Russia. One result of the British influence was the arrival of increasing numbers of **Indian traders** from the 1860s onwards, most of them working as representatives of British companies in India. In 1892 a new sequence of treaties were signed granting Britain the right to directly control all aspects of the rulers' foreign affairs – effectively relinquishing external sovereignty in exchange for British protection.

Iranian influence

The uncanny ability of Dubai's Maktoum rulers to seize advantage of changing local and global commercial conditions and turn them to spectacular profit is one of the recurrent motifs in Dubai's history, first exemplified by the leadership of **Sheikh Maktoum bin Hasher** (ruled 1894–1906).

Dubai's sudden opportunity came as the result of changing circumstances across the Gulf in Iran. Increasingly punitive taxes and other regulations in the flourishing Iranian port of **Lingah** (or Bandar Lengeh, as it's now called) were the key. Lingah was home to a large and prosperous community of Qawasim-descended merchants who were being increasingly targeted by the government in Tehran suspicious of their foreign origins. Seeing an opportunity of attracting an expert commercial workforce in search of a new home, Sheikh Maktoum took drastic measures, abolishing customs duty and licences for vessels, and turning Dubai into a free port, while sending emissaries to Lingah to talk up

Dubai's commercial opportunities and offer free plots of land alongside the Creek for refugee merchants to establish new homes. Not surprisingly, many Qawasim decided to return to their ancestral homelands in Ras al Khaimah and Sharjah, although a significant number (along with many Indian traders previously based in Lingah) opted to set up shop in Dubai.

The results of Sheikh Maktoum bin Hasher's initiative changed the cultural and commerical face of the city forever. By 1901, five hundred of Lingah's Qawasim-descended Iranian merchants had settled in Dubai and the town had overtaken both Abu Dhabi and Sharjah as the region's largest port, while the new Iranian quarter the settlers established in **Bastakiya**, with its elaborate wind-towered houses, provided a model of modern urban development in a city which still largely consisted of primitive palm-thatch shacks. The arrival of the Iranians also established Dubai as the leading overseas conduit for Iranian trade, channelling vast sums of money and merchandise through the city, which would henceforth play a role relative to Iran not unlike that which British Hong Kong played in relation to mainland China. Persian-descended Emiratis, or *ajamis*, still make up a sizeable proportion of the local population today.

Famine and democracy

The massive commercial fillip provided by the arrival of the Iranian merchants and Dubai's emergence as the southern Gulf's leading port lent the city a new economic and cultural vibrancy which lasted for the best part of three decades. Further waves of merchants arrived in Dubai during the 1920s and 1930s from Iran, Abu Dhabi and Sharjah, attracted by the city's low-tax and trade-friendly environment.

But the new-found prosperity was not to last, and the city's continued over-reliance on the pearling industry (which had been increasingly hamstrung by protectionist British regulations prohibiting the use of modern technology and diving equipment) proved fatal. The onset of the **Great Depression** in 1929 signalled the beginning of the end. Overseas demand for precious stones dried up overnight, and the industry's death-knell was sounded shortly afterwards, when Japanese scientists discovered a reliable method for creating cultured pearls, instantly wiping out traditional pearling in Dubai and elsewhere. The effect on Dubai's economy was catastrophic. Many of the city's businesses went bankrupt, Indian traders returned post-haste to Bombay and the fledgling educational system collapsed. Food shortages and occasional famine became a recurrent feature, with locals reduced to catching and frying the swarms of locusts which periodically infested the city.

The ongoing economic crisis had major social consequences. Anger was widespread, much of it directed at the city's kindly but ineffectual ruler **Sheikh Saeed** (ruled 1912–1958). As living conditions plummeted organized opposition to Sheikh Saeed's leadership gained momentum, with widespread demonstrations and two attempted coups. Ironically, despite widespread local poverty, Sheikh Saeed himself was earning an increasingly extravagant income through lucrative arrangements with the British relating to the right to prospect for oil, for landing rights for seaplanes on the Creek and other perks and privileges – part of the so-called **rentier system** whereby Britain sought to confirm the ruling sheikhs in power, while protecting their own interests.

As economic conditions systematically worsened, opposition to autocratic Maktoum rule expressed itself in the remarkable **merchant's majlis**, established in 1938 and led by a cousin of Sheikh Saeed – the closest approach to a genuine democracy ever seen in Dubai. The *majlis* set up a fifteen-member council which sought to enact a series of progressive reforms ranging from education and healthcare through to rubbish collection – as well as demanding that Sheikh Saeed hand over 85 percent of his personal income for public use. As tensions rose, the city reached a point of de facto civil war, with Sheikh Saeed and his loyal troop of Bedouin soldiers retaining control of Bur Dubai, while the rebels seized Deira.

The crisis was finally resolved in extraordinary circumstances (which tend, not surprisingly, to be glossed over in official histories of the city). The occasion was the 1939 wedding of Sheikh Saeed's eldest son – and future Dubai ruler – **Sheikh Rashid** to a daughter of a former ruler of Abu Dhabi, Sheikha Latifa, who had fled to Dubai some years previously. The rebels agreed to a temporary truce in order to allow Sheikh Rashid's wedding to go ahead at Sheikha Latifa's home, which happened to be located in rebel-held Deira. Sheikh Rashid arrived with his traditional entourage of rifle-toting Bedouin retainers, who took advantage of the truce to gun down a large proportion of the rebel *majlis*'s leaders. Many of those who survived were blinded in one eye and forced to "buy" their remaining eye on payment of a large ransom.

Deira was thus returned to Maktoum control, and Dubai's most promising democratic movement was annihilated. The wedding went ahead following the carnage. This was a notable event in its own right, in that it cemented relationships between the region's two major Bani Yas communities. Latifa would subsequently bear nine children by Rashid, including two future rulers of Dubai, meaning that the leaders of the city would henceforth be cousins of the ruling Al Nahyan family in Abu Dhabi.

Sheikh Rashid and the rise of modern Dubai

The wedding massacre in Deira in 1939 marked the arrival on the Dubai political scene of the charismatic, visionary and occasionally ruthless **Sheikh Rashid**, the man often described as the father of modern Dubai, and the ruler who (with the possible exception of his own son, Sheikh Mohammed – see below) did more than anyone else to put modern Dubai on the global map.

During the 1940s, Sheikh Rashid gradually took over the management of the city from his increasingly enfeebled father, Sheikh Saeed. Despite quashing the merchant's *majlis*, however, Sheikh Rashid was confronted with growing resistance centred on the international **Arab nationalism** movement, inspired by Egyptian president Gamal Nasser and promulgated in Dubai by the city's many well-educated foreign schoolteachers from Egypt, Iraq, Syria, Lebanon and Yemen. Local pan-Arabists called for a new socialist democracy, with an end to Maktoum rule and the ending of all ties with Britain. Not surprisingly, this agenda found little favour with Sheikh Rashid and his followers, despite a series of riots and increasing political dissent throughout the 1940s and 1950s.

Sheikh Saeed died in 1958, with leadership of the city formally passing to Sheikh Rashid. One of Rashid's first acts was the characteristically bold decision to **dredge the Creek**, which had began to silt up, meaning that larger boats could no longer enter it (the water, in places, was just two foot deep), striking at the heart of Dubai's commercial lifeblood. Despite its challenging cost and complexity Rashid pressed ahead with the project, raising money from local merchants and overseas bonds. By 1961 the Creek had been cleared, widened and deepened, establishing the city as pre-eminent port in the region and kickstarting a trade bonanza between Dubai, neighbouring Gulf emirates, Iran and destinations further afield (Sharjah, by contrast, allowed its harbour to silt up, losing virtually all its shipping business to Dubai as a result).

Shortly afterwards, Sheikh Rashid's leadership received an additional boost when **oil** was finally discovered in Dubai. The first commercially important deposits were discovered at the Fateh (Fortune) oilfield 15 miles offshore in 1966, with the first exports beginning in 1969. Although only ever a modest amount of oil compared to the vast reserves found in Abu Dhabi (see p.186), the new revenues allowed Rashid to undertake a visionary series of **infrastructure developments** which laid the basis for Dubai's current prosperity. Many of these were derided at the time as being hopelessly ambitious, and yet in virtually every case history has proved Rashid's judgement to be faultless.

One of Rashid's first acts was to provide the city with its own **airport**, opened in 1960 (characteristically, the first in the Gulf to have its own duty free shop), while the two sides of the Creek were finally connected with the opening of the **Maktoum Bridge** in 1963. Yet Rashid's most famous – and successful – gamble concerned the creation of a new **deep water port**. Original plans were drawn up in 1967 for a port with four berths, based on future trade predictions. Ignoring the predictions, Rashid ordered the port's capacity to be doubled, and then doubled again. Rashid was vindicated when the port finally opened in 1971 with sixteen berths – and was immediately oversubscribed.

Dubai's rising prosperity during the 1960s had an important **social pay-off**. As the city grew increasingly wealthy, the pan-Arabist reforming fervour of the 1940s and 1950s began to cool. People gave up socialism and turned to shopping instead. Oil revenues allowed Rashid to exempt his subjects from all forms of taxation and to provide basic levels of free healthcare and housing for less well off citizens. Dubai's leading merchant families and other bigwigs (including many prominent members of the reform movement) were bought off by being granted lucrative and exclusive trading licences and other concessions – a clever arrangement which stopped short of outright bribery, but which offered a virtual licence to print money, as well as ensuring that the people concerned would henceforth have a vested interest in maintaining the status quo.

By the mid-1960s, the population of Dubai had topped 100,000. Some four thousand dhows were registered in the city, carrying a wide range of goods including textiles, gold and electronics, some of which were exported legally, although much was smuggled (the protectionist policies of India's Nehru government, in particular, were a godsend to Dubai's gold and textile merchants).

Independence

Further political challenges, however, lay just around the corner. In 1968, the British government suddenly announced plans to withdraw from the Gulf within three years. The ruling sheikhs, who had lived safely under the umbrella of British protection since 1820, were understandably alarmed, fearing that their tiny emirates might fall prey to much larger and more powerful states (Saudi Arabia, for example, had long claimed parts of Abu Dhabi emirate, while Iran has made a similar claim for Bahrain and other places in the Gulf). In a reversal of the usual colonial scenario, both Sheikh Zayed of Abu Dhabi and Sheikh Rashid urgently requested Britain to keep its military forces in the area beyond the proposed withdrawal date, even offering to pay for the cost of the troops themselves; the British rejected the appeal on the grounds that it would cast their armed forces in a somewhat mercenary light.

The British encouraged the sheikhs to seek safety in numbers and to enter into a loose **confederation**, consisting of the seven emirates which now form the UAE, plus Qatar and Bahrain. Yet tensions between Qatar and Bahrain (then the most populous of the Gulf states) threw up irreconcilable differences and both withdrew from the proposed union, choosing to go it alone. Abu Dhabi and Dubai, however, agreed to unite, 135 years after their original split, along with Sharjah, Ras al Khaimah, Ajman, Umm al Quwain and Fujairah. Sheikh Rashid (who the British had expected to lead the new union) requested that Sheikh Zayed become the **first president** of the new country, perhaps realizing Abu Dhabi's much larger size and far richer oil reserves made him the natural choice of leader.

Independence duly arrived on December 1, 1971, with the newly formed country taking the name of the **United Arab Emirates** (Ras al Khaimah withdrew from the union at the last minute, but rejoined soon afterwards). Locally and abroad, there was a general sense of pessimism over the survival prospects of the fledgling country. The USSR initially refused to recognize the country, as did Saudi Arabia. Even worse, a few hours before Independence Iranian forces occupied the two small Tunbs islands belonging to Ras al Khaimah, and another, Abu Musa, belonging to Sharjah (and, indeed, continue to occupy them to this day). British warships stationed nearby signally failed to intervene.

Sheikh Mohammed and the boom years

Despite the initial misgivings, the newly independent UAE prospered. Political leadership continued to rest with the Al Nahyan family in Abu Dhabi, but Dubai remained easily the largest and most commercially vibrant city in the new country. Sheikh Rashid continued to plough oil revenues into further infrastructure developments including the landmark World Trade Centre (see p.71), as well as Jebel Ali Port and the new Shindagha Tunnel linking Deira and Bur Dubai. One of Sheikh Rashid's last major acts as ruler was to commission the city's new **dry docks**, opened in 1983. As ever, his timing was faultless. Within a year of the docks' opening, fighting broke out between Iran and Iraq, creating a steady supply of war-damaged vessels limping into Dubai to be repaired.

In 1982 Rashid suffered a severe stroke, and although he remained official ruler until his death in 1990, the increasingly infirm leader began to hand power over to his four sons. The eldest, the capable but low-key Sheikh Maktoum, was officially anointed heir to the throne, but over the following years it became increasingly apparent that it was Rashid's third son, **Sheikh Mohammed**, who had inherited his father's vision and who was the driving force behind the city's ongoing development.

Under Mohammed, the already brisk pace of change became a whirlwind. During the 1980s and 1990s, as Mohammed's influence grew, the city began increasingly to diversify from its original base as a regional trade and shipping entrepot. One key growth area was the development of the city's **tourism** industry. In the mid-1980s the city had 42 hotels with 4600 rooms; by 2008 it had around 40,000, a tenfold increase. In 1985, following a dispute with Gulf Air, Mohammed also launched **Emirates airline** in a bid to free Dubai from its dependence on other air carriers (Emirates has gone on to become one of the world's most successful airlines and, as with many of Mohammed's schemes, has also been widely imitated by neighbouring emirates, including Abu Dhabi).

Many other businesses were lured to the city by the creation of assorted **free trade zones** in which much of the UAE's normal red tape would be relaxed, including the ban on foreign ownership of the majority of any UAE business. The first free trade zone was established at **Jebel Ali**. This was followed by a string of more specialized hi-tech enclaves. The first two, **Internet City** and **Media City**, succeeded in attracting dozens of top international organizations to the city, ranging from Microsoft to the BBC. At the same time, the opening of the **Burj al Arab** in 1999 provided the city with an iconic landmark whose

Oil in Dubai

The idea that Dubai is some kind of mega-rich oil sheikhdom is often heard, but has little basis in fact. The UAE as a whole sits on top of the world's fifth-largest discovered oil reserves and is the world's third-largest oil exporter. Ninety-five percent of these reserves, however, are in Abu Dhabi, which struck oil in 1958 and has been living off it very comfortably ever since.

Dubai, by contrast, had to wait until 1966 to find a commercially viable source of oil and even this amounted to very little when compared with its neighbour's oil wealth, just four percent of total UAE deposits (further small fields were also discovered in Sharjah and Ras al Khaimah – the rest of the emirates got nothing). Despite the relatively modest finds, oil played a brief but **vital role** in the city's development, allowing Sheikh Rashid to invest in a range of infrastructure projects (see p.185). The oil boom was brief, however. In 1975, oil accounted for almost two-thirds of the national GDP; a decade later it had dropped to fifty percent. Today the figure is under five percent, and falling, while according to latest estimates the emirate's reserves are expected to have been exhausted within twenty years.

distinctive sail-shaped outline has probably done more than anything else to stamp Dubai on the global consciousness.

As the new millennium arrived, the city went into overdrive. Sheikh Mohammed's ongoing attempts to position Dubai as a major global **financial centre** began to take shape with the opening of the Dubai Stock Exchange and Dubai International Financial Centre (DIFC). More importantly, in 2002 restrictions on foreign ownership of property were lifted, meaning that expats could suddenly buy their own homes and foreign investors could enter the local property market. A massive **real estate boom** ensued. Foreign money poured in and construction companies went beserk, turning large parts of the city into an enormous building site – during the mid-noughties it was estimated that a quarter of all the world's cranes could be found in Dubai. At the same time work began on **Palm Jumeirah**, the first of the four artificial islands planned to line the coast, and other landmark developments including the gargantuan new Atlantis resort and the **Burj Khalifa** (or Burj Dubai, as it was then known), the world's tallest building.

The credit crunch

November 2008 saw the spectacular opening of the grandiose new Atlantis resort, Dubai's latest mega-attraction – the launch party alone cost over $20 million dollars, the most expensive in history, with a million fireworks, a gaggle of A-list of celebrities ranging from Robert de Niro to Richard Branson, and Kylie Minogue on stage. It marked, by all accounts, the end of an era.

Even while the Atlantis extravaganza was in progress, serious questions were being asked about Dubai's financial future. As 2008 became 2009, the global recession began to hit Dubai with alarming force. Overseas investors pulled their funds out, tourists stopped arriving and the city's burgeoning real-estate market, which had been one of the biggest drivers of local economic growth, suddenly collapsed, with up to half the value of some properties being wiped off in a few weeks. Major developers like Nakheel, Emar and Damac announced that various landmark projects were being put on indefinite hold or cancelled. The Dubai Stock Market lost fifty percent of its value, while a sixty percent fall in the price of oil didn't help either. Rumours circulated that the airport car parks were being left full of vehicles abandoned by their expat owners as they flew back home to avoid bankruptcy and possible imprisonment.

Then, in November 2009, **Dubai World**, the city's biggest government company, with debts of $59 billion, sparked worldwide financial panic when it announced that it would be unable to make scheduled debt repayments. The possible collapse of the Dubai economy suddenly became one of the major talking points in the ongoing global financial meltdown, raising the possibility that should Dubai default on its loans (which are owed to a wide range of institutions worldwide, including a significant number of UK banks), the global recession would enter a new and even more toxic phase.

Dubai's sky-high ambition had suddenly turned into a colossal mountain of debt – around $80 billion in total. And given that most of this was chalked up against government-owned firms, there seemed a genuine possibility that the entire emirate would go bankrupt, as had recently happened to Iceland. Foreign journalists lined up to take spiteful swipes at the struggling city while the financial world held its breath waiting to see whether the oil-rich government in Abu Dhabi would, as expected, come to the aid of its beleaguered neighbour. This it eventually did, to an estimated tune of around $20 billion, although not before making Dubai sweat for a while. Rumours abounded that Abu Dhabi had been holding out for a stake in Dubai's prized Emirates airline and other key assets in return for the bail-out, although instead they got naming rights to the Burj Khalifa (see p.73). Another glitterati-packed launch party heralded the opening of this landmark structure in early 2010, although it appeared somewhat valedictory: a symbol of the magnificent ambition which the city no longer has the cash to underwrite, and named after the ruler of a rival state. All of which points to the fact that bankruptcy may have been averted, although the city's prestige and financial standing will take slightly longer to recover.

It seems that the next few years will be quieter for Dubai. Many of its more speculative projects (see p.86) are likely to be shelved temporarily or permanently, although the city's creaking infrastructure received a further boost in 2009 with the opening of the huge new metro system and the massive airport Terminal 3. As of early 2010 the punch-drunk city appeared to have dragged itself back up off the canvas. Tourists had begun returning to the city, the real-estate market was showing slight signs of recovery, while the discovery of a new offshore oilfield added a further note of (cautious) optimism. In short, reports of Dubai's demise have almost certainly been exaggerated, and despite recent financial woes the city still boasts an infrastructure and a widely diversified array of business and tourist facilities which have few equals anywhere else on the planet. The party may have slowed down, but it is still far from over.

Contemporary Dubai

Dubai is the modern world's most extraordinary urban experiment: an attempt to create a global city, from scratch, within the space of a few decades. Not surprisingly, there have been growing pains along the way, as Dubai attempts to enact its own vision of history on fast-forward. The city's landmark achievements and record-busting mega-projects have received plenty of coverage, although in the past few years foreign media have focused increasingly on Dubai's darker side, including **human-rights** issues, **environmental concerns** and the city's alleged role in international terrorist networks. The uniquely multicultural expat society – and its relationship with its Emirati hosts – is another ongoing source of tension and potential instability, as the city's rulers and citizens argue over Dubai's identity, culture and eventual destination.

Demographic diversity

Dubai is perhaps the most **cosmopolitan** city on the planet, with residents from over 200 countries calling it home. The emirate's population is overwhelmingly foreign, and native Emiratis – or "nationals" – find themselves in an increasingly small minority. Of the UAE's population of around six million, under twenty percent are nationals; the figure is even lower in Dubai itself – some estimates put it at below five percent. Dubai's Emiratis thus find themselves forming just one small strand in the city's diverse cultural fabric, a situation which has led to increasing social tensions (see opposite).

The remainder of the city's populace is a veritable kaleidoscope of cultures. Nearly two-thirds are from **South Asia**, mainly Indian (around 1.7 million, including particularly large numbers from the state of Kerala), plus 1.25 million Pakistanis. Most of these are employed as low-skilled construction workers, taxi drivers and in various other menial positions, although there are also a significant number of wealthy and well-established Indian trading families. A further quarter of the population comes from other Arab countries (mainly Palestinian, Lebanese, Syrian, Egyptian and Somali) and Iran – Iranian merchants have traditionally provided the city with much of its commercial dynamism, while expat Arabs can be found in a wide range of jobs in the city's business and leisure sectors. There are also large number of Filipinas (who provide the city with many of its waitresses, housemaids and nannies) plus a smaller but economically significant number of expat Europeans who supply essential financial, tourism and engineering expertise. As such, Dubai is not really a single city, but an agglomeration of dozens of self-contained ethnic enclaves, geographically contiguous, but culturally quite separate. All of which lends the city its fascinatingly varied, but also decidedly dysfunctional, flavour.

The UAE's other demographic oddity is its **gender imbalance**. This is one of the most male-dominated countries on the planet. The situation in Dubai is particularly uneven, with men forming some 75 percent of the population, making it one of the world's most sexually lopsided cities – and also providing one of the root causes of its widespread prostitution industry (see p.39).

The ruling bargain: Emiratis and expats

Dubai has never been a **democracy** and, apart from a brief period in the 1930s (see p.182) has never looked like becoming one. The old tribal system of government by the ruling sheikh and his family remains deeply entrenched, regardless of the city's other impeccably modernist credentials. Despite appearances, the original system was not as autocratic as it might appear. Sheikhs were allowed to rule on the assumption that they acted in the best interests of their subjects, and did their best to provide for them – the so-called **ruling bargain**. Unpopular or incompetent leaders who failed to deliver their share of the bargain could be replaced, and often were. This simple but effective system of tribal democracy was somewhat undermined by the British, who tended to confirm the position and privileges of whichever family was in power, irrespective of their abilities. Fortunately the UAE, and Dubai in particular, has been blessed with a number of unusually effective and often prescient leaders – sheikhs Zayed of Abu Dubai and sheikhs Rashid and Mohammed of in particular – and there's certainly no way in which Dubai could have pursued its spectacularly rapid road to modernization under a traditional democracy.

The ruling bargain is still very much in force, in terms of the financial benefits which the sheikhs are expected to hand down to their subjects. Emirati **citizenship** is jealously guarded, and Dubai's native population benefit from a range of perks estimated to be worth over $50,000 per year, including free land, university education, building grants and so on – not to mention a complete lack of income tax, as well as the possibility of earning easy additional money through renting out property or sponsoring foreign companies. The downside of this sheikhly nanny-state model is that it has increasingly tended to mollycoddle its citizens into a state of privileged insensibility. Given their various guaranteed state subsidies and welfare benefits, around twenty percent of Emiratis simply decline to work, while those that do gravitate towards well-paid, low-skilled government jobs. The result is a notable lack of educated and entrepreneurial locals – which tends to place even more of the reins of economic power in the hands of foreigners (more than 99 percent of employees in private companies are expats). The situation has particularly concerned Sheikh Mohammed and his ruling circles, who have launched an ongoing **Emiratisation** programme over the past decade in order to encourage locals to acquire skills and get more nationals into senior positions at private companies, although so far with relatively little success.

The rulers' disappointment in the apathy of their local workforce is one side of the equation. The flipside is the increasing resentment among some local Emiratis with what they see as the **sell-out** of their country and its traditional culture, and the fact that they now find themselves virtual strangers in their own homes. Despite Dubai's cosmopolitan make-up, there has been a remarkable lack of racial tension, although this may change. Increasing popular disgust at the insensitive behaviour of certain local Western expats and visitors (such as the "sex on the beach" couple Michelle Palmer and Vince Acors – see p.31) is increasingly hardening local attitudes against foreigners.

Dubai's **expats**, in turn, find themselves in an ambivalent position. Emirati citizenship (with all its associated financial perks) is only very rarely granted to outsiders. Even those who have lived in the country for decades, including many people who were born in Dubai, have no rights to citizenship or even residence, instead holding the nationality of their parents' country – which they might never have visited. As such, Dubai is largely a city of transients, with foreigners living in Dubai on a sequence of three-year working visas, and with residence dependent on keeping their jobs and not falling foul of the authorities. Those from Europe, North America, Australia and New Zealand often come to Dubai, see out their contracts, and then go home again, giving the city's "western" community its peculiarly rootless and impermanent flavour.

Human rights and wrongs

Dubai's expat community runs through a huge range of ethnic and economic groups. At the bottom of the heap lie the **Indian and Pakistani labourers**, the city's most unsung and exploited community, who have provided the manpower to build modern Dubai, but who are denied any of its rewards. Most of the abuses are related to the **construction industry**, and its workforce of largely Subcontinental labourers. The majority of these immigrants live in labour camps in the most basic conditions, often working in dangerous circumstances in the heat of the Gulf sun, with fatalities all too common (an estimated 800 in 2007 alone). Workers' passports are routinely confiscated to prevent them from absconding, while pay is often held for months in arrears for the same reason. In addition, workers have no freedom of movement, being obliged by the terms of their visas to work for the employer who sponsored their arrival in Dubai. Pretty much all labourers also owe large sums of money to the employment agents in India who arranged their jobs for them, and spend much of their first year or two just paying off these fees. Workers are also routinely promised one wage in India, but arrive in Dubai to find that their actual salary is far lower. What money they do manage to earn is sent back home to support their families. In Dubai itself, attempts are made to ensure that the workers remain largely invisible, prevented by security guards from entering the shopping malls and skyscrapers they helped to build.

Such workers are effectively little better than modern-day slaves. The principal offenders are the Gulf's large construction companies (including, ironically, a number of Indian firms) and employment agents in the Subcontinent, although the Dubai government has acted with uncharacteristic lethargy in addressing the problems, and seems to regard it as more of a PR headache than a fundamental issue of human rights. Improvements are being made, but slowly. The ultimate challenge which forces Dubai to improve labour conditions may come from outside, however. Increasingly upbeat economic conditions in the Subcontinent mean that in future many Indians (if not Pakistanis) will be able to find better pay and working conditions at home. Which will be Dubai's loss – and India's gain.

The plight of the city's **housemaids** is sometimes even worse than that of its construction workers, as they risk suffering serious abuse in the privacy of their employer's home. **Human-trafficking** and forced prostitution (see p.39) is another major concern.

Terrorism and dirty money

Dubai's role in the international terrorist network is another issue that is frequently discussed, if little understood. The city's position is strangely ambiguous. On one hand, it is often held up as a potential target for Islamic extremists on account of its extremely liberal and western-leaning regime. On the other, it's also often cited as a hub for international terrorist activities, and as the conduit through which terrorist finances are laundered and sent overseas. Repeated **threats** have been made against the city, but nothing has yet materialized (there seems to be no basis in the popular rumour that Dubai hasn't yet been attacked because it's paying protection money to Al Qaeda). The main possible trigger for an attack isn't Dubai's liberal regime, bars or (relatively) scantily clad western women, but the presence of over a thousand US troops, including at the Jebel Ali Port. The country is protected by a very well-developed (and largely invisible) security system, while potentially troublesome local Islamist publications and organizations are routinely supressed.

Dubai is also often cited as some kind of international **terrorist hub**. Certainly, the city's loose regulation and free-wheeling commercial atmosphere (not to mention its proximity to Afghanistan, East Africa and, particularly, Iran – see p.181) have made it a valuable transit point for money, arms, gold and drugs. Al Qaeda and other terrorist organizations have apparently used Dubai as a conduit for money-laundering, while the city has also been used as a base for various arms deals and dealers – including the notorious Victor Bout, the so-called "Merchant of Death" who banked in Dubai and operated a fleet of fifty cargo planes from Sharjah, shipping guns and weaponry around the region to repressive regimes such as Charles Taylor's Liberia. The city was also an international centre for nuclear weapons technology, which was smuggled from here to secret nuclear programs in Iran, Libya and North Korea. Increasing government vigilance has succeeded in stamping out at least some of this traffic, and Dubai is no more guilty of actively harbouring and encouraging terrorists than London, Hamburg or New York. As is often pointed out, although two of the 9/11 terrorists may have come from the UAE, most of the hijackers learnt to fly in the US.

Environmental disaster in the making?

Lingering concerns have also been raised about the city's **ecological credentials**. The facts make unpleasant reading. The UAE has the largest per capita environmental footprint of any country in the world (slightly above the US, almost double that of the UK, and three times times the global average). Part of the reason can be found in Dubai's challenging climate, and the need for almost year-round air-conditioning, and its lack of natural water supplies, which have to be created using extremely energy-intensive desalination plants. Other causes of environmental over-consumption include the city's car-centred culture and inefficient public transport networks. Energy-busting city landmarks also burn up a prodigious amount of fuel: it's been estimated that the Burj Khalifa requires cooling energy equivalent to that provided by 10,000 tons of melting ice per day. Dubai's innumerable skyscrapers are particularly to blame: running elevators or pumping water up to the top of a forty-storey high-rise burns huge quantities of energy, while the glass-walled style favoured by most of the city's architects means that each building acts as a kind of giant greenhouse, thereby massively increasing air-conditioning requirements. Other forms of physical damage to the environment are also commonplace; the possible environmental problems associated with the construction of the Palm Jumeirah (see p.90) have been widely publicized, while preliminary work on the Palm Jebel Ali involved burying an entire national marine park under the island's foundations.

The profligate attitude towards energy-consumption is perhaps a result of Dubai's location in one of the world's most oil-rich regions, while low-cost (or free) energy and water is provided as a matter of course to nationals, further encouraging waste. As a result, Dubai now actually consumes more energy than it produces and could soon find itself a victim of its own ecological rapaciousness, with its landmark string of artificial islands particularly at risk from rising sea levels. Ironically, it is oil-rich Abu Dhabi which has for once out-thought its neighbour, with schemes such as the vast new Masdar project, a low-rise, carbon-neutral development which will eventually serve as home to some 50,000 people.

A modern Córdoba?

In many ways, Dubai is a victim of its own success, and many aspects of the modern city which concern outsiders – its role in arms smuggling, money-laundering and human trafficking, for example – are a direct consequence of the *laissez faire* policies which made the city such a huge hit in the first place. Meanwhile its extremely sensitive geopolitical situation at the heart of one of the world's most volatile regions has frequently put it under the international microscope and made it the object of negative – and frequently vituperative – media coverage in the west.

What is less widely appreciated are Dubai's massive achievements, of which the landmark skyscrapers, artificial islands and supersized malls are merely the most obvious, and superficial, expression. More important than any of these widely trumpeted (and just as frequently derided) mega-projects is Dubai's intangible contribution to Arab pride and Middle Eastern stability, and its role in providing an example of a (until lately) stable and successful city based on commercial acumen, cultural liberalism and religious tolerance at the heart of one of the world's most dysfunctional regions. Sheikh Mohammed himself has suggested tenth-century Córdoba as a possible example of what the city may eventually become, alluding to the illustrious history of what was then one of Europe's more culturally and socially advanced cities, hosting a vibrant community of Muslims, Christians and Jews, and boasting some of the era's most spectacular architectural achievements. It's far too early to judge Dubai yet, or to decide whether it will suceed in living up to such lofty aspirations. Even so, it's worth bearing in mind that the city which is widely derided for its lack of culture and character could well turn out to be the focal point for a twenty-first-century Middle Eastern cultural and political renaissance, and a new and invaluable bridge between east and west.

Books

There aren't many books about Dubai, although the past couple of years have seen the publication of several interesting studies of the modern city. Don't expect to find any of these for sale in Dubai itself, however. Local booksellers appear averse to stocking anything that might ruffle offical feathers. Several of the authors below have encountered trouble with the authorities: Christopher Davidson's book was at one point apparently on the UAE's list of banned publications, while Syed Ali was actually deported while researching his. Books marked with the symbol are particularly recommended.

Syed Ali *Dubai: Gilded Cage*. Detailed study of contemporary Dubai's relations with its massive expat community, from exploited Indian labourers to wealthy European expats, plus a good chapter on the social position of the city's Emiratis. Ploddingly written, but makes some sound points about the political and social structures which shape life in the city.

Raymond Barrett *Dubai Dreams: Inside the Kingdom of Bling*. Despite the tabloid-style title (and lurid cover), this is a serious attempt to discover what makes modern-day Dubai tick, with an eclectic blend of travelogue, history and contemporary reportage. There are some interesting and entertaining moments en route, with particularly strong coverage of the city's reclusive Emirati community and Islamic heritage, although it's a mixed bag overall, and rather one-dimensional compared to Jim Krane's book (see below).

Anne Coles and Peter Jackson *Windtower: Houses of the Bastaki*. This beautiful coffee-table book offers a marvellous visual memento of old Dubai, with superb photographs of the architecture and inhabitants of Bastakiya back in the 1970s, accompanied by absorbing text.

Christopher M. Davidson *Dubai: the Vulnerability of Success*. Detailed scholarly study of the history of Dubai, plus chapters on the city's social, political and economic workings, current challenges and future prospects. Full of fascinating detail, although rather a turgid read for non-specialists. Davidson has also provided a similarly in-depth account of Dubai's great rival in *Abu Dhabi: Oil and Beyond*.

Maha Gargash *The Sand Fish: a novel from Dubai*. A rare novel from a native Dubaian, *The Sand Fish* is set in Dubai and the northern UAE in the 1950s. Narrated through the eyes of rebellious seventeen-year-old Noora, the third-wife of an older man, it offers a vivid portrait of the city and its culture at the moment of transition from the traditional to modern era.

Edward Henderson *Arabian Destiny*. Published in 1988, *Arabian Destiny* describes Henderson's sojourn in the Gulf during the late 1940s and 1950s while working for the Petroleum Development Trucial Coast. Much of the book is devoted to various events in neighbouring Oman, but there's a fascinating chapter on life in old Dubai, as well as forays into Al Ain and Abu Dhabi. Widely available in Dubai itself, although difficult to get hold of abroad.

Jim Krane *Dubai: the Story of the World's Fastest City* (published in North America as *City of Gold: Dubai and the Dream of Capitalism*). Far and away the best book on modern Dubai, packed with fascinating insights and offering a sympathetic but balanced account of the city's huge successes – and occasional failures. Krane systematically tackles pretty much every important aspect of Dubai's past and present, with absorbing accounts of the city's history and the personalities and achievements of its charismatic rulers through to vexed contemporary issues such as human-rights abuses and environmental concerns, condensing a vast mass of detail into a compellingly readable roller coaster of a narrative.

Robin Moore *Dubai*. Rollicking Middle Eastern blockbuster by *French Connection* author Robin Moore, describing the gold-smuggling, oil-politicking and ladykilling exploits of disgraced US soldier James Fitzroy Lodd in late-1960s Dubai. The gung-ho narrative is of minimal literary value, admittedly, but paints a nice picture of pre-oil Dubai, while much of the historical background is surprisingly accurate, complete with cameo appearances by sheikhs Rashid and Zayed. An excellent poolside read.

Jonathan Raban *Arabia*. Published in 1979, and still one of the best books ever written about the Middle East. It covers Raban's travels through the recently independent Gulf emirates, including chapters on Dubai and Abu Dhabi, before heading west to Yemen, Jordan and Egypt, with perceptive and entertaining accounts of the people and places encountered en route, all described in Raban's inimitable prose. Inevitably dated, but offers a wonderful portrait of the region at a moment of huge historical change.

Wilfred Thesiger *Arabian Sands*. This classic of desert exploration covers Thesiger's two traverses of the Empty Quarter in the late 1940s, including accounts of Al Ain and Abu Dhabi, plus a brief visit to Dubai en route.

Language

Language

Language

Language in Dubai is as complicated as the ethnic patchwork of people who inhabit the city. The city's official language is **Arabic**, spoken by nearly a third of the population, including local Emiratis, other Gulf Arabs and various Arabic-speaking expats from countries like Lebanon, Syria, Jordan and further afield. **Hindi and Urdu** are the mother tongue of many of the city's enormous number of Indian and Pakistani expats, although other Indian languages, most notably **Malayalam**, the native tongue of Kerala, as well as Tamil and Sinhalese (the majority language of Sri Lanka) are also spoken. Other Asian languages are also common, most notably **Tagalog**, the first language of the city's large Filipino community.

In practice, the city's most widely understood language is actually **English**, (even if most speak it only as a second or third language) which serves as a link between all the city's various ethnic groups, as well as the principal language of the European expat community and the business and tourism sectors.

Relatively few of the people you come into contact with as a tourist in Dubai will be Arabic speakers, except in the city's Middle Eastern restaurants. And unless you're pretty fluent, trying to speak Arabic (or indeed any other language) in Dubai is mainly an exercise in diplomacy rather than a meaningful attempt to communicate, since the person you're addressing will almost certainly speak much better English than you do Arabic (or Hindi, or whatever). Still, there's no harm in giving it a go, and the person you're speaking to may be pleasantly entertained by your attempts to address him or her in their own language.

Useful Arabic words and phrases

Hello (formal)	a'salaam alaykum (response: wa alaykum a'salaam)
Hello (informal)	marhaba/ahlan wasahlan/ya hala/ salaam!
Good morning	sabah al kheer
Good evening	masaa al kheer
Good night (to a man)	tisbah al kher
(to a woman)	tisbahi al kher
Goodbye	ma'assalama/fi aman allah
Yes	na'am/aiwa
No	la
Please (to a man)	minfadlack
(to a woman)	minfadlick
Excuse me	afwan
Thank you	shukran
You're welcome	afwan
Sorry	afwan/muta'assef/ assef
OK	n'zayn
How much?	bikaim?
Do you speak English?	teh ki ingelezi?
I don't speak Arabic	ma ah'ki arabi
I understand	ana fahim (fem: ana fahma)
I don't understand	ana ma fahim (fem: ana ma fahma)
My name is…	Ismi…
What is your name?	Sho ismak?
God willing!	Inshallah
I'm British	ana Britani
Irish	Irlandee

American	Amerikanee	**here/there**	hina/hunak
Canadian	Canadee	**open/closed**	maftooh/mseeker
Australian	Ostralee	**big/small**	kabeer/saghir
New Zealand	Noozeelandee	**old/new**	kadeem/jadeed
Where are you from?	min wayn inta?	**day/night**	yoom/layl
Where is?	wayn?	**today/tomorrow**	al yoom/bokra
in	fi	**perhaps**	mumkin
near/far	gareeb/ba'eed		

Numbers

1	wahid	**9**	tissa
2	ithnayn	**10**	ashra
3	theletha	**20**	aishreen
4	arba'a	**30**	thelatheen
5	khamsa	**40**	arba'aeen
6	sitta	**50**	khamseen
7	saba'a	**100**	maya
8	themanya	**1000**	elf

Food glossary

The traditional Middle Eastern meal consists of a wide selection of small dishes known as **mezze** (or *meze*) shared between a number of diners. Most or all of the following dishes, dips and other ingredients are found in the city's better Middle Eastern (or "Lebanese", as they are usually described) restaurants and cafés, although note that vagaries in the transliteration from Arabic script to English can result in considerable variations in spelling.

baba ghanouj all-purpose dip made from grilled eggplant (aubergine) mixed with ingredients like tomato, onion, lemon juice and garlic

burghul cracked wheat, often used as an ingredient in Middle Eastern dishes such as tabouleh

falafel deep-fried balls of crushed chickpeas mixed with spices; usually served with bread and salad

fatayer miniature triangular pastries, usually filled with either cheese or spinach

fatteh dishes containing pieces of fried or roasted bread

fattoush salad made of tomatoes, cucumber, lettuce and mint mixed up with crispy little squares of deep-fried flatbread

foul madamas smooth dip made from fava beans (*foul*) blended with lemon juice, chillis and olive oil

jebne white cheese

halloumi grilled cheese

hammour common Gulf fish which often crops up on local menus; a bit like cod

humous crushed chickpeas blended with tahini, garlic and lemon; served as a basic side dish and eaten with virtually everything, from bread and vegetables through to meat dishes

kibbeh small ovals of deep-fried minced lamb mixed with cracked wheat and spices

labneh thick, creamy Arabian yoghurt, often flavoured with garlic or mint

loubia salad of green beans with tomatoes and onion

moutabal a slightly creamier version of *baba ghanouj*, thickened using yoghurt or tahini

saj Lebanese style of thin, round flatbread

saj manakish (or *mana'eesh*) pieces of *saj* spinkled with herbs and oil – a kind of Middle Eastern mini-pizza

sambousek miniature pastries, filled with meat or cheese and then fried

shwarma chicken or lamb kebabs, cut in narrow strips off a big hunk of meat roasted on a vertical spit (like the Turkish doner kebab) and served wrapped in flatbread with salad

shisha waterpipe (also known as hubbly-bubbly). Tobacco is filtered through the glass water-container at the base of the pipe, and so is much milder (and less harmful) than normal cigarettes. Tobacco is usually available either plain or in various flavoured varieties; the best shisha cafés may have as many as twenty varieties.

shish taouk basic chicken kebab, with small pieces of meat grilled on a skewer and often served with garlic sauce

tabouleh finely chopped mixture of tomato, mint and cracked wheat

tahini paste made from sesame seeds

waraq aynab vine leaves stuffed with a mixture of rice and meat

zaatar a widely used seasoning made from a mixture of dried thyme (or oregano), salt and sesame seeds

zatoon olives

Glossary

abbeya black, full-length women's traditional robe

abra small boat used to ferry passengers across the Creek (see p.23 & p.48)

attar traditional perfume

bahar sea

barasti palm thatch used to construct traditional houses

bayt/bait house

burj tower

dar house

dhow generic term loosely used to describe all types of traditional wooden Arabian boat (see p.67)

dishdasha See *kandoura* below.

Eid Al Fitr Festival celebrating the end of Ramadan (see p.29)

falaj traditional irrigation technique used to water date plantations, with water drawn from deep underground and carried to its destination along tiny earthen canals

funduk hotel

ghutra men's headscarf, usually white or red-and-white check

haj pilgrimage to Mecca

hosn/hisn fort

iftar the breaking of the fast after dark during Ramadan

iqal the rope-like black cords used to keep the ghutra on the head (traditionally used to tie together the legs of camels to stop them running off)

jebel hill or mountain

kandoura the full-length traditional robe worn by Gulf Arabs (also known as dishdashas). A decorative tassel, known as the *farokha* (or *tarboush*) often hangs from the collar. A long robe, or *basht*, is sometimes worn over the dishdasha on formal occasions, denoting the authority of the wearer.

khanjar traditional curved dagger, usually made of silver

Al Khor The Creek

Al Khaleej The Gulf (translated locally as the Arabian Gulf, never as the Persian Gulf)

majlis meeting/reception room in a traditional Arabian house; the place where local or family problems were discussed and decisions taken.

masjid mosque

mina port

nakheel palm tree

oud Arabian lute

qasr palace or castle

qibla the direction of Mecca, usually indicated by a sign or sticker in most hotel rooms in the city (and in mosques by a recessed niche known as the *mihrab*)

Ramadan see p.29

shayla women's black headscarf, worn with an abbeya

wadi dry river bed or valley

Travel store

Small print and
Index

A Rough Guide to Rough Guides

Published in 1982, the first Rough Guide – to Greece – was a student scheme that became a publishing phenomenon. Mark Ellingham, a recent graduate in English from Bristol University, had been travelling in Greece the previous summer and couldn't find the right guidebook. With a small group of friends he wrote his own guide, combining a highly contemporary, journalistic style with a thoroughly practical approach to travellers' needs.

The immediate success of the book spawned a series that rapidly covered dozens of destinations. And, in addition to impecunious backpackers, Rough Guides soon acquired a much broader and older readership that relished the guides' wit and inquisitiveness as much as their enthusiastic, critical approach and value-for-money ethos.

These days, Rough Guides include recommendations from shoestring to luxury and cover more than 200 destinations around the globe, including almost every country in the Americas and Europe, more than half of Africa and most of Asia and Australasia. Our ever-growing team of authors and photographers is spread all over the world, particularly in Europe, the US and Australia.

In the early 1990s, Rough Guides branched out of travel, with the publication of Rough Guides to World Music, Classical Music and the Internet. All three have become benchmark titles in their fields, spearheading the publication of a wide range of books under the Rough Guide name.

Including the travel series, Rough Guides now number more than 350 titles, covering: phrasebooks, waterproof maps, music guides from Opera to Heavy Metal, reference works as diverse as Conspiracy Theories and Shakespeare, and popular culture books from iPods to Poker. Rough Guides also produce a series of more than 120 World Music CDs in partnership with World Music Network.

Visit www.roughguides.com to see our latest publications.

Rough Guide credits

Text editor: Harry Wilson
Layout: Sachin Gupta
Cartography: Rajesh Mishra
Picture editor: Mark Thomas
Production: Louise Daly
Proofreader: Serena Stephenson
Cover design: Nicole Newman, Dan May, Chloë Roberts
Photographer: Gavin Thomas
Editorial: **London** Andy Turner, Keith Drew, Edward Aves, Alice Park, Lucy White, Jo Kirby, James Smart, Natasha Foges, Róisín Cameron, James Rice, Lara Kavanagh, Emma Beatson, Emma Gibbs, Kathryn Lane, Monica Woods, Mani Ramaswamy, Harry Wilson, Lucy Cowie, Alison Roberts, Eleanor Aldridge, Ian Blenkinsop, Joe Staines, Matthew Milton, Tracy Hopkins, Ruth Tidball; **Delhi** Madhavi Singh, Lubna Shaheen, Jalpreen Kaur Chhatwal
Design & Pictures: **London** Scott Stickland, Dan May, Diana Jarvis, Mark Thomas, Nicole Newman, Sarah Cummins, Emily Taylor; **Delhi** Umesh Aggarwal, Ajay Verma, Jessica Subramanian, Ankur Guha, Pradeep Thapliyal, Sachin Tanwar, Anita Singh, Nikhil Agarwal
Production: Rebecca Short, Liz Cherry, Erika Pepe
Cartography: **London** Ed Wright, Katie Lloyd-Jones; **Delhi** Rajesh Chhibber, Ashutosh Bharti, Animesh Pathak, Jasbir Sandhu, Karobi Gogoi, Swati Handoo, Deshpal Dabas, Lokamata Sahu
Online: **London** Faye Hellon, Jeanette Angell, Fergus Day, Justine Bright, Clare Bryson, Aine Fearon, Adrian Low, Ezgi Celebi; **Delhi** Amit Verma, Rahul Kumar, Narender Kumar, Ravi Yadav, Debojit Borah, Rakesh Kumar, Ganesh Sharma, Shisir Basumatari
Marketing & Publicity: **London** Liz Statham, Jess Carter, Vivienne Watton, Anna Paynton, Rachel Sprackett, Laura Vipond; **New York** Katy Ball; **Delhi** Aman Arora
Digital Travel Publisher: Peter Buckley
Reference Director: Andrew Lockett
Operations Assistant: Becky Doyle
Operations Manager: Helen Atkinson
Publishing Director (Travel): Clare Currie
Commercial Manager: Gino Magnotta
Managing Director: John Duhigg

Publishing information

This first edition published November 2010 by
Rough Guides Ltd,
80 Strand, London WC2R 0RL
11, Community Centre, Panchsheel Park, New Delhi 110017, India
Distributed by the Penguin Group
Penguin Books Ltd,
80 Strand, London WC2R 0RL
Penguin Group (USA)
375 Hudson Street, NY 10014, USA
Penguin Group (Australia)
250 Camberwell Road, Camberwell, Victoria 3124, Australia
Penguin Group (NZ)
67 Apollo Drive, Mairangi Bay, Auckland 1310, New Zealand
This paperback edition published in Canada in 2010. Rough Guides is represented in Canada by Tourmaline Editions Inc., 662 King Street West, Suite 304, Toronto, Ontario, M5V 1M7
Cover concept by Peter Dyer.
Typeset in Bembo and Helvetica to an original design by Henry Iles.
Printed in Singapore

216pp includes index
A catalogue record for this book is available from the British Library
ISBN: 978-1-84836-586-5

1 3 5 7 9 8 6 4 2

Help us update

We've gone to a lot of effort to ensure that the first edition of **The Rough Guide to Dubai** is accurate and up-to-date. However, things change – places get "discovered", opening hours are notoriously fickle, restaurants and rooms raise prices or lower standards. If you feel we've got it wrong or left something out, we'd like to know, and if you can remember the address, the price, the hours, the phone number, so much the better.

Please send your comments with the subject line "**Rough Guide Dubai Update**" to mail@roughguides.com. We'll credit all contributions and send a copy of the next edition (or any other Rough Guide if you prefer) for the very best emails.

Find more travel information, connect with fellow travellers and book your trip on www.roughguides.com

SMALL PRINT

Acknowledgements

The author wishes to thank Mohammed Alaoui, Abigail Frommeyer, Fatma Yousuf Salem and Frances Linzee Gordon. Particular thanks to Harry Wilson, my editor at Rough Guides, for all his input, and to Lejla Charif and Ulrike Baumann at Jumeirah for all their assistance with this and previous volumes. And, of course, to Allison, for letting me go in the first place, and then for coming out in person and teaching me how to shop properly.

Photo credits

All photos by Gavin Thomas © Rough Guides except the following:

Introduction

Burj Khalifa with Dubai Fountain in foreground © dblight/istock
Sheikh Zayed Road © Nikada/istock
Detail of minaret © Hilary Schacht
Outdoor tables, Madinat Jumeirah © Simeone Giovanni/4Corners
Beach, Dubai Marina © Amanda Hall/Getty Images
Camel safari © Frances Stephane/4Corners

Things not to miss

01 Wind-towered houses, Bastakiya © Keren Su/ Getty Images
02 Dubai Museum © Jon Hikcs/Alamy
03 Burj Khalifa © Gavin Thomas
06 Sheikh Zayed Mosque © Gavin Thomas
08 Sheikh Zayed Road © Gavin Thomas
09 Desert safari © Schmid Reinhard/4Corners
10 Arabian food © Photolibrary
11 Palm trees, Al Ain Oasis © Michele Falzone/ Alamy
13 Ski Dubai © Caro/Alamy
14 Dhows on Dubai Creek © Christopher Allan/ Getty Images
15 Deira Gold Souk © Maremagnum/Getty Images
16 Wafi and Khan Murjan Souk © Gavin Thomas
17 Sharjah Museum of Islamic Civilization © Gavin Thomas
18 Sheikh Saeed al Maktoum House © Gavin Thomas
20 Burj al Arab © Pankaj & Insy Shah/Getty Images

Futuristic Dubai colour section

Burj Khalifa, lake and Dubai Mall © Nikada/istock
Dubai Marina © Nikada/istock
Palm Jumeirah © Grafenhain Gunter/4Corners Images
Burj al Arab © Hugh Sitton Photographer/Getty Images
Dubai metro © travelstock44/Alamy
Burj Khalifa © Getty Images

Traditional Dubai colour section

Bastakiya alley © Megapress/Alamy
Abras on the Creek © travelib asia/Alamy

Black and whites

p.72 Sheikh Zayed Road © Mark Horn/Getty Images
p.171 Emirates Palace Hotel © Motivate Publishing/Getty Images

Index

Map entries are in colour.

B

C

D

E

F

G

H

I

J

K

L

M

N

O

P

Q

R

S

T

U

V

W

X

INDEX

Map symbols

maps are listed in the full index using coloured text

- Chapter boundary
- International boundary
- Road
- Tunnel
- Path
- Metro line
- Ferry route
- Waterway
- Wall
- Bridge
- River boat
- Mosque
- Golf course
- Mountain
- Peak
- Point of interest
- Hospital
- Tourist office
- Post office
- Fountain
- Airport
- Hotel
- Building
- Muslim cemetery
- Beach
- Park

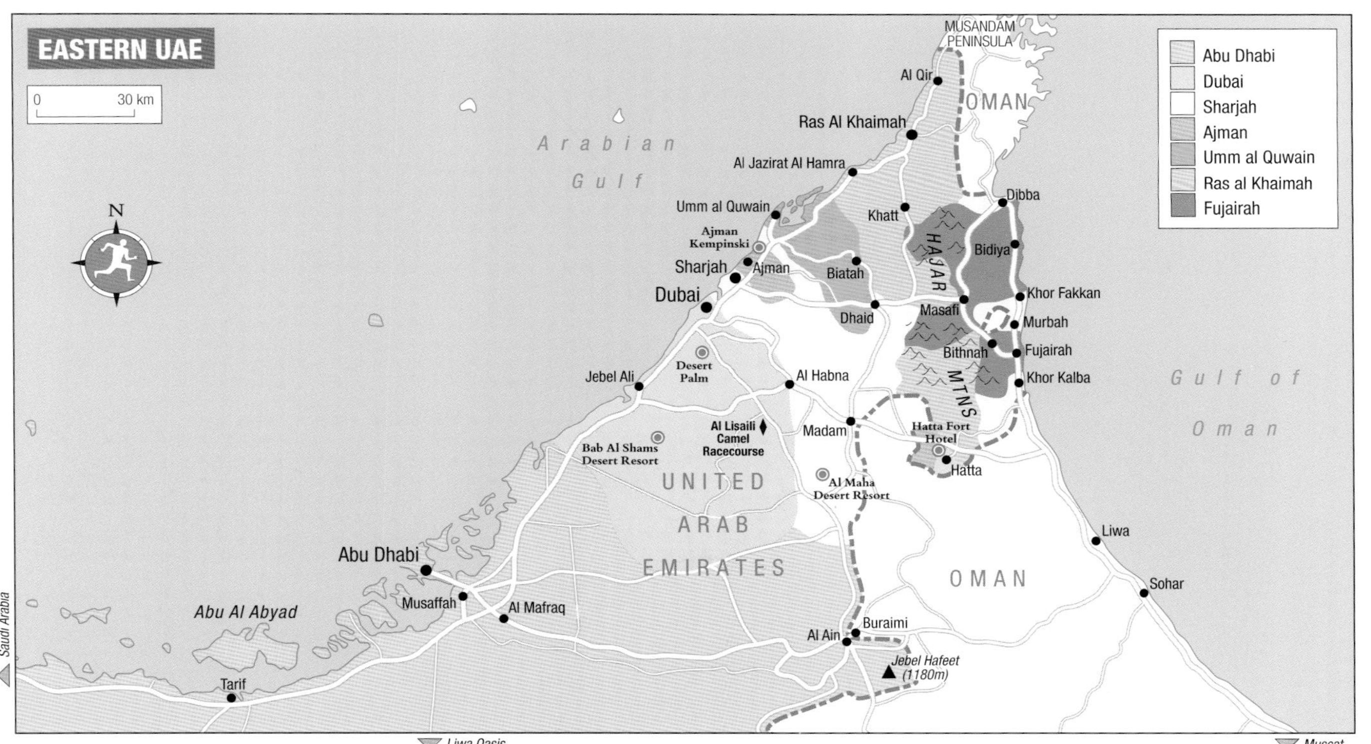

EASTERN UAE
0
30 km
N
Abu Dhabi
Dubai
Sharjah
Ajman
Umm al Quwain
Ras al Khaimah
Fujairah
MUSANDAM PENINSULA
OMAN
Al Qir
Ras Al Khaimah
Arabian Gulf
Al Jazirat Al Hamra
Umm al Quwain
Ajman Kempinski
Sharjah
Ajman
Dubai
Khatt
Biatah
Dhaid
HAJAR MTNS
Dibba
Bidiya
Khor Fakkan
Masafi
Murbah
Bithnah
Fujairah
Khor Kalba
Gulf of Oman
Desert Palm
Jebel Ali
Al Habna
Al Lisaili Camel Racecourse
Bab Al Shams Desert Resort
Madam
Hatta Fort Hotel
Hatta
Al Maha Desert Resort
UNITED ARAB EMIRATES
OMAN
Liwa
Sohar
Abu Dhabi
Musaffah
Al Mafraq
Abu Al Abyad
Tarif
Buraimi
Al Ain
Jebel Hafeet (1180m)
Saudi Arabia
Liwa Oasis
Muscat

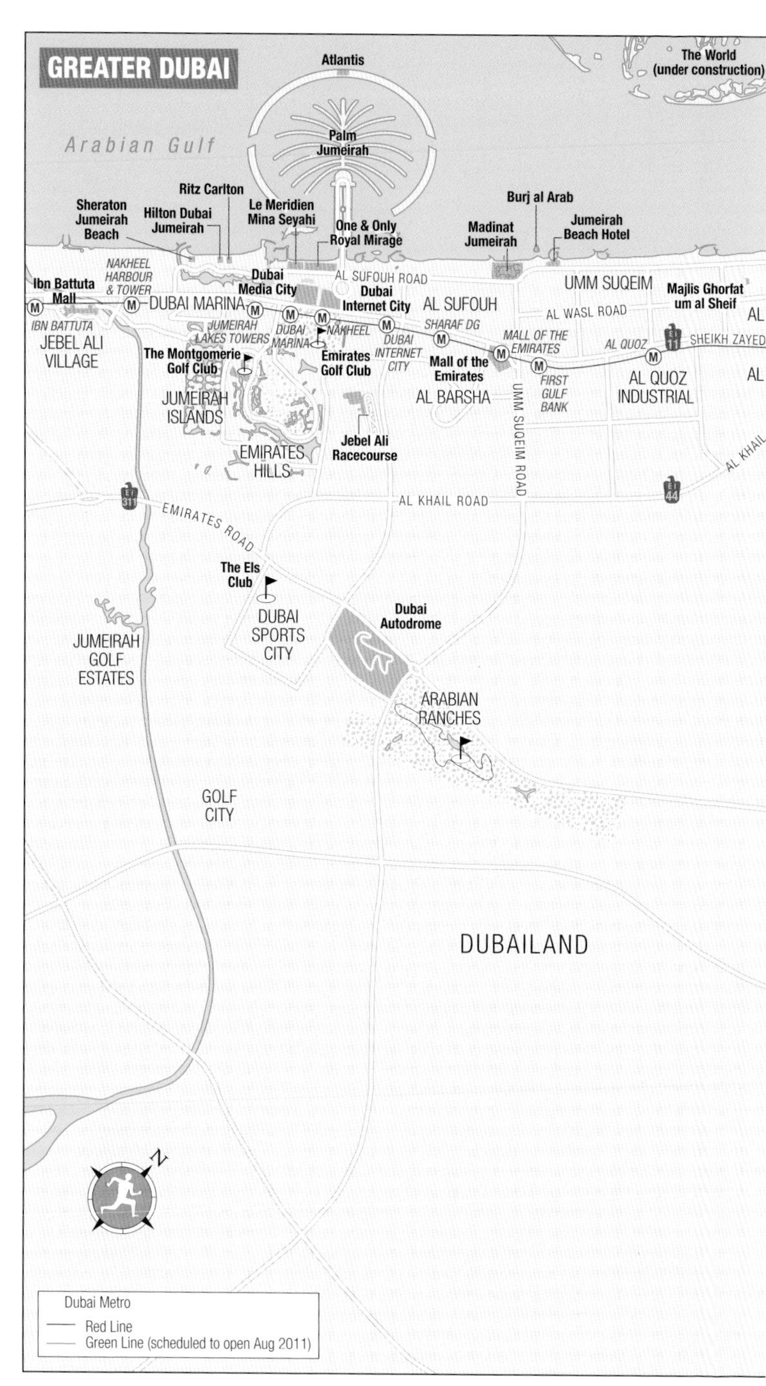

GREATER DUBAI
Atlantis
The World (under construction)
Arabian Gulf
Palm Jumeirah
Ritz Carlton
Sheraton Jumeirah Beach
Hilton Dubai Jumeirah
Le Meridien Mina Seyahi
One & Only Royal Mirage
Burj al Arab
Madinat Jumeirah
Jumeirah Beach Hotel
NAKHEEL HARBOUR & TOWER
AL SUFOUH ROAD
Ibn Battuta Mall
Dubai Media City
Dubai Internet City
UMM SUQEIM
Majlis Ghorfat um al Sheif
DUBAI MARINA
AL SUFOUH
AL WASL ROAD
IBN BATTUTA
JUMEIRAH LAKES TOWERS
DUBAI MARINA
NAKHEEL
DUBAI INTERNET CITY
SHARAF DG
MALL OF THE EMIRATES
AL QUOZ
SHEIKH ZAYED
JEBEL ALI VILLAGE
The Montgomerie Golf Club
Emirates Golf Club
Mall of the Emirates
FIRST GULF BANK
AL QUOZ INDUSTRIAL
AL BARSHA
JUMEIRAH ISLANDS
UMM SUQEIM ROAD
Jebel Ali Racecourse
EMIRATES HILLS
AL KHAIL
AL KHAIL ROAD
EMIRATES ROAD
The Els Club
DUBAI SPORTS CITY
Dubai Autodrome
JUMEIRAH GOLF ESTATES
ARABIAN RANCHES
GOLF CITY
DUBAILAND
N
Dubai Metro
Red Line
Green Line (scheduled to open Aug 2011)

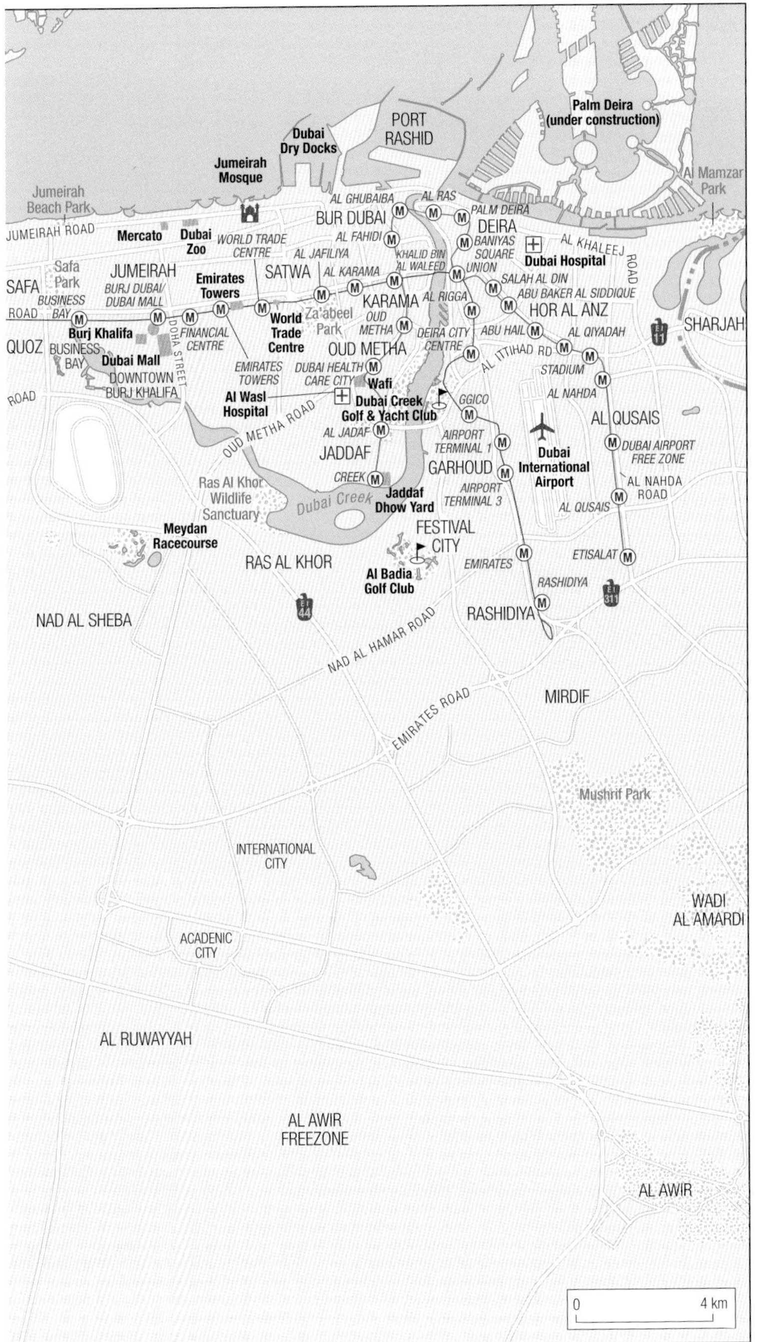

Palm Deira
(under construction)
PORT
RASHID
Dubai
Dry Docks
Jumeirah
Mosque
Al Mamzar
Park
Jumeirah
Beach Park
AL GHUBAIBA
AL RAS
PALM DEIRA
BUR DUBAI
DEIRA
JUMEIRAH ROAD
Mercato
Dubai
Zoo
WORLD TRADE
CENTRE
AL FAHIDI
BANIYAS
SQUARE
Dubai Hospital
AL KHALEEJ ROAD
Safa
Park
JUMEIRAH
AL JAFILIYA
KHALID BIN
AL WALEED
UNION
SATWA
AL KARAMA
SALAH AL DIN
SAFA
BUSINESS
BAY
BURJ DUBAI/
DUBAI MALL
Emirates
Towers
KARAMA
AL RIGGA
ABU BAKER AL SIDDIQUE
HOR AL ANZ
ROAD
World
Trade
Centre
Za'abeel
Park
OUD
METHA
SHARJAH
Burj Khalifa
FINANCIAL
CENTRE
DOHA STREET
DEIRA CITY
CENTRE
ABU HAIL
AL QIYADAH
QUOZ
BUSINESS
BAY
OUD METHA
AL ITTIHAD RD
Dubai Mall
DOWNTOWN
BURJ KHALIFA
EMIRATES
TOWERS
DUBAI HEALTH
CARE CITY
Wafi
STADIUM
AL NAHDA
ROAD
Al Wasl
Hospital
Dubai Creek
Golf & Yacht Club
GGICO
AL QUSAIS
OUD METHA ROAD
AL JADAF
AIRPORT
TERMINAL 1
Dubai
International
Airport
DUBAI AIRPORT
FREE ZONE
JADDAF
GARHOUD
CREEK
AIRPORT
TERMINAL 3
AL NAHDA
ROAD
Ras Al Khor
Wildlife
Sanctuary
Dubai Creek
Jaddaf
Dhow Yard
AL QUSAIS
FESTIVAL
CITY
Meydan
Racecourse
ETISALAT
RAS AL KHOR
EMIRATES
Al Badia
Golf Club
RASHIDIYA
NAD AL SHEBA
RASHIDIYA
NAD AL HAMAR ROAD
EMIRATES ROAD
MIRDIF
Mushrif Park
INTERNATIONAL
CITY
WADI
AL AMARDI
ACADENIC
CITY
AL RUWAYYAH
AL AWIR
FREEZONE
AL AWIR
0
4 km

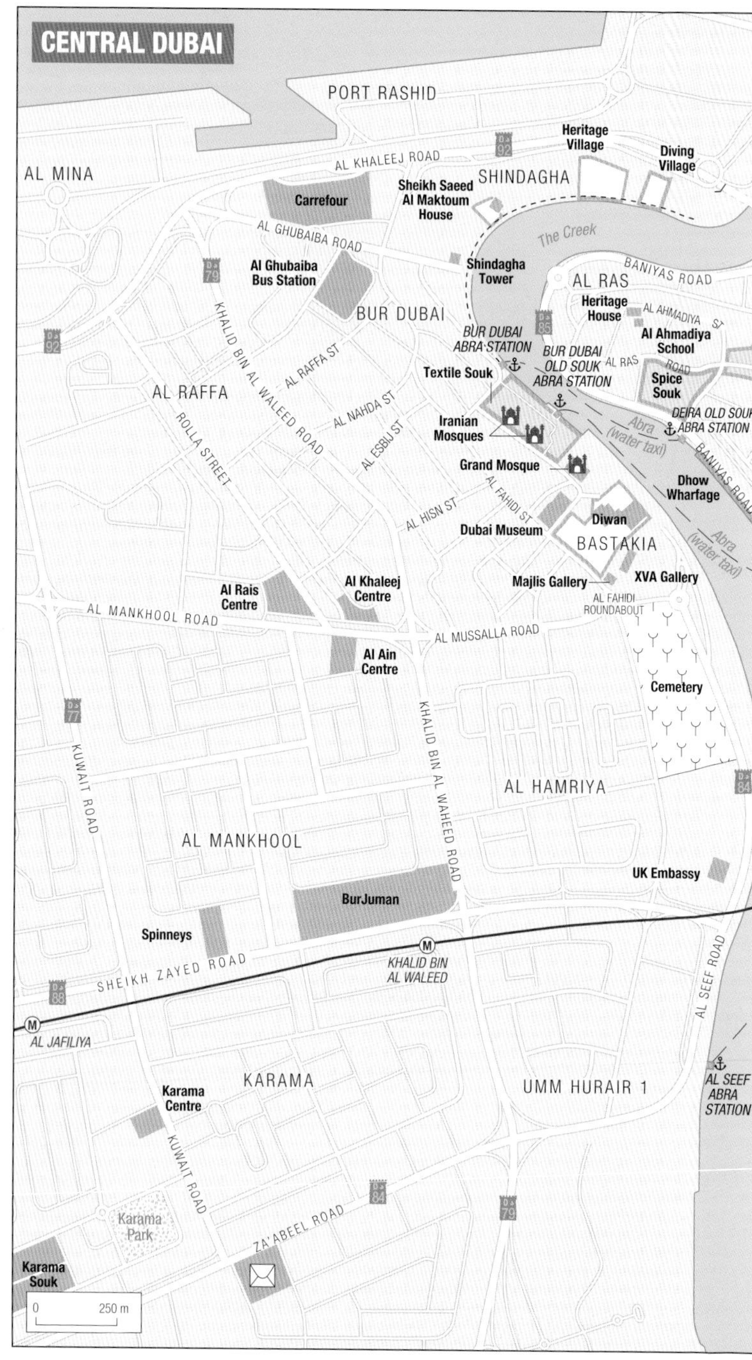
CENTRAL DUBAI
PORT RASHID
AL MINA
AL KHALEEJ ROAD
Heritage Village
Diving Village
SHINDAGHA
Sheikh Saeed Al Maktoum House
Carrefour
AL GHUBAIBA ROAD
The Creek
Al Ghubaiba Bus Station
Shindagha Tower
BANIYAS ROAD
AL RAS
Heritage House
AL AHMADIYA ST
BUR DUBAI
Al Ahmadiya School
BUR DUBAI ABRA STATION
BUR DUBAI OLD SOUK ABRA STATION
AL RAS ROAD
KHALID BIN AL WALEED ROAD
AL RAFFA ST
Textile Souk
Spice Souk
AL RAFFA
AL NAHDA ST
Iranian Mosques
DEIRA OLD SOUK ABRA STATION
Abra (water taxi)
ROLLA STREET
AL ESBIJ ST
Grand Mosque
Dhow Wharfage
BANIYAS ROAD
AL FAHIDI ST
AL HISN ST
Diwan
Dubai Museum
BASTAKIA
Majlis Gallery
XVA Gallery
Al Rais Centre
Al Khaleej Centre
AL FAHIDI ROUNDABOUT
AL MANKHOOL ROAD
AL MUSSALLA ROAD
Al Ain Centre
Cemetery
KUWAIT ROAD
KHALID BIN AL WAHEED ROAD
AL HAMRIYA
AL MANKHOOL
UK Embassy
BurJuman
Spinneys
SHEIKH ZAYED ROAD
KHALID BIN AL WALEED
AL SEEF ROAD
AL JAFILIYA
KARAMA
Karama Centre
UMM HURAIR 1
AL SEEF ABRA STATION
KUWAIT ROAD
ZA'ABEEL ROAD
Karama Park
Karama Souk
0 250 m

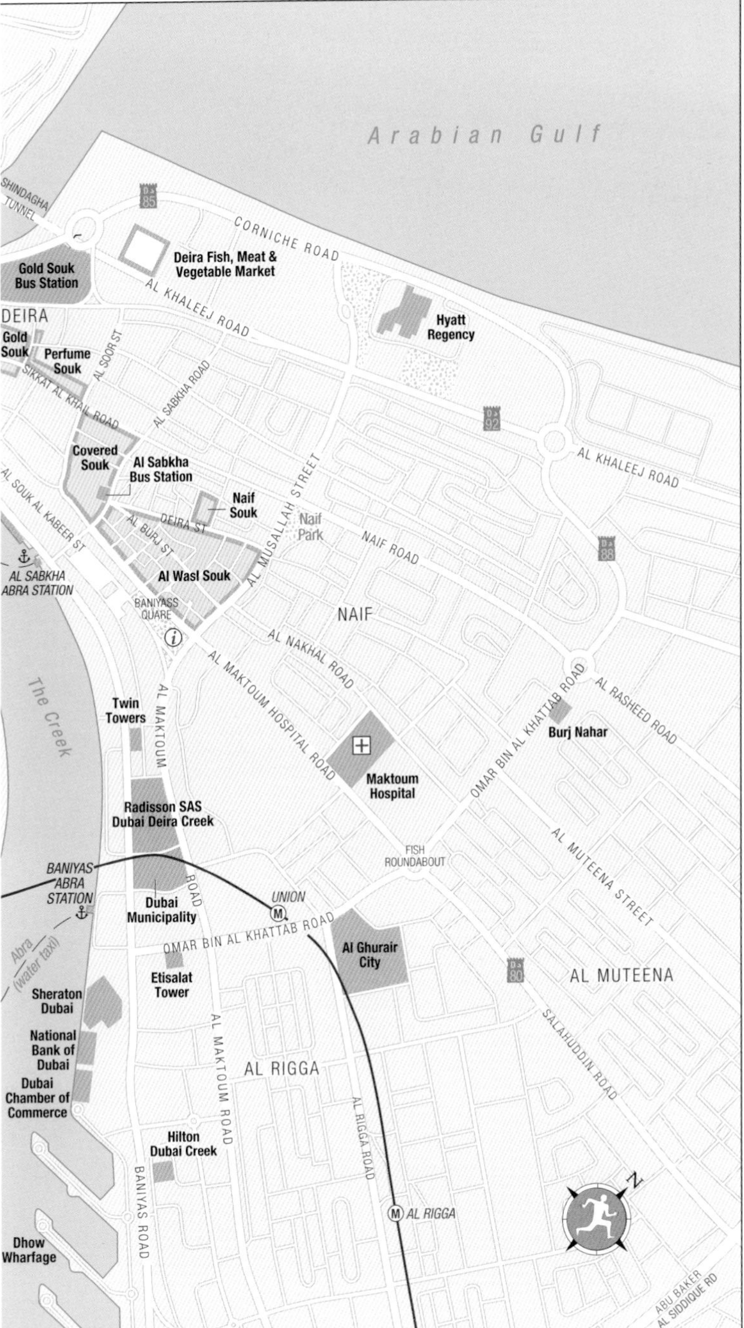

Arabian Gulf
SHINDAGHA TUNNEL
D 85
CORNICHE ROAD
Deira Fish, Meat & Vegetable Market
Gold Souk Bus Station
AL KHALEEJ ROAD
DEIRA
Gold Souk
Perfume Souk
AL SOOR ST
Hyatt Regency
AL SABKHA ROAD
SIKKAT AL KHAIL ROAD
D 92
Covered Souk
Al Sabkha Bus Station
AL KHALEEJ ROAD
AL MUSALLAH STREET
Naif Souk
DEIRA ST
Naif Park
AL SOUK AL KABEER ST
AL BURJ ST
NAIF ROAD
D 88
AL SABKHA ABRA STATION
Al Wasl Souk
BANIYASS QUARE
NAIF
AL NAKHAL ROAD
AL MAKTOUM HOSPITAL ROAD
The Creek
Twin Towers
AL MAKTOUM ROAD
OMAR BIN AL KHATTAB ROAD
AL RASHEED ROAD
Burj Nahar
Maktoum Hospital
Radisson SAS Dubai Deira Creek
AL MUTEENA STREET
FISH ROUNDABOUT
BANIYAS ABRA STATION
UNION
Dubai Municipality
OMAR BIN AL KHATTAB ROAD
Abra (water taxi)
Al Ghurair City
D 80
AL MUTEENA
Etisalat Tower
Sheraton Dubai
SALAHUDDIN ROAD
National Bank of Dubai
AL MAKTOUM ROAD
AL RIGGA
Dubai Chamber of Commerce
AL RIGGA ROAD
Hilton Dubai Creek
BANIYAS ROAD
N
AL RIGGA
Dhow Wharfage
ABU BAKER AL SIDDIQUE RD

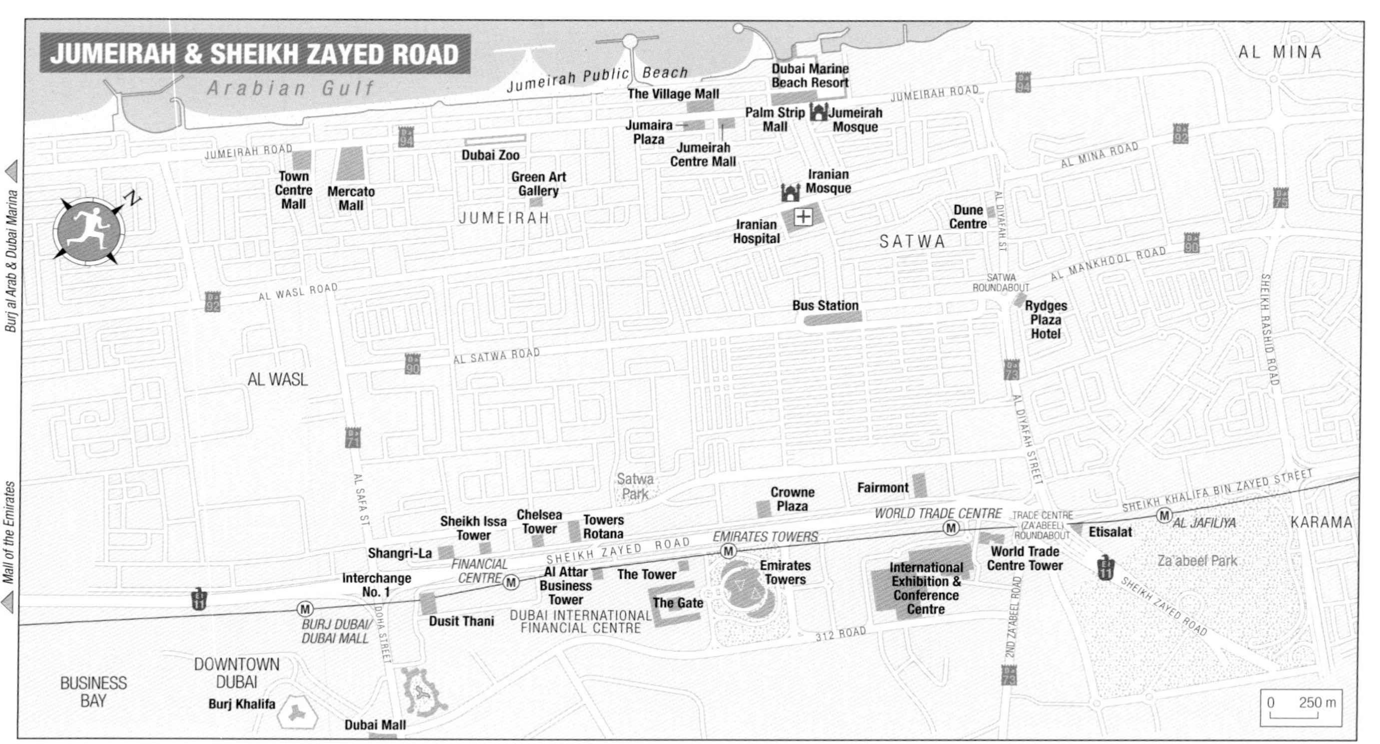
JUMEIRAH & SHEIKH ZAYED ROAD
Arabian Gulf
Jumeirah Public Beach
AL MINA
JUMEIRAH ROAD
Dubai Marine Beach Resort
The Village Mall
Palm Strip Mall
Jumeirah Mosque
Jumaira Plaza
Jumeirah Centre Mall
Dubai Zoo
Town Centre Mall
Mercato Mall
Green Art Gallery
Iranian Mosque
Iranian Hospital
JUMEIRAH
SATWA
Dune Centre
AL MINA ROAD
AL DIYAFAH ST
AL MANKHOOL ROAD
SATWA ROUNDABOUT
SHEIKH RASHID ROAD
AL WASL ROAD
Bus Station
Rydges Plaza Hotel
AL SATWA ROAD
AL WASL
AL DIYAFAH STREET
AL SAFA ST
Satwa Park
Crowne Plaza
Fairmont
SHEIKH KHALIFA BIN ZAYED STREET
WORLD TRADE CENTRE
TRADE CENTRE (ZA'ABEEL) ROUNDABOUT
Etisalat
AL JAFILIYA
KARAMA
Sheikh Issa Tower
Chelsea Tower
Towers Rotana
EMIRATES TOWERS
Shangri-La
SHEIKH ZAYED ROAD
World Trade Centre Tower
Za'abeel Park
FINANCIAL CENTRE
Al Attar Business Tower
The Tower
Emirates Towers
International Exhibition & Conference Centre
Interchange No. 1
The Gate
SHEIKH ZAYED ROAD
BURJ DUBAI/ DUBAI MALL
DOHA STREET
Dusit Thani
DUBAI INTERNATIONAL FINANCIAL CENTRE
312 ROAD
2ND ZA'ABEEL ROAD
DOWNTOWN DUBAI
BUSINESS BAY
Burj Khalifa
Dubai Mall
0 250 m
Burj al Arab & Dubai Marina
Mall of the Emirates
N
94
92
75
90
73
71
11